Efficient Learning Machines

Theories, Concepts, and Applications for Engineers and System Designers

Mariette Awad

Rahul Khanna

Efficient Learning Machines: Theories, Concepts, and Applications for Engineers and System Designers

Mariette Awad and Rahul Khanna

ISBN-13 (pbk): 978-1-4302-5989-3

ISBN-13 (electronic): 978-1-4302-5990-9

Managing Director: Welmoed Spahr
Lead Editors: Jeffrey Pepper (Apress); Steve Weiss (Apress); Patrick Hauke (Intel)
Acquisitions Editor: Robert Hutchinson
Developmental Editor: Douglas Pundick
Technical Reviewers: Abishai Daniel, Myron Porter, Melissa Stockman
Coordinating Editor: Rita Fernando
Copyeditor: Lisa Vecchione

Distributed to the book trade worldwide by Springer Science+Business Media New York, 233 Spring Street, 6th Floor, New York, NY 10013. Phone 1-800-SPRINGER, fax (201) 348-4505, e-mail orders-ny@springer-sbm.com, or visit www.springeronline.com.

For information on translations, please e-mail rights@apress.com, or visit www.apress.com.

About ApressOpen

What Is ApressOpen?

- ApressOpen is an open access book program that publishes high-quality technical and business information.

- ApressOpen eBooks are available for global, free, noncommercial use.

- ApressOpen eBooks are available in PDF, ePub, and Mobi formats.

- The user-friendly ApressOpen free eBook license is presented on the copyright page of this book.

To my family, and especially Edwin, my sunshine. —Mariette

To my family, and especially my mother, Udesh, who always believed in me. —Rahul

Contents at a Glance

Contents

About the Authors

Mariette Awad is an assistant professor in the Department of Electrical and Computer Engineering at the American University of Beirut. She was also a visiting professor at Virginia Commonwealth University, Intel (Mobile and Communications Group), and the Massachusetts Institute of Technology and was invited by the Computer Vision Center at the Autonomous University of Barcelona, Google, and Qualcomm to present her work on machine learning and image processing. Additionally, she has published in numerous conference proceedings and journals. Prior to her academic position, she was with the IBM Systems and Technology Group, in Essex Junction, Vermont, as a wireless product engineer. Over the years, her technical leadership and innovative spirit have earned her management recognition and several business awards as well as multiple IBM patents. Mariette holds a PhD in Electrical Engineering from the University of Vermont.

Rahul Khanna is currently a principal engineer working as a platform architect at Intel involved in the development of energy-efficient algorithms. Over the past 20 years he has worked on server system software technologies, including platform automation, power/thermal optimization techniques, reliability, and predictive methodologies. He has authored numerous technical papers and book chapters on energy optimization, platform wireless interconnect, sensor networks, interconnect reliability, predictive modeling, motion estimation, and security and has coauthored a book on platform autonomy. He holds 33 patents. He is also the coinventor of the Intel Interconnect Built-in Self-Test (IBIST), a methodology for high-speed interconnect testing. His research interests include machine learning–based power/thermal optimization algorithms, narrow-channel high-speed wireless interconnects, and information retrieval in dense sensor networks. Rahul is a member of the Institute of Electrical and Electronic Engineers and the recipient of three Intel Achievement Awards for his contributions in areas related to the advancement of platform technologies.

About the Technical Reviewers

Abishai Daniel is a staff reliability engineer with Intel's Datacenter Group. He works in the areas of device, component, architectural reliability, and input-output (I/O) signal integrity, with a focus on statistical predictive model development based on reliability data and the application of machine learning techniques to reliability modeling. He has served as both program committee member and session chair for various Institute of Electrical and Electronic Engineer conferences, mainly on the topics of reliability and design for reliability, and has published more than 15 papers. Abishai has an AB from Wabash College and an MSEE and a PhD from the University of Michigan.

Myron Porter has served in a variety of roles at Intel, including systems programmer, manager, board validation program manager, and technical writer. Previously, he had positions at other Fortune 500 companies. He has lived in Bush Alaska and Sakha (Russian Yakutia) but was raised in the Ozarks. He got his start in business selling Christmas cards door-to-door at the age of eight. Myron later sold fireworks and has worked as a cabdriver, a pollster/political interviewer, a grant writer, a cook, a substitute teacher, a fuel truck deliveryman, a college English instructor, a copywriter, a restaurant manager, an ESL teacher, and a technical contractor. Additionally, he has done volunteer work for a veterinarian and two college radio stations and as technical support to a regional women's shelter.

Melissa Stockman is currently in the Division of Surgery at the American University of Beirut Medical Center, focusing on the analysis of medical data. She also worked as a senior software engineer in the United States and was the director, for more than 10 years, of Information Technology Infrastructure and Support at the Lebanese American University. She holds a PhD in Electrical and Computer Engineering from the American University of Beirut as well as a BA in Mathematics from New York University and an MA in Computer Science from George Mason University. Melissa's research areas include machine learning, support vector machines, and computer architecture.

Acknowledgments

Many thanks to Yara Rizk (Chapter 7), Nadine Hajj (Chapter 8), Nicolas Mitri (Chapter 9), and Obada Al Zoubi (Chapter 9) for their contributions to this book.

We would also like to thank Kshitij Doshi, Christian Le, John J. Jaiber, Martin Dimitrov, and Karthik Kumar, who helped develop the concepts of phase detection and workload fingerprinting detailed in Chapter 11.

CHAPTER 1

■ ■ ■

Machine Learning

Nature is a self-made machine, more perfectly automated than any automated machine.
To create something in the image of nature is to create a machine, and it was by learning
the inner working of nature that man became a builder of machines.

—Eric Hoffer, *Reflections on the Human Condition*

Machine learning (ML) is a branch of artificial intelligence that systematically applies algorithms to synthesize the underlying relationships among data and information. For example, ML systems can be trained on automatic speech recognition systems (such as iPhone's Siri) to convert acoustic information in a sequence of speech data into semantic structure expressed in the form of a string of words.

ML is already finding widespread uses in web search, ad placement, credit scoring, stock market prediction, gene sequence analysis, behavior analysis, smart coupons, drug development, weather forecasting, big data analytics, and many more applications. ML will play a decisive role in the development of a host of user-centric innovations.

ML owes its burgeoning adoption to its ability to characterize underlying relationships within large arrays of data in ways that solve problems in big data analytics, behavioral pattern recognition, and information evolution. ML systems can moreover be trained to categorize the changing conditions of a process so as to model variations in operating behavior. As bodies of knowledge evolve under the influence of new ideas and technologies, ML systems can identify disruptions to the existing models and redesign and retrain themselves to adapt to and coevolve with the new knowledge.

The computational characteristic of ML is to generalize the *training experience* (or examples) and output a hypothesis that estimates the target function. The generalization attribute of ML allows the system to perform well on unseen data instances by accurately predicting the future data. Unlike other optimization problems, ML does not have a well-defined function that can be optimized. Instead, training errors serve as a catalyst to test learning errors. The process of generalization requires classifiers that input discrete or continuous feature vectors and output a class.

The goal of ML is to predict future events or scenarios that are unknown to the computer. In 1959, Arthur Samuel described ML as the "field of study that gives computers the ability to learn without being explicitly programmed" (Samuel 1959). He concluded that programming computers to learn from experience should eventually eliminate the need for much of this detailed programming effort. According to Tom M. Mitchell's definition of ML: "A computer program is said to learn from experience E with respect to some class of tasks T and performance measure P, if its performance at tasks in T, as measured by P, improves with experience E." Alan Turing's seminal paper (Turing 1950) introduced a benchmark standard for demonstrating machine intelligence, such that a machine has to be intelligent and responsive in a manner that cannot be differentiated from that of a human being.

The learning process plays a crucial role in generalizing the problem by acting on its historical experience. Experience exists in the form of training datasets, which aid in achieving accurate results on new and unseen tasks. The training datasets encompass an existing problem domain that the learner uses to build a general model about that domain. This enables the model to generate largely accurate predictions in new cases.

Key Terminology

To facilitate the reader's understanding of the concept of ML, this section defines and discusses some key multidisciplinary conceptual terms in relation to ML.

- *classifier*. A method that receives a new input as an unlabeled instance of an observation or feature and identifies a category or class to which it belongs. Many commonly used classifiers employ statistical inference (probability measure) to categorize the best label for a given instance.

- *confusion matrix* (aka *error matrix*). A matrix that visualizes the performance of the classification algorithm using the data in the matrix. It compares the predicted classification against the actual classification in the form of false positive, true positive, false negative and true negative information. A confusion matrix for a two-class classifier system (Kohavi and Provost, 1998) follows:

Confusion Matrix		Predicted	
		Positive	Negative
Actual	Positive	TP	FN
	Negative	FP	TN

➢ TP = Outcome is correctly identified as positive.
➢ TN = Outcome is correctly identified as negative.
➢ FP = Outcome is incorrectly identified as positive.
➢ FN = Outcome is incorrectly identified as negative

- *accuracy* (aka *error rate*). The rate of correct (or incorrect) predictions made by the model over a dataset. Accuracy is usually estimated by using an independent test set that was not used at any time during the learning process. More complex accuracy estimation techniques, such as *cross-validation* and *bootstrapping*, are commonly used, especially with datasets containing a small number of instances.

$$\text{Accuracy (AC)} = \frac{TP + TN}{TP + TN + FN + FP} \tag{1-1}$$

$$\text{Precision (P)} = \frac{TP}{TP + FP} \tag{1-2}$$

$$\text{Recall} \left(R, \text{true positive rate} \right) = \frac{TP}{TP + FN} \tag{1-3}$$

$$\text{F} - \text{Measure} = \frac{\left(\beta^2 + 1 \right) \cdot P \cdot R}{\beta^2 \cdot P + R}, \tag{1-4}$$

where β has a value from 0 to infinity (∞) and is used to control the weight assigned to P and R.

- *cost*. The measurement of performance (or accuracy) of a model that predicts (or evaluates) the outcome for an established result; in other words, that quantifies the deviation between predicted and actual values (or class labels). An optimization function attempts to minimize the cost function.

- *cross-validation*. A verification technique that evaluates the generalization ability of a model for an independent dataset. It defines a dataset that is used for testing the trained model during the training phase for overfitting. Cross-validation can also be used to evaluate the performance of various prediction functions. In k-*fold cross-validation*, the training dataset is arbitrarily partitioned into k mutually exclusive subsamples (or *folds*) of equal sizes. The model is trained k times (or *folds*), where each iteration uses one of the k subsamples for testing (cross-validating), and the remaining k-1 subsamples are applied toward training the model. The k results of cross-validation are averaged to estimate the accuracy as a single estimation.

- *data mining*. The process of knowledge discovery (q.v.) or pattern detection in a large dataset. The methods involved in data mining aid in extracting the accurate data and transforming it to a known structure for further evaluation.

- *dataset*. A collection of data that conform to a schema with no ordering requirements. In a typical dataset, each column represents a feature and each row represents a member of the dataset.

- *dimension*. A set of attributes that defines a property. The primary functions of dimension are filtering, classification, and grouping.

- *induction algorithm*. An algorithm that uses the training dataset to generate a model that generalizes beyond the training dataset.

- *instance*. An object characterized by feature vectors from which the model is either trained for generalization or used for prediction.

- *knowledge discovery*. The process of abstracting knowledge from structured or unstructured sources to serve as the basis for further exploration. Such knowledge is collectively represented as a schema and can be condensed in the form of a model or models to which queries can be made for statistical prediction, evaluation, and further knowledge discovery.

- ***model***. A structure that summarizes a dataset for description or prediction. Each model can be tuned to the specific requirements of an application. Applications in big data have large datasets with many predictors and features that are too complex for a simple parametric model to extract useful information. The learning process synthesizes the parameters and the structures of a model from a given dataset. Models may be generally categorized as either *parametric* (described by a finite set of parameters, such that future predictions are independent of the new dataset) or *nonparametric* (described by an infinite set of parameters, such that the data distribution cannot be expressed in terms of a finite set of parameters). Nonparametric models are simple and flexible, and make fewer assumptions, but they require larger datasets to derive accurate conclusions.

- ***online analytical processing*** (**OLAP**). An approach for resolving multidimensional analytical queries. Such queries index into the data with two or more attributes (or dimensions). OLAP encompasses a broad class of business intelligence data and is usually synonymous with *multidimensional OLAP* (MOLAP). OLAP engines facilitate the exploration of multidimensional data interactively from several perspectives, thereby allowing for complex analytical and ad hoc queries with a rapid execution time. OLAP commonly uses intermediate data structures to store precalculated results on multidimensional data, allowing fast computation. *Relational OLAP* (ROLAP) uses relational databases of the base data and the dimension tables.

- ***schema***. A high-level specification of a dataset's attributes and properties.

- ***supervised learning***. Learning techniques that extract associations between independent attributes and a designated dependent attribute (the label). Supervised learning uses a training dataset to develop a prediction model by consuming input data and output values. The model can then make predictions of the output values for a new dataset. The performance of models developed using supervised learning depends upon the size and variance of the training dataset to achieve better generalization and greater predictive power for new datasets. Most induction algorithms fall into the supervised learning category.

- ***unsupervised learning***. Learning techniques that group instances without a prespecified dependent attribute. This technique generally involves learning structured patterns in the data by rejecting pure unstructured noise. Clustering and dimensionality reduction algorithms are usually unsupervised.

- ***feature vector***. An n-dimensional numerical vector of explanatory variables representing an instance of some object that facilitates processing and statistical analysis. Feature vectors are often weighted to construct a predictor function that is used to evaluate the quality or fitness of the prediction. The dimensionality of a feature vector can be reduced by various dimensionality reduction techniques, such as *principal component analysis* (PCA), *multilinear subspace reduction, isomaps,* and *latent semantic analysis* (LSA). The vector space associated with these vectors is often called the *feature space.*

Developing a Learning Machine

Machine learning aids in the development of programs that improve their performance for a given task through experience and training. Many big data applications leverage ML to operate at highest efficiency. The sheer volume, diversity, and speed of data flow have made it impracticable to exploit the natural capability of human beings to analyze data in real time. The surge in social networking and the wide use of Internet-based applications have resulted not only in greater volume of data, but also increased complexity of data. To preserve data resolution and avoid data loss, these streams of data need to be analyzed in real time.

The heterogeneity of the big data stream and the massive computing power we possess today present us with abundant opportunities to foster learning methodologies that can identify best practices for a given business problem. The sophistication of modern computing machines can handle large data volumes, greater complexity, and terabytes of storage. Additionally, intelligent program-flows that run on these machines can process and combine many such complex data streams to develop predictive models and extract intrinsic patterns in otherwise noisy data. When you need to predict or forecast a target value, supervised learning is the appropriate choice. The next step is to decide, depending on the target value, between *clustering* (in the case of discrete target value) and *regression* (in the case of numerical target value).

You start the development of ML by identifying all the metrics that are critical to a decision process. The processes of ML synthesize models for optimizing the metrics. Because the metrics are essential to developing the solution for a given decision process, they must be selected carefully during conceptual stages.

It is also important to judge whether ML is the suitable approach for solving a given problem. By its nature, ML cannot deliver perfect accuracy. For solutions requiring highly accurate results in a bounded time period, ML may not be the preferred approach. In general, the following conditions are favorable to the application of ML: (a) very high accuracy is not desired; (b) large volumes of data contain undiscovered patterns or information to be synthesized; (c) the problem itself is not very well understood owing to lack of knowledge or historical information as a basis for developing suitable algorithms; and (d) the problem needs to adapt to changing environmental conditions.

The process of developing ML algorithms may be decomposed into the following steps:

1. *Collect the data.* Select the subset of all available data attributes that might be useful in solving the problem. Selecting all the available data may be unnecessary or counterproductive. Depending upon the problem, data can either be retrieved through a data-stream API (such as a CPU performance counters) or synthesized by combining multiple data streams. In some cases, the input data streams, whether raw or synthetic, may be statistically preprocessed to improve usage or reduce bandwidth.

2. *Preprocess the Data.* Present the data in a manner that is understood by the consumer of the data. Preprocessing consists of the following three steps:

    i. *Formatting.* The data needs to be presented in a useable format. Using an industry-standard format enable plugging the solution with multiple vendors that in turn can mix and match algorithms and data sources such as XML, HTML, and SOAP.

    ii. *Cleaning.* The data needs to be cleaned by removing, substituting, or fixing corrupt or missing data. In some cases, data needs to be normalized, discretized, averaged, smoothened, or differentiated for efficient usage. In other cases, data may need to be transmitted as integers, double precisions, or strings.

    iii. *Sampling.* Data need to be sampled at regular or adaptive intervals in a manner such that redundancy is minimized without the loss of information for transmission via communication channels.

3. *Transform the data.* Transform the data specific to the algorithm and the knowledge of the problem. Transformation can be in the form of feature scaling, decomposition, or aggregation. Features can be decomposed to extract the useful components embedded in the data or aggregated to combine multiple instances into a single feature.

4. *Train the algorithm.* Select the training and testing datasets from the transformed data. An algorithm is trained on the training dataset and evaluated against the test set. The transformed training dataset is fed to the algorithm for extraction of knowledge or information. This trained knowledge or information is stored as a model to be used for cross-validation and actual usage. Unsupervised learning, having no target value, does not require the training step.

5. *Test the algorithm.* Evaluate the algorithm to test its effectiveness and performance. This step enables quick determination whether any learnable structures can be identified in the data. A trained model exposed to test dataset is measured against predictions made on that test dataset which are indicative of the performance of the model. If the performance of the model needs improvement, repeat the previous steps by changing the data streams, sampling rates, transformations, linearizing models, outliers' removal methodology, and biasing schemes.

6. *Apply reinforcement learning.* Most control theoretic applications require a good feedback mechanism for stable operations. In many cases, the feedback data are sparse, delayed, or unspecific. In such cases, supervised learning may not be practical and may be substituted with *reinforcement learning* (RL). In contrast to supervised learning, RL employs dynamic performance rebalancing to learn from the consequences of interactions with the environment, without explicit training.

7. *Execute.* Apply the validated model to perform an actual task of prediction. If new data are encountered, the model is retrained by applying the previous steps. The process of training may coexist with the real task of predicting future behavior.

Machine Learning Algorithms

Based on underlying mappings between input data and anticipated output presented during the learning phase of ML, ML algorithms may be classified into the following six categories:

- *Supervised learning* is a learning mechanism that infers the underlying relationship between the observed data (also called *input data*) and a target variable (a dependent variable or label) that is subject to prediction (Figure 1-1). The learning task uses the labeled training data (training examples) to synthesize the model function that attempts to generalize the underlying relationship between the feature vectors (input) and the supervisory signals (output). The feature vectors influence the direction and magnitude of change in order to improve the overall performance of the function model. The training data comprise observed input (feature) vectors and a desired output value (also called the *supervisory signal* or *class label*). A well-trained function model based on a supervised learning algorithm can accurately predict the class labels for hidden phenomena embedded in unfamiliar or unobserved data instances. The goal of learning algorithms is to minimize the error for a given set of inputs (the training set). However, for a poor-quality training set that is influenced by the accuracy and versatility of the labeled examples, the model may encounter the problem of overfitting, which typically represents poor generalization and erroneous classification.

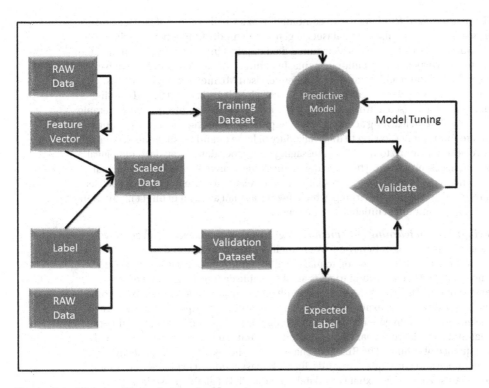

Figure 1-1. *High-level flow of supervised learning*

- ***Unsupervised learning algorithms*** are designed to discover hidden structures in unlabeled datasets, in which the desired output is unknown. This mechanism has found many uses in the areas of data compression, outlier detection, classification, human learning, and so on. The general approach to learning involves training through probabilistic data models. Two popular examples of unsupervised learning are *clustering* and *dimensionality reduction*. In general, an unsupervised learning dataset is composed of inputs $x_1, x_2, x_3 \cdots x_n$, but it contains neither target outputs (as in supervised learning) nor rewards from its environment. The goal of ML in this case is to hypothesize representations of the input data for efficient decision making, forecasting, and information filtering and clustering. For example, unsupervised training can aid in the development of phase-based models in which each phase, synthesized through an unsupervised learning process, represents a unique condition for opportunistic tuning of the process. Furthermore, each phase can act as a state and can be subjected to forecasting for proactive resource allocation or distribution. Unsupervised learning algorithms centered on a probabilistic distribution model generally use *maximum likelihood estimation* (MLE), *maximum a posteriori* (MAP), or Bayes methods. Other algorithms that are not based on probability distribution models may employ statistical measurements, quantization error, variance preserving, entropy gaps, and so on.

- ***Semi-supervised learning*** uses a combination of a small number of labeled and a large number of unlabeled datasets to generate a model function or classifier. Because the labeling process of acquired data requires intensive skilled human labor inputs, it is expensive and impracticable. In contrast, unlabeled data are relatively inexpensive and readily available. Semi-supervised ML methodology operates somewhere between the guidelines of unsupervised learning (unlabeled training data) and supervised learning (labeled training data) and can produce considerable improvement in learning accuracy. Semi-supervised learning has recently gained greater prominence, owing to the availability of large quantities of unlabeled data for diverse applications to web data, messaging data, stock data, retail data, biological data, images, and so on. This learning methodology can deliver value of practical and theoretical significance, especially in areas related to human learning, such as speech, vision, and handwriting, which involve a small amount of direct instruction and a large amount of unlabeled experience.

- ***Reinforcement learning (RL) methodology*** involves exploration of an adaptive sequence of actions or behaviors by an intelligent agent (*RL-agent*) in a given environment with a motivation to maximize the cumulative reward (Figure 1-2). The intelligent agent's action triggers an observable change in the state of the environment. The learning technique synthesizes an adaptation model by training itself for a given set of experimental actions and observed responses to the state of the environment. In general, this methodology can be viewed as a control-theoretic trial-and-error learning paradigm with rewards and punishments associated with a sequence of actions. The RL-agent changes its policy based on the collective experience and consequent rewards. RL seeks past actions it explored that resulted in rewards. To build an exhaustive database or model of all the possible action-reward projections, many unproven actions need to be tried. These untested actions may have to be attempted multiple times before ascertaining their strength. Therefore, you have to strike a balance between exploration of new possible actions and likelihood of failure resulting from those actions. Critical elements of RL include the following:

    - The *policy* is a key component of an RL-agent that maps the control-actions to the perceived state of the environment.

    - The *critic* represents an estimated value function that criticizes the actions that are made according to existing policy. Alternatively, the critic evaluates the performance of the current state in response to an action taken according to current policy. The critic-agent shapes the policy by making continuous and ongoing corrections.

    - The *reward function* estimates the instantaneous desirability of the perceived state of the environment for an attempted control-action.

    - *Models* are planning tools that aid in predicting the future course of action by contemplating possible future situations.

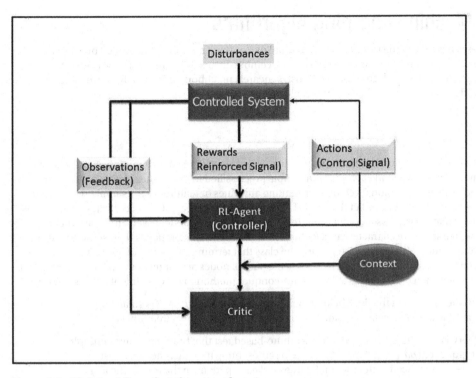

Figure 1-2. High-level flow of reinforcement learning

- ***Transductive learning*** (aka *transductive inference*) attempts to predict exclusive model functions on specific test cases by using additional observations on the training dataset in relation to the new cases (Vapnik 1998). A local model is established by fitting new individual observations (the training data) into a single point in space—this, in contrast to the global model, in which new data have to fit into the existing model without postulating any specific information related to the location of that data point in space. Although the new data may fit into the global model to a certain extent (with some error), thereby creating a global model that would represent the entire problem, space is a challenge and may not be necessary in all cases. In general, if you experience discontinuities during the model development for a given problem space, you can synthesize multiple models at the discontinuous boundaries. In this case, newly observed data are the processed through the model that fulfill the boundary conditions in which the model is valid.

- ***Inductive inference*** estimates the model function based on the relation of data to the entire hypothesis space, and uses this model to forecast output values for examples beyond the training set. These functions can be defined using one of the many representation schemes, including linear weighted polynomials, logical rules, and probabilistic descriptions, such as Bayesian networks. Many statistical learning methods start with initial solutions for the hypothesis space and then evolve them iteratively to reduce error. Many popular algorithms fall into this category, including SVMs (Vapnik 1998), *neural network* (NN) models (Carpenter and Grossberg 1991), and neuro-fuzzy algorithms (Jang 1993). In certain cases, one may apply a *lazy learning* model, in which the generalization process can be an ongoing task that effectively develops a richer hypothesis space, based on new data applied to the existing model.

Popular Machine Learning Algorithms

This section describes in turn the top 10 most influential data mining algorithms identified by the IEEE International Conference on Data Mining (ICDM) in December 2006: C4.5, *k*-means, SVMs, Apriori, estimation maximization (EM), PageRank, AdaBoost, *k*–nearest neighbors (*k*-NN), naive Bayes, and classification and regression trees (CARTs) (Wu et al. 2008).

C4.5

C4.5 classifiers are one of the most frequently used categories of algorithms in data mining. A C4.5 classifier inputs a collection of cases wherein each case is a sample preclassified to one of the existing classes. Each case is described by its *n*-dimensional vector, representing attributes or features of the sample. The output of a C4.5 classifier can accurately predict the class of a previously unseen case. C4.5 classification algorithms generate classifiers that are expressed as decision trees by synthesizing a model based on a tree structure. Each node in the tree structure characterizes a feature, with corresponding branches representing possible values connecting features and leaves representing the class that terminates a series of nodes and branches. The class of an instance can be determined by tracing the path of nodes and branches to the terminating leaf.

Given a set *S* of instances, C4.5 uses a divide-and-conquer method to grow an initial tree, as follows:

- If all the samples in the list *S* belong to the same class, or if the list *S* is small, then create a leaf node for the decision tree and label it with the most frequent class.

- Otherwise, the algorithm selects an attribute-based test that branches *S* into multiple subbranches (*partitions*) (*S1*, *S2*, ...), each representing the outcome of the test. The tests are placed at the root of the tree, and each path from the root to the leaf becomes a *rule script* that labels a class at the leaf. This procedure applies to each subbranch recursively.

- Each partition of the current branch represents a child node, and the test separating *S* represents the branch of the tree.

This process continues until every leaf contains instances from only one class or further partition is not possible. C4.5 uses tests that select attributes with the highest normalized information gain, enabling disambiguation of the classification of cases that may belong to two or more classes.

k-Means

The k-*means* algorithm is a simple iterative clustering algorithm (Lloyd 1957) that partitions *N* data points into *K* disjoint subsets S_j so as to minimize the sum-of-squares criterion. Because the sum of squares is the squared Euclidean distance, this is intuitively the "nearest" mean,

$$J = \sum_{j=1}^{K} \sum_{n \in S_j} |x_n - \mu_j|^2, \tag{1-5}$$

where
x_n = vector representing the nth data point
μ_j = geometric centroid of the data points in S_j

The algorithm consists of a simple two-step re-estimation process:

1. *Assignment*: Data points are assigned to the cluster whose centroid is closest to that point.

2. *Update*: Each cluster centroid is recalculated to the center (mean) of all data points assigned to it.

These two steps are alternated until a stopping criterion is met, such that there is no further change in the assignment of data points. Every iteration requires $N \times K$ comparisons, representing the time complexity of one iteration.

Support Vector Machines

Support vector machines (SVMs) are supervised learning methods that analyze data and recognize patterns. SVMs are primarily used for classification, regression analysis, and novelty detection. Given a set of training data in a two-class learning task, an SVM training algorithm constructs a model or classification function that assigns new observations to one of the two classes on either side of a hyperplane, making it a nonprobabilistic binary linear classifier (Figure 1-3). An SVM model maps the observations as points in space, such that they are classified into a separate partition that is divided by the largest distance to the nearest observation data point of any class (the *functional margin*). New observations are then predicted to belong to a class based on which side of the partition they fall. Support vectors are the data points nearest to the hyperplane that divides the classes. Further details of support vector machines are given in Chapter 4.

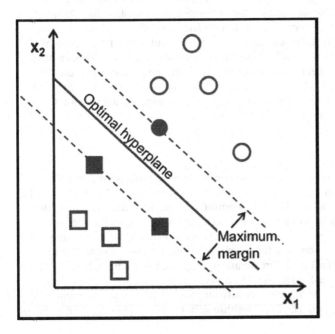

Figure 1-3. *The SVM algorithm finds the hyperplane that maximizes the largest minimum distance between the support vectors*

Apriori

Apriori is a data mining approach that discovers frequent itemsets by using candidate generation (Agrawal and Srikant 1994) from a transactional database and highlighting association rules (general trends) in the database. It assumes that any subset of a frequently occurring pattern must be frequent. Apriori performs breadth-first search to scan frequent 1-itemsets (that is, itemsets of size 1) by accumulating the count for each item that satisfies the minimum support requirement. The set of frequent 1-itemsets is used to find the set of frequent 2-itemsets, and so on. This process iterates until no more frequent k-itemsets can be found. The Apriori method that identifies all the frequent itemsets can be summarized in the following three steps:

1. Generate candidates for frequent $k + 1$-itemsets (of size $k + 1$) from the frequent k-itemsets (of size k).

2. Scan the database to identify candidates for frequent $k + 1$-itemsets, and calculate the support of each of those candidates.

3. Add those itemsets that satisfy the minimum support requirement to frequent itemsets of size $k + 1$.

Thanks in part to the simplicity of the algorithm, it is widely used in data mining applications. Various improvements have been proposed, notably, the *frequent pattern growth* (FP-growth) extension, which eliminates candidate generation. Han et al. (Han, Pei, and Yin 2000) propose a *frequent pattern tree* (FP-tree) structure, which stores and compresses essential information to interpret frequent patterns and uses FP-growth for mining the comprehensive set of frequent patterns by pattern fragment growth. This Apriori technique enhancement constructs a large database that contains all the essential information and compresses it into a highly condensed data structure. In the subsequent step, it assembles a *conditional-pattern base* which represents a set of counted patterns that co-occur relative to each item. Starting at the frequent header table, it traverses the FP-tree by following each frequent item and stores the prefix paths of those items to produce a conditional pattern base. Finally, it constructs a *conditional FP-tree* for each of the frequent items of the conditional pattern base. Each node in the tree represents an item and its count. Nodes sharing the same label but residing on different subtrees are conjoined by a node–link pointer. The position of a node in the tree structure represents the order of the frequency of an item, such that a node closer to the root may be shared by more transactions in a transactional database.

Estimation Maximization

The *estimation–maximization* (EM) algorithm facilitates parameter estimation in probabilistic models with incomplete data. EM is an iterative scheme that estimates the MLE or MAP of parameters in statistical models, in the presence of hidden or latent variables. The EM algorithm iteratively alternates between the steps of performing an expectation (E), which creates a function that estimates the probability distribution over possible completions of the missing (unobserved) data, using the current estimate for the parameters, and performing a maximization (M), which re-estimates the parameters, using the current completions performed during the E step. These parameter estimates are iteratively employed to estimate the distribution of the hidden variables in the subsequent E step. In general, EM involves running an iterative algorithm with the following attributes: (a) observed data, X; (b) latent (or missing) data, Z; (c) unknown parameter, θ; and (d) a likelihood function, $L(\theta; X, Z) = P(X, Z|\theta)$. The EM algorithm iteratively calculates the MLE of the marginal likelihood using a two-step method:

1. *Estimation (E)*: Calculate the expected value of the log likelihood function, with respect to the conditional distribution of Z, given X under the current estimate of the parameters $\theta(t)$, such that

$$Q(\theta \,|\, \theta(t)) = E_{Z|X,\theta(t)}\big[\log L(\theta; X, Z)\big]. \tag{1-6}$$

2. *Maximization (M)*: Find the parameter that maximizes this quantity:

$$\theta(t+1) = \arg_\theta \max Q(\theta \,|\, \theta(t)).$$ (1-7)

PageRank

PageRank is a link analysis search algorithm that ranks the elements of hyperlinked documents on the World Wide Web for the purpose of measuring their importance, relative to other links. Developed by Larry Page and Sergey Bin, PageRank produces static rankings that are independent of the search queries. PageRank simulates the concept of prestige in a social network. A hyperlink to a page counts as a vote of support. Additionally, PageRank interprets a hyperlink from source page to target page in such a manner that the page with the higher rank improves the rank of the linked page (the source or target). Therefore, backlinks from highly ranked pages are more significant than those from average pages. Mathematically simple, PageRank can be calculated as

$$r(P) = \sum_{Q \in B_p} \frac{r(Q)}{|Q|},$$ (1-8)

where
$r(P)$ = rank of the page P
B_p = the set of all pages linking to page P
$|Q|$ = number of links from page Q
$r(Q)$ = rank of the page Q

AdaBoost (Adaptive Boosting)

AdaBoost is an ensemble method used for constructing strong classifiers as linear combinations of simple, weak classifiers (or rules of thumb) (Freund and Schapire 1997). As in any ensemble method, AdaBoost employs multiple learners to solve a problem with better generalization ability and more accurate prediction. The strong classifier can be evaluated as a linear combination of weak classifiers, such that

$$H(x) = \sum_{t=1}^{T} \beta_t \cdot h_t(x),$$

where
$H(x)$ = strong classifier
$h_t(x)$ = weak classifier (*feature*)

The Adaboost algorithm may be summarized as follows:

Input:
Data-Set $I = \{(x_1, y_1), (x_2, y_2), (x_3, y_3), \cdots, (x_m, y_m)\}$,
Base learning algorithm L
Number of learning rounds T

Process:
$$D_1^i = \frac{1}{m}$$ *// Initialize weight distribution*
FOR (t = 1 to T) DO   *// **Run the loop for t = T iterations***
$h_t = L(I, D_t)$ *// Train a weak learner h_t from I using D_t*
$\epsilon_t = \sum_i D_t^i |h_t(x_i) - y_i|$ *// calculate the error of h_t*

13

$$\beta_t = \frac{1}{2}\ln\left(\frac{1-\epsilon_t}{\epsilon_t}\right) \qquad // \text{ calculate the weight of } h_t$$

$$D_{t+1}^i = \frac{D_t^i}{Z_t}\cdot e^{(-\beta_t\, y_i\, h_t(x_i))} \qquad // \text{ Update the distribution,}$$
$$// \; Z_t \text{ is the normalization factor}$$

END

Output:

$$H(x) = sign\left(\sum_{t=1}^{T}\beta_t h_t(x)\right) \; // \text{ Strong classifier}$$

The AdaBoost algorithm is adaptive, inasmuch as it uses multiple iterations to produce a strong learner that is well correlated with the true classifier. As shown above, it iterates by adding weak learners that are slightly correlated with the true classifier. As part of the adaptation process, the weighting vector adjusts itself to improve upon misclassification in previous rounds. The resulting classifier has a greater accuracy than the weak learners' classifiers. AdaBoost is fast, simple to implement, and flexible insofar as it can be combined with any classifier.

k-Nearest Neighbors

The k-*nearest neighbors* (k-*NN*) classification methodology identifies a group of k objects in the training set that are closest to the test object and assigns a label based on the most dominant class in this neighborhood. The three fundamental elements of this approach are

- an existing set of labeled objects
- a distance metric to estimate distance between objects
- the number of nearest neighbors (k)

To classify an unlabeled object, the distances between it and labeled objects are calculated and its k-nearest neighbors are identified. The class labels of these nearest neighbors serve as a reference for classifying the unlabeled object. The k-*NN* algorithm computes the similarity distance between a training set, $(x, y) \in I$, and the test object, $z = (\hat{x},\hat{y})$, to determine its nearest-neighbor list, I_z. x represents the training object, and y represents the corresponding training class. $\hat{x}$ and $\hat{y}$ represent the test object and its class, respectively. The algorithm may be summarized as follows:

Input:
Training object $(x, y) \in I$ and test object $z = (\hat{x},\hat{y})$

Process:
Compute distance $d = (\hat{x}, x)$ between z and every object $(x, y) \in I$.
Select $I_z \subseteq I$, the set of k closest training objects to z.

Output (Majority Class):
$$\hat{y} = \arg_v max \sum_{(x_i, y_i)\in I_z} F(v = y_i)$$

$F(.) = 1$ if argument (.) is TRUE and 0 otherwise, v is the class label.
The value of k should be chosen carefully. A smaller value can result in noisy behavior, whereas a larger value may include too many points from other classes.

Naive Bayes

Naive Bayes is a simple probabilistic classifier that applies Bayes' theorem with strong (naive) assumption of independence, such that the presence of an individual feature of a class is unrelated to the presence of another feature.

Assume that input features $x_1, x_2 \cdots x_n$ are conditionally independent of each other, given the class label Y, such that

$$P(x_1, x_2 \cdots x_n | Y) = \prod_{i=1}^{n} P(x_i | Y) \tag{1-9}$$

For a two-class classification ($i = 0,1$), we define $P(i|x)$ as the probability that measurement vector $x = \{x_1, x_2 \cdots x_n\}$ belongs to class i. Moreover, we define a classification score

$$\frac{P(1|x)}{P(0|x)} = \frac{\prod_{j=1}^{n} f(x_j|1)P(1)}{\prod_{j=1}^{n} f(x_j|0)P(0)} = \frac{P(1)}{P(0)} \prod_{j=1}^{n} \frac{f(x_j|1)}{f(x_j|0)} \tag{1-10}$$

$$\ln \frac{P(1|x)}{P(0|x)} = \ln \frac{P(1)}{P(0)} + \sum_{j=1}^{n} \ln \frac{f(x_j|1)}{f(x_j|0)}, \tag{1-11}$$

where $P(i|x)$ is proportional to $f(x|i)P(i)$ and $f(x|i)$ is the conditional distribution of x for class i objects.

The naive Bayes model is surprisingly effective and immensely appealing, owing to its simplicity and robustness. Because this algorithm does not require application of complex iterative parameter estimation schemes to large datasets, it is very useful and relatively easy to construct and use. It is a popular algorithm in areas related to text classification and spam filtering.

Classification and Regression Trees

A *classification and regression tree* (CART) is a nonparametric decision tree that uses a binary recursive partitioning scheme by splitting two child nodes repeatedly, starting with the root node, which contains the complete learning sample (Breiman et al. 1984). The tree-growing process involves splitting among all the possible splits at each node, such that the resulting child nodes are the "purest." Once a CART has generated a "maximal tree," it examines the smaller trees obtained by pruning away the branches of the maximal tree to determine which contribute least to the overall performance of the tree on training data. The CART mechanism is intended to yield a sequence of nested pruned trees. The right-sized, or "honest," tree is identified by evaluating the predictive performance of every tree in the pruning sequence.

Challenging Problems in Data Mining Research

Data mining and knowledge discovery have become fields of interdisciplinary research in the areas related to database systems, ML, intelligent information systems, expert systems, control theory, and many others. Data mining is an important and active area of research but not one without theoretical and practical challenges from working with very large databases that may be noisy, incomplete, redundant, and dynamic in nature. A study by Yang and Wu (2006) reviews the most challenging problems in data mining research, as summarized in the following sections.

Scaling Up for High-Dimensional Data and High-Speed Data Streams

Designing classifiers that can handle very high-dimensional features extracted through high-speed data streams is challenging. To ensure a decisive advantage, data mining in such cases should be a continuous and online process. But, technical challenges prevent us from computing models over large amounts streaming data in the presence of *environment drift* and *concept drift*. Today, we try to solve this problem with incremental mining and offline model updating to maintain accurate modeling of the current data stream. Information technology challenges are being addressed by developing in-memory databases, high-density memories, and large storage capacities, all supported by high-performance computing infrastructure.

Mining Sequence Data and Time Series Data

Efficient classification, clustering, and forecasting of sequenced and time series data remain an open challenge today. Time series data are often contaminated by noise, which can have a detrimental effect on short-term and long-term prediction. Although noise may be filtered, using signal-processing techniques or smoothening methods, lags in the filtered data may result. In a closed-loop environment, this can reduce the accuracy of prediction, because we may end up overcompensating or underprovisioning the process itself. In certain cases, lags can be corrected by differential predictors, but these may require a great deal of tuning the model itself. Noise-canceling filters placed close to the data I/O block can be tuned to identify and clean the noisy data before they are mined.

Mining Complex Knowledge from Complex Data

Complex data can exist in many forms and may require special techniques to extract the information useful for making real-world decisions. For example, information may exist in a graphical form, requiring methods for discovering graphs and structured patterns in large data. Another complexity may exist in the form of *non—independent-and-identically-distributed* (non-iid) data objects that cannot be mined as an independent single object. They may share relational structures with other data objects that should be identified.

State-of-the-art data mining methods for unstructured data lack the ability to incorporate domain information and knowledge interface for the purpose of relating the results of data mining to real-world scenarios.

Distributed Data Mining and Mining Multi-Agent Data

In a distributed data sensing environment, it can be challenging to discover distributed patterns and correlate the data streamed through different probes. The goal is to minimize the amount of data exchange and reduce the required communication bandwidth. Game-theoretic methodologies may be deployed to tackle this challenge.

Data Mining Process-Related Problems

Autonomous data mining and cleaning operations can improve the efficiency of data mining dramatically. Although we can process models and discover patterns at a fast rate, major costs are incurred by preprocessing operations such as data integration and data cleaning. Reducing these costs through automation can deliver a much greater payoff than attempting to further reduce the cost of model-building and pattern-finding.

Security, Privacy, and Data Integrity

Ensuring users' privacy while their data are being mined is critical. Assurance of the knowledge integrity of collected input data and synthesized individual patterns is no less essential.

Dealing with Nonstatic, Unbalanced, and Cost-Sensitive Data

Data is dynamic and changing continually in different domains. Historical trials in data sampling and model construction may be suboptimal. As you retrain a current model based on new training data, you may experience a learning drift, owing to different selection biases. Such biases need to be corrected dynamically for accurate prediction.

Summary

This chapter discussed the essentials of ML through key terminology, types of ML, and the top 10 data mining and ML algorithms. Owing to the explosion of data on the World Wide Web, ML has found widespread use in web search, advertising placement, credit scoring, stock market prediction, gene sequence analysis, behavior analysis, smart coupons, drug development, weather forecasting, big data analytics, and many more such applications. New uses for ML are being explored every day. Big data analytics and graph analytics have become essential components of cloud-based business development. The new field of data analytics and the applications of ML have also accelerated the development of specialized hardware and accelerators to improve algorithmic performance, big data storage, and data retrieval performance.

References

Agrawal, Rakesh, and Ramakrishnan Srikant. "Fast Algorithms for Mining Association Rules in Large Databases." In *Proceedings of the 20th International Conference on Very Large Data Bases (VLDB '94), September 12–15, 1994, Santiago de Chile, Chile,* edited by Jorge B. Bocca, Matthias Jarke, and Carlo Zaniolo. San Francisco: Morgan Kaufmann (1994): 487–499.

Breiman, Leo, Jerome H. Friedman, Richard A. Olshen, and Charles J. Stone. *Classification and Regression Trees.* Belmont, CA: Wadsworth, 1984.

Carpenter, Gail A., and Stephen Grossberg. *Pattern Recognition by Self-Organizing Neural Networks.* Massachusetts: Cambridge, MA: Massachusetts Institute of Technology Press, 1991.

Freund, Yoav, and Robert E. Schapire. "A Decision-Theoretic Generalization of On-Line Learning and an Application to Boosting." *Journal of Computer and System Sciences* 55, no. 1 (1997): 119–139.

Han, Jiawel, Jian Pei, and Yiwen Yin. "Mining Frequent Patterns without Candidate Generation." In *SIGMOD/PODS '00: ACM international Conference on Management of Data and Symposium on Principles of Database Systems, Dallas, TX, USA, May 15–18, 2000,* edited by Weidong Chen, Jeffrey Naughton, Philip A. Bernstein. New York: ACM (2000): 1–12.

Jang, J.-S. R. "ANFIS: Adaptive-Network-Based Fuzzy Inference System." *IEEE Transactions on Systems, Man and Cybernetics* 23, no. 3 (1993): 665–685.

Kohavi, Ron, and Foster Provost. "Glossary of Terms." *Machine Learning* 30, no. 2–3 (1998): 271–274.

Lloyd, Stuart P. "Least Squares Quantization in PCM," in special issue on quantization, *IEEE Transactions on Information Theory*, IT-28, no. 2(1982): 129–137.

Samuel, Arthur L. "Some Studies in Machine Learning Using the Game of Checkers," *IBM Journal of Research and Development* 44:1.2 (1959): 210–229.

Turing, Alan M. "Computing machinery and intelligence." *Mind* (1950): 433–460.

Vapnik, Vladimir N. *Statistical Learning Theory*. New York: Wiley, 1998.

Wu, Xindong, Vipin Kumar, Ross Quinlan, Joydeep Ghosh, Qiang Yang, Hiroshi Motoda, Geoffrey J. McLachlan, Angus Ng, Bing Liu, Philip S. Yu, Zhi-Hua Zhou, Michael Steinbach, David J. Hand, and Dan Steinberg. "Top 10 Algorithms in Data Mining." *Knowledge and Information Systems* 14 (2008): 1–37.

Yang, Qiang, and Xindong Wu. "10 Challenging Problems in Data Mining Research." *International Journal of Information Technology and Decision Making* 5, no. 4 (2006): 597–604.

CHAPTER 2

■ ■ ■

Machine Learning and Knowledge Discovery

When you know a thing, to hold that you know it; and when you do not know a thing, to allow that you do not know it—this is knowledge.

—Confucius, *The Analects*

The field of data mining has made significant advances in recent years. Because of its ability to solve complex problems, data mining has been applied in diverse fields related to engineering, biological science, social media, medicine, and business intelligence. The primary objective for most of the applications is to characterize patterns in a complex stream of data. These patterns are then coupled with knowledge discovery and decision making. In the Internet age, information gathering and dynamic analysis of spatiotemporal data are key to innovation and developing better products and processes. When datasets are large and complex, it becomes difficult to process and analyze patterns using traditional statistical methods. *Big data* are data collected in volumes so large, and forms so complex and unstructured, that they cannot be handled using standard database management systems, such as DBMS and RDBMS. The emerging challenges associated with big data include dealing not only with increased volume, but also the wide variety and complexity of the data streams that need to be extracted, transformed, analyzed, stored, and visualized. Big data analysis uses inferential statistics to draw conclusions related to dependencies, behaviors, and predictions from large sets of data with low information density that are subject to random variations. Such systems are expected to model knowledge discovery in a format that produces reasonable answers when applied across a wide range of situations. The characteristics of big data are as follows:

- *Volume*: A great quantity of data is generated. Detecting relevance and value within this large volume is challenging.

- *Variety*: The range of data types and sources is wide.

- *Velocity*: The speed of data generation is fast. Reacting in a timely manner can be demanding.

- *Variability*: Data flows can be highly inconsistent and difficult to manage, owing to seasonal and event-driven peaks.

- *Complexity*: The data need to be linked, connected, and correlated to infer nonlinear relationships and causal effects.

Modern technological advancements have enabled the industry to make inroads into big data and big data analytics. Affordable open source software infrastructure, faster processors, cheaper storage, virtualization, high throughput connectivity, and development of unstructured data management tools, in conjunction with cloud computing, have opened the door to high-quality information retrieval and faster analytics, enabling businesses to reduce costs and time required to develop newer products with customized offerings.

Big data and powerful analytics can be integrated to deliver valuable services, such as these:

- *Failure root cause detection*: The cost of unplanned shutdowns resulting from unexpected failures can run into billions of dollars. *Root cause analysis* (RCA) identifies the factors determinative of the location, magnitude, timing, and nature of past failures and learns to associate actions, conditions, and behaviors that can prevent the recurrence of such failures. RCA transforms a reactive approach to failure mitigation into a proactive approach of solving problems before they occur and avoids unnecessary escalation.

- *Dynamic coupon system*: A dynamic coupon system allows discount coupons to be delivered in a very selective manner, corresponding to factors that maximize the strategic benefits to the product or service provider. Factors that regulate the delivery of the coupon to selected recipients are modeled on existing locality, assessed interest in a specific product, historical spending patterns, dynamic pricing, chronological visits to shopping locations, product browsing patterns, and redemption of past coupons. Each of these factors is weighted and reanalyzed as a function of competitive pressures, transforming behaviors, seasonal effects, external factors, and dynamics of product maturity. A coupon is delivered in real time, according to the recipient's profile, context, and location. The speed, precision, and accuracy of coupon delivery to large numbers of mobile recipients are important considerations.

- *Shopping behavior analysis*: A manufacturer of a product is particularly interested in the understanding the heat-map patterns of its competitors' products on the store floor. For example, a manufacturer of large-screen TVs would want to ascertain buyers' interest in features offered by other TV manufacturers. This can only be analyzed by evaluating potential buyers' movements and time spent in proximity to the competitors' products on the floor. Such reports can be delivered to the manufacturer on an individual basis, in real time, or collectively, at regular intervals. The reports may prompt manufacturers to deliver dynamic coupons to influence potential buyers who are still in the decision-making stage as well as help the manufacturer improve, remove, retain, or augment features, as gauged by buyers' interest in the competitors' products.

- *Detecting fraudulent behavior*: Various types of fraud related to insurance, health care, credit cards, and identity theft cost consumers and businesses billions of dollars. Big data and smart analytics have paved the way for developing real-time solutions for identifying fraud and preventing it before it occurs. Smart analytics generate models that validate the patterns related to spending behavior, geolocation, peak activity, and insurance claims. If a pattern cannot be validated, a corrective, preventive, or punitive action is initiated. The accuracy, precision, and velocity of such actions are critical to the success of isolating the fraudulent behavior. For instance, each transaction may evaluate up to 500 attributes, using one or more models in real time.

- *Workload resource tuning and selection in datacenter*: In a cloud service management environment, *service-level agreements* (SLAs) define the expectation of *quality of service* (QoS) for managing performance loss in a given service-hosting environment composed of a pool of computing resources. Typically, the complexity of resource interdependencies in a server system results in suboptimal behavior, leading to performance loss. A well-behaved model can anticipate demand patterns and proactively react to dynamic stresses in a timely and optimized manner. Dynamic characterization methods can synthesize a self-correcting workload fingerprint codebook that facilitates phase prediction to achieve continuous tuning through proactive workload allocation and load balancing. In other words, the codebook characterizes certain features, which are continually reevaluated to remodel workload behavior to accommodate deviation from an anticipated output. It is possible, however, that the most current model in the codebook may not have been subjected to newer or unidentified patterns. A new workload is hosted on a compute node (among thousands of potential nodes) in a manner that not only reduces the thermal hot spots, but also improves performance by lowering the resource bottleneck. The velocity of the analysis that results in optimal hosting of the workload in real time is critical to the success of workload load allocation and balancing.

Knowledge Discovery

Knowledge extraction gathers information from structured and unstructured sources to construct a knowledge database for identifying meaningful and useful patterns from underlying large and semantically fuzzy datasets. *Fuzzy datasets* are sets whose elements have a degree of membership. *Degree of membership* is defined by a *membership function* that is valued between 0 and 1.

The extracted knowledge is reused, in conjunction with source data, to produce an enumeration of patterns that are added back to the knowledge base. The process of *knowledge discovery* involves programmatic exploration of large volumes of data for patterns that can be enumerated as knowledge. The knowledge acquired is presented as models to which specific queries can be made, as necessary. Knowledge discovery joins the concepts of computer science and machine learning (such as databases and algorithms) with those of statistics to solve user-oriented queries and issues. Knowledge can be described in different forms, such as classes of actors, attribute association models, and dependencies. Knowledge discovery in big data uses core machine algorithms that are designed for *classification, clustering, dimensionality reduction*, and *collaborative filtering* as well as scalable distributed systems. This chapter discusses the classes of machine learning algorithms that are useful when the dataset to be processed is very large for a single machine.

Classification

Classification is central to developing predictive analytics capable of replicating human decision making. Classification algorithms work well for problems with well-defined boundaries in which inputs follow a specific set of attributes and in which the output is categorical. Generally, the classification process develops an *archive of experiences* entailing evaluation of new inputs by matching them with previously observed patterns. If a pattern can be matched, the input is associated with the predefined predictive behavioral pattern. If a pattern cannot be matched, it is quarantined for further evaluation to determine if it is an undiscovered valid pattern or an unusual pattern. Machine-based classification algorithms follow supervised-learning techniques, in which algorithms learn through examples (also called training sets) of accurate decision making, using carefully prepared inputs. The two main steps involved in classification are synthesizing a model, using a learning algorithm, and employing the model to categorize new data.

Clustering

Clustering is a process of knowledge discovery that groups items from a given collection, based on similar attributes (or characteristics). Members of the same cluster share similar characteristics, relative to those belonging to different clusters. Generally, clustering involves an iterative algorithm of trial and error that operates on an assumption of similarity (or dissimilarity) and that stops when a termination criterion is satisfied. The challenge is to find a function that measures the *degree of similarity* between two items (or data points) as a numerical value. The parameters for clustering—such as the clustering algorithm, the distance function, the density threshold, and the number of clusters—depend on the applications and the individual dataset.

Dimensionality Reduction

Dimensionality reduction is the process of reducing random variables through feature selection and feature extraction. Dimensionality reduction allows shorter training times and enhanced generalization and reduces overfitting. *Feature selection* is the process of synthesizing a subset of the original variables for model construction by eliminating redundant or irrelevant features. *Feature extraction*, in contrast, is the process of transforming the high-dimensional space to a space of fewer dimensions by combining attributes.

Collaborative Filtering

Collaborative filtering (CF) is the process of filtering for information or patterns, using collaborative methods between multiple data sources. CF explores an area of interest by gathering preferences from many users with similar interests and making recommendations based on those preferences. CF algorithms are expected to make satisfactory recommendations in a short period of time, despite very sparse data, increasing numbers of users and items, synonymy, data noise, and privacy issues.

Machine learning performs predictive analysis, based on established properties learned from the training data (models). Machine learning assists in exploring *useful knowledge* or *previously unknown knowledge* by matching new information with historical information that exists in the form of patterns. These patterns are used to filter out new information or patterns. Once this new information is validated against a set of linked behavioral patterns, it is integrated into the existing knowledge database. The new information may also correct existing models by acting as additional training data. The following sections look at various machine learning algorithms employed in knowledge discovery, in relation to clustering, classification, dimensionality reduction, and collaborative filtering.

Machine Learning: Classification Algorithms

Logistic Regression

Logistic regression is a probabilistic statistical classification model that predicts the probability of the occurrence of an event. Logistic regression models the relationship between a categorical dependent variable X and a dichotomous categorical outcome or feature Y. The logistic function can be expressed as

$$P(Y \mid X) = \frac{e^{\beta_0 + \beta_1 X}}{1 + e^{\beta_0 + \beta_1 X}}.$$

(2-1)

The logistic function may be rewritten and transformed as the inverse of the logistic function—called *logit* or *log-odds*—which is the key to generating the coefficients of the logistic regression,

$$logit(P(Y \mid X)) = \ln\left(\frac{P(Y \mid X)}{1 - P(Y \mid X)}\right) = \beta_0 + \beta_1 X. \tag{2-2}$$

As depicted in Figure 2-1, the logistic function can receive a range of input values ($\beta_0 + \beta_1 X$) between negative infinity and positive infinity, and the output ($P(Y|X)$ is constrained to values between 0 and 1.

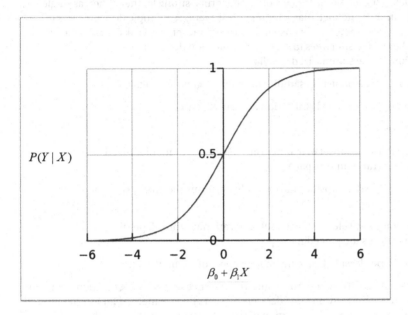

Figure 2-1. *The logistic function*

The logit transform of $P(Y|X)$ provides a dynamic range for linear regression and can be converted back into odds. The logistic regression method fits a regression curve, using the regression coefficients β_0 and β_1, as shown in Equation 2-1, where the output response is a binary (dichotomous) variable, and X is numerical. Because the logistic function curve is nonlinear, the logit transform (see Equation 2-2) is used to perform linear regression, in which $P(Y|X)$ is the probability of success (Y) for a given value of X. Using the generalized linear model, an estimated logistic regression equation can be formulated as

$$logit(P(Y = 1 \mid X_1, X_2, X_3 \ldots X_n)) = \beta_0 + \sum_{k=1}^{n} \beta_k X_k. \tag{2-3}$$

The coefficients β_0 and β_k ($k = 1, 2, ..., n$) are estimated, using *maximum likelihood estimation* (MLE) to model the probability that the dependent variable Y will take on a value of 1 for given values of X_k (k = 1, 2, ..., n).

Logistic regression is widely used in areas in which the outcome is presented in a binary format. For example, to predict blood cholesterol based on *body mass index* (BMI), you would use linear regression, because the outcome is continuous. If you needed to predict the odds of being diabetic based on BMI, you would use logistic regression, because the outcome is binary.

Random Forest

Random forest (Breiman 2001) is an ensemble learning approach for classification, in which "weak learners" collaborate to form "strong learners," using a large collection of decorrelated decision trees (the random forest). Instead of developing a solution based on the output of a single deep tree, however, random forest aggregates the output from a number of shallow trees, forming an additional layer to bagging. *Bagging* constructs n predictors, using independent successive trees, by bootstrapping samples of the dataset. The n predictors are combined to solve a classification or estimation problem through averaging. Although individual classifiers are weak learners, all the classifiers combined form a strong learner. Whereas single decision trees experience high variance and high bias, random forest averages multiple decision trees to improve estimation performance. A decision tree, in ensemble terms, represents a weak classifier. The term *forest* denotes the use of a number of decision trees to make a classification decision.

The random forest algorithm can be summarized as follows:

1. To construct B trees, select n bootstrap samples from the original dataset.

2. For each bootstrap sample, grow a classification or regression tree.

3. At each node of the tree:

    – m predictor variables (or subset of features) are selected at random from all the predictor variables (random subspace).

    – The predictor variable that provides the best split performs the binary split on that node.

    – The next node randomly selects another set of m variables from all predictor variables and performs the preceding step.

4. Given a new dataset to be classified, take the majority vote of all the B subtrees.

By averaging across the ensemble of trees, you can reduce the variance of the final estimation. Random forest offers good accuracy and runs efficiently on large datasets. It is an effective method for estimating missing data and maintains accuracy, even if a large portion of the data is missing. Additionally, random forest can estimate the relative importance of a variable for classification.

Hidden Markov Model

A *hidden Markov model* (HMM) is a doubly stochastic process, in which the system being modeled is a Markov process with unobserved (hidden) states. Although the underlying stochastic process is hidden and not directly observable, it can be seen through another set of stochastic processes that produces the sequence of observed symbols. In traditional Markov models, states are visible to an observer, and state transitions are parameterized, using transition probabilities. Each state has a probability distribution over output emissions (observed variables). HMM-based approaches correlate the system observations and state transitions to predict the most probable state sequence. The states of the HMM can only be inferred from the observed emissions—hence, the use of the term *hidden*. The sequence of output emissions generated by an HMM is used to estimate the sequence of states. HMMs are generative models, in which the joint distribution of observations and hidden states is modeled. To define a hidden Markov model, the following attributes have to be specified (see Figure 2-2):

- Set of states: $\{S_1, S_2 ..., S_n\}$

- Sequence of states: $\mathbf{Q} = q_1, q_2, ..., q_t$

- Markov chain property: $P(q_{t+1} = S_j \mid q_t = S_i, q_{t-1} = S_k, \cdots, q_0 = S_0) = P(q_{t+1} = S_j \mid q_t = S_i)$

- Set of observations: $\mathbf{O} = \{o_1, o_2, o_3, \ldots, o_M\}$

- Transition probability matrix: $\mathbf{P} = \{p_{ij}\}$, $p_{ij} = P(q_{t+1} = S_j \mid q_t = S_i)$

- Emission probability matrix: $\mathbf{B} = \{b_j(k)\}$, $b_j(k) = P(x_t = o_k \mid q_t = S_j)$

- Initial probability matrix: $\pi = \{\pi_i\}$, $\pi_i = P(q_1 = S_i)$

- HMM: $\mathbf{M} = (\mathbf{A}, \mathbf{B}, \pi)$

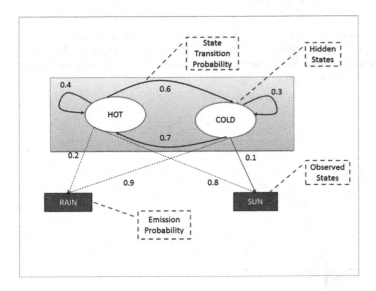

Figure 2-2. *Attributes of an HMM*

The three fundamental problems addressed by HMMs can be summarized as follows:

- *Model evaluation*: Evaluate the likelihood of a sequence of observations for a given HMM ($\mathbf{M} = (\mathbf{A}, \mathbf{B}, \pi)$).

- *Path decoding*: Evaluate the optimal sequence of model states ($\mathbf{Q}$) (hidden states) for a given sequence of observations and HMM model $\mathbf{M} = (\mathbf{A}, \mathbf{B}, \pi)$.

- *Model training*: Determine the set of model parameters that best accounts for the observed signal.

HMMs are especially known for their application in temporal pattern recognition, such as speech, handwriting, gesture recognition, part-of-speech tagging, musical score following, partial discharges, and bioinformatics. For further details on the HMM, see Chapter 5.

Multilayer Perceptron

A *multilayer perceptron* (*MLP*) is a feedforward network of simple neurons that maps sets of input data onto a set of outputs. An MLP comprises multiple layers of nodes fully connected by directed graph, in which each node (except input nodes) is a neuron with a nonlinear activation function.

The fundamental component of an MLP is the neuron. In an MLP a pair of neurons is connected in two adjacent layers, using weighted edges. As illustrated in Figure 2-3, an MLP comprises at least three layers of neurons, including one input layer, one or more hidden layers, and one output layer. The number of input neurons depends on the dimensions of the input features; the number of output neurons is determined by the number of classes. The number of hidden layers and the number of neurons in each hidden layer depend on the type of problem being solved. Fewer neurons result in inefficient learning; a larger number of neurons results in inefficient generalization. An MLP uses a supervised-learning technique called *backpropagation* for training the network. In its simple instantiation the perceptron computes an output y by processing a linear combination of weighted real-valued inputs through a nonlinear activation function,

$$y = \varphi \left(\sum_{i=1}^{n} w_i x_i + b \right),$$ (2-4)

where $\mathbf{w}$ represents the weights vector, $\mathbf{x}$ is the input vector, b is the bias, and φ is the activation function. Generally, MLP systems choose the logistic sigmoid function $1/(1+e^{-x})$ or the hyperbolic tangent $\tanh(x)$ as the activation functions. These functions offer statistical convenience, because they are linear near the origin and saturate quickly when moved away from the origin.

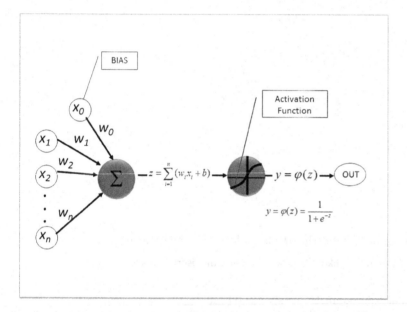

Figure 2-3. *The MLP is fed the input features to the input layer and gets the result from the output layer; the results are calculated in a feedforward approach from the input layer to the output layer*

The MLP learning process adjusts the weights of the hidden layer, such that the output error is reduced. Starting with the random weights, MLP feeds forward the input pattern signals through the network and backpropagates the error signal, starting at the output. The backpropagating error signal is made up of of the difference between actual $(O_n(t))$ and desired (T_n) values. Error function may be summarized as

$$E(O_n(t)) = T_n - O_n(t).$$ (2-5)

The goal of the learning process is to minimize the error function. To find the minimum value of the error function, differentiate it, with respect to the weight matrix. The learning algorithm comprises the following steps:

1. Initialize random weights within the interval [1, –1].

2. Send an input pattern to the network.

3. Calculate the output of the network.

4. For each node n in the output layer:

    a. Calculate the error on output node n: $E(O_n(t))=T_n-O_n(t)$.

    b. Add $E(O_n(t))$ to all the weights that connect to node n.

5. Repeat step 2.

To influence the convergence rate and thereby reduce the step sizes at which weights undergo an adaptive change, a learning parameter η (< 1) is used. The i-th weight connected to j-th output can be updated by the following rule:

$$w_{ij}(t+1) - w_{ij}(t) = \eta E(O_j(t)).$$ (2-6)

Equation 2-6 represents an iterative weight adaptation, in which a fraction of output error at iteration $(t+1)$ is added to the existing weight from iteration t.

MLPs are commonly used for supervised-learning pattern recognition processes. There is renewed interest in MLP backpropagation networks, owing to the successes of deep learning. *Deep learning* is an approach for effectively training an MLP, using multiple hidden layers. With modern advancements in silicon technology, deep learning is being developed to unlock the enormous big data analytics potential in areas in which highly varying functions can be represented by deep architecture.

Machine Learning: Clustering Algorithms
k-Means Clustering

k-*means clustering* is an unsupervised-learning algorithm of vector quantization that partitions n observations into k clusters. The algorithm defines k centroids, which act as prototypes for their respective clusters. Each object is assigned to a cluster with the nearest centroid when measured with a specific distance metric. The step of assigning objects to clusters is complete when all the objects have been applied to one of the k clusters. The process is repeated by recalculating centroids, based on previous $S = \{S_1, S_1, ..., S_k\}$ allocations, and reassigning objects to the nearest new centroids. The process continues until there is no movement of centroids of any k cluster. Generally, a k-means clustering algorithm classifies objects according to their features into k groups (or clusters) by minimizing the sum of squares of the distances between the object data and the cluster centroid.

For a given set of d-dimensional observations vectors $(x_1, x_2, ..., x_n)$, k-means clustering partitions n observations into $k(\leq n)$ cluster sets so as to minimize the sum of squares,

$$\arg\min_{S} \sum_{i=1}^{k} \sum_{\mathbf{x} \in S_i} \| \mathbf{x} - \mu_i \|^2,$$ (2-7)

where μ_i is the mean of the points in S_i.

The k-means clustering algorithm is easy to implement on large datasets. It has found many uses in areas such as market segmentation, computer vision, profiling applications and workloads, optical character recognition, and speech synthesis. The algorithm is often used as the preprocessing step for other algorithms in order to find the initial configuration.

Fuzzy k-Means (Fuzzy c-Means)

Fuzzy k-*means* (also called *fuzzy* c-*means* [FCM]) (Dunn 1973; Bezdek 1981) is an extension of the k-means algorithm that synthesizes soft clusters, in which an object can belong to more than one cluster with a certain probability. This algorithm provides increased flexibility in assigning data objects to clusters and allowing the data objects to maintain partial membership in multiple neighboring clusters. FCM uses the fuzzification parameter m in range [1, n], which determines the degree of fuzziness in the clusters. Whereas $m = 1$ signifies crisp clustering, $m > 1$ suggests a higher degree of fuzziness among data objects in decision space. The FCM algorithm is based on minimization of the objective function

$$J_m = \sum_x \sum_{j=1}^{C} w_k(x)^m \, \|c_j - x\|^2, \tag{2-8}$$

where x is the d-dimensional data object, c_j is the d-dimensional centroid of the cluster j (see Equation 2-10), and $w_k(x)$ is the degree of membership of x in the cluster k dependent on the fuzzification parameter m, which controls the weighting accorded the closest centroid:

$$w_k(x) = \frac{1}{\sum_{j=1}^{C} \left(\dfrac{\|c_k - x\|}{\|c_j - x\|} \right)^{2/(m-1)}}. \tag{2-9}$$

With FCM the d-dimensional centroid of a kth cluster (c_k) is the mean of all points, weighted by their degree of membership to that cluster:

$$c_k = \frac{\sum_x w_k(x)^m \, x}{\sum_x w_k(x)^m}. \tag{2-10}$$

The c-means clustering algorithm synthesizes cluster centers and the degree to which data objects are assigned to them. This does not translate into hard membership functions. FCM is used in image processing for clustering objects in an image.

Streaming k-Means

Streaming k-means is a two-step algorithm, consisting of a *streaming step* and a *ball* k-*means step*. A streaming step traverses the data objects of size n in one pass and generates an optimal number of centroids—which amounts to $k\log(n)$ clusters, where k is expected number of clusters. The attributes of these clusters are passed on to the ball k-means step, which reduces the number of clusters to k.

Streaming Step

A streaming-step algorithm steps through the data objects one at a time and makes a decision to either add the data object to an existing cluster or create a new one. If the distance between the centroid of the cluster and a data point is smaller than the distance cutoff threshold, the algorithm adds the data to an existing cluster or creates a new cluster with a probability of $d/(distancecutoff)$. If the distance exceeds the cutoff, the algorithm creates a new cluster with a new centroid. As more data objects are processed, the centroids of the existing clusters may change their position. This process continues to add new clusters until the number of existing clusters reaches a cluster cutoff limit. The number of clusters can be reduced by increasing the distance cutoff threshold. This step is mainly used for dimensionality reduction. The output of this step is a reduced dataset in the form of multiple clusters that are proxies for a large amount of the original data.

Ball K-Means Step

A ball k-means algorithm consumes the output of a streaming step (X = set of centroids > k) and performs multiple independent runs to synthesize k clusters by selecting the best solution. Each run selects k centroids, using a seeding mechanism, and runs the ball k-means algorithm iteratively to refine the solution.

The seeding process may invoke the k-means++ algorithm for optimal spreading of k clusters. The k-means++ seeding algorithm is summarized as follows:

1. Choose center c_1 uniformly at random from X.

2. Select a new center c_i by choosing $x \in X$ with probability, $P(x)$, and add it to $\bar{X}$,

$$P(x) = \frac{D(x)^2}{\sum_{i \in X} D(i)^2},$$

where $D(x)$ is the distance between x and the nearest center that has already been chosen.

3. Repeat step 2 until k centers $c_1, c_2, \cdots, c_k \in \bar{X}$ are selected.

4. Randomly pick two centers $\hat{c}_1, \hat{c}_2 \in \bar{X}$ with probability proportional to $norm \| \hat{c}_1 - \hat{c}_2 \|^2$.

5. For each $\hat{c}_i$, create a ball of radius $\| \hat{c}_1 - \hat{c}_2 \| / 3$ around it.

6. Recompute the new centroids $\bar{c}_1, \bar{c}_2$ by using the elements of $\bar{X}$ contained within the ball.

This algorithm is particularly useful in applications with a large number of data objects. The algorithm reduces the dimensionality of the original dataset by employing the streaming operation and replacing that data with a reduced proxy data composed of $k \cdot log(n)$ centroids of the original data. The reduced data act as input to the ball k-means algorithm, which synthesizes and refines k centroids for their respective clusters.

Machine Learning: Dimensionality Reduction

Machine learning works through a large number of features to train most regression or classification problems. This compounds the complexity, raises the computational requirement, and increases the time needed to converge to a solution. A useful approach for mitigating these problems is to reduce the dimensional space of the original features by synthesizing a lower-dimensional space. In this new, lower-dimensional space the most important features are retained, hidden correlations between features are exposed, and unimportant features are discarded. One of the simplest, most straightforward, and least supervised feature-reduction approaches involves variants of matrix decomposition: singular value decomposition, eigen decomposition, and nonnegative matrix factorization. The following sections consider some of the methods commonly used in statistical dimensionality reduction.

Singular Value Decomposition

Singular value decomposition (SVD) performs matrix analysis to synthesize low-dimensional representation of a high-dimensional matrix. SVD assists in eliminating less important parts of matrix representation, leading to approximate representation with the desired number of dimensions. This helps in creating a smaller representation of a matrix that closely resembles the original. SVD is useful in dimensionality reduction, owing to the following characteristics:

- SVD transforms correlated variables into a set of uncorrelated ones that exposes corresponding relationships between the data items.

- SVD identifies dimensions along which data points exhibit the most variation.

Once you identify the points with distinct variations, you can approximate original data points with fewer dimensions. You can define thresholds below which variations can be ignored, thereby leading to a highly reduced dataset without degradation of the information related to inherent relationships and interests within data points.

If M is an $m \times n$ matrix, then you can break it down into the product of three matrices U, Σ, and V^T with the following characteristics:

- U is a column-orthogonal matrix. The columns of U are orthonormal eigenvectors of MM^T.

- V^T is a transpose of orthogonal matrix V. The columns of V are orthonormal eigenvectors of M^TM.

- Σ is a diagonal matrix, where all elements except diagonal are 0. Σ contains square roots of eigenvalues from U or V, in descending order.

In its exact form, M can be rewritten as

$$M = U \Sigma V^T. \tag{2-11}$$

In the process of dimensionality reduction, you synthesize U and V, such that they contain elements accounted for in the original data, in descending order of variation. You may delete elements representing dimensions that do not exhibit meaningful variation. This can be done by setting the smallest eigenvalue to 0. Equation 2-11 can be rewritten in its best rank-l approximate form as

$$\hat{M} = \sum_{i}^{l} u_i \cdot \lambda_i \cdot v_i^T \quad \lambda_1 \geq \lambda_2, \geq \cdots, \lambda_1, \tag{2-12}$$

where u_i and v_i are the ith columns of U and V, respectively, and λ_i is the ith element of the diagonal matrix Σ.

Principal Component Analysis

When you have a swarm of points in space, the coordinates and axes you use to represent such points are arbitrary. The points have certain variances, relative to the direction of axes chosen, indicating the spread around the mean value in that direction. In a two-dimensional system the model is constrained by the perpendicularity of the second axis to the first axis. But, in three-dimensional cases and higher, you can position the nth axis perpendicular to the plane constructed by any two axes. The model is constrained by the position of the first axis, which is positioned in the direction with the highest variance. This results in a new feature space that compresses the swarm of points into the axes of high variance. You may select the axes with higher variances and eliminate the axes with lower variances. Figure 2-4 illustrates the new feature space, reduced from a dataset with 160 featuresto 59 components (axes). Each component is associated with a certain percentage of variance, relative to other components. The first component has the highest variance, followed by second component, and so on.

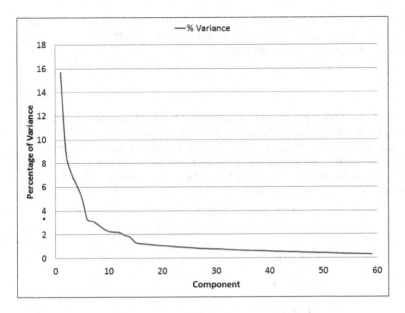

Figure 2-4. *The percentage of variance of a principal component transform of a dataset with 160 features reduced to 59 components*

Principal component analysis (PCA) is a widely used analytic technique that identifies patterns to reduce the dimensions of the dataset without significant loss of information. The goal of PCA is to project a high-dimensional feature space into a smaller subset to decrease computational cost. PCA computes new features, called *principal components* (PCs), which are uncorrelated linear combinations of the original features projected in the direction of greater variability. The key is to map the set of features into a matrix M and synthesize the eigenvalues and eigenvectors for MM^T or M^TM. Eigenvectors facilitate simpler solutions to problems that can be modeled using linear transformations along axes by stretching, compressing, or flipping. Eigenvalues provide a factor (length and magnitude of eigenvectors) whereby such transformation occurs. Eigenvectors with larger eigenvalues are selected in the new feature space because they enclose more information than eigenvectors with lower eigenvalues for a data distribution. The first PC has the greatest possible variance (i.e., the largest eigenvalues) compared with the next PC (uncorrelated, relative to the first PC), which is computed under the constraint of being orthogonal to the first component. Essentially, the ith PC is the linear combination of the maximum variance that is uncorrelated with all previous PCs.

PCA comprises the following steps:

1. Compute the d-dimensional mean of the original dataset.

2. Compute the covariance matrix of the features.

3. Compute the eigenvectors and eigenvalues of the covariance matrix.

4. Sort the eigenvectors by decreasing eigenvalue.

5. Choose k eigenvectors with the largest eigenvalues.

Eigenvector values represent the contribution of each variable to the PC axis. PCs are oriented in the direction of maximum variance in m-dimensional points.

PCA is one of the most widely used multivariate methods for uncovering new, informative, uncorrelated features; it reduces dimensionality by rejecting low-variance features and is useful in reducing the computational requirements for classification and regression analysis.

Lanczos Algorithm

The *Lanczos algorithm* is a low-cost eigen-decomposition technique identical to truncated SVD, except that it does not explicitly compute singular values/vectors of the matrix. The Lanczos algorithm uses a small number of Lanczos vectors that are eigenvectors of $M^T M$ or MM^T, where M is a symmetrical $n \times n$ matrix.

Lanczos starts by seeding an arbitrary nonzero vector x_0 with cardinality equal to the number of columns of matrix M. The mth ($m<<n$) step of the algorithm transforms the matrix M into a tridiagonal matrix T_{mm}. The iterative process can be summarized as follows:

Initialize

$$\bar{M} = MM^T$$

$$q_0 = 0, \ \beta_0 = 0$$

$$v_1 = \frac{x_0}{\|x_0\|}$$

Algorithm

FOR $i = 1,2,3,4,\cdots,m-1,$

$$u_i = \bar{M}q_i$$

$$\alpha_i = q_i^H u_i$$

$$u_i = u_i - \beta_{i-1}v_{i-1} - \alpha_i v_i$$

$$\beta_i = \|u_i\|$$

IF $\beta_i = 0$, then STOP

$$v_{i+1} = \frac{u_i}{\beta_i}$$

END

After m iterations are completed, you get α_i and β_i, which are the diagonal and subdiagonal entries, respectively, of the symmetrical tridiagonal matrix T_{mm}. The resulting tridiagonal matrix is orthogonally similar to $\bar{M}$:

$$T_{mm} = \begin{pmatrix} \alpha_1 & \beta_2 & & 0 \\ \beta_2 & \ddots & \ddots & \\ & \ddots & \ddots & \beta_m \\ 0 & & \beta_m & \alpha_m \end{pmatrix}. \tag{2-13}$$

The symmetrical tridiagonal matrix represents the projections of given matrices onto a subspace spanned by corresponding sets of Lanczos vectors V_m. The eigenvalues of these matrices are the eigenvalues of the mapped subspace of the original matrix. Lanczos iterations by themselves do not directly produce eigenvalues or eigenvectors; rather, they produce a tridiagonal matrix (see Equation 2-13) whose eigenvalues and eigenvectors are computed by another method (such as the QR algorithm) to produce Ritz values and vectors. For the eigenvalues, you may compute the k smallest or largest eigenvalues of T_{mm} if the number of Lanczos iterations is large compared with k. The Lanczos vectors v_i so generated then construct the transformation matrix,

$$V_m = (v_i, v_2, v_3, \cdots, v_m),$$

which can be used to generate the *Ritz eigenvectors* ($V_m \cdot u_m$), the approximate eigenvectors to the original matrix.

Machine Learning: Collaborative Filtering

Collaborative filtering (CF is used by *recommender systems*, whose goal is to forecast the user's interest in a given item, based on collective user experience (*collaboration*). The main objective is to match people with similar interests to generate personalized recommendations. Let's say, for instance, that there are M items and N users. This gives us an $M \times N$ user–item matrix X, where $x_{m,n}$ represents n^{th} user recommendations for item m. The following sections discuss some of the CF systems used in recommender systems.

User-Based Collaborative Filtering

User-based CF forecasts the user's interest in an item, based on collective ratings from similar user profiles. The user–item matrix can be written as

$$\mathbf{X} = [\mathbf{u}_1, \mathbf{u}_2, \cdots, \mathbf{u}_N]^T$$

$$\mathbf{u_n} = [x_{1,n}, x_{2,n}, \cdots x_{M,n}]^T, \ n = 1, 2, 3, \cdots, N.$$

The first step in user-based CF is to evaluate the similarity between users and arrange them according to their nearest neighbor. For example, to evaluate the similarity between two users, you may use a cosine similarity matrix $\mathbf{u_n}, \mathbf{u_a}$:

$$sim(\mathbf{u_n}, \mathbf{u_a}) = \frac{\sum_{m=1}^{M} x_{m,n} x_{m,a}}{\sqrt{\sum_{m=1}^{M} x_{m,n}^2} \cdot \sqrt{\sum_{m=1}^{M} x_{m,a}^2}}. \tag{2-14}$$

Finally, the predicted rating $\hat{x}_{m,a}$ of test item m by test user a is computed as

$$\hat{x}_{m,a} = \bar{u}_a + \frac{\sum_{n=1}^{N} sim(\mathbf{u_n}, \mathbf{u_a})(x_{m,n} - \bar{u}_n)}{\sum_{n=1}^{N} sim(\mathbf{u_n}, \mathbf{u_a})}, \tag{2-15}$$

where $\bar{u}_n$ and $\bar{u}_a$ denote the average rating made by users n and a, respectively. As seen from Equations 2-14 and 2-15, processing CF is a compute-intensive job function and may require large resource pools and faster computing machines. Therefore, it is recommended that you leverage a Hadoop platform for better performance and scalability.

Item-Based Collaborative Filtering

Item-based CF computes the similarity between items and selects the best match. The idea is to isolate users that have reviewed both items and then compute the similarity between them. The user–item matrix is represented as

$$X = [\mathbf{i}_1, \mathbf{i}_2, \cdots \mathbf{i_M}]^T$$

$$\mathbf{i_m} = [x_{m,1}, x_{m,2}, \cdots x_{m,N}]^T, \quad m = 1, 2, \dots, M,$$

where $\mathbf{i_m}$ corresponds to an item's ratings by all users m, which results in item-based recommendation algorithms.

The first step in item-based CF is to evaluate the similarity between items and arrange them according to their nearest neighbor. For instance, you may use the cosine similarity matrix to evaluate the similarity between two items $\mathbf{i_m}, \mathbf{i_b}$. To remove the difference in rating scale between users when computing the similarity, the cosine similarity is adjusted by subtracting the user's average rating $\bar{x}_n$ (Sarwar 2001) from each co-rated pair:

$$sim(\mathbf{i}_m, \mathbf{i}_b) = \frac{\sum_{n=1}^{N}(x_{m,n} - \bar{x}_n)(x_{b,n} - \bar{x}_n)}{\sqrt{\sum_{n=1}^{N}(x_{m,n} - \bar{x}_n)^2} \cdot \sqrt{\sum_{n=1}^{N}(x_{b,n} - \bar{x}_n)^2}}. \tag{2-16}$$

Finally, the predicted rating $\hat{x}_{m,a}$ of test item m by test user a is computed as

$$\hat{x}_{m,a} = \frac{\sum_{b=1}^{N} sim(\mathbf{i}_b, \mathbf{i}_m)(x_{b,a})}{\sum_{b=1}^{M} sim(\mathbf{i}_b, \mathbf{i}_m)}. \tag{2-17}$$

The rating of an item by a user can be estimated by averaging the ratings of similar items evaluated by the same user.

Alternating Least Squares with Weighted-λ-Regularization

The *alternating-least-squares with weighted-λ-regularization* (ALS-WR) algorithm factors the user–item matrix into the user–factor matrix and the item–factor matrix. This algorithm strives to uncover the latent factors that rationalize the observed user-item ratings and searches for optimal factor weights to minimize the least squares between predicted and actual ratings (Zhou 2008).

If you have multiple users and items, you will need to learn the feature vectors that represent each item and each user in the feature space. The objective is to uncover features that associate each user u with a user–factor vector $x_u \in \mathbb{R}^f$, and each item i with an item–factor vector $y_i \in (\mathbb{R})^f$. Ratings are described by the inner dot product $p_{ui} = x_u^T y_i$ of the user–factor vector and the item–factor vector. The idea is to perform matrix factorization, such that users and items can be mapped into common latent factors, whereby they can be directly compared. Because the rating matrix is sparse and not fully defined, the factorization has to be done using known ratings only. The quality of the solution is measured not only with respect to the observed data, but also with respect to a generalization of the unobserved data. You have to find a set of user and item feature vectors that minimizes the following cost function:

$$\sum_{u,i}(p_{ui} - x_u^T y_i)^2 - \lambda \left(\sum_u n_u^x \| x_u \|^2 + \sum_i n_i^y \| y_i \|^2 \right), \tag{2-18}$$

where n_u^x and n_i^y represent the number of ratings of user u and item i, respectively. The regularization term $\lambda(...)$ avoids overfitting the training data. The parameter λ depends on the data and is tuned by cross-validation in the dataset for better generalization. Because the search space is very large (multiple users and items), it prevents application of traditional direct optimization techniques, such as stochastic gradient descent.

The cost function assumes a quadratic form when either the user–factor or the item–factor is fixed, which allows computation of a global minimum. This in turn allows ALS optimization, in which user–factors and item–factors are alternately recomputed by fixing each other. This algorithm is designed for large-scale CF for large datasets.

Machine Learning: Similarity Matrix

A *similarity matrix* scores the similarity between data points. Similarity matrices are strongly related to their counterparts: distance matrices and substitution matrices. The following sections look at some of the commonly used similarity calculation methods.

Pearson Correlation Coefficient

Pearson correlation measures the linear dependence between two variables. The *Pearson correlation coefficient* is the covariance of the two variables (X and Y) divided by the product of their standard deviations:

$$r = \frac{\sum_{i=1}^{n}(X_i - \bar{X})(Y_i - \bar{Y})}{\sqrt{\sum_{i=1}^{n}(X_i - \bar{X})^2}\sqrt{\sum_{i=1}^{n}(Y_i - \bar{Y})^2}}. \tag{2-19}$$

The Pearson correlation coefficient ranges from -1 to 1. A value of 1 validates a perfect linear relationship between X and Y, in which the data variability of X tracks that of Y. A value of -1 indicates a reverse relationship between X and Y, such that the data variability of Y is opposite to that of X. A value of 0 suggests lack of linear correlation between the variables X and Y.

Although the Pearson coefficient reflects the strength of the linear relationship, it is highly sensitive to extreme values and outliers. The low relationship strength may be misleading if two variables have a strong curvilinear relationship instead of a strong linear relationship. The coefficient may also be misleading if X and Y have not been analyzed in terms of their full ranges.

Spearman Rank Correlation Coefficient

The Spearman correlation coefficient performs statistical analysis of the strength of a monotonic relationship between the paired variables X and Y. Spearman correlation calculates Pearson correlation for the ranked values of the paired variables. Ranking (from low to high) is obtained by assigning a rank of 1 to the lowest value, 2 to the next lowest, and so on, such that

$$r_s = 1 - \frac{6\sum d_i^2}{n(n^2 - 1)}, \tag{2-20}$$

where n is the sample size, and d is the distance between the statistical ranks of the variable pairs given by

$$d_i = x_i - y_i.$$

The sign of the Spearman correlation coefficient signifies the direction of the association between the dependent and independent variables. The coefficient is positive if the dependent variable Y increases (or decreases) in the same direction as the independent variable X. The coefficient is negative if the dependent variable Y increases (or decreases) in the reverse direction, relative to the independent variable X. A Spearman correlation of 0 signifies that the variable Y has no inclination to either increase or decrease, relative to X. Spearman correlation increases in magnitude as X and Y move closer to being perfect monotone functions. Spearman correlation can only be computed if the data are not truncated. Although less sensitive to extreme values, it relies only on rank instead of observation.

Euclidean Distance

The *Euclidean distance* is the square root of the sum of squared differences between the vector elements of the two variables:

$$d(\mathbf{X}, \mathbf{Y}) = \sqrt{\sum_{i=1}^{n}(X_i - Y_i)^2}. \tag{2-21}$$

A Euclidean distance is valid if both variables are measured on the same scale. You can transform the distance in Equation 2-21 to an inverse form (see Equation 2-22), such that it returns a value of 1 if X and Y (X – Y = 0) are similar and trend to 0 if the similarity decreases:

$$\hat{d}(\mathbf{X}, \mathbf{Y}) = \frac{1}{1 + d(\mathbf{X}, \mathbf{Y})}. \tag{2-22}$$

You can verify that $\hat{d}(\mathbf{X}, \mathbf{Y})$ calculates to the value of 1 if the distance d(**X**,**Y**) = 0 (indicating similarity), and $\hat{d}(\mathbf{X}, \mathbf{Y})$ decreases to 0 if d(**X**,**Y**) increases (indicating dissimilarity).

Jaccard Similarity Coefficient

The Jaccard similarity coefficient gauges similarity between finite sample sets X and Y by measuring overlapping between them. Sets X and Y do not have to be of same size. Mathematically, the coefficient can be defined as the ratio of the intersection to the union of the sample sets (X, Y):

$$J(X,Y) = \frac{X \cap Y}{X \cup Y}, \quad 0 \le J(X,Y) \le 1 \tag{2-23}$$

$$J(X,X) = 1.$$

The Jaccard distance measures the dissimilarity between sample sets and is obtained by subtracting the Jaccard coefficient from 1:

$$d_J(X,Y) = 1 - J(X,Y). \tag{2-24}$$

The Jaccard coefficient is commonly used in measuring keyword similarities, document similarities, news article classification, *natural language processing* (NLP), and so on.

Summary

The solution to a complex problem relies on intelligent use of machine learning techniques. The precision, speed, and accuracy of the solution can be improved by employing techniques that not only reduce the dimensionality of the features, but also train the models specific to a unique behavior. Distinct behavioral attributes can be clustered into phases by using one of the clustering techniques, such as k-means. Reduced data points corresponding to each cluster label are separated and trained to solve a regression or classification problem. In a normal posttraining operation, once phases are identified, the trained model associated with that phase is employed to forecast (or estimate) the output of the feedback loop.

Figure 2-5 summarizes a process control system capable of sensing a large number of sensors in order to control an environmental process (e.g., cooling in the datacenter). The first step is to reduce the dimensionality of the data. The new data are fed into clustering methods, which discover a group's items from a given collection, based on similar attributes and distinctive properties. Data corresponding to each cluster label are segregated and trained individually for classification. Phase identification allows the application of a model function, which associates with the identified phase. The output of the phase-specific model triggers the process control functions, which act on the environment and change the sensor outputs. Additionally, this procedure lets us actively predict the current phase duration and the upcoming phase and accordingly forecast the output for proactive control.

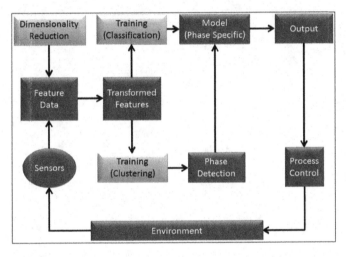

Figure 2-5. *Machine learning–based feedback control system: features are transformed and fed into phase detectors; the data classification process employs models trained on the detected phase*

References

Bezdek, James C. *Pattern Recognition with Fuzzy Objective Function Algorithms*. Norwell, MA: Kluwer, 1981.

Breiman, Leo. "Random Forests." *Machine Learning* 45, no. 1 (2001): 5–32.

Dunn, J. C. "A Fuzzy Relative of the Isodata Process and Its Use in Detecting Compact Well-Separated Clusters." Cybernetics 3 (1973): 32–57.

Sarwar, Badrul, George Karypis, Joseph Konstan, and John Riedl. "Item-Based Collaborative Filtering Recommendation Algorithms." In *Proceedings of the 10th International Conference on the World Wide Web*, 285–295. New York: ACM, 2001.

Zhou, Yunhong, Dennis Wilkinson, Robert Schreiber, and Rong Pan. "Large-Scale Parallel Collaborative Filtering for the Netflix Prize." In *Algorithmic Aspects in Information and Management, Proceedings of the 4th International Conference, AAIM 2008, Shanghai, China, June 23–25, 2008*, edited by Rudof Fleischer and Jinhui Xu, 337–348. Berlin: Springer, 2008.

■ ■ ■

CHAPTER 3

Support Vector Machines for Classification

Science is the systematic classification of experience.

—George Henry Lewes

This chapter covers details of the *support vector machine* (SVM) technique, a sparse kernel decision machine that avoids computing posterior probabilities when building its learning model. SVM offers a principled approach to *machine learning* problems because of its mathematical foundation in statistical learning theory. SVM constructs its solution in terms of a subset of the training input. SVM has been extensively used for classification, regression, novelty detection tasks, and feature reduction. This chapter focuses on SVM for supervised classification tasks only, providing SVM formulations for when the input space is linearly separable or linearly nonseparable and when the data are unbalanced, along with examples. The chapter also presents recent improvements to and extensions of the original SVM formulation. A case study concludes the chapter.

SVM from a Geometric Perspective

In classification tasks a discriminant machine learning technique aims at finding, based on an *independent and identically distributed* (*iid*) training dataset, a discriminant function that can correctly predict labels for newly acquired instances. Unlike generative machine learning approaches, which require computations of conditional probability distributions, a discriminant classification function takes a data point x and assigns it to one of the different classes that are a part of the classification task. Less powerful than generative approaches, which are mostly used when prediction involves outlier detection, discriminant approaches require fewer computational resources and less training data, especially for a multidimensional feature space and when only posterior probabilities are needed. From a geometric perspective, learning a classifier is equivalent to finding the equation for a multidimensional surface that best separates the different classes in the feature space.

SVM is a discriminant technique, and, because it solves the convex optimization problem analytically, it always returns the same optimal hyperplane parameter—in contrast to *genetic algorithms* (*GAs*) or *perceptrons*, both of which are widely used for classification in machine learning. For perceptrons, solutions are highly dependent on the initialization and termination criteria.

For a specific kernel that transforms the data from the input space to the feature space, training returns uniquely defined SVM model parameters for a given training set, whereas the perceptron and GA classifier models are different each time training is initialized. The aim of GAs and perceptrons is only to minimize error during training, which will translate into several hyperplanes' meeting this requirement.

If many hyperplanes can be learned during the training phase, only the optimal one is retained, because training is practically performed on samples of the population even though the test data may not exhibit the same distribution as the training set. When trained with data that are not representative of the overall data population, hyperplanes are prone to poor generalization.

Figure 3-1 illustrates the different hyperplanes obtained with SVM, perceptron, and GA classifiers on two-dimensional, two-class data. Points surrounded by circles represent the support vector, whereas the hyperplanes corresponding to the different classifiers are shown in different colors, in accordance with the legend.

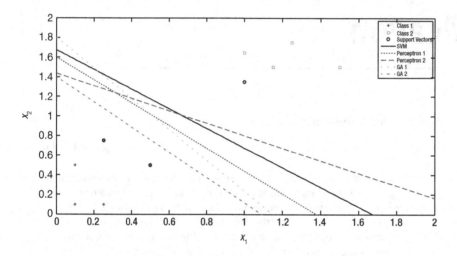

Figure 3-1. *Two-dimensional, two-class plot for SVM, perceptron, and GA hyperplanes*

■ **Note SVM vs. ANN**   Generally speaking, SVM evolved from a robust theory of implementation, whereas *artificial neural networks* (*ANN*) moved heuristically from application to theory.

SVM distinguishes itself from ANN in that it does not suffer from the classical multilocal minima—the double curse of dimensionality and overfitting. Overfitting, which happens when the machine learning model strives to achieve a zero error on all training data, is more likely to occur with machine learning approaches whose training metrics depend on variants of the sum of squares error. By minimizing the structural risk rather than the empirical risk, as in the case of ANN, SVM avoids overfitting.

SVM does not control model complexity, as ANN does, by limiting the feature set; instead, it automatically determines the model complexity by selecting the number of support vectors.

SVM Main Properties

Deeply rooted in the principles of statistics, optimization, and machine learning, SVM was officially introduced by Boser, Guyon, and Vapnik (1992) during the Fifth Annual Association for Computing Machinery Workshop on Computational Learning Theory. [Bartlett (1998) formally revealed the statistical bounds of the generalization of the hard-margin SVM. SVM relies on the complexity of the hypothesis space and empirical error (a measure of how well the model fits the training data). *Vapnik-Chervonenkis (VC)* theory proves that a VC bound on the risk exists. VC is a measure of the complexity of the hypothesis space. The VC dimension of a hypothesis $\mathcal{H}$ relates to the maximum number of points that can be shattered by $\mathcal{H}$. $\mathcal{H}$ shatters N points, if $\mathcal{H}$ correctly separates all the positive instances from the negative ones. In other words, the VC capacity is equal to the number of training points N that the model can separate into 2^N different labels. This capacity is related to the amount of training data available. The VC dimension h affects the generalization error, as it is bounded by $\| w \|$ where w is the weight vector of the separating hyperplane and the radius of the smallest sphere R that contains all the training points, according to: $h < \dfrac{R^2}{\| w \|^2}$. The overall error of a machine learning model consists of $\varepsilon = \varepsilon_{emp} + \varepsilon_g$, where ε_{emp} is the training error, and ε_g is the generalization error. The empirical risk of a model f is $\varepsilon_{emp}[f] = \dfrac{1}{N} \sum_{i=1}^{N} \dfrac{1}{2} |y_i - f(.)|$.

The lower bound for risk is $\varepsilon[f] \le \varepsilon_{emp}[f] + \sqrt{\dfrac{1}{N}\left(h\left(\ln \dfrac{2N}{h} + 1 \right) - \ln \dfrac{\eta}{4} \right)}$ where $1 - \eta$ is the probability of his bound's being true for any function in the class of function with VC dimension h, independent of the data distribution.

■ **Note** There are 2^N different learning problems that can be defined, as N points can be labeled in 2^N manners as positive or negative. For instance, for three points, there are 24 different labels and 8 different classification boundaries that can be learned. Thus, the VC dimension in R^2 is 3.

SVM elegantly groups multiple features that were already being proposed in research in the 1960s to form what is referred to as the *maximal margin classifier*. SVM borrows concepts from large-margin hyperplanes (Duda 1973; Cover 1995; Vapnik and Lerner 1963; Vapnik and Chervonenkis 1964); kernels as inner products in the feature space (Aizermann, Braverman, and Rozonoer 1964); kernel usage (Aizermann, Braverman, and Rozonoer 1964; Wahba 1990; Poggio 1990) and sparseness (Cover 1995). Mangasarian (1965) also proposed an optimization approach similar to the one adopted by SVM. The concept of slack, used to address noise in data and nonseparability, was originally introduced by Smith (1968) and was further enhanced by Bennett and Mangasarian (1992). Incorporated into SVM formulation by Cortes (1995), soft-margin SVM represents a modification of the hard-margin SVM through its adoption of the concept of slack to account for noisy data at the separating boundaries. (For readers interested in delving into the foundations of SVM, see Vapnik 1998, 1999, for an exhaustive treatment of SVM theory.)

Known for their robustness, good generalization ability, and unique global optimum solutions, SVMs are probably the most popular machine learning approach for supervised learning, yet their principle is very simple. In his comparison of SVM with 16 classifiers, on 21 datasets, Meyer, Leisch, and Hornik (2003) showed that SVM is one of the most powerful classifiers in machine learning. Since their introduction in 1992, SVMs have found their way into a myriad of applications, such as weather prediction, power estimation stock prediction, defect classification, speaker recognition, handwriting identification, image and audio processing, video analysis, and medical diagnosis.

What makes SVM an attractive machine learning framework can be summarized by the following properties:

- *SVM is a sparse technique.* Like nonparametric methods, SVM requires that all the training data be available, that is, stored in memory during the training phase, when the parameters of the SVM model are learned. However, once the model parameters are identified, SVM depends only on a subset of these training instances, called *support vectors*, for future prediction. Support vectors define the margins of the hyperplanes. Support vectors are found after an optimization step involving an objective function regularized by an error term and a constraint, using *Lagrangian relaxation*.[1] The complexity of the classification task with SVM depends on the number of support vectors rather than the dimensionality of the input space. The number of support vectors that are ultimately retained from the original dataset is data dependent and varies, based on the data complexity, which is captured by the data dimensionality and class separability. The upper bound for the number of support vectors is half the size of the training dataset, but in practice this is rarely the case. The SVM model described mathematically in this chapter is written as a weighted sum of the support vectors, which gives the SVM framework the same advantages as parametric techniques in terms of reduced computational time for testing and storage requirements.

- *SVM is a kernel technique.* SVM uses the kernel trick to map the data into a higher-dimensional space before solving the machine learning task as a convex optimization problem in which optima are found analytically rather than heuristically, as with other machine learning techniques. Often, real-life data are not linearly separable in the original input space. In other words, instances that have different labels share the input space in a manner that prevents a linear hyperplane from correctly separating the different classes involved in this classification task. Trying to learn a nonlinear separating boundary in the input space increases the computational requirements during the optimization phase, because the separating surface will be of at least the second order. Instead, SVM maps the data, using predefined kernel functions, into a new but higher-dimensional space, where a linear separator would be able to discriminate between the different classes. The SVM optimization phase will thus entail learning only a linear discriminant surface in the mapped space. Of course, the selection and settings of the kernel function are crucial for SVM optimality.

- *SVM is a maximum margin separator.* Beyond minimizing the error or a cost function, based on the training datasets (similar to other discriminant machine learning techniques), SVM imposes an additional constraint on the optimization problem: the hyperplane needs to be situated such that it is at a maximum distance from the different classes. Such a term forces the optimization step to find the hyperplane that would eventually generalize better because it is situated at an equal and maximum distance from the classes. This is essential, because training is done on a sample of the population, whereas prediction is to be performed on yet-to-be-seen instances that may have a distribution that is slightly different from that of the subset trained on.

---

[1]Established in the 1970s, Lagrangian relaxation provides bounds for the branch-and-bound algorithm and has been extensively used in scheduling and routing. Lagrangian relaxation converts many hard integer-programming problems into simpler ones by emphasizing the constraints in the objective function for optimization via Lagrange multipliers. (For a more in-depth discussion on Lagrangian relaxation, see Fisher 2004.)

SVM uses structural risk minimization (SRM) and satisfies the duality and convexity requirements. SRM (Vapnik 1964) is an inductive principle that selects a model for learning from a finite training dataset. As an indicator of capacity control, SRM proposes a trade-off between the VC dimensions, that is, the hypothesis of space complexity and the empirical error. SRM's formulation is a convex optimization with n variables in the cost function to be maximized and m constraints, solvable in polynomial time. SRM uses a set of models sequenced in an increasing order of complexity. Figure 3-2 shows how the overall model error varies with the complexity index of a machine learning model. For non- complex models, the error is high because a simple model cannot capture all the complexity of the data which results in an underfitting situation. As the complexity index increases, the error reaches its minimum for the optimal model indexed h^* before it starts increasing again. For high model indices, the structure starts adapting its learning model to the training data which results in an overfitting that reduces the training error value and increases the model VC however, at the expense of a deterioration in the test error.

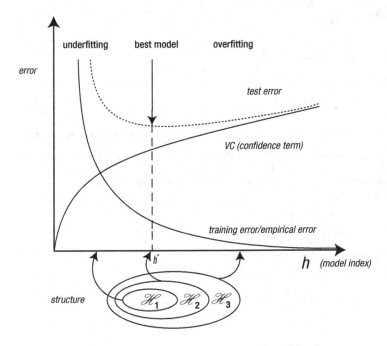

Figure 3-2. *Relationship between error trends and model index*

Hard-Margin SVM

The SVM technique is a classifier that finds a hyperplane or a function $g(x) = w^T x + b$ that correctly separates two classes with a maximum margin. Figure 3-3 shows a separating hyperplane corresponding to a hard-margin SVM (also called a *linear SVM*).

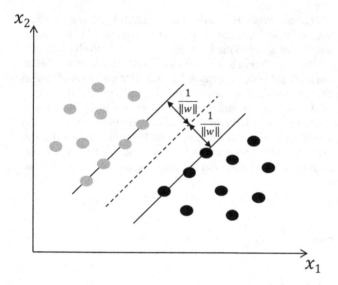

Figure 3-3. *Hard-maximum-margin separating hyperplane*

Mathematically speaking, given a set of points x_i that belong to two linearly separable classes ω_1, ω_2, the distance of any instance from the hyperplane is equal to $\frac{|g(x)|}{\|w\|}$. SVM aims to find w, b, such that the value of $g(x)$ equals 1 for the nearest data points belonging to class ω_1 and –1 for the nearest ones of ω_2.

This can be viewed as having a margin of

$$\frac{1}{\|w\|} + \frac{1}{\|w\|} = \frac{2}{\|w\|},$$

whereas $w^T x + b = 1$ for $x \in \omega_1$, and $w^T x + b = -1$ for $x \in \omega_2$.

This leads to an optimization problem that minimizes the objective function

$$J(w) = \frac{1}{2}\|w\|^2,$$

subject to the constraint

$$y_i\left(w_i^T x + b\right) \geq 1, \ i = 1, 2, \ldots, N.$$

When an optimization problem—whether minimization or maximization—has constraints in the variables being optimized, the cost or error function is augmented by adding to it the constraints, multiplied by the Lagrange multipliers.

In other words, the Lagrangian function for SVM is formed by augmenting the objective function with a weighted sum of the constraints,

$$\mathcal{L}(w, b, \lambda) = \frac{1}{2}w^T w - \sum_{i=1}^{N}\lambda_i\left[y_i\left(w^T x_i + b\right) - 1\right]$$

where w and b are called primal variables, and λ_i's the Lagrange multipliers.

These multipliers thus restrict the solution's search space to the set of feasible values, given the constraints. In the presence of inequality constraints, the *Karush-Kuhn-Tucker* (KKT) conditions generalize the Lagrange multipliers.

The *KKT* conditions are

1. Primal constraints

$$-\left[y_i\left(w^T x_i + b\right) - 1\right] \leq 0 \quad \forall i = 1, \ldots, N$$

2. Dual constraints

$$\lambda_i \geq 0 \ \forall i = 1, \ldots, N$$

3. Complementarity slackness

$$\lambda_i\left[y_i\left(w^T x_i + b\right) - 1\right] = 0 \quad \forall i = 1, \ldots, N$$

4. Gradient of the Lagrangian (zero, with respect to primal variables)

$$\nabla \mathcal{L}(w, b, \lambda) = \begin{bmatrix} w - \sum_{i=1}^{N} \lambda_i y_i x_i \\ -\sum_{i=1}^{N} \lambda_i y_i \end{bmatrix} = 0$$

Based on the KKT conditions,

$$w = \sum_{i=1}^{N} \lambda_i y_i x_i,$$

$$\sum_{i=1}^{N} \lambda_i y_i = 0.$$

■ **Note**   Appearing in a study by Kuhn and Tucker (1951), these conditions are also found in the unpublished master's thesis of Karush (1939).

Since most linear programming problems come in pairs, a primal problem with n variables and m constraints can be rewritten in the Wolfe dual form with m variables and n constraints while the same solution applies for both primal and dual formulations. The duality theorem formalizes this by stating that the number of variables in one form is equal to the number of constraints in the complementary form. The complementary slackness is the relationship between the primal and dual formulation: when added to inequalities, slack variables transform them into equalities.

The dual problem of SVM optimization is to find

$$\max_{\lambda} \left(\sum_{i=1}^{N} \lambda_i - \frac{1}{2} \sum_{i,j} \lambda_i \lambda_j y_i y_j x_i x_j \right),$$

subject to

$$\sum_{i=1}^{N} \lambda_i y_i = 0,$$

$$\lambda_i \geq 0 \quad \forall i.$$

■ **Note** This last constraint is essential for solution optimality. At optimality, the dual variables have to be nonnegative, as dual variables are multiplied by a positive quantity. Because negative Lagrange multipliers decrease the value of the function, the optimal solution cannot have negative Lagrange multipliers. Active or binding constraints have a corresponding nonzero multiplier, whereas nonbinding ones are zero and do not affect the problem solution. SVM hyperplane parameters are thus defined by the active, binding constraints, which correspond to the nonzero Lagrange multipliers, that is, the support vector.

Solving the duality of the aforementioned problem is useful for several reasons. First, even if the primal is not convex, the dual problem will always have a unique optimal solution. Second, the value of the objective function is a lower bound on the optimal function value of the primal formulation. Finally, the number of dual variables may be significantly less than the number of primal variables; hence, an optimization problem formulated in the dual form can be solved faster and more efficiently.

Soft-Margin SVM

When the data are not completely separable, as with the points marked by a X in Figure 3-4, slack variables ξ_i are introduced to the SVM objective function to allow error in the misclassification. SVM, in this case, is not searching for the hard margin, which will classify all data flawlessly. Instead, SVM is now a soft-margin classifier; that is, SVM is classifying most of the data correctly, while allowing the model to misclassify a few points in the vicinity of the separating boundary.

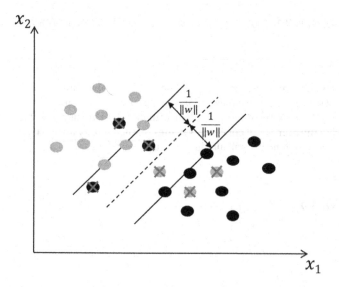

Figure 3-4. A few misclassifications, as part of soft-margin SVM

The problem in primal form now is a minimization of the objective function

$$J(w,b,\xi) = \frac{1}{2}\|w\|^2 + C\sum_{i=1}^{N}\xi_i,$$

subject to these two constraints:

$$y_i\left[w_i^T x_i + b\right] \geq 1 - \xi_i, \quad i = 1, 2, \dots, N,$$

$$\xi_i \geq 0, \quad i = 1, 2, \dots, N.$$

The *regularization term* or *box constraint, C,* is a parameter that varies, depending on the optimization goal. As C is increased, a tighter margin is obtained, and more emphasis is placed on minimizing the number of misclassifications. As C is decreased, more violations are allowed, because maximizing the margin between the two classes becomes the SVM aim. Figure 3-5 captures the effect of the regularization parameter, with respect to margin width and misclassification. For $C_1 < C_2$, fewer training points are within the margin for C_2 than for C_1, but the latter has a wider margin.

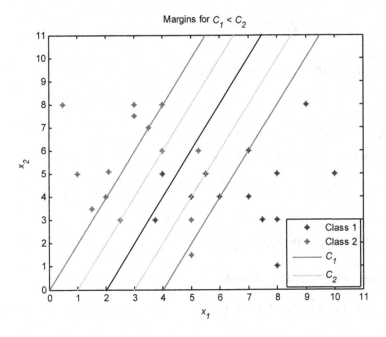

Figure 3-5. *The box constraint effect on SVM performance*

In dual form the soft margin SVM formulation is

$$\max_{\lambda}\left(\sum_{i=1}^{N}\lambda_i - \frac{1}{2}\sum_{i,j}\lambda_i\lambda_j y_i y_j x_i x_j\right),$$

subject to

$$\sum_{i=1}^{N}\lambda_i y_i = 0,$$

$$0 \leq \lambda_i \leq C, \quad i = 1, 2, \dots, N.$$

The soft-margin dual problem is equivalent to the hard-margin dual problem, except that the dual variable is upper bounded by the regularization parameter C.

Kernel SVM

When a problem is not linearly separable in input space, soft-margin SVM cannot find a robust separating hyperplane that minimizes the number of misclassified data points and that generalizes well. For that, a kernel can be used to transform the data to a higher-dimensional space, referred to as *kernel space*, where data will be linearly separable. In the kernel space a linear hyperplane can thus be obtained to separate the different classes involved in the classification task instead of solving a high-order separating hypersurface in the input space. This is an attractive method, because the overhead on going to kernel space is insignificant compared with learning a nonlinear surface.

A kernel should be a Hermitian and positive semidefinite matrix and needs to satisfy Mercer's theorem, which translates into evaluating the kernel or Gram matrix on all pairs of data points as positive and semidefinite, forming

$$K(x,u) = \sum_r \varphi_r(x)\varphi_r(u),$$

where $\varphi(x)$ belongs to the Hilbert space.

In other words, $\iint K(x,u)g(x)g(u)dxdu \geq 0 \quad \forall g(x)$, where $\int g^2(x)dx < +\infty$.

Some popular kernel functions include

- *Linear kernel*: $K(x,u) = \mathrm{x}^T.u$

- *Polynomial function*: $K(x,u) = \left(ax^Tu + c\right)^q$, $q > 0$

- *Hyperbolic tangent (sigmoid)*: $K(x,u) = \tanh\left(\beta x^Tu + \gamma\right)$

- *Gaussian radial basis function (RBF)*: $K(x,u) = \exp\left(-\dfrac{\|x-u\|^2}{\sigma^2}\right)$

- *Laplacian radial basis function*: $K(x,u) = \exp\left(-\dfrac{\|x-u\|}{\sigma}\right)$

- *Randomized blocks analysis of variance (ANOVA RB) kernel*:

$$K(x,u) = \sum_{k=1}^{n}\exp(-\sigma(x^k - u^k)^2)^d$$

- *Linear spline kernel in 1D*:

$$K(x,u) = 1 + x.u.\min(x,u) - \frac{x+u}{2}(\min(x,u)^2 + \frac{1}{3}\min(x,u)^3)$$

Kernel selection is heavily dependent on the data specifics. For instance, the linear kernel—the simplest of all—is useful in large sparse data vectors. However, it ranks behind the polynomial kernel, which avoids zeroing the Hessian. The polynomial kernel is widely used in image processing, whereas the ANOVA RB kernel is usually reserved for regression tasks. The Gaussian and Laplace RBFs are general-purpose kernels that are mostly applied in the absence of prior knowledge. A kernel matrix that ends up being diagonal indicates that the feature space is redundant and that another kernel should be tried after feature reduction.

Note that when kernels are used to transform the feature vectors from input space to kernel space for linearly nonseparable datasets, the kernel matrix computation requires massive memory and computational resources, for big data.

Figure 3-6 displays the two-dimensional exclusive OR (XOR) data, a linearly nonseparable distribution in input space (upper-left) as well as in the feature space. In the latter, 16 points (for different sets) are created for the four inputs when the kernel is applied. The choice of the Gaussian RBF kernel-smoothing parameter σ^2 affects the distribution of the data in the kernel space. Because the choice of parameter value is essential for transforming the data from a linearly nonseparable space to a linearly separable one, grid searches are performed to find the most suitable values.

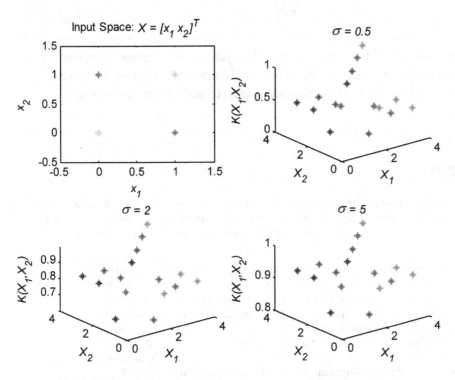

Figure 3-6. *Two-dimensional XOR data, from input space to kernel space*

The primal formulation of the kernel SVM is

$$\min_{w,\xi}\frac{1}{2}w^T w + C\sum_{i=1}^{N}\xi_i,$$

subject to $y_i\left(w^T\varphi(x_i)+b\right)\geq1-\xi_i$ and $\xi_i\geq0, \forall i$,
where $\varphi(x_i)$ is such that $\mathrm{K}\left(x_i,x_j\right)=\varphi(x_i).\varphi(x_j)$.

Again, the SVM solution should satisfy the KKT conditions, as follows:

1. $w=\sum_{i=1}^{N}\lambda_i y_i\varphi(x_i)$

2. $\sum_{i=1}^{N}\lambda_i y_i=0$

3. $C-\mu_i-\lambda_i=0\ i=1,2,...,N$

4. $\lambda_i\left[y_i\left(w^T\varphi(x_i)+b\right)-1+\xi_i\right]=0\ i=1,2,...,N$

5. $\mu_i\xi_i=0\ i=1,2,...,N$

6. $\mu_i,\xi_i>0\ i=1,2,...,N$

As mentioned earlier, the dual formulation of this problem is more efficient to solve and is used in most implementations of SVM:

$$\max_{\lambda} \left(\sum_{i=1}^{N} \lambda_i - \frac{1}{2} \sum_{i=1}^{N} \lambda_i \lambda_j y_i y_j x_i x_j \right),$$

subject to

$$\sum_i \lambda_i y_i$$

■ **Note** For a dataset size of N, the kernel matrix has N^2 entries. Therefore, as N increases, computing the kernel matrix becomes inefficient and even unfeasible, making SVM impractical to solve. However, several algorithms have alleviated this problem by breaking the optimization problem into a number of smaller problems.

Multiclass SVM

The early extensions of the SVM binary classification to the multiclass case were the work of Weston and Watkins (1999) and Platt (2000). Researchers devised various strategies to address the multiclassification problem, including one-versus-the-rest, pair-wise classification, and the multiclassification formulation, discussed in turn here.

- *One-versus-the-rest* (also called *one-against-all* [*OAA*]) is probably the earliest SVM multiclass implementation and is one of the most commonly used multiclass SVMs. It constructs c binary SVM classifiers, where c is the number of classes. Each classifier distinguishes one class from all the others, which reduces the case to a two-class problem. There are c decision functions: $w_1^T \varphi(x_i) + b_1; \ldots; w_c^T \varphi(x_i) + b_c$. The initial formulation of the OAA method assigns a data point to a certain class if and only if that class has accepted it, while all other classes have not, which leaves undecided regions in the feature space when more than one class accepts it or when all classes reject it. Vapnik (1998) suggested assigning data points to the class with the highest value, regardless of sign. The final label output is given to the class that has demonstrated the highest output value:

$$class\ of\ x \equiv \arg max_{i=1,\ldots,c}(w_i^T \varphi(x) + b_i).$$

- Proposed by Knerr, Personnaz, and Dreyfus (1990), and first adopted in SVM by Friedman (1996) and Kressel (1999), *pair-wise classification* (also called *one-against-one* [*OAO*]) builds $c(c-1)/2$ binary SVMs, each of which is used to discriminate two of the c classes only and requires evaluation of $(c-1)$ SVM classifiers. For training data from the kth and j^{th} classes, the constraints for (x_t, y_t) are

$$\left(w_{kj}^T \varphi(x_t) + b_{kj} \right) \geq 1 - \xi_{kj}^t,\ \text{for}\ y_t = k,$$

$$\left(w_{kj}^T \varphi(x_t) + b_{kj} \right) \leq -1 + \xi_{kj}^t,\ \text{for}\ y_t = j,$$

$$\xi_{kj}^t \geq 0.$$

- The *multiclassification objective function* probably has the most compact form, as it optimizes the problem in a single step. The decision function is the same as that of the OAA technique. The multiclassification objective function constructs c two-class rules, and c decision functions solve the following constraints:

$$w_{y_i}^T \varphi(\mathbf{x}_i) + b_{y_i} \geq w_m^T \varphi(\mathbf{x}_i) + b_m + 2 - \xi_i^m, \ \xi_i^m \geq 0 \ .$$

For reasonable dataset sizes, the accuracy of the different multiclassification techniques is comparable. For any particular problem, selection of the optimal approach depends partly on the required accuracy and partly on the development and training time goals. For example, from a computational cost perspective, OAA and OAO are quite different. Let's say, for instance, that there are c different classes of N instances and that $T(N_1)$ represents the time for learning one binary classifier. Using N_1 examples, OAA will learn in cN^3, whereas OAO will require $4(c-1)N^3/ c^2$.

Although the SVM parametric model allows for adjustments when constructing the discriminant function, for multiclass problems these parameters do not always fit across the entire dataset. For this reason, it is sometimes preferable to partition the data into subgroups with similar features and derive the classifier parameters separately. This process results in a *multistage SVM* (*MSVM*), or *hierarchical SVM*, which can produce greater generalization accuracy and reduce the likelihood of overfitting, as shown by Stockman (2010). A graphical representation of a single SVM and an MSVM is presented in Figure 3-7.

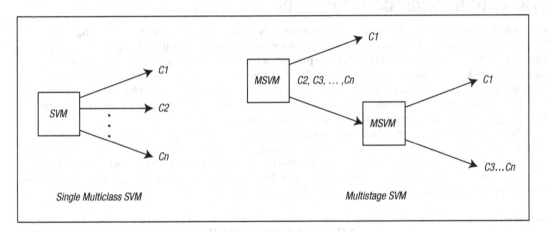

Figure 3-7. Single multiclass SVM and MSVM flows

With a multistage approach, different kernel and tuning parameters can be optimized for each stage separately. The first-stage SVM can be trained to distinguish between a single class and the rest of the classes. At the next stage, SVM can tune a different kernel to further distinguish among the remaining classes. Thus, there will be a binary classifier, with one decision function to implement at each stage.

Hierarchical SVM as an alternative for multiclass SVM has merit in terms of overall model error. SVM accuracy approaches the Bayes optimal rule as an appropriate kernel choice and in smoothing metaparameter values. Also, by definition, for a multiclass problem with $M \, c_1$ classes, and an input vector x, $\sum_{i=1}^{M} P(c_i|x) = 1$, because classes should cover all the search space. When the classes being considered are not equiprobable, the maximum $P(c_i|x)$ has to be greater than $1/M$; otherwise, the sum will be less than 1. Let's say, for example, that the probability of correct classification is

$$P_c = \sum_{i=1}^{M} P(x \in R_i, c_i) = \sum_{i=1}^{M} P(c_i) \int_{R_i} p(x|c_i) dx,$$

where R_i is the region of the feature space in which the decision is in favor of c_i. Because of the definition of region R_i,

$$P_c = \sum_{i=1}^{M} \int_{R_i} P(x|c_i) p(x) dx \geq \frac{1}{M} \sum_{i=1}^{M} \int_{R_i} p(x) dx,$$

$$\Rightarrow P_c \geq \frac{1}{M};$$

hence, the probability of multiclassification error is

$$P_e = 1 - P_c \leq 1 - \frac{1}{M} = \frac{M-1}{M}.$$

As the number of classes M increases, P_e increases for a multiclassification flat formulation. For a hierarchical classification the multiclassification task is reduced at each stage to a binary one, with $P_e = \frac{1}{2}$. Thus, the cumulative error for the hierarchical task is expected to converge asymptotically to a lower value than with a flat multiclassification task.

SVM with Imbalanced Datasets

In many real-life applications and nonsynthetic datasets, the data are *imbalanced*; that is, the important class—usually referred to as the *minority class*—has many fewer samples than the other class, usually referred to as the *majority class*. Class imbalance presents a major challenge for classification algorithms whenever the risk loss for the minority class is higher than for the majority class. When the minority data points are more important than the majority ones, and the main goal is to classify those minority data points correctly, standard machine learning that is geared toward optimized overall accuracy is not ideal; it will result in hyperplanes that favor the majority class and thus generalize poorly.

When dealing with imbalanced datasets, overall accuracy is a biased measure of classifier goodness. Instead, the confusion matrix, and the information on true positive (TP) and false positive (FP) that it holds, are a better indication of classifier performance. Referred to as *matching matrix* in unsupervised learning, and as *error matrix* or *contingency matrix* in fields other than machine learning, a confusion matrix provides a visual representation of actual versus predicted class accuracies.

ACCURACY METRICS

A confusion matrix is as follows:

Predicted/Actual Class	Positive Class	Negative Class
Positive Class	TP	FP
Negative Class	FN	TN

Accuracy is the number of data points correctly classified by the classification algorithm:

$$Accuracy = \frac{TP + TN}{TP + TN + FN + FP}.$$

The positive class is the class that is of utmost importance to the designer and usually is the minority class.

True positive (*TP*) (also called *recall* in some fields) is the number of data points correctly classified from the positive class.

False positive (*FP*) is the number of data points predicted to be in the positive class but in fact belonging to the negative class.

True negative (*TN*) is the number of data points correctly classified from the negative class.

False negative (*FN*) is the number of data points predicted to be in the negative class but in fact belonging to the positive class.

Sensitivity (also called *true positive rate* [*TPR*] or *recall rate* [*RR*]) is a measure of how well a classification algorithm classifies data points in the positive class:

$$Sensitivity = \frac{TP}{TP + FN}.$$

Specificity (also called *true negative rate* [*TNR*]) is a measure of how well a classification algorithm classifies data points in the negative class:

$$Specificity = \frac{TN}{TN + FP}.$$

Receiver operating characteristic (*ROC*) curves offer another useful graphical representation for classifiers operating on imbalanced datasets. Originally developed during World War II by radar and electrical engineers for communication purposes and target prediction, ROC is also embraced by diagnostic decision making. Fawcett (2006) provided a comprehensive introduction to ROC analysis, highlighting common misconceptions.

The original SVM formulation did not account for class imbalance during its supervised learning phase. But, follow-up research proposed modifications to the SVM formulation for classifying imbalanced datasets.

Previous work on SVM addressed class imbalance either by preprocessing the data or by proposing algorithmic modification to the SVM formulation. Kubat (1997) recommended balancing a dataset by randomly undersampling the majority class instead of oversampling the minority class. However, this results in information loss for the majority class. Veropoulos, Campbell, and Cristianini (1999) introduced different loss functions for the positive and negative classes to penalize the misclassification of minority data points. Tax and Ruin (1999) solved the class imbalance by using the *support vector data description* (*SVDD*), which aims at finding a sphere that encompasses the minority class and separates it from the outliers as optimally as possible. Feng and Williams (1999) suggested *general scaled SVM* (*GS-SVM*), another variation of SVM, which introduces a translation of the hyperplane after training the SVM. The translation distance is added to the SVM formulation; translation distance is computed by projecting the data points on the normal vector of the trained hyperplane and finding the distribution scales of the whole dataset (Das 2012). Chang and Lin (2011) proposed *weighted scatter degree SVM* (WSD-SVM), which embeds the global information in the GS-SVM by using the scatter of the data points and their weights, based on their location.

Many efforts have been made to learn imbalanced data at the level of both the data and the algorithm. Preprocessing the data before learning the classifier was done through oversampling of the minority class to balance the class distribution by replication or undersampling of the larger class, which balances the data by eliminating samples randomly from that class (Kotsiantis, Kanellopoulos, and Pintelas 2006). Tang et al. (2009) recommended the granular SVM repetitive undersampling (GSVM-RU) algorithm, which, instead of using random undersampling of the majority class to obtain a balanced dataset, uses SVM itself—the idea being to form multiple majority information granules, from which local majority support vectors are extracted and then aggregated with the minority class. Another resampling method for learning classifiers from imbalanced data was suggested by Ou, Hung, and Oyang (2006) and Napierała, Stefanowski, and Wilk (2010). These authors concluded that only when the data suffered severely from noise or borderline examples would their proposed resampling methods outperform the known oversampling methods. The synthetic minority oversampling technique (SMOTE) algorithm (Chawla et al. (2002) oversamples the minority class by introducing artificial minority samples between a given minority data point and its nearest minority neighbors. Extensions of the SMOTE algorithm have been developed, including one that works in the distance space (Koknar-Tezel and Latecki 2010). Cost-sensitive methods for imbalanced data learning have also been used. These methods define a cost matrix for misclassifying any data sample and fit the matrix into the classification algorithm (He and Garcia 2009).

Tax and Duin (2004) put forward the one-class SVM, which tends to learn from the minority class only. The one-class SVM aims at estimating the probability density function, which gives a positive value for the elements in the minority class and a negative value for everything else.

By introducing a multiplicative factor z to the support vector of the minority class, Imam, Ting, and Kamruzzaman (2006) posited that the bias of the learned SVM will be reduced automatically, without providing any additional parameters and without invoking multiple SVM trainings.

Akbani, Kwek, and Japkowicz (2004) proposed an algorithm based on a combination of the SMOTE algorithm and the different error costs for the positive and negative classes. Wang and Japkowicz (2010) also aggregated the different penalty factors as well as using an ensemble of SVM classifiers to improve the error for a single classifier and treat the problem of the skewed learned SVM. In an attempt to improve classification of imbalanced datasets using SVM standard formulation, Ajeeb, Nayal, and Awad (2013) suggested a novel *minority SVM* (*MinSVM*), which, with the addition of one constraint to the SVM objective function, separates boundaries that are closer to the majority class. Consequently, the minority data points are favored, and the probability of being misclassified is smaller.

Improving SVM Computational Requirements

Despite the robustness and optimality of the original SVM formulation, SVMs do not scale well computationally. Suffering from slow training convergence on large datasets, SVM online testing time can be suboptimal; SVMs write the classifier hyperplane model as a sum of support vectors whose number cannot be estimated ahead of time and may total as much as half the datasets. Thus, it is with larger datasets that SVM fails to deliver efficiently, especially in the case of nonlinear classification. Large datasets impose heavy computational time and storage requirements during training, sometimes rendering SVM even slower than ANN, itself notorious for slow convergence. For this reason, support vector set cardinality may be a problem when online prediction requires real-time performance on platforms with limited computational and power supply capabilities, such as mobile devices.

Many attempts have been made to speed up SVM. A survey related to SVM and its variants reveals a dichotomy between speedup strategies. The first category of techniques applies to the training phase of the SVM algorithm, which incurs a heftier computational cost in its search for the optimal separator. The intent of these algorithms is to reduce the cardinality of the dataset and speed up the optimization solver. The second category of techniques aims to accelerate the testing cycle. With the proliferation of power-conscious mobile devices, and the ubiquity of computing pushed from the cloud to these terminals, reducing the SVM testing cycle can be useful in applications in which computational resources are limited and real-time prediction is necessary. For example, online prediction on mobile devices would greatly benefit from reducing the computations required to perform a prediction.

To reduce the computational complexity of the SVM optimization problem, Platt (1998) developed the sequential minimal optimization (SMO) method, which divides the optimization problem into two quadratic program (QP) problems. This decomposition relieves the algorithm of large memory requirements and makes it feasible to train SVM on large datasets. Therefore, this algorithm grows alternately linearly and quadratically, depending on dataset size. SMO speeds up the training phase only, with no control over the number of support vectors or testing time. To achieve additional acceleration, many parallel implementations of SMO (Zeng et al. 2008; Peng, Ma, and Hong 2009; Catanzaro et al. 2008; Alham et al. 2010; Cao et al. 2006) were developed on various parallel programming platforms, including graphics processing unit (GPU) (Catanzaro et al. 2008), Hadoop MapReduce (Alham et al. 2010), and message passing interface (MPI) (Cao et al. 2006).

Using the Cholesky factorization (Gill and Murray 1974), Fine (2002) approximated the kernel matrix by employing a low-rank matrix that requires updates that scale linearly with the training set size. The matrix is then fed to a QP solver to obtain an approximate solution to the SVM classification problem. Referred to as the *Cholesky product form QP*, this approach showed significant training time reduction, with its approximation of the optimal solution provided by SMO. However, if the training set contains redundant features, or if the support vectors are scaled by a large value, this method fails to converge (Fine and Scheinberg 2002).

Instead of decomposing the optimization problem, Lee (2001a) reformulated the constraint optimization as an unconstrained, smooth problem that can be solved using the Newton-Armijo algorithm in quadratic time. This reformulation resulted in improved testing accuracy of the standard SVM formulation (Vapnik 1999) on several databases (Lee 2001). Furthermore, Lee (2001) argued that this reformulation allows random selection of a subset of vectors and forces creation of more support vectors, without greatly affecting the prediction accuracy of the model.

Margin vectors were identified by Kong and Wang (2010) by computing the self and the mutual center distances in the feature space and eliminating the statistically insignificant points, based on the ratio and center distance of those points. The training set was forced to be balanced, and results were compared with those found using reduced SVM (RSVM) on three datasets from the University of California, Irvine, Machine Learning Repository (Frank and Asuncion 2010). The authors found that the model resulted in better generalization performance than with RSVM but that it required slightly more training time, owing to the overhead of computing the ratios and center distances.

Zhang (2008) identified boundary vectors, using the k-nearest neighbors (k-NN algorithm. With this method the distance between each vector and all other vectors is computed, and the vectors that have among their k-NN a vector of opposing class are retained. For linearly nonseparable problems, k-NN is applied in the kernel space, where the dataset is linearly separable. The preextract boundary vectors are used to train SVM. Because this subset is much smaller than the original dataset, training will be faster, and the support vector set will be smaller.

Downs, Gates, and Masters (2002) attempted to reduce the number of support vectors used in the prediction stage by eliminating vectors from the support vector set produced by an SMO solver that are linearly dependent on other support vectors. Hence, the final support vector set is formed of all linearly independent support vectors in the kernel space obtained by using row-reduced echelon form. Although this method produced reduction for polynomial kernels, and RBF with large sigma values, the number of, support vectors reduced could not be predicted ahead of time and was dependent on the kernel and the problem.

Nguyen (2006) reduced the support vector set by iteratively replacing the two nearest support vectors belonging to the same class, using a constructed support vector that did not belong to the original training set. The algorithm was applied after training the SVM on the training set and obtaining the support vector set. The algorithm was tested on the United States Postal Service database (Le Cun 1990) and achieved significant reduction in support vector set cardinality, with little reduction in prediction accuracy.

Rizk, Mitri, and Awad (2013) proposed a *local mixture–based SVM* (*LMSVM*), which exploits the increased separability provided by the kernel trick, while introducing a one-time computational cost. LMSVM applies kernel k-means clustering to the data in kernel space before pruning unwanted clusters, based on a mixture measure for label heterogeneity. Extending this concept, Rizk, Mitri, and Awad (2014) put forward *knee-cut SVM* (*KCSVM*) and *knee-cut ordinal optimization–inspired SVM* (*KCOOSVM*), with a soft trick of ordered kernel values and uniform subsampling to reduce the computational complexity of SVM, while maintaining an acceptable impact on its generalization capability.

Case Study of SVM for Handwriting Recognition

Automated *handwriting recognition* (*HWR*) is becoming popular in several offline and online sensing tasks. Developing robust yet computationally efficient algorithms is still a challenging problem, given the increased awareness of energy-aware computing. *Offline sensing* occurs by optically scanning words and then transforming those images to letter code usable in the computer software environment. *Online recognition* automatically converts the writing on a graphics tablet or pen-based computer screen into letter code. HWR systems can also be classified as *writer dependent* or *writer independent*, with dependent systems' having a higher recognition rate, owing to smaller variance in the provided data.

Because isolated-letter HWR is an essential step for online HWR, we present here a case study on developing an efficient writer-independent HWR system for isolated letters, using pen trajectory modeling for feature extraction and an MSVM for classification (Hajj and Awad 2012). In addition to underlining the importance of the application, this case study illustrates how stationary features are created from sequential data and how a multiclass task is converted into a hierarchical one. Usually, hidden Markov models (HMM) are better for modeling and recognizing sequential data, but with an appropriate feature generation scheme, an SVM model can be used to model variable sequence length for moderate handwriting vocabularies.

The proposed HWR workflow is composed of preprocessing; feature extraction; and a hierarchical, three-stage classification phase.

Preprocessing

The UJIpenchars database can be transformed into a sequence of points suitable for feature extraction in a way similar to preprocessing performed a step typically found in many HWR systems. The preprocessing comprises correcting the slant; normalizing the dimensions of the letter; and shifting the coordinates, with respect to the center of mass.

To correct the slant, the input, consisting of a sequence of collected points, is first written in the form of a series of vectors with polar coordinates, and then only vectors with an angle equal to or less than 50 degrees with the vertical are considered. The slant is computed by averaging the angles of the significant vectors. Next, the letter is rotated by the slant angle, and the data are normalized so that all letters have the same dimensions. Finally, the shifting of the coordinates, with respect to the center of mass, fits the letter into a square of unit dimension with a centroid with the coordinates (0, 0).

Figure 3-8 shows two letters before (left) and after (right) the preprocessing stage.

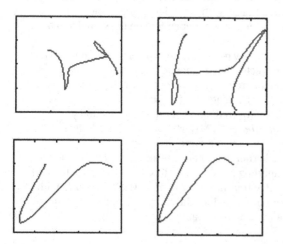

Figure 3-8. *Examples of letters before (left) and after (right) preprocessing*

Feature Extraction

To obtain different representations of the letters, a set of feature vectors of fixed length should be computed. The preprocessed data, consisting of strokes of coordinate pairs $[x(t), y(t)]$, can be modeled, using a pen trajectory technique (Jaeger 2008), and the set of features is obtained after averaging the following functions:

- *Writing direction*: Defined by

$$\cos\alpha(t)=\frac{\Delta x(t)}{\Delta s(t)};\ \sin\alpha(t)=\frac{\Delta y(t)}{\Delta s(t)},$$

where Δx, Δy, and Δs are defined as

$$\Delta x(t)=x(t-1)-x(t+1),$$

$$\Delta y(t)=y(t-1)-y(t+1),$$

$$\Delta s(t)=\sqrt{\Delta x(t)^2+\Delta y(t)^2}.$$

- *Curvature*: Defined by the sine and cosine of the angle defined by the points $(x(t-2)$, $y(t-2))$; $(x(t), y(t))$; and $(x(t+2), y(t+2))$. Curvature can be calculated from the writing direction, using the following equations:

$$\cos\beta(t)=\cos\alpha(t-1)\cos\alpha(t+1)+\sin\alpha(t-1)\sin\alpha(t+1),$$

$$\sin\beta(t)=\cos\alpha(t-1)\sin\alpha(t+1)-\sin\alpha(t-1)\cos\alpha(t+1).$$

- *Aspect of the trajectory*: Computed according to the equation

$$A(t)=\frac{\left(\Delta y(t)-\Delta x(t)\right)}{\left(\Delta y(t)+\Delta x(t)\right)}.$$

- *Curliness*: Describes the deviation of the points from a straight line formed by the previous and following points in the sequence by the equation

$$C(t)=L(t)/max(\Delta x,\Delta y)-2,$$

where $L(t)$ represents the length of the trajectory from point $(x(t-1), y(t-1))$ to point $(x(t+1), y(t+1))$.

In addition to the previous functions, the following global features are computed:

- *Linearity*: Measured by the average distance from each point of the sequence to the straight line joining the first and last points in the sequence:

$$LN=\frac{1}{N}\sum d_i.$$

- *Slope of the sequence*: Measured by the cosine and sine of the angle formed by the straight line joining the first and last points in the sequence and a horizontal line.

- *Ascenders and descenders*: Describes the number of points of the sequence below (descenders) or above (ascenders) the *baseline* (the straight horizontal line on which the letter is written), each weighted by its distance to the baseline.

- *Variance of coordinates* (for both dimensions): Measures the expansion of the points around the center of mass.

- *Ratio of variances*: Represents the proportion of the width to the height of the letter.

- *Cumulative distance*: The sum of the length of the segments of line joining consecutive points of the sequence.

- *Average distance to the center*, The mean of the distances from each point of the sequence to the center of mass of the letter.

Hierarchical, Three-Stage SVM

After the preprocessing and feature extraction stages, a three-stage classifier recognizes one of the 52 classes (26 lowercase and 26 uppercase letters).

- Using a binary SVM classifier, the first stage classifies the instance as one of two classes: uppercase or lowercase letter.

- Using OAA SVM, the second stage classifies the instance as one of the manually determined clusters shown in Table 3-1.

Table 3-1. *Lower- and Uppercase Clusters*

Lowercase Clusters	Uppercase Clusters
Cluster 1: a c e o	Cluster 9: A B P R
Cluster 2: b d l t	Cluster 10: C D G O Q
Cluster 3: f h k	Cluster 11: E F I L
Cluster 4: g z j	Cluster 12: J K T
Cluster 5: p q	Cluster 13: M N H
Cluster 6: i r s	Cluster 14: S Y Z X
Cluster 7: u v w x	Cluster 15: U V W
Cluster 8: m n	

- Using OAA SVM, with a simple majority vote, the third stage identifies the letter as one of the 52 classes (or subclusters). Figure 3-9 displays the hierarchy of the three-stage system.

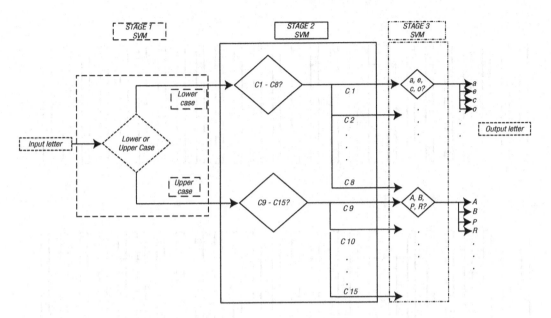

Figure 3-9. *Hierarchical, three-stage SVM*

Experimental Results

Experimental results, implemented with the MATLAB R2011a SVM toolbox, showed (using a four-fold cross-validation) an average accuracy of 91.7 percent—or, an error rate of 8.3 percent, compared with an error rate of 10.85 percent, using 3NN (Prat et al. 2009). The three stages of the classifier achieved, respectively, 99.3 percent, 95.7 percent, and 96.5 percent accuracy. The kernel used for the three stages was an RBF with parameters tuned using a grid search algorithm. Our proposed preprocessing helped improve the general accuracy of the recognizer by approximately 1.5 percent to 2 percent.

Figure 3-10 presents a confusion histogram demonstrating the occurrence of the predicted classified labels, along with their true labels. For example, in the first column, of the six letter *a*'s, five were correctly recognized, and one was mistaken for *c*. Generally, no particular trend was observed in this confusion matrix, and the error may be assumed to be randomly distributed among all classes.

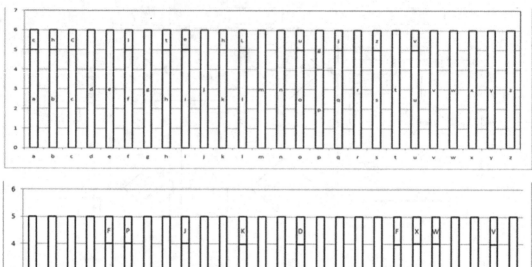

Figure 3-10. Confusion plot for classified label versus true label

Because a flat SVM architecture may seem computationally less expensive, it was compared with the proposed three-stage SVM, using OAO and OAA SVM techniques. Table 3-2 shows the recognition rates obtained using the proposed architecture, compared with a flat SVM technique as well as the3NN algorithm. The accuracy attained ranged from 65 percent, using OAA, to 82 percent, using OAO, whereas the hierarchical SVM structure reached 91.7 percent. This is due to the fact that, with a three-stage SVM, both the metaparameters of SVM (i.e., the regularization parameter between the slack and hyperplane parameters) and the kernel specifics can be better modified independently during each phase of training and better tailored to the resulting data subsets than a flat SVM model can be for the whole dataset.

Table 3-2. Recognition Rate Comparison

Architecture	Recognition Rate (%)
Flat SVM OAA	65
Flat SVM OAO	82
3NN (Prat et al. 2009)	89.15
Three-Stage SVM	91.8

Complexity Analysis

Tables 3-3 and 3-4, respectively, provide the required operations for the preprocessing and feature extraction stages of the three-stage SVM, where a letter is represented by a sequence of strokes of length N, with M being the number of significant vectors, and K, the data size.

Table 3-3. *Required Operations for the Preprocessing Stage*

Step	Total Operations
Representing letter in a sequence of vector	$8N$
Computing slant	$M + 1$
Rotating letter	N
Normalizing dimensions	$2N$
Shifting to center of mass	$4N + 2$

Table 3-4. *Required Operations for the Feature Extraction Stage*

Feature	Total Operations
Writing direction	$7N$
Curvature	$6N$
Aspect	$2N$
Curliness	$14N$
Linearity	$6N + 1$
Slope	7
Ascenders and descenders	$6N$
Variance	$8N + 4$
Ratio of variances	1
Cumulative distance	$5N - 5$
Average distance	$4N$

Table 3-5 compares the required operations for the classification process using three-stage SVM and the 3NN algorithm . Both SVM optimal hyperplane coefficients and support vectors were computed during the training process. Given an input pattern represented by a multidimensional (11) vector x and a w vector representing the decision boundary (hyperplane), the decision function for the classification phase is reduced to a sign function.

Table 3-5. *Comparison of Three-Stage SVM and 3NN Classifiers*

Classifier	Decision Function	Total Operations
Three-Stage SVM	$C(\underline{x}) = \underline{w}^T \underline{x} + w_0$	12 operations per classifier; in total, 168 operations (the class requiring the most classifiers)
3NN (Prat et al. 2009)	$D(\underline{x}, \underline{z}) = \sqrt{\left(x_1 - z_1\right)^2 + \ldots + \left(x_{50} - z_{50}\right)^2}$	150 operations per distance measure; in total, 3 50 * K = 150 * K

The online classification task is much costlier using a 3NN classifier compared with a hierarchical SVM. In fact, every classification task requires the Euclidian distance calculation to all points in the dataset, which would be an expensive cost to incur in the presence of a large dataset. Additionally, with the lack of a classification model, the k-NN technique is a non parametric approach and requires access to all the data each time an instance is recognized. With SVM, in contrast, separating class boundaries is learned offline, during the training phase, and at runtime the computational cost of SVM training is not present. Only preprocessing, feature extraction, and a simple multiplication operation with the hyperplane parameters are involved in the online testing process. An advantage of 3NN, however, is that no training is required, as opposed to the complex SVM classification step.

References

Aizerman, M., E. Braverman, and L. Rozonoer. "Theoretical Foundations of the Potential Function Method in Pattern Recognition Learning." *Automation and Remote Control* 25 (1964): 821–837.

Ajeeb, N., A. Nayal, and M. Awad. "Minority SVM for Linearly Separable and Imbalanced Datasets." In *IJCNN 2013: Proceedings of the 2013 International Joint Conference on Neural Networks*, 1–5. Piscataway, NJ: Institute for Electrical and Electronics Engineers, 2013.

Akbani, Rehan, Stephen Kwek, and Nathalie Japkowicz. "Applying Support Vector Machines to Imbalanced Datasets." In *Machine Learning: ECML 2004: 15th European Conference on Machine Learning, Pisa, Italy, September 2004*, edited by Jean-François Boulicaut, Floriana Esposito, Fosca Giannotti, and Dino Pedreschi, 39–50. Berlin: Springer, 2004.

Alham, N. K., Maozhen Li, S. Hammoud, Yang Liu, and M. Ponraj. "A Distributed SVM for Image Annotation." In *FSKD 2010: Proceedings of the Seventh International Conference on Fuzzy Systems and Knowledge Discovery*, edited by Maozhen Li, Qilian Liang, Lipo Wang and Yibin Song, 2983–2987. Piscataway, NJ: Institute of Electrical and Electronics Engineers, 2010.

Aronszajn, N. "Theory of Reproducing Kernels." *Transactions of the American Mathematical Society* 68, no. 3 (1950): 337–404.

Bartlett, P. and J. Shawe-Taylor, "Generalization Performance of Support Vector Machines and Other Pattern Classifiers", Advances in Kernel Methods: Support Vector Learning, 1999.

Ben-Hur, Asa, and Jason Weston. "A User's Guide to Support Vector Machines." *Data Mining Techniques for Life Sciences*, edited by Oliviero Carugo and Frank Eisenhaber, 223-239. New York: Springer, 2010.

Bennett, Kristen P., and O. L. Mangasarian. "Robust Linear Programming Discrimination of Two Linearly Inseparable Sets." *Optimization Methods and Software* 1, no. 1: (1992): 23–34.

Boser, Bernard E., Isabelle M. Guyon, and Vladimir N. Vapnik. "A Training Algorithm for Optimal Margin Classifiers." In *COLT '92: Proceedings of the Fifth Annual Workshop on Computational Learning Theory*, edited by David Haussler, 144–152. New York: ACM, 1992.

Cao, L. J., S. S. Keerthi, Chong-Jin Ong, J. Q. Zhang, U. Periyathamby, Xiu Ju Fu, and H. P. Lee. "Parallel Sequential Minimal Optimization for the Training of Support Vector Machines." *IEE Transactions on Neural Networks* 17, no. 4 (2006): 1039–1049.

Catanzaro, Bryan Christopher, Narayanan Sundaram, and Kurt Keutzer. "Fast Support Vector Machine Training and Classification on Graphics Processors." In *ICML '08: Proceedings of the 25th International Conference on Machine Learning*, edited by William Cohen, Andrew McCallum, and Sam Roweis, 104–111. New York: ACM, 2008.

Chang, Chih-Chung, and Chih-Jen Lin. "LIBSVM: A Library for Support Vector Machines," in "Large-Scale Machine Learning," edited by Huan Liu and Dana Nau, special issue, *ACM Transactions on Intelligent Systems and Technology* 2, no. 3 (2011).

Chawla, Nitesh V., Kevin W. Bowyer, Lawrence O. Hall, and W. Philip Kegelmeyer. "SMOTE: Synthetic Minority Over-Sampling Technique." *Journal of Artificial Intelligence Research* 16 (2002): 321–357.

Cover, Thomas M. "Geometrical and Statistical Properties of Systems of Linear Inequalities with Applications in Pattern Recognition." *IEEE Transactions on Electronic Computers* 14 (1995): 326–334.

Das, Barnan. "Implementation of SMOTEBoost Algorithm Used to Handle Class Imbalance Problem in Data," 2012. www.mathworks.com/matlabcentral/fileexchange/37311-smoteboost.

Downs, Tom, Kevin E. Gates, and Annette Masters. "Exact Simplification of Support Vector Solutions." *Journal of Machine Learning Research* 2 (2002): 293–297.

Duda, Richard O., and Peter E. Hart. *Pattern Classification and Scene Analysis*. New York: Wiley, 1973.

Fawcett, Tom. "An Introduction to ROC Analysis. "*Pattern Recognition Letters 27* (2006): 861–874.

Feng, Jianfeng, and P. Williams. "The Generalization Error of the Symmetric and Scaled Support Vector Machines." *IEEE Transactions on Neural Networks* 12, no. 5 (1999): 1255–1260.

Fine, Shai, and Katya Scheinberg. "Efficient SVM Training Using Low-Rank Kernel Representations." *Journal of Machine Learning Research* 2 (2002): 243–264.

Fisher, Marshall L. "The Lagrangian Relaxation Method for Solving Integer Programming Problems. "*Management Science* 50, no. 12 (2004):1861–1871.

Frank, A., and A. Asuncion. University of California, Irvine, Machine Learning Repository. Irvine: University of California, 2010. www.ics.uci.edu/`mlearn/MLRepository.html.

Friedman, J. "Another Approach to Polychotomous Classification." Technical report, Stanford University, 1996.

Hajj, N., and M. Awad." Isolated Handwriting Recognition via Multi-Stage Support Vector Machines." In *Proceedings of the 6th IEEE International Conference on Intelligent Systems,"* edited by Vladimir Jotsov, Krassimir Atanassov, 152–157. Piscataway, NJ: Institute for Electrical and Electronic Engineers, 2012.

He, Heibo, and Edwardo A. Garcia. "Learning from Imbalanced Data." *IEEE Transactions on Knowledge and Data Engineering* 21, no. 9(2009):1263–1284.

Gill, Philip E., and Walter Murray. "Newton-Type Methods for Unconstrained and Linearly Constrained Optimization." *Mathematical Programming* 7 (1974): 311–350.

Imam, Tasadduq, Kai Ming Ting, and Joarder Kamruzzaman. "z-SVM: An SVM for Improved Classification of Imbalanced Data." In *AI 2006: Advances in Artificial Intelligence; Proceedings of the 19th Australian Joint Conference on Artificial Intelligence, Hobart, Australia, December 4-8, 2006*, edited by Abdul Sattar and Byeong-Ho Kang, 264–273, 2006. Berlin: Springer, 2006.

S. Jaeger, S. Manke, J. Reichert, A. Waibel, "Online Handwriting Recognition: the NPen++ Recognizer", International Journal on Document Analysis and Recognition, vol.3, no.3, 169-180, March 2008.

Jin, A-Long, Xin Zhou, and Chi-Zhou Ye. "Support Vector Machines Based on Weighted Scatter Degree." In *Artificial Intelligence and Computational Intelligence: Proceedings of the AICI Third International Conference, Taiyuan, China, September 24–25, 2011, Part III*, edited by Hepu Deng, Duoqian Miao, Jingsheng Lei, and Fu Lee Wang, 620–629. Berlin: Springer, 2011.

Karush, William. "Minima of Functions of Several Variables with Inequalities as Side Constraints." Master's thesis, University of Chicago, 1939.

Knerr, S., L. Personnaz, and G. Dreyfus. "Single-Layer Learning Revisited: A Stepwise Procedure for Building and Training a Neural Network." In *Neurocomputing: Algorithms, Architectures and Applications; NATO Advanced Workshop on Neuro-Computing, Les Arcs, Savoie, France, 1989*, edited by Françoise Fogelman Soulié and Jeanny Hérault, 41–50. Berlin: Springer, 1990.

Koknar-Tezel, S., and L. J. Latecki. "Improving SVM Classification on Imbalanced Data Sets in Distance Spaces." In *ICDM '09: Proceedings of the Ninth IEEE International Conference on Data Mining*, edited by Wei Wang, Hillol Kargupta, Sanjay Ranka, Philip S. Yu, and Xindong Wu, 259–267. Piscataway, NJ: Institute for Electrical and Electronics Engineers, 2010.

Kong, Bo, and Hong-wei Wang. "Reduced Support Vector Machine Based on Margin Vectors." In *CiSE 2010 International Conference on Computational Intelligence and Software Engineering,*" 1–4. Piscataway, NJ: Institute for Electrical and Electronic Engineers, 2010.

Kotsiantis, Sotiris, Dimitris Kanellopoulos, and Panayiotis Pintelas. "Handling Imbalanced Datasets: A Review."*GESTS International Transactions on Computer Science and Engineering* 30, no. 1 (2006): 25–36.

Kressel, Ulrich H.-G. "Pairwise Classification and Support Vector Machines." In *Advances in Kernel Methods: Support Vector Learning,* edited by Bernhard Schölkopf, Christopher J. C. Burges, and Alexander J. Smola, 255–268. Cambridge, MA: Massachusetts Institute of Technology Press, 1999.

Kuhn, H. W., and A. W. Tucker. "Nonlinear Programming." In *Proceedings of the Second Berkeley Symposium on Mathematical Statistics and Probability*, edited by Jerzy Neyman, 481–492. Berkeley: University of California Press, 1951.

Le Cun, Y., B. Boser, J. S. Denker, D. Henderson, R. E. Howard, W. Hubbard and L. D. Jackel. "Handwritten Digit Recognition with a Back-Propagation Network." In *Advances in Neural Information Processing Systems*, edited by D. S. Touretzky, 396–404. San Mateo, CA: Morgan Kaufmann, 1990.

Lee, Yuh-Jye, and O. L. Mangasarian. "SSVM: A Smooth Support Vector Machine for Classification." *Computational Optimization and Applications* 20 (2001a): 5–22.

Lee, Yuh-Jye, and Olvi L. Mangasarian. "RSVM: Reduced Support Vector Machines." In *Proceedings of the First SIAM International Conference on Data Mining*, edited by Robert Grossman and Vipin Kumar, 5–7. Philadelphia: Society for Industrial and Applied Mathematics, 2001b .

Liu, Xin, and Ying Ding. "General Scaled Support Vector Machines." In *ICMLC 2011: Proceedings of the 3rd International Conference on Machine Learning and Computing*. Piscataway, NJ: Institute of Electrical and Electronics Engineers, 2011.

Mangasarian, O. L. "Linear and Nonlinear Separation of Patterns by Linear Programming." *Operations Research* 13, no. 3 (1965): 444–452.

Meyer, David, Friederich Leisch, and Kurt Hornik." The Support Vector Machine Under Test." *Neurocomputing* 55, nos. 1–2 (2003): 169–186.

Napierała, Krystyna, Jerzy Stefanowski, and Szyman Wilk. "Learning from Imbalanced Data in Presence of Noisy and Borderline Examples." In *Rough Sets and Current Trends in Computing: Proceedings of the 7th RSCTC International Conference, Warsaw, Poland, June 2010,*edited by Marcin Szczuka, Marzena Kryszkiewicz, Sheela Ramanna, Richard Jensen, and Qinghua Hu, 158–167. Berlin: Springer, 2010.

Nguyen, Duc Dung, and Tuo Bao Ho. "A Bottom-Up Method for Simplifying Support Vector Solutions." *IEEE Transactions on Neural Networks*. 17, no. 3 (2006): 792–796.

Ou, Yu-Yen, Hao-Geng Hung, and Yen-Jen Oyang, "A Study of Supervised Learning with Multivariate Analysis on Unbalanced Datasets." In *IJCNN '06: Proceedings of the 2006 International Joint Conference on Neural Networks*, 2201–2205. Piscataway, NJ: Institute for Electrical and Electronic Engineers, 2006.

Peng, Peng, Qian-Lee Ma, and Lei-Ming Hong. "The Research of the Parallel SMO Algorithm for Solving SVM." In *ICMLC 2009: Proceedings of the 2009 International Conference on Machine Learning and Cybernetics*, 1271–1274. Piscataway, NJ: Institute for Electrical and Electronics Engineers, 2009.

Platt, John C. "Sequential Minimal Optimization: A Fast Algorithm for Training Support Vector Machines." Technical report MSR-TR-98-14, 1998.

Platt, John C., Nello Cristianini, and John Shawe-Taylor. "Large Margin DAGs for Multiclass Classification." In *Advances in Neural Information Processing Systems 12 (NIPS '99)*, edited S. A. Solla, T. K. Leen, and K.-R. Müller, 547–553. Cambridge, MA: Massachusetts Institute of Technology Press, 2000.

Poggio, Tomaso, and Federico Girosi. "Networks for Approximation and Learning." *Proceedings of the IEEE* 78, no. 9 (1990): 1481–1497.

Prat, Federico, Andrés Marzal, Sergio Martín, Rafael Ramos-Garijo, and María José Castro. "A Template-Based Recognition System for On-line Handwritten Characters." *Journal of Information Science and Engineering* 25 (2009): 779–791.

Rizk, Y., N. Mitri, and M. Awad. "A Local Mixture Based SVM for an Efficient Supervised Binary Classification." In *IJCNN 2013: Proceedings of the International Joint Conference on Neural Networks*, 1–8. Piscataway, NJ: Institute for Electrical and Electronics Engineers, 2013.

Rizk, Y., N. Mitri, and M. Awad. "An Ordinal Kernel Trick for a Computationally Efficient Support Vector Machine." In *IJCNN 2014: Proceedings of the 2014 International Joint Conference on Neural Networks*, 3930–3937. Piscataway, NJ: Institute for Electrical and Electronics Engineers, 2014.

Schölkopf, B., John C. Platt, John C. Shawe-Taylor, Alex J. Smola, and Robert C. Williamson. "Estimating the Support of a High-Dimensional Distribution." *Neural Computation* 13, no. 7 (2001):1443–1471.

Smith, F. W. "Pattern Classifier Design by Linear Programming." *IEEE Transactions on Computers*, C-17. no. 4 (1968): 367–372.

Stockman, M., and M. Awad. "Multistage SVM as a Clinical Decision Making Tool for Predicting Post Operative Patient Status." *IKE '10: Proceedings of the 2010 International Conference on Information and Knowledge Engineering*. Athens, GA: CSREA, 2010.

Suykens, J. A. K. Suykens, and J. Vandewalle. "Least Squares Support Vector Machine Classifiers." *Neural Processing Letters* 9, no. 3 (1999): 293–300.

Tang, Yuchun, Yan-Qing Zhang, Nitesh V. Chawla, and Sven Krasser. "SVMs Modeling for Highly Imbalanced Classification." *Journal of Latex Class Files* 1, no. 11 (2002). www3.nd.edu/~dial/papers/SMCB09.pdf.

Tang, Yuchun, Yan-Qing Zhang, N. V. Chawla, and Sven Krasser. "SVMs Modeling for Highly Imbalanced Classification." *Systems, Man, and Cybernetics B: IEEE Transactions on Cybernetics* 39, no. 1 (2009): 281–288.

Tax, David M. J., and Robert P. W. Ruin. "Support Vector Domain Description." *Pattern Recognition Letters* 20 (1999): 1191–1199.

Tax, David M. J., and Robert P. W. Duin. "Support Vector Data Description." *Machine Learning* 54 (2004): 45–66.

Vapnik, Vladimir N. *The Nature of Statistical Learning Theory*. New York: Springer, 1995.

Vapnik, Vladimir N. Statistical Learning Theory. New York: Wiley, 1998.

Vapnik, Vladimir N. *The Nature of Statistical Learning Theory, Second Edition.* New York: Springer, 1999.

Vapnik, V., and A. Chervonenkis. "A Note on One Class of Perceptrons." *Automation and Remote Control* 25 (1964).

Vapnik, V., and A. Lerner. "Pattern Recognition Using Generalized Portrait Method." *Automation and Remote Control* 24 (1963): 774–780.

Veropoulos, K., C. Campbell, and N. Cristianini. "Controlling the Sensitivity of Support Vector Machines." In *IJCAI '99: Proceedings of the 16th International Joint Conference on Artificial Intelligence*, edited by Thomas Dean, 55–60. San Francisco: Morgan Kaufmann, 1999.

Wahba, Grace. *Spline Models for Observational Data.* CBMS-NSF Regional Conference Series in Applied Mathematics 59. Philadelphia: Society for Industrial and Applied Mathematics, 1990.

Wang, Benjamin X., and Nathalie Japkowicz. "Boosting Support Vector Machines for Imbalanced Data Sets." *Knowledge and Information Systems* 25, no. 1 (2010): 1–20.

Weston, J., and C. Watkins. Support Vector Machines for Multi-Class Pattern Recognition. In *ESANN 1999: Proceedings of the 7th European Symposium on Artificial Neural Networks, Bruges, Belgium, 21–23 April 1999*, 219–224. 1999. https://www.elen.ucl.ac.be/Proceedings/esann/esannpdf/es1999-461.pdf.

Zeng, Zhi-Qiang, Hong-Bin Yu, Hua-Rong Xu, Yan-Qi Xie, and Ji Gao. "Fast Training Support Vector Machines Using Parallel Sequential Minimal Optimization." In *ISKE 2008: Proceedings of the 3rd International Conference on Intelligent System and Knowledge Engineering*, edited by Shaozi Li, Tianrui Li, and Da Ruan, 997–1001. Piscataway, NJ: Institute for Electrical and Electronics Engineers, 2008.

Zhang, Li, Ning Ye, Weida Zhou, and Licheng Jiao. "Support Vectors Pre-Extracting for Support Vector Machine Based on K Nearest Neighbour Method." In *ICIA 2008: Proceedings of the 2008 International Conference on Information and Automation*, 1353–1358. Piscataway, NJ: Institute of Electrical and Electronics Engineers, 2008.

Zhang, Xuegong. "Using Class-Center Vectors to Build Support Vector Machines." *Neural Networks for Signal Processing IX: Proceedings of the 1999 IEEE Signal Processing Society Workshop*, edited by Yu-Hen Hu, Jan Larsen, Elizabeth Wilson, and Scott Douglas, 3–11. Piscataway, NJ: Institute for Electrical and Electronic Engineers, 1999.

Zhuang, Ling, and Honghua Dai. "Parameter Optimization of Kernel-Based One-Class Classifier on Imbalance Text Learning." *Journal of Computers* 1, no. 7 (2006): 32–40.

CHAPTER 4

■ ■ ■

Support Vector Regression

The key to artificial intelligence has always been the representation.

—Jeff Hawkins

Rooted in statistical learning or Vapnik-Chervonenkis (VC) theory, *support vector machines* (SVMs) are well positioned to generalize on yet-to-be-seen data. The SVM concepts presented in Chapter 3 can be generalized to become applicable to regression problems. As in classification, *support vector regression* (SVR) is characterized by the use of kernels, sparse solution, and VC control of the margin and the number of *support vectors*. Although less popular than SVM, SVR has been proven to be an effective tool in real-value function estimation. As a supervised-learning approach, SVR trains using a symmetrical loss function, which equally penalizes high and low misestimates. Using Vapnik's ε-insensitive approach, a flexible tube of minimal radius is formed symmetrically around the estimated function, such that the absolute values of errors less than a certain threshold ε are ignored both above and below the estimate. In this manner, points outside the tube are penalized, but those within the tube, either above or below the function, receive no penalty. One of the main advantages of SVR is that its computational complexity does not depend on the dimensionality of the input space. Additionally, it has excellent generalization capability, with high prediction accuracy.

This chapter is designed to provide an overview of SVR and Bayesian regression. It also presents a case study of a modified SVR applicable to circumstances in which it is critically necessary to eliminate or strictly limit underestimating a function.

SVR Overview

The regression problem is a generalization of the classification problem, in which the model returns a continuous-valued output, as opposed to an output from a finite set. In other words, a regression model estimates a continuous-valued multivariate function.

SVMs solve binary classification problems by formulating them as convex optimization problems (Vapnik 1998). The optimization problem entails finding the maximum margin separating the hyperplane, while correctly classifying as many training points as possible. SVMs represent this optimal hyperplane with support vectors. The sparse solution and good generalization of the SVM lend themselves to adaptation to regression problems. SVM generalization to SVR is accomplished by introducing an ε-insensitive region around the function, called the ε-tube. This tube reformulates the optimization problem to find the tube that best approximates the continuous-valued function, while balancing model complexity and prediction error. More specifically, SVR is formulated as an optimization problem by first defining a convex ε-insensitive loss function to be minimized and finding the flattest tube that contains most of the training instances. Hence, a multiobjective function is constructed from the loss function and the geometrical properties of the tube.

Then, the convex optimization, which has a unique solution, is solved, using appropriate numerical optimization algorithms. The hyperplane is represented in terms of support vectors, which are training samples that lie outside the boundary of the tube. As in SVM, the support vectors in SVR are the most influential instances that affect the shape of the tube, and the training and test data are assumed to be *independent and identically distributed* (iid), drawn from the same fixed but unknown probability distribution function in a supervised-learning context.

SVR: Concepts, Mathematical Model, and Graphical Representation

SVR problem formulation is often best derived from a geometrical perspective, using the one-dimensional example in Figure 4-1. The continuous-valued function being approximated can be written as in Equation 4-1. For multidimensional data, you augment x by one and include b in the w vector to simply the mathematical notation, and obtain the multivariate regression in Equation 4-2.

$$y = f(x) = \, <w, x> + b = \sum_{j=1}^{M} w_j x_j + b, \; y, b \in \mathbb{R}, x, w \in \mathbb{R}^M \tag{4-1}$$

$$f(x) = \begin{bmatrix} w \\ b \end{bmatrix}^T \begin{bmatrix} x \\ 1 \end{bmatrix} = w^T x + b \quad x, w \in \mathbb{R}^{M+1} \tag{4-2}$$

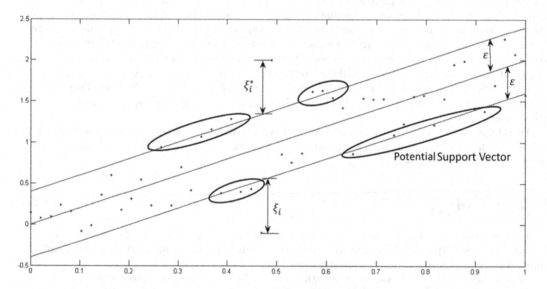

Figure 4-1. One-dimensional linear SVR

SVR formulates this function approximation problem as an optimization problem that attempts to find the narrowest tube centered around the surface, while minimizing the prediction error, that is, the distance between the predicted and the desired outputs. The former condition produces the objective function in Equation 4-3, where $\| w \|$ is the magnitude of the normal vector to the surface that is being approximated:

$$\min_{w} \frac{1}{2} \| w \|^2. \tag{4-3}$$

To visualize how the magnitude of the weights can be interpreted as a measure of flatness, consider the following example:

$$f(x, w) = \sum_{i=1}^{M} w_i x^i, x \in \mathbb{R}, w \in \mathbb{R}^M.$$

Here, M is the order of the polynomial used to approximate a function. As the magnitude of the vector w increases, a greater number of w_i are nonzero, resulting in higher-order solutions, as shown in Figure 4-2. The horizontal line is a 0th-order polynomial solution and has a very large deviation from the desired outputs, and thus, a large error. The linear function, a 1st-order polynomial, produces better approximations for a portion of the data but still underfits the training data. The 6th-order solution produces the best tradeoff between function flatness and prediction error. The highest-order solution has zero error but a high complexity and will most likely overfit the solution on yet to be seen data. The magnitude of w acts as a regularizing term and provides optimization problem control over the flatness of the solution.

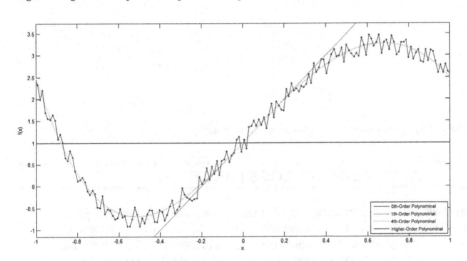

Figure 4-2. *Solutions with various orders*

The constraint is to minimize the error between the predicted value of the function for a given input and the actual output. SVR adopts an ε-insensitive loss function, penalizing predictions that are farther than ε from the desired output. The value of ε determines the width of the tube; a smaller value indicates a lower tolerance for error and also affects the number of support vectors and, consequently, the solution sparsity. Intuitively, the latter can be visualized for Figure 4-1. If ε is decreased, the boundary of the tube is shifted inward. Therefore, more datapoints are around the boundary, which indicates more support vectors. Similarly, increasing ε will result in fewer points around the boundary.

Because it is less sensitive to noisy inputs, the ε-insensitive region makes the model more robust. Several loss functions can be adopted, including the linear, quadratic, and Huber ε, as shown in Equations 4-4, 4-5, and 4-6, respectively. As demonstrated in Figure 4-3, the Huber loss function is smoother than the linear and quadratic functions, but it penalizes all deviations from the desired output, with greater penalty as the error increases. The choice of loss function is influenced by a priori information about the noise distribution affecting the data samples (Huber 1964), the model sparsity sought, and the training computational complexity. The loss functions presented here are symmetrical and convex. Although asymmetrical loss functions can be adopted to limit either underestimation or overestimation, the loss functions should be convex to ensure that the optimization problem has a unique solution that can be found in a finite number of steps. Throughout this chapter, the derivations will be based on the linear loss function of Equation 4-4.

$$L_\varepsilon\big(y,f(x,w)\big)=\begin{cases} 0 & |y-f(x,w)|\le\varepsilon; \\ |y-f(x,w)|-\varepsilon & \text{otherwise}, \end{cases} \tag{4-4}$$

$$L_\varepsilon\big(y,f(x,w)\big)=\begin{cases} 0 & |y-f(x,w)|\le\varepsilon; \\ \big(|y-f(x,w)|-\varepsilon\big)^2 & \text{otherwise}, \end{cases} \tag{4-5}$$

$$L\big(y,f(x,w)\big)=\begin{cases} c|y-f(x,w)|-\dfrac{c^2}{2} & |y-f(x,w)|>c \\ \dfrac{1}{2}|y-f(x,w)|^2 & |y-f(x,w)|\le c \end{cases} \tag{4-6}$$

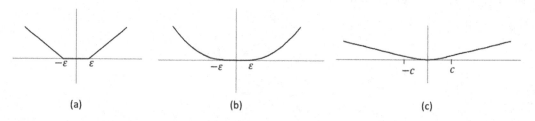

(a) (b) (c)

Figure 4-3. *Loss function types: (a) linear, (b) quadratic, and (c) Huber*

ASYMMETRICAL LOSS FUNCTIONS

Some researchers have proposed modification to loss functions to make them asymmetrical. Shim, Yong, and Hwang (2011) used an asymmetrical ε-insensitive loss function in support vector quantile regression (SVQR) in an attempt to decrease the number of support vectors. The authors altered the insensitivity according to the quantile and achieved a sparser model. Schabe (1991) proposed a two-sided quadratic loss function and a quasi-quadratic s-loss function for Bayes parameter estimation, and Norstrom (1996) replaced the quadratic loss function with an asymmetrical loss function to derive a general class of functions that approach infinity near the origin for Bayesian risk analysis. Nath and Bhattacharyya (2007) presented a maximum margin classifier that bounds misclassification for each class differently, thus allowing for different tolerances levels. Lee, Hsieh, and Wang (2005) reformulated the typical SVR approach into a nonconstrained problem, thereby only solving a system of linear equations rather than a convex quadratic one. Pan and Pan (2006) compared three* different loss functions for economic tolerance design: Taguchi's quadratic loss function, inverted normal loss function, and revised inverted normal loss function.

Adopting a soft-margin approach similar to that employed in SVM, slack variables ξ, ξ^* can be added to guard against outliers. These variables determine how many points can be tolerated outside the tube illustrated in Figure 4-1.

Based on Equations 4-3 and 4-4, the optimization problem in Equation 4-7 is obtained; C is a regularization—thus, a tuneable parameter that gives more weight to minimizing the flatness, or the error, for this multiobjective optimization problem. For example, a larger C gives more weight to minimizing the error. This constrained quadratic optimization problem can be solved by finding the Lagrangian (see Equation 4-8). The Lagrange multipliers, or dual variables, are λ, λ^*, α, α^* and are nonnegative real numbers.

$$\min \frac{1}{2}\|w\|^2 + C\sum_{i=1}^{N} \xi_i + \xi_i^*, \tag{4-7}$$

subject to

$$y_i - w^T x_i \le \varepsilon + \xi_i^* \quad i=1...N$$

$$w^T x_i - y_i \le \varepsilon + \xi_i \quad i=1...N$$

$$\xi_i, \xi_i^* \ge 0 \quad i=1...N$$

$$\mathcal{L}\left(w, \xi^*, \xi, \lambda, \lambda^*, \alpha, \alpha^*\right) = \frac{1}{2}\|w\|^2 + C\sum_{i=1}^{N} \xi_i + \xi_i^* + \sum_{i=1}^{N} \alpha_i^* \left(y_i - w^T x_i - \varepsilon - \xi_i^*\right)$$
$$+ \sum_{i=1}^{N} \alpha_i \left(-y_i + w^T x_i - \varepsilon - \xi_i\right) - \sum_{i=1}^{N} \lambda_i \xi_i + \lambda_i^* \xi_i^* \tag{4-8}$$

The minimum of Equation 4-8 is found by taking its partial derivatives with respect to the variables and setting them equal to zero, based on the *Karush-Kuhn-Tucker* (KKT) conditions. The partial derivatives with respect to the Lagrange multipliers return the constraints, which have to be less than or equal to zero, as illustrated in Equation 4-9. The final KKT condition states that the product of the Lagrange multipliers and the constraints is equal to zero (see Equation 4-10). The Lagrange multipliers that are equal to zero correspond to data inside the tube, whereas the support vectors have nonzero-valued Lagrange multipliers. The solution is written in terms of the support vector only—hence, the solution sparsity. The function approximation is represented in Equation 4-12. By replacing Equation 4-9 in Equation 4-8, the dual form of the optimization problem can be written as shown in Equation 4-13.

$$\frac{\delta \mathcal{L}}{\delta w} = w - \sum_{i=1}^{N} (\alpha_i^* - \alpha_i) x_i = 0$$

$$\frac{\delta \mathcal{L}}{\delta \xi_i^*} = C - \lambda_i^* - \alpha_i^* = 0$$

$$\frac{\delta \mathcal{L}}{\delta \xi_i} = C - \lambda_i - \alpha_i = 0$$

$$\frac{\delta \mathcal{L}}{\delta \lambda_i^*} = \sum_{i=1}^{N} \xi_i^* \le 0 \tag{4-9}$$

$$\frac{\delta \mathcal{L}}{\delta \lambda_i} = \sum_{i=1}^{N} \xi_i \le 0$$

$$\frac{\delta \mathcal{L}}{\delta \alpha_i^*} = y_i - w^T x_i - \varepsilon - \xi_i^* \le 0$$

$$\frac{\delta \mathcal{L}}{\delta \alpha_i} = -y_i + w^T x_i - \varepsilon - \xi_i \le 0$$

$$\alpha_i \left(-y_i + w^T x_i - \varepsilon - \xi_i\right) = 0$$
$$\alpha_i^* \left(y_i - w^T x_i - \varepsilon - \xi_i^*\right) = 0 \qquad \forall i \tag{4-10}$$
$$\lambda_i \xi_i = 0,$$
$$\lambda_i^* \xi_i^* = 0$$

$$w = \sum_{i=1}^{N_{sv}} \left(\alpha_i^* - \alpha_i\right) x_i \tag{4-11}$$

$$f(x) = \sum_{i=1}^{N_{SV}} \left(\alpha_i^* - \alpha_i \right) x_i^T x, \alpha_i, \alpha_i^* \in [0,C] \tag{4-12}$$

$$\max_{\alpha,\alpha^*} -\varepsilon \sum_{i=1}^{N_{SV}} \left(\alpha_i + \alpha_i^* \right) + \sum_{i=1}^{N_{SV}} \left(\alpha_i^* - \alpha_i \right) y_i - \frac{1}{2} \sum_{j=1}^{N_{SV}} \sum_{i=1}^{N_{SV}} \left(\alpha_i^* - \alpha_i \right) \left(\alpha_j^* - \alpha_j \right) x_i^T x_j, \tag{4-13}$$

subject to

$$\sum_{i=1}^{N_{SV}} \left(\alpha_i^* - \alpha_i \right) = 0, \ \alpha_i, \alpha_i^* \in [0,C]$$

At the beginning of this section, the weights vector w was augmented with the scalar b, and the derivation of the SVR's mathematical formulation was carried out, disregarding the explicit computation of b (see Equation 4-2). However, b could have been calculated from the KKT conditions, as shown next.

Training data that belong to the outside of the boundary of the tube will have nonzero α_i or α_i^*; they cannot both be zero, because that would mean that the instance (x_i, y_i) belongs to the lower and upper boundary, which is not possible. Therefore, the corresponding constraints will be satisfied with equality, as demonstrated in Equation 4-14. Furthermore, because the point is not outside the tube, $\xi_i = 0$, leading to the result in Equation 4-15 when $\alpha \in (0,C)$. Equation 4-16 computes b. Performing the same analysis for α_i^*, one gets Equations 4-17 and 4-18.

$$y_i - w^T x_i - b - \varepsilon - \xi_i = 0 \tag{4-14}$$

$$y_i - w^T x_i - b - \varepsilon = 0 \tag{4-15}$$

$$b = y_i - w^T x_i - \varepsilon \tag{4-16}$$

$$-y_i + w^T x_i - b - \varepsilon = 0 \tag{4-17}$$

$$b = -y_i + w^T x_i - \varepsilon \tag{4-18}$$

Instead of using the KKT conditions, one could have also computed b, while solving the optimization problem, using the interior-point method, which can converge to an optimal solution in logarithmic time by navigating along the central path of the feasible region. The central path is determined by solving the primal and dual optimization problems simultaneously.

Kernel SVR and Different Loss Functions: Mathematical Model and Graphical Representation

The previous section dealt with data in the feature space, assuming $f(x)$ is linear. For non linear functions, the data can be mapped into a higher dimensional space, called kernel space, to achieve a higher accuracy, using kernels that satisfy Mercer's condition (see Figure 4-4), as discussed previously for classification. Therefore, replacing all instances of x in Equations 4-1–4-18 with $k(x, x)$ yields the primal formulation shown in Equation 4-19, where $\varphi(.)$ is the transformation from feature to kernel space. Equation 4-20 describes the new weight vector in terms of the transformed input. The dual problem is represented in Equation 4-21, and the function approximation $f(x)$ is in Equation 4-22, where $k(.,.)$, the kernel, is as illustrated in Equation 4-23.

$$\min \frac{1}{2}\|w\|^2 + C \sum_{i=1}^{N} \xi_i + \xi_i^*, \tag{4-19}$$

subject to

$$y_i - w^T \varphi(x_i) \le \varepsilon + \xi_i^* \quad i = 1,...,N$$

$$w^T \varphi(x_i) - y_i \le \varepsilon + \xi_i \quad i = 1,...,N$$

$$\xi_i, \xi_i^* \ge 0 \quad i = 1,...,N$$

$$w = \sum_{i=1}^{N_{SV}} \left(\alpha_i^* - \alpha_i\right) \varphi(x_i) \tag{4-20}$$

$$\max_{\alpha,\alpha^*} -\varepsilon \sum_{i=1}^{N_{SV}} \left(\alpha_i + \alpha_i^*\right) + \sum_{i=1}^{N_{SV}} \left(\alpha_i^* - \alpha_i\right) y_i - \frac{1}{2} \sum_{j=1}^{N_{SV}} \sum_{i=1}^{N_{SV}} \left(\alpha_i^* - \alpha_i\right)\left(\alpha_j^* - \alpha_j\right) k\left(x_i, x_j\right) \tag{4-21}$$

$$\alpha_i, \alpha_i^* \in [0, C], i = 1,...,N_{SV}, \sum_{i=1}^{N_{SV}} \left(\alpha_i^* - \alpha_i\right) = 0$$

$$f(x) = \sum_{i=1}^{N_{SV}} \left(\alpha_i^* - \alpha_i\right) k\left(x_i, x\right) \tag{4-22}$$

$$k\left(x_i, x\right) = \varphi\left(x_i\right).\varphi(x) \tag{4-23}$$

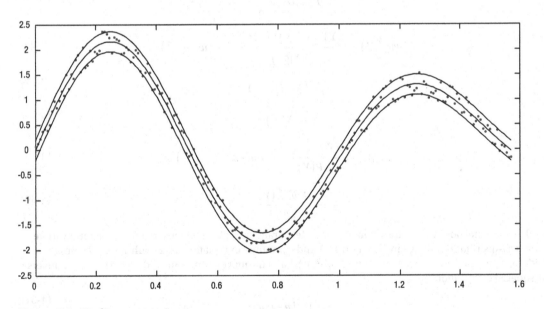

Figure 4-4. *Nonlinear regression*

Bayesian Linear Regression

Unlike SVR, *Bayesian linear regression* is a generative, as opposed to discriminant, method, that builds linear regression models based on Bayesian inference. After specifying a model, the method computes the posterior distribution of parameters and model predictions. This statistical analysis allows the method to determine model complexity during training, which results in a model that is less likely to overfit.

For simplicity, assume that a single output $y_p \in \mathbb{R}$ are predicted using the model parameters w learned from a set of predictor variables X sized $k \times 1$ and observations Y sized $n \times 1$. The observations Y are assumed to have the distribution in Equation 4-24, where σ^2 is the variance of the uncertainty in the observations:

$$P(Y|w,\sigma^2,X) \sim \mathcal{N}(Xw,\sigma^2 I) \tag{4-24}$$

Once the model has been specified, the model parameters' posterior distributions can be estimated. This is done by first assuming a prior distribution of the model parameters (see Equation 4-25). Given the model variance and observations, the posterior distribution of the model parameters (which is Gaussian) is as shown in Equation 4-26, with the mean computed in Equation 4-27, and the standard deviation scale factor, in Equation 4-28. The mean is simply the Moore-Penrose pseudoinverse of the predictive variables multiplied by the observations. Given some observations, the posterior probability of the model variance is computed, and an inverse chi-squared distribution (see Equation 4-29), with $n-k$ degrees of freedom and a scale factor s^2 (see Equation 4-30), is obtained. The scale factor is the error between the model's predicted output and an observation.

$$P(w,\sigma^2) \propto \frac{1}{\sigma^2} \tag{4-25}$$

$$P(w|\sigma^2,Y) = \frac{P(Y|w,\sigma^2,X)P(w|\sigma^2)}{P(Y|\sigma^2)} \sim \mathcal{N}(w_E,v_w\sigma^2) \tag{4-26}$$

$$w_E = (X^T X)^{-1} X^T Y \tag{4-27}$$

$$v_w = (X^T X)^{-1} \tag{4-28}$$

$$P(\sigma^2|Y) = \frac{P(Y|\sigma^2)P(\sigma^2)}{P(Y)} \sim inv - \mathcal{X}^2(n-k,s^2) \tag{4-29}$$

$$s^2 = \frac{(Y-Xw_E)^T(Y-Xw_E)}{n-k} \tag{4-30}$$

The marginal posterior distribution of the model parameters, given the observations, is a multivariate Student's t-distribution, shown in Equation 4-31 and computed in Equation 4-32, with $n-k$ degrees of freedom, w_E mean, and s^2 scale factor, as $P(w|\sigma^2,Y)$ has a normal distribution, and $P(\sigma^2|Y)$ has an inverse chi-squared distribution.

$$P(w|Y) \sim t(n-k,w_E,s^2) \tag{4-31}$$

$$P(w|Y) = \int_{\sigma^2} P(w|\sigma^2,Y)P(\sigma^2|Y)d\sigma^2 \tag{4-32}$$

Given the model parameter probability distributions and a set of predictive variables X_p, the marginal posterior predictive distribution Y_p, which is a multivariate Student's t-distribution (see Equation 4-33) can be determined. The mean is computed in Equation 4-34, and the variance, in Equation 4-35. The predictive distribution variance depends on the uncertainty in the observed data and the model parameters.

$$P(Y_p|Y) \sim t\left(n-k, E(Y_p|Y), var(Y_p|\sigma^2, Y)\right) \tag{4-33}$$

$$E(Y_p|Y) = X_p w_E \tag{4-34}$$

$$var(Y_p|\sigma^2, Y) = \left(I + X_p v_w X_p^T\right)\sigma^2 \tag{4-35}$$

The concept of Bayesian regression is displayed in Figure 4-5, in which the sample input data available during training would have been generated by a Gaussian distribution. If these instances represent their population well, the regression model is expected to generalize well.

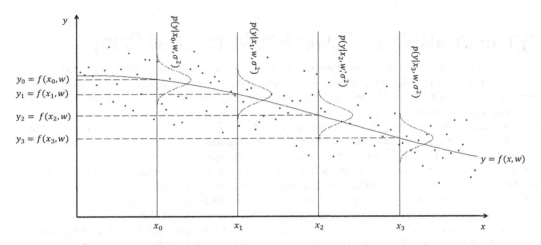

Figure 4-5. *One-dimensional regression example illustrating the Gaussian conditional probability distributions of the output on the input and model parameters*

DISCRIMINANT VS. GENERATIVE MODELS

A *generative approach* models the joint probability distribution of the data and class labels $p(x, C_k)$, based on the prior probability distributions of the class labels $p(C_k)$ and the likelihood probability distribution $p(x|C_k)$. The joint distribution computes the posterior probability distributions $p(C_k|k)$, which will be used to map datapoints to class labels.

A *discriminant approach* directly computes the posterior probability distributions $p(C_k|x)$ without computing the joint probability distribution $p(x, C_k)$. A discriminant approach produces a mapping from the datapoints to the class labels without computing probability distributions. Therefore, this approach performs the inference and decision stages in one step.

	Advantages	Disadvantages
Generative	• Robust to outliers • Can easily update decision model • Allows combination of classifiers trained on different types of data by applying probability rules • Can improve prediction accuracy by measuring confidence in classification based on posterior distributions and not making predictions when confidence is low	• Computationally demanding • Requires a lot of training data • Suffers from the curse of dimensionality
Discriminant	• Computationally less demanding • Simple to implement	• Sensitive to noisy data and outliers • Requires retraining for any changes in the decision model

Asymmetrical SVR for Power Prediction: Case Study

Justification: In many instances of approximation, there is an uneven consequence of misprediction, based on whether the error is above or below the target value (Stockman et al. 2012a, 2012b). For example, in power prediction an incorrect low estimate may be of much more concern than an overestimate. Underpredicting can lead to insufficient cooling of datacenters, inadequate uninterruptible power supply (UPS), unavailable processor resources, needless powering down of chip components, and so on. In the case of forest fire behavior prediction, a lower estimate of the threat can lead to greater property damage as well as loss of life, owing to a lack of adequate supply of personnel and equipment.

In these instances, it is crucial to minimize misestimates on one side of a boundary, even at the risk of reducing the accuracy of the entire estimation. It is necessary to restrict the loss function so that a minimal number of under- or overestimates occur. This leads to an asymmetrical loss function for training, in which a greater penalty is applied when the misestimate is on the wrong side of the boundary.

Approach: *Asymmetrical and lower-bounded SVR* (ALB-SVR) was proposed by Stockman, Awad, and Khanna (2012a). This approach modifies the SVR loss functions and corresponding error functions, such that the ε-tube is only above the function, as demonstrated in Figure 4-6. The penalty parameter C is split into $C+$ and $C-$ so that different penalties can be applied to the upper and lower mispredictions.

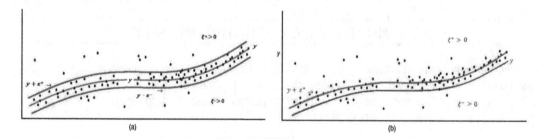

Figure 4-6. *(a) SVR and (b) ALB-SVR (Source: Intel, 2012)*

ALB-SVR uses the Huber insensitive loss function (Popov and Sautin 2008). This function is similar to the ε-insensitive loss function; however, it increases quadratically for small errors outside the ε-bound but below a certain threshold $\partial > \varepsilon$ and then linearly beyond ∂. This makes it robust with respect to outliers. The Huber insensitive loss function is represented by:

$$L_{\varepsilon\partial HuberSVR}(t,y) = \begin{cases} 0 & if \; |t-y| \le \varepsilon \\ (|t-y|-\varepsilon)^2 & if \; \varepsilon < |t-y| < \partial \\ (\partial-\varepsilon)(2|t-y|-\partial-\varepsilon) & if \; |t-y| \ge \partial. \end{cases}$$

ALB-SVR modifies the Huber insensitive loss function as follows:

$$L_{\varepsilon\partial HuberALB-SVR}(t,y) = \begin{cases} 0 & if \; 0 \ge (t-y) \le \varepsilon \\ (t-y)^2 & if \; (t-y) < 0 \\ ((t-y)-\varepsilon)^2 & if \; \varepsilon < (t-y) < \partial \\ (\partial-\varepsilon)(2|t-y|-\partial-\varepsilon) & if \; |t-y| \ge \partial. \end{cases}$$

Thus, the solution is:

$$\max_{\alpha^+,\alpha^-} \left[\begin{array}{c} \sum_{i=1}^{L}(\alpha_i^+ - \alpha_i^-)t_i - \frac{1}{2C}\sum_{i=1}^{L}(\varepsilon\alpha_i^{+2} - \alpha_i^{-2}) \\ -\frac{1}{2}\sum_{i,j}(\alpha_i^+ - \alpha_i^-)(\alpha_i^+ - \alpha_i^-)x_i \cdot x_j \end{array} \right],$$

and the resulting optimization problem:

$$\max_{\alpha^+,\alpha^-} \left[\begin{array}{c} -\sum_{i=1}^{L}(\alpha_i^+ - \alpha_i^-)t_i + \frac{1}{2C}\sum_{i=1}^{L}(\varepsilon\alpha_i^{+2} - \alpha_i^{-2}) \\ +\frac{1}{2}\sum_{i,j}(\alpha_i^+ - \alpha_i^-)(\alpha_i^+ - \alpha_i^-)x_i \cdot x_j \end{array} \right]$$

$$-C \le (\alpha_i^+ - \alpha_i^-) \le C \quad i = 1..L$$

$$\sum_{1}^{L}(\alpha_i^+ - \alpha_i^-) = 0.$$

By substituting the new loss function, ALB-SVR's empirical risk becomes

$$R_{emp}(y) = \frac{1}{L}\sum_{i=1}^{L}L_{\varepsilon-ALB-SVR}(t_i, y_i).$$

The maximum additional empirical risk for ALB-SVR can be computed as

$$\sum_{i\in(y-t)\le\varepsilon}^{L}(y-t) + \sum_{i\in(y-t)>\varepsilon}^{L}\varepsilon.$$

Validation: ALB-SVR was tested on a dataset used by David et al. (2010) and Stockman et al. (2010) that consists of 17,765 samples of five attributes of memory activity counters, with the actual corresponding power consumed in watts, as measured directly by a memory power riser. The memory power model attributes are *activity, read, write, CKE = high*, and *CKE = low*. ALB-SVR was implemented with a modified version of LIBSVM (Chang and Lin 2011) for ALB-SVR. Simulation results (see Figures 4-7 – 4-9) took the average of ten runs of threefold cross-validation of a radial basis function (RBF) kernel, with a combination of grid search and heuristic experimentation to find the best metaparameters ε, g, C^+, and C^-.

Type	C^+	C^-	g	ε	∂	% Error	% Out of Bound
Huber insensitive SVR	512	–	128	0.1	1.0e-06	1.03	67.07
Huber insensitive ALB-SVR	10,000,000	1,000	128	0.1	1.0e-06	1.50	0.24

Figure 4-7. *Comparative results of SVR versus ALB-SVR (Source: Intel, 2012)*

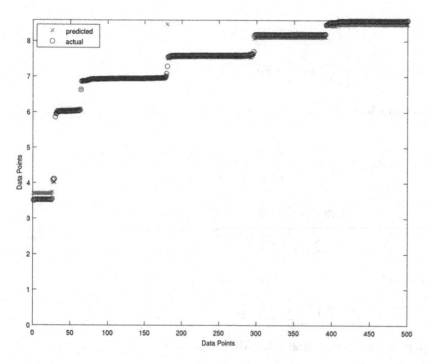

Figure 4-8. *Power estimates for running average power limit (RAPL) data with Huber insensitive SVR (Source: Intel, 2012)*

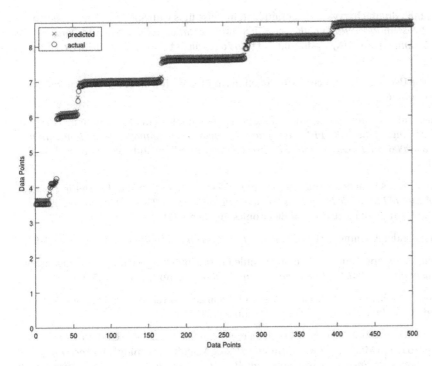

Figure 4-9. *Power estimates for RAPL data with Huber insensitive ALB-SVR (Source: Intel, 2012)*

In SVR, support vectors are those points that lie outside the ε-tube. The smaller the value of ε, the more points that lie outside the tube and hence the greater the number of support vectors. With ALB-SVR the ε-tube is cut in half, and the lower ε-bound is dropped. Therefore, for the same g and ε parameters, more points lie outside the tube, and there are a larger number of support vectors. This means that the number of support vectors is greater for ALB-SVR than for SVR. This increase in the number of support vectors indicates that using ALB-SVR has some negative effects on the complexity of the estimating function. Although the percentage relative error data set was higher (5.06 percent), this is acceptable, because the main purpose was to reduce the number of underestimates and this was achieved.

References

Chang, Chih-Chung, and Chih-Jen Lin. "LIBSVM: A Library for Support Vector Machines," in "Large-Scale Machine Learning," edited by C. Ling, special issue, *ACM Transactions on Intelligent Systems and Technology* 2, no. 3 (2011). www.csie.ntu.edu.tw/~cjlin/papers/libsvm.pdf.

David, Howard, Eugene Gorbatov, Ulf R. Hanebutte, Rahul Khanna, and Christian Le. "RAPL: Memory Power Estimation and Capping." In *Proceedings of the 2010 ACM/IEEE International Symposium on Low-Power Electronics and Design (ISLPED), August 18–20, 2010, Austin, TX*, 189–194. Piscataway, NJ: Institute for Electrical and Electronics Engineers, 2010.

Huber, Peter J. "Robust Estimation of a Location Parameter." *Annals of Mathematical Statistics* 35, no. 1 (1964): 73–101.

Lee, Yuh-Jye, Wen-Feng Hsieh, and Chien-Ming Huang. "ε-SSVR: A Smooth Support Vector Machine for ε-Insensitive Regression." *IEEE Transactions on Knowledge and Data Engineering* 17, no. 5 (2005): 678–685.

Nath, J. Saketha, and Chiranjib Bhattacharyya. "Maximum Margin Classifiers with Specified False Positive and False Negative Error Rates." In *Proceedings of the Seventh SIAM International Conference on Data Mining, April 26-28, 2007, Minneapolis, MN*, 35-46. 2007. http://dblp.uni-trier.de/rec/bibtex/conf/sdm/NathB07.

Norstrom, Jan Gerhard. "The Use of Precautionary Loss Functions in Risk Analysis." *IEEE Transactions on Reliability* 45, no. 3 (1996): 400-403.

Pan, Jeh-Nan, and Jianbiao Pan. "A Comparative Study of Various Loss Functions in the Economic Tolerance Design." In *Proceedings of the 2006 IEEE International Conference on Management of Innovation and Technology, June 21-23, 2006, Singapore, China*, 783-787. Piscataway, NJ: Institute of Electrical and Electronics Engineers, 2006.

Popov, A. A, and A. S. Sautin. "Loss Functions Analysis in Support Vector Regression," *9th International Conference on Actual Problems of Electronic Instrument Engineering*, September 23-25, 2008, Novosibirsk, Russia, 198. Piscataway, NJ: Institute of Electrical and Electronics Engineers, 2008.

Schabe, H. "Bayes Estimates Under Asymmetric Loss." *IEEE Transactions on Reliability* 40, no. 1 (1991): 63-67.

Shim, Joo Yong, and Chang Ha Hwang. "Support Vector Quantile Regression Using Asymmetric ε-Insensitive Loss Function." *Communications for Statistical Applications and Methods* 18, no. 2 (2011): 165-170.

Stockman, Melissa, Mariette Awad, and Rahul Khanna. "Asymmetrical and Lower Bounded Support Vector Regression for Power Prediction." *Intel Technology Journal* 16, no. 2 (2012a).

Stockman, Melissa, Mariette Awad, Rahul Khanna, Christian Le, Howard David, Eugene Gorbatov, and Ulf R. Hanebutte. "A Novel Approach to Memory Power Estimation Using Machine Learning." In *Proceedings of the 2010 International Conference on Energy Aware Computing (ICEAC), December 16-18, 2010, Cairo, Egypt*, 1-3. Piscataway, NJ: Institute for Electrical and Electronics Engineers, 2010.

Stockman, Melissa, Randa S. El Ramli, Mariette Awad, and Rabih Jabr. "An Asymmetrical and Quadratic Support Vector Regression Loss Function for Beirut Short Term Load Forecast." In*2012 IEEE International Conference on Systems, Man, and Cybernetics (SMC), October 14-17, 2012, Seoul, Korea*, 651-656. Piscataway, NJ: Institute of Electrical and Electronics Engineers, 2012b.

Vapnik, Vladimir N. *Statistical Learning Theory*. New York: Wiley, 1998.

CHAPTER 5

■ ■ ■

Hidden Markov Model

The best thing about the future is that it comes one day at a time.

—Abraham Lincoln

Real-time processes produce observations that can be discrete, continuous, stationary, time variant, or noisy. The fundamental challenge is to characterize the observations as a parametric random process, the parameters of which should be estimated, using a well-defined approach. This allows us to construct a theoretical model of the underlying process that enables us to predict the process output as well as distinguish the statistical properties of the observation itself. The *hidden Markov model* (HMM) is one such statistical model. HMM interprets the (nonobservable) process by analyzing the pattern of a sequence of observed symbols. An HMM consists of a doubly stochastic process, in which the underlying (or hidden) stochastic process can be indirectly inferred by analyzing the sequence of observed symbols of another set of stochastic processes. HMM comprises (hidden) states that represent an unobservable, or latent, attribute of the process being modeled. HMM-based approaches are widely used to analyze features or observations, such as usage and activity profiles and transitions between different states of the process, to predict the most probable sequence of states. The HMM can be represented as a stochastic model of discrete events and a variation of the *Markov chain*, a chain of linked states or events, in which the next state depends only on the current state of the system. The states of an HMM are hidden (or can only be inferred from the observed symbols). For a given model and sequence of observations, HMM is used to analyze the solution to problems related to model selection, state-sequence determination, and model training (for more details, see the section "The Three Basic Problems of HMM").

- The fundamental theory of HMMs was developed on the basis of pioneering work by Baum and colleagues (Baum and Petrie 1966; Baum and Eagon 1967; Baum and Sell 1968; Baum et al. 1970; Baum 1972). Earlier work in this area is credited to Stratonovich (1960), who proposed an optimal nonlinear filtering model, based on the theory of conditional Markov processes. A recent contribution to the application of HMM was made by Rabiner (1989), in the formulation of a statistical method of representing speech. The author established a successful implementation of an HMM system, based on discrete or continuous density parameter distributions.

- This chapter describes HMM techniques, together with their real-life applications, in such management solutions as intrusion detection, workload optimization, and fault prediction.

Discrete Markov Process

A system may be described at any time as being in one of the states S_1, S_2, S_n (see Figure 5-1). When the system undergoes a change from state S_i to S_j at regular time intervals with a certain probability p_{ij}, this can be described by a simple stochastic process, in which the distribution of future states depends only on the present state and not on how the system arrived at the present state. The matrix **P**, with elements p_{ij}, is called the *transition probability matrix* of the Markov chain. In other words, we can describe a *discrete Markov process* as a phenomenon evolving in regularly spaced intervals, such that, for a given present state, past and future are statistically independent. Conventionally, a time-evolving phenomenon in which only the present state affects the future state, is called a *dynamic system*. The exclusive dependence of future states on present states allows us to model the solutions, using random variables instead of deterministic objects. A random variable defines a set of possible outcomes (the sample space Ω) and a probability distribution that associates each outcome with a probability.

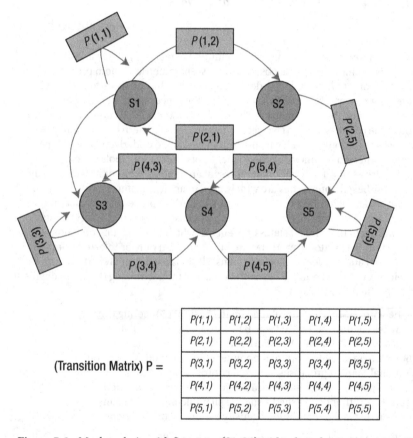

P(1,1)	P(1,2)	P(1,3)	P(1,4)	P(1,5)
P(2,1)	P(2,2)	P(2,3)	P(2,4)	P(2,5)
P(3,1)	P(3,2)	P(3,3)	P(3,4)	P(3,5)
P(4,1)	P(4,2)	P(4,3)	P(4,4)	P(4,5)
P(5,1)	P(5,2)	P(5,3)	P(5,4)	P(5,5)

(Transition Matrix) P =

Figure 5-1. *Markov chain with five states (S1–S5) with selected state transitions P(i, j)*

A simple example of a discrete Markov process—a Markov chain—is a random walk in one dimension. In this case, an individual may move forward or backward with a certain probability. Formally, you can define independent random variables $q_1, q_2 \cdots$, where each variable is either +1 (forward movement) or –1 (backward movement), with a 50 percent probability for each value. Statistically, you may define a random walk as a sequence Q_t of random variables that increments, using independent and identically distributed (iid) random variables S, such that

$$Q_n = \sum_{t=1}^{n} q_t \quad ; Q_0 = 0,$$

where expectation $E(Q_n) = 0$, and variance $E(Q_n^2) = n$. If $S_1, S_2, \cdots, S_N$ is the sequence of integers, then

$$\mathbb{P}(q_{t+1} = S_j \mid q_t = S_i, q_{t-2} = S_k, \cdots) = \mathbb{P}(q_{t+1} = S_j \mid q_t = S_i). \tag{5-1}$$

This equation tells us that the probability that the random walk will be at S_j at time $t + 1$ depends only on its current value and not on how it got there. Formally, the discrete Markov process admits three definitions, described in the following sections.

Definition 1

A Markov chain on Ω is a stochastic process $\{q_0, q_1, \ldots, q_t\}$, with each $q_i \in \Omega$, such that

$$\mathbb{P}(q_{t+1} = S_j \mid q_t = S_i, q_{t-1} = S_k, \cdots, q_0 = S_0)$$
$$=> \mathbb{P}(q_{t+1} = S_j \mid q_t = S_i) := \mathbb{P}(i,j) := p_{ij}. \tag{5-2}$$

You construct $\Omega \times \Omega$ transition matrix $\mathbf{P}$, whose (i, j) th entry represents $\mathbb{P}(i, j)$, with the following properties:

$$\forall (i,j) \in \Omega, \mathbb{P}(i,j) \geq 0$$
$$\forall i \in \Omega, \sum_{j \in \Omega} \mathbb{P}(i,j) = 1$$

A matrix $\mathbf{P}$ with these properties is called a *stochastic matrix*.

Definition 2

The (ij) th entry $P^n(i, j)$ of the matrix P^n gives the probability that the Markov chain, starting in state i, will be in state j after n steps.

Definition 3

Let $u^{(0)}$ be the probability vector that represents the starting distribution. Then, the probability that the chain is in state j after n steps is the jth entry in the vector:

$$u^{(n)} = u^{(0)}\mathbf{P}^{(n)}$$

If you want to examine the behavior of the chain under the assumption that it starts in a certain state i, you simply choose u to be the probability vector, with ith entry equal to 1 and all other entries equal to 0. The stochastic process defined in the following sections can also be characterized as an observable Markov model, because each state can be represented as physical event.

Introduction to the Hidden Markov Model

The previous sections discussed a stochastic process characterized by a Markov model in which states correspond to an observable physical phenomenon. This model may be too restrictive to be of practical use in realistic problems in which states cannot directly correspond to a physical event. To improve its flexibility, you expand the model into one in which the observed output is a probabilistic function of a state. Each state can produce a number of outputs, according to a unique probability distribution, and each distinct output can potentially be generated at any state. The resulting model is the doubly embedded stochastic model referred to as the HMM. The underlying stochastic process in the HMM produces a state sequence that is not directly observable and that can only be approximated through another set of stochastic processes that produces the sequence of observations.

Figure 5-2 illustrates an extension of a discrete Markov process into a doubly stochastic HMM. The new HMM allows observation symbols to be emitted from each state, with a finite probability distribution. This lets the model be more expressive and flexible than the simple Markov chain. Additionally, as illustrated in Figure 5-3, you can model physical processes through a sequence of observed symbols that is true in most practical cases. The key difference from a conventional Markov chain is that, in analyzing the sequence of observed states, you cannot say exactly which state sequence produced these observations; you can, however, calculate the likelihood of a certain state sequence's having produced them. This indicates that state sequence is hidden and can only be observed through a sequence of observed states or symbols.

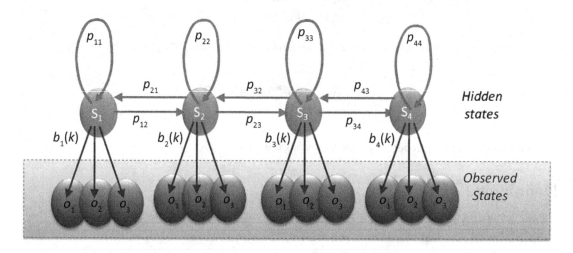

p_{ij} = [Transition Model] Transition Probability from Hidden State i to Hidden State j
$b_j(k)$ = [Observation Model] Observation probability Distribution for State j
$k = \{O_1, O_2, O_3 ..... O_n\}$

Figure 5-2. Hidden Markov model with four hidden states and three observed states

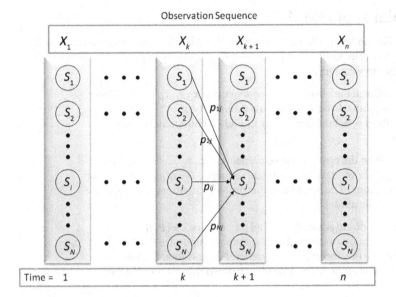

Figure 5-3. *Hidden Markov model: trellis representation*

Essentials of the Hidden Markov Model

A complete specification of the HMM (Rabiner 1989) requires formal definition of the following elements:

- *Number of hidden states:* (N) in the model. Individual states are represented as $S = \{S_1, S_2, S_3, \cdots, S_N\}$; the state at time t is represented as q_t.

- *State transition probability distribution:* $\mathbf{P} = \{p_{ij}\}$, to represent state transition from state i to state j, where $p_{ij} = \mathbb{P}(q_{t+1} = S_j \mid q_t = S_i), 1 \le i, j \le N, p_{ij} \ge 0$. This property is similar to Definition 5-1 of a Markov chain.

- *Observation symbol probability distribution:* ($\mathbf{B} = \{b_j(k)\}$) for state j, where $b_j(k) = \mathbb{P}(x_t = o_k \mid q_t = S_j), 1 \le j \le N, 1 \le k \le M$.

- *Initial state distribution:* ($\pi = \{\pi_i\}$), where $\pi_i = \mathbb{P}(q_1 = S_i), 1 \le i \le N$.

Once the HMM parameters are defined for a physical process by appropriate values of N, M, $\mathbf{P}$, $\mathbf{B}$, π, you can analyze an observation sequence (output) $x_1, x_2, x_3, \cdots$, in which each x_t is one of the symbols from observation matrix $\mathbf{O}$ at time t.

Formally, an HMM can be defined by specifying model parameters N and M, observation symbols O, and three probability matrices $\mathbf{P}$, $\mathbf{B}$, and π. For simplicity, you can use the compact form,

$$\lambda = (\mathbf{P}, \mathbf{B}, \pi), \tag{5-3}$$

to indicate the complete parameter set of the model. The HMM described here makes two assumptions:

- *Markov assumption:* The current state is dependent only on the previous state; this represents the memory of the model.

- *Independence assumption:* Output observation o_t at time t is dependent only on the current state; it is independent of previous observations and states.

The Three Basic Problems of HMM

The preceding section described the model for HMM. This section identifies the basic problems that need to be solved to apply the model to real-world problems.

These basic problems fall into three categories:

> **Problem 1.** *Evaluation*: Given the observation sequence $X = x_1, x_2, x_3, \cdots, x_t$ and an HMM model $\lambda = (P, B, \pi)$, how do we compute the probability of X? The solution to this problem allows us to select the competing model that best matches the observation sequence.

> **Problem 2.** *Decoding*: Given the observation sequence $X = x_1, x_2, x_3, \cdots, x_t$ and an HMM model $\lambda = (P, B, \pi)$, how do we find the state sequence $Q = q_1, q_2, q_3, \cdots, q_t$ that best explains the observations? The solution to this problem attempts to uncover the hidden part of the stochastic model.

> **Problem 3.** *Learning*: How do we adjust the model parameters $\lambda = (P, B, \pi)$ to maximize $\mathbb{P}(X \mid \lambda)$? The solution to this problem attempts to optimize the model parameters to best describe the observation sequence. Furthermore, the solution allows us to adapt the model parameters, according to the observed training data sequence.

Consider the problem of failure prediction, which assesses the risk of failure in future time. In a typical system, components have underlying dependencies that allow an error to propagate from one component to another. Additionally, there exist *health states* that cannot be cannot be measured but that can induce errors among dependable components. These health states progress through *normal performance state*, *subperformance state, attention-needed state*, and, ultimately, *failure state*. It is therefore essential to identify the operational states accurately to avoid a reactive shutdown of the system. In this scenario, health states correspond to hidden states, and observations correspond to a sequence of error conditions. This lets the system administrator schedule preventive maintenance ahead of a complete system failure. Because faults are hidden (and so cannot be measured) and produce symbols corresponding to errors, you can model the problem of failure prediction to an HMM. For the sake of simplicity, you may assume that faults can be predicted by identifying unique patterns of errors that can be measured, using system counters.

Although the complete system can be modeled, using a *normal* state and *failed* states, such models do not provide component-level granularity for tracking the progression of failure through dependent components. For this reason, system architects categorize failure into multiple domains to attribute the prediction of a failure to a specific component and thus avoid a system-level catastrophic shutdown.

The first task is performed by using the solution to Problem 3, in which individual models for each failure domain ($\Lambda = \lambda_1, \lambda_2, \cdots$) are constructed through a training process. This process assigns the HMM parameters to the descriptive model that enables an optimal match between error patterns and the corresponding transition to a fault state by the system. In a computer system this training can be supported by system event-log information, which contains error information as well as failure descriptions.

To understand the physical meaning of the *model states*, you identify the solution to Problem 2. In this case, the statistical properties of error counters translate into the sequence of observations occurring in each health state of the models. The definition and the number of states are dependent on the objectives and characteristics of the application. This process allows us to fine-tune the model to improve its capability to represent the various states that characterize system health. Normal state and failure state are the two end states of the HMM; intermediate states are added as needed to help predict the progression of the faulty behavior. Adding intermediate states affords modeling of predictive and critical scenarios that facilitate incorporation of repair mechanisms in anticipation of an actual failure.

Once you have the set of HMMs (Λ) designed and optimized, recognition of a component health state is performed by using the solution to Problem 1.

Solutions to the Three Basic Problems of HMM

The following sections present the solutions to the three fundamental problems of HMM. The solutions to these problems are critical to building a probabilistic framework.

Solution to Problem 1

The solution to Problem 1 involves evaluating the probability of observation sequence $X = x_1, x_2, x_3, \cdots, x_t$ given the model λ; that is, $\mathbb{P}(X \mid \lambda)$. Consider a state sequence $Q = q_1, q_2, q_3, \cdots, q_t$, where q_1 and q_t are initial and final states, respectively. The probability of an observation X sequence for a state sequence Q and a model λ can be represented as

$$\mathbb{P}(X \mid Q, \lambda) = \prod_{t=1}^{n} \mathbb{P}(x_t \mid q_t, \lambda) = b_{x_1}(q_1) . b_{x_2}(q_2) . b_{x_3}(q_3) \cdots b_{x_n}(q_n). \tag{5-4}$$

From the property of a Markov chain, you can represent the probability of the state sequence as

$$\mathbb{P}(Q \mid \lambda) = \pi_{q_1} \cdot p_{q_1,q_2} \cdot p_{q_2,q_3} \cdots p_{q_{n-1},q_n}. \tag{5-5}$$

Summation over all possible state sequences is as follows:

$$\mathbb{P}(X \mid \lambda) = \sum_{Q} \mathbb{P}(X, Q \mid \lambda) = \mathbb{P}(X \mid Q, \lambda) . \mathbb{P}(Q \mid \lambda)$$

$$\mathbb{P}(X \mid \lambda) = \sum_{Q} \pi_{q_1} \cdot b_{x_1}(q_1) \cdot p_{q_1,q_2} \cdot b_{x_2}(q_2) . p_{q_2,q_3} \cdot b_{x_3}(q_3) \cdots p_{q_{n-1},q_n} b_{x_n}(q_n). \tag{5-6}$$

Unfortunately, direct computation is not very practical, because it requires $2nN^n$ multiplications. At every $t = 1, 2, 3, \cdots, n$, N possible states can be reached, which turns out to be a large number. For example, at $n = 100$ (number of observation sequences) and $N = 5$ (states), there can be $2 \cdot 100 \cdot 5^{100} \approx 10^{72}$ possible computations. Fortunately, an efficient approach, called the *forward algorithm*, achieves the same result.

Forward Algorithm

Consider a forward variable $\alpha_t(i)$ that represents the probability of a partial observation sequence up to time t, such that the underlying Markov process is in state S_i at time t, given the HMM model λ:

$$\alpha_t(i) = \mathbb{P}(x_1, x_2, x_3, \cdots, x_t, q_t = S_i \mid \lambda).$$

You can compute $\alpha_t(i)$ recursively via the following steps:

1. Initialize the forward probability as a joint probability of state S_i and initial observation x_1. Let $\alpha_1(i) = \pi_i \, b_i(x_1)$ for $1 \leq i \leq N$.

2. Compute $\alpha_n(j)$ for all states j and $t = n$, using the induction procedure, substituting $t = 1, 2, 3, \cdots, n$:

$$\alpha_{t+1}(j) = \left[\sum_{i=1}^{N} \alpha_t(i) \cdot p_{ij} \right] b_j(x_t), 1 \leq t \leq (n-1), 1 \leq j \leq N.$$

3. Using the results from the preceding step, compute $\mathbb{P}(X \mid \lambda) = \sum_{j=1}^{N} \alpha_n(j)$.

The total number of computations involved in evaluating the forward probability is $N^2 n$ rather than $2nN^n$, as required by direct computation. For $n = 100$ and $N = 5$ the total number of computations is 2,500, which is 10^{69} times smaller in magnitude.

Backward Algorithm

For the forward algorithm you can also define a backward variable $\beta_t(i)$ that represents the probability of a partial observation sequence from time $t+1$ to the end (instead of up to t. as in the forward algorithm), where the Markov process is in state S_i at time t for a given model λ. Mathematically, you can represent the backward variable as

$$\beta_t(i) = \mathbb{P}(x_{t+1}, x_{t+2}, \cdots, x_n \mid q_t = S_i, \lambda).$$

You can compute $\alpha_t(i)$ recursively via the following steps:

1. Define $\beta_n(i) = 1$ for $1 \le i \le N$.
2. Compute $\beta_t(i) = \sum_{j=1}^{N} p_{ij} b_j(x_{t+1}) \beta_{t+1}(j).$

Scaling

A practical impediment in modeling long sequences of HMMs is the numerical scaling of conditional probabilities. Efficient computation of conditional probabilities helps in estimating the most likely sequence of states for a given model. For a sufficiently large sequence the probability of observing a long sequence tends to be so extremely small that numerical instability occurs. In most cases, the resulting computations exceed the precision range of essentially any machine (including double-precision). The most common approach for mitigating this situation is to rescale the conditional probabilities, using efficient scaling mechanisms.

For example, let's revisit the forward variable equation,

$$\alpha_{t+1}(j) = \left[\sum_{i=1}^{N} \alpha_t(i) \cdot p_{ij} \right] b_j(x_t).$$

In the case of forward variable $\alpha_t(i)$, you obtain the new value $\alpha_{t+1}(i)$ by multiplying by p_{ij} and $b_j(x_t)$. These probabilities tend to be small and can underflow. Logarithms may not be helpful, because you are dealing with the sum of products. Furthermore, logarithms require computation of the logarithm and exponential for each addition. Basic scaling procedure multiplies $\alpha_t(i)$ with the scaling coefficient, with the goal of keeping the scaled $\alpha_t(i)$ within the dynamic precision range of the machine. At the end of computation, scaling coefficients are canceled out. The scaling coefficients need not be applied at every t-step but can be used whenever necessary.

Solution to Problem 2

Unlike the solution of Problem 1, identifying the optimal state sequence is a complex problem, because there can be many criteria. Part of the complexity originates from the definition of the measure of optimality, in which several unique criteria are possible. One solution is to identify the states q_t that are most likely to occur individually at time t. This solution attempts to maximize the expected number of correct individual states. To implement the solution to Problem 2, you define the variable $\gamma_t(i)$ as the probability of being in state S_i at time t, given the observation sequence X and model λ, such that

$$\gamma_t(i) = \mathbb{P}(q_t = S_i \mid X, \lambda).$$

Using the definition of conditional probability, you can express this equation as

$$\gamma_t(i) = \frac{\mathbb{P}(X, q_t = S_i \mid \lambda)}{\mathbb{P}(X \mid \lambda)} = \frac{\mathbb{P}(X, q_t = S_i \mid \lambda)}{\sum_{i}^{N} \mathbb{P}(X, q_t = S_i \mid \lambda)}. \qquad (5\text{-}7)$$

You can rewrite Equation 5-7, using the forward-backward variable, as

$$\gamma_t(i) = \frac{\alpha_t(i) \cdot \beta_t(i)}{\displaystyle\sum_i^N \alpha_t(i) \cdot \beta_t(i)},$$
(5-8)

where $\alpha_t(i)$ defines the probability of partial observation $x_1, x_2, x_3, \cdots, x_t$ and state S_i at time t, and $\beta_t(i)$ defines the remainder of the probability of observation $x_{t+1}, x_{t+2}, x_{t+3}, \cdots, x_n$ and state S_i at time t. Using $\gamma_t(i)$, you can solve for the individually most likely state q_t^* at each time t by calculating the highest probability of being in state S_i at time t, as expressed by the following equation:

$$q_t^* = \underset{1 \le i \le N}{argmax}\big[\gamma_t(i)\big] \text{ for } \forall t = 1 \cdots n.$$
(5-9)

Although this equation maximizes the expected number of correct states by choosing the most likely state at each time interval, the state sequence itself may not be valid. For instance, in the case of the individually most likely states in the sequence $q_t = S_i$ and $q_{t+1} = S_j$, the transition probability p_{ij} may be 0 and hence not valid. This solution identifies the individually most likely state at any time t without giving any consideration as to the probability of the occurrence of the sequence of states.

One way to address this issue is to maximize the occurrence of a sequence of more than one state. This allows automatic evaluation of valid occurrences of states, while evaluating for the most likely sequence. One widely used scheme is to find the single most likely sequence of states that ultimately results in maximizing $\mathbb{P}(X, Q \mid \lambda)$. This technique, which is based on dynamic programming, is called a *Viterbi algorithm*. To find the single best state sequence, you define a variable $\delta_t(i)$ that represents the highest probability along one state sequence (path) that accounts for first t observations and that ends in state S_i, as follows:

$$\delta_t(i) = \underset{q_1, q_2, \cdots, q_{t-1}}{max}(q_1, q_2, \cdots, q_t = S_i, x_1, x_2, \cdots, x_t \mid \lambda).$$

You can compute $\delta_{t+1}(j)$ by induction, as

$$\delta_{t+1}(j) = \underset{i}{max}\big[\delta_t(i) \cdot p_{ij}\big] \cdot b_j(x_{t+1}),$$

from which it is clear that to retrieve the state sequence, you need to track the state that maximizes $\delta_t(i)$ at each time t. This is done by constructing an array $\psi_{t+1}(j)$ that defines the state at time t from which a transition to state S_j maximizes the probability $\delta_{t+1}(j)$. Mathematically, this can be represented as

$$\psi_{t+1}(j) - \underset{1 \le i \le N}{argmax}\big[\delta_t(i) \ p_{ij}\big].$$

The complete procedure for finding the best state sequence consists of the following steps:

Initialization

$$\delta_1(i) = \pi_i \cdot b_i(x_1); 1 \leq I \leq N$$
$$\psi_1(i) = 0$$

Recursion

$$\delta_t(j) = \max_{1 \leq i \leq N}\left[\delta_{t-1} \cdot p_{ij}\right] \cdot b_j(x_t); 1 \leq j \leq N; 2 \leq t \leq n$$
$$\psi_t(j) = \underset{1 \leq i \leq N}{\operatorname{argmax}}\left[\delta_{t-1}(i) \cdot p_{ij}\right]; 1 \leq j \leq N; 2 \leq t \leq n$$

Termination

$$P^* = \max_{1 \leq i \leq N}\left[\delta_n(i)\right]$$
$$q_n^* = \underset{1 \leq i \leq N}{\operatorname{argmax}}\left[\delta_n(i)\right]$$

State Sequence Backtracking

$$q_t^* = \psi_{t+1}(q_{t+1}^*); t = n-1, n-2, n-3, \cdots, 1$$

The Viterbi algorithm is similar to the forward procedure, except that it uses maximization over previous states instead of a summation.

Solution to Problem 3

The solution to Problem 3 involves a method for adjusting the model parameters (P,B,π) to maximize the probability of an observation sequence for a given model. In practice there is no well-known method that maximizes the probability of observation sequence. However, you can select $\lambda = (P,B,\pi)$, such that $P(X|\lambda)$ is locally maximized, using an iterative method, such as the Baum-Welch algorithm.

To specify the reestimation of HMM parameters, you define the variable $\gamma_t(i,j)$ as the probability of being in state S_i at time t and in S_j at time $t + 1$ for a given model λ and observation sequence X, such that

$$\gamma_t(i,j) = \mathbb{P}(q_t = S_i, q_{t+1} = S_j \mid X, \lambda). \tag{5-10}$$

Using the definition of the forward-backward algorithm, you can rewrite Equation 5-10 as

$$\gamma_t(i,j) = \frac{\alpha_t(i) \cdot p_{ij} \cdot b_j(x_{t+1}) \cdot \beta_{t+1}(j)}{\mathbb{P}(X \mid \lambda)} \tag{5-11}$$

$$\gamma_t(i,j) = \frac{\alpha_t(i) \cdot p_{ij} \cdot b_j(x_{t+1}) \cdot \beta_{t+1}(j)}{\sum_i^N \sum_j^N \alpha_t(i) \cdot p_{ij} \cdot b_j(x_{t+1}) \cdot \beta_{t+1}(j)}. \tag{5-12}$$

As defined by Equation 5-8, $\gamma_t(i)$ is the probability of being in state S_i at time t, given the observation sequence and model. Using this equation, you can relate $\gamma_t(i)$ to $\gamma_t(i, j)$ by summing over j as

$$\gamma_t(i) = \sum_{j}^{N} \gamma_t(i, j).$$

By summing $\gamma_t(i)$ over time t, you can quantify the number of times state S_i is visited or, alternatively, the expected number of transitions made from state S_i. Similarly, summation of $\gamma_t(i, j)$ over time t reveals the expected number of transitions from state S_i to state S_j. Given $\gamma_t(i)$, $\gamma_t(i, j)$, and the current model λ, you can build the method to reestimate the parameters of the HMM model $(\bar{\lambda})$. The method can be broken down as follows:

1. At time $t = 1$ the expected frequency at state S_i is given
    by $\bar{\pi}_i = \gamma_1(i)$ $\forall i = (1,2,3,\cdots,N)$.

2. The probability of transiting from state S_i to state S_j, which is the desired
    value of $\overline{p_{ij}}$, is given by

$$\overline{p_{ij}} = \frac{\sum_{t=1}^{n-1} \gamma_t(i, j)}{\sum_{t=1}^{n-1} \gamma_t(i)} \quad \forall i, j = (1,2,3,\cdots,N).$$

    The numerator is the reestimated value of the expected number of transitions
    from state S_i to state S_j; the denominator is the expected number of transitions
    from S_i to any state.

3. The probability of observing symbol k, given that the model is in state S_j,
    is given by

$$\overline{b_j}(k) = \frac{\sum_{t=1, x_t=k}^{n} \gamma_t(j)}{\sum_{t=1}^{n} \gamma_t(j)} \quad \forall k = (1,2,\cdots,M).$$

    The numerator of the reestimated $\overline{b_j}(k)$ is the expected number of times the
    model is in state S_j with observation symbol k; the denominator is the expected
    number of times the model is in state S_j.

With this method, you use the current model $\lambda(P,B,\pi)$ to reestimate the new model $\bar{\lambda}(\bar{P},\bar{B},\bar{\pi})$, as described by the previous three steps. The reestimation process is an iterative method consisting of the following steps:

1. Initialize $\lambda(P,B,\pi)$ with a best guess or random value, or use the existing model.

2. Compute $\alpha_t(i), \beta_t(i), \gamma_t(i), \gamma_t(i, j)$.

3. Reestimate the model $\bar{\lambda}(\bar{P},\bar{B},\bar{\pi})$.

4. If $\mathbb{P}(X \mid \bar{\lambda}) > \mathbb{P}(X \mid \lambda)$, repeat step 2.

The final result of this reestimation process is called the *maximum likelihood estimation* (MLE) of the parameters of the HMM. The forward-backward algorithm yields only the local maximum.

Continuous Observation HMM

The previous sections considered a scenario in which observations are discrete symbols from a finite alphabet, enabling use of the discrete probability density for each state in the system. For many practical implementations, however, observations are continuous vectors. Although it is possible to quantize continuous vectors via codebooks, and so on, quantization may entail degradation. Therefore, it is advantageous to have an HMM with continuous observations, whose *probability density function* (PDF) is evaluated as a convex combination of other distribution functions—a mixture distribution, with an associated mixture weight. The number of components is restricted to being finite. For a given pool of observations, mixture distributions are employed to make statistical inferences about the properties of the subpopulations without requiring the label identifying the subpopulation to which the observation belongs. The number of components M (subpopulations) depends on the number of observation clusters (learned through unsupervised algorithms, such as k-means) that group the pool of observations. Generally, each mixture component represents an m-dimensional categorical distribution, where each of the M possible outcomes is specified with the probability of each outcome. Each mixture component follows the similar distributions (normal, log-normal, and so on) and represents a unique qualification for classifying the set of continuous observations at any time instance as a unique symbol (similar to discrete observations). Mixture components that are trained using the EM algorithm are able to self-organize to fit a data set. The continuous observation model produces sequences of hidden clusters (or a mixture symbol) at each time step of the HMM state transition, according to a state-to-cluster-emission probability distribution. Clusters (or mixture symbols) can be considered the hidden symbols embedded in the hidden states. For example, a hidden state may represent a specific workload, and a symbol may represent a specific attribute of the workload, based resource utilization.

You start with the representation of the *probability density function* (PDF) that allows its parameters to be reestimated in a consistent manner. The most general form of PDF that can be used for the reestimation process is given by a multivariate normal distribution or a mixture of Gaussian distributions:

$$b_j(X) = \sum_{m=1}^{M} c_{jm} \, \aleph(X, \mu_{jm}, U_{jm}) \; 1 \le j \le N,$$

(5-13)

where

X = observation vector ($x_1, x_2, x_3, \cdots, x_D$)

M = number of mixture densities

c_{jm} = weight of the mth mixture in the jth state

$\aleph$ = any elliptically symmetrical density function (e.g., a Gaussian)

μ_{jm} = mean vector for the mth mixture in the jth state

U_{jm} = covariance matrix for the mth mixture and jth state

$$c_{jm} \ge 0, 1 \le j \le N, 1 \le m \le M$$

$$\sum_{m-1}^{M} c_{jm} = 1, 1 \le j \le N$$

$$\int_{-\infty}^{\infty} b_j(x) dx = 1, 1 \le j \le N$$

In statistics a mixture model is a probabilistic model in which the underlying data belong to a mixture distribution. In a mixture distribution the density function is a convex combination (i.e., a linear combination in which all coefficients or weights sum to 1) of other PDFs. It can be shown (Liporace 2006; Hwang 1986) that reestimation of the coefficients for mixture density (c_{jm}, μ_{jm}, U_{jm}) can be represented as

$$\overline{c_{jk}} = \frac{\sum_{t=1}^{n} \varepsilon_t(j,k)}{\sum_{t=1}^{n}\sum_{k=1}^{M} \varepsilon_t(j,k)}$$

$$\overline{\mu_{jk}} = \frac{\sum_{t=1}^{n} \varepsilon_t(j,k) \cdot x_t}{\sum_{t=1}^{n} \varepsilon_t(j,k)} \tag{5-14}$$

$$\overline{U_{jk}} = \frac{\sum_{t=1}^{n} \varepsilon_t(j,k) \cdot (x_t - \mu_{jk}) \cdot (x_t - \mu_{jk})^T}{\sum_{t=1}^{n} \varepsilon_t(j,k)},$$

where $(X_t-\mu_{jk})^T$ represents the vector transpose, and $\varepsilon_t(j,k)$, the probability of being in state j at time t with the kth mixture accounting for X_t:

$$\varepsilon_t(j,k) = \left[\frac{\alpha_t(j)\beta_t(j)}{\sum_{j=1}^{N}\alpha_t(j)\beta_t(j)}\right]\left[\frac{c_{jk}\aleph(X_t,\mu_{jk},U_{jk})}{\sum_{m=1}^{M}c_{jm}\aleph(X_t,\mu_{jm},U_{jm})}\right]. \tag{5-15}$$

The reestimation formula for p_{ij} is similar to that defined for discrete observation density. The reestimation formula for c_{jk} is the ratio of the expected number of times the system is in state j, using the kth mixture component to the expected number of times the system is in state j.

To reduce computational complexity, an alternate approach is semicontinuous HMM (SCHMM), which is a special form of continuous observation HMM (CHMM). SCHMM uses state mixture densities that are tied to a general set of mixture densities. All states share the same mixture, and only the mixture density component weights c_{jk} remain state-specific states.

Multivariate Gaussian Mixture Model

In the CHMM, $b_j(X)$ is a continuous PDF that is often a mixture of multivariate Gaussian distributions of L-dimensional observations. *Gaussian mixture model* (GMM) density is defined as the weighted sum of Gaussian densities. The choice of the Gaussian distribution is natural and very widespread when dealing with a natural phenomenon. For the Gaussian mixture, $\aleph$ in Equation 5-13 can be substituted by Gaussian distribution to take the mathematical form of an emission density,

$$b_j(X) = \sum_{k=1}^{M} c_{jk}\left(\frac{1}{(2\pi)^{L/2}|U_{jk}|^{1/2}}\exp\left(-\frac{1}{2}\left(X-\mu_{jk}\right)^T U_{jk}^{-1}\left(X-\mu_{jk}\right)\right)\right). \tag{5-16}$$

Each Gaussian mixture is defined by its set of parameters, which includes the mixture distribution c_{jk}, the mean vectors μ_{jk}, and the covariance matrices U_{jk}. Note that a CHMM with finite mixtures of Gaussian PDFs as conditional densities is equivalent to one with simple Gaussian PDFs as conditional densities. Using a Gaussian mixture PDF, you can transform a state with a mixture density into a net of multiple single-density states. Figure 5-4 depicts a scenario in which the state $S2$, corresponding to a two-component mixture PDF, has been expanded into two states $S2_a$ and $S2_b$ with single-component PDFs and adjusted transition probabilities.

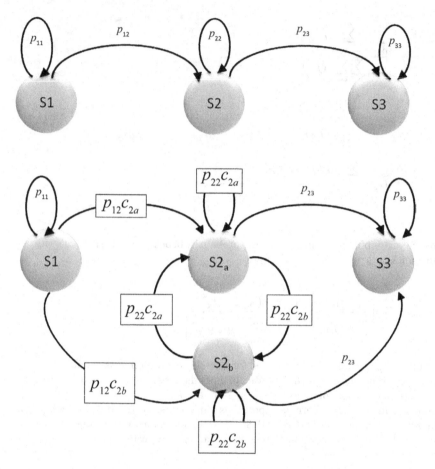

Figure 5-4. *Two-component Gaussian mixture model for state S2 expanded into single-component Gaussian model with two new states (S2$_a$, S2$_b$)*

Example: Workload Phase Recognition

Recent computer architecture research has demonstrated that program execution exhibits phase behavior that can be characterized on the largest of scales (Perelman et al. 2002). In the majority of cases, workload behavior is neither homogeneous nor totally random; it is well structured, with a class of phases. As you transition between phases, you can initiate a reconfiguration by reusing configuration information for recurring phases.

Trends in datacenter and cloud computing pose interesting challenges related to power optimization and power control in a server system. A system can be represented as a set of components whose cooperative interaction produces useful work. These components may be heterogeneous in nature and may vary in their power consumption and power control mechanisms. A server system with several central processing unit (CPU), memory, and input/output (I/O) components may coordinate power control actions, using embedded controllers or special hardware. The accuracy and agility of control actions are critical in proactive tuning for performance. Observing how variations in a workload affect the power drawn by different server components provides critical data for analysis and for building models relating quality of service (QoS) expectations to power consumption. Therefore, you need an autonomous system that can extract the workload features and proactively tune the system, according to the phase of operation. The following sections present one such approach that uses performance data in a server platform to model the runtime behavior of a system. We describe a trained model that analyzes the behavioral attributes of a workload and that identifies the present and predicts with reasonable accuracy the future phase of workload characteristics, using a CHMM.

Predictive systems are devised for recognition of workload patterns and early detection of phases for characterization. The knowledge base (model) recommends appropriate actions. These systems are self-correcting and require continuous training to adapt to the previously known as well as evolutionary behavior over a period of time. The phase detection model can assist in predicting performance states and proactively adapts by tuning its parameters to meet system constraints.

Monitoring and Observations

Monitoring and measuring events from system activities is the basis for characterizing system phases and predicting the future. Modern processors have built-in performance-monitoring counters that measure real-time access patterns to processor and memory events and that help in designing analytical intelligence for a variety of dynamic decisions. Trends such as memory access patterns, rate of instruction execution, and pipeline stalls can be studied statistically for patterns, hidden correlations, and time-dependent behaviors. Measured events (resource utilization, temperature, energy consumption, performance) can be considered multiple dimensions of observed emissions. Extracted phases can be seen as predictable system characteristics, based on dynamic models that maximize the probability of the sequence of observations. Once you identify the current workload phase of operation and the most likely future phase, you can tune and provision the system with adequate resources and avoid reactive resource allocation. The CHMM-based phase characterization process uses built-in performance counters and sensors. Additionally, synthetic counters are used to abstract time-varying behavior of the workload.

Workload and Phase

Workloads are applications with specialized objectives (queries, searches, analysis, and so on) that undergo phases of execution, while operating under multiple constraints. These constraints are related to power consumption, heat generation, and QoS requirements. Optimal system operation involves complex choices, owing to a variety of degrees of freedom for power and performance parameter tuning. The process involves modeling methodology, implementation choices, and dynamic tuning. Phase detection in a workload acts as an essential ingredient, capturing time-varying behavior of dynamically adaptable systems. This ability aids in reconfiguring hardware and software ahead of variation in demand and enables reuse of trained models for recurring phases. Phase identification also helps predict future phases during workload execution, which prevents reactive response to changes in workload behavior. In this context a phase is a stage of execution in which a workload demonstrates similar power, temperature, and performance characteristics.

CHMM-assisted methodology identifies a phase's boundaries, which are represented by a latent component of Gaussian density mixture function in the presence of system sensors and performance counters. A state's variable can be used as a process control parameter that is fed back to the process control loop. For instance, you can feed back the workload phase (or behavioral attributes) to control thermal behavior proactively, because the physical dynamics of the temperature can be represented as a function of utilization of various system components. In general, the HMM is particularly useful, as it can exploit the underlying pattern in a sequence of events and perform state-space analysis. You may use Gaussian observations as an indicator of correctly identifying phase boundaries in a time-varying workload behavior. These phase boundaries can further be used to extract the relationship with various states of physical phenomena, such as server demand projection and thermal variation projection. Figure 5-5 for example displays a test of CPU utilization versus a workload phase that is estimated statistically at regular intervals. This function can be expanded by using more than one variable.

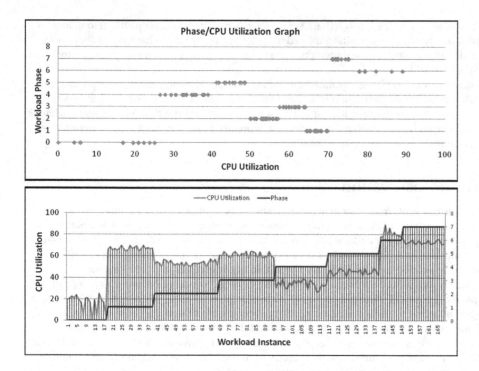

Figure 5-5. *CPU utilization versus phase model. The workload is composed of eight phases with phase-specific power, thermal, and performance characteristics. The red line (bottom graph) identifies the phase number that corresponds to the running average power limit (RAPL) (blue line) for each instance of workload. For example, average utilization of 65–70 percent results in phase 1*

Compared with aggregate workload analysis, CHMM-assisted analysis is more accurate and informative. In general, effective tuning of system hardware and software helps in building efficient systems that minimize power and thermal dissipation for given performance constraints. Various attributes of systems can benefit from phase identification:

- For a given performance constraint, you can tune the system components (CPU, memory, I/O) for minimum power usage. Upon identifying a new phase, power is allocated (or deallocated) in a manner such that performance degradation is minimized.

- Proactive compensation for anticipated performance variation aids in avoiding reactive state changes and thus reactive latencies, improving performance.

- Available power is distributed to system components in a way that maximizes overall performance. One strategy may involve individual allocation (or deallocation), according to each component's share in performance gain.

- Activity vectors are employed to perform thermally balanced computing, thus preventing hot spots. Activity data can also be used to coschedule tasks in a contention-free and energy-efficient manner.

- You can profile task characteristics related to (1) task priority, (2) energy and thermal profile, and (2) optimization methodology regarding latency targets proportional to task priority.

Workload phases can be exploited for adaptive architectures, guiding performance and power optimization through predictive state feedback. Because HMM uses and correlates observations with objective oriented states (such as average temperature or utilization), it may very well be a consideration in system design. Observation points can be characterized by using a reasonable set of system-wide performance counters and sensors. Hidden states that predict a control objective (such as server temperature) are measured by extracting workload phases, using feature extraction techniques. Furthermore, states share probabilistic relationships with these observations. These probabilistic relationships (also called *profiles*), harden and evolve with the constant use of the workload over its lifetime. If you consider a normal workload behavior to be a pattern of an observed sequence, an HMM should be appropriate for mapping such patterns to one of several states. Furthermore, it is essential to build an adaptive strategy, based on embedding numerous policies that are informed by contextual and environmental inputs. The policies govern various behavioral attributes, enhancing flexibility to maximize efficiency and performance in the presence of high levels of environmental variability. HMM-based approaches correlate the system observations (usage, activity profiles) to predict the most probable system state. HMM training, using initial data and continuous reestimation, creates a profile that consists of component models, transition probabilities, and observation symbol probabilities. CHMM aids in estimating workload phases by clustering the homogeneous behavior of multiple components. Workload phases can be interpreted by a d-dimensional Gaussian (observation vector) model of k mixtures by maximizing the probability of the sequence of observations.

Mixture Models for Phase Detection

The foremost objective of HMM-based methodology is to predict the state of the process by establishing various phase execution boundaries in the presence of time-varying behavior. Unlike traditional approaches, which study aggregate behavior, HMM-based methods can extract representative phases and workload classification, using *Gaussian mixture models* (GMMs). For instance, HMM can be modeled by training itself against workloads and the corresponding phases that are characterized by an inherent behavioral pattern. These phases can be considered latent symbols (as they cannot be observed directly) that are embedded in the hidden states, which, in this case, is a *workload*. In a trained model these latent phase patterns can be identified through sets of observed phenomena modeled through a combination of individual mixture component probability densities, along with the presence of a hidden state (evaluated using a state transition matrix). The observations exist in the form of synthetic counters and sensors that measure the performance and power characteristics of the system as well as system components. Various functional blocks that assist in workload phase detection are described in turn in the following sections.

Sensor Block

In autonomic system instrumentation, endpoints (sensors/controllers) are spread all over the platform (see Figure 5-6), and the characteristics of these endpoints can differ from one platform to another. In typical server management architecture a *sensor block* comprises a mix of performance counters and temperature, airflow, and power sensors. These sensors are accessed through a variety of interfaces, such as PCI Express, SMBus, PECI Bus, and CPU model specific registers (MSR). The output of the sensors is statistically processed and used as feedback. The relative importance of instrumentation may vary, according to the user requirements. In some cases, because of cost constraints, instrumentation is synthesized in lieu of physical sensors by correlating the sensor data with a different set of variables. In other cases, the instrumentation accuracy of physical sensors may vary over the operating region, outside of which it may be highly inaccurate. In such cases, sensitivity is not constant over the entire operating range of the sensor, and nonlinearity results. Nonlinearity depends on the deviation of the sensor output from the ideal behavior over the full range of the sensor. It may be necessary to calibrate the sensor within the linear operating range and then use the calibrated parameters and functions for the rest of the nonlinear operating region. Sensor data can also observe long-term drift, owing to the aging of sensor properties over a long period of time. With digital sensors, you can also have digitization error, because the measured data are an approximation of the actual data. Additionally, limitations on sampling frequency can lead to dynamic error in the measured data. The ability of an application to measure or control an aspect of the platform depends significantly on where it is hosted and its connectivity to the instrumentation endpoint.

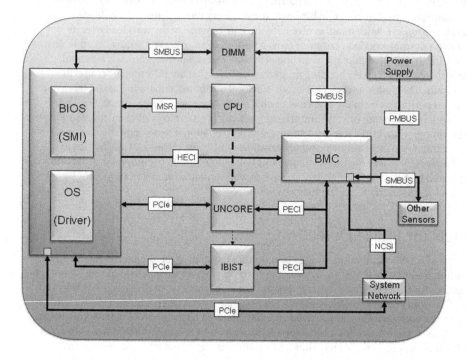

Figure 5-6. *Instrumentation telemetry in a typical Intel Xeon server platform*

Power, thermal, and performance variations in a system can result in suboptimal behavior that may need correction for platform policy compliance. This behavior must be predicted well in advance so that corrective action can be employed within a window of opportunity. Such conditions can be predicted, using a set of sensors that together can act as component Gaussians to model the overall feature density. In a platform these sensors are available as activity counters; temperature, power, and performance monitors; and so on. Classes of sensor data are as follows:

- *CPU performance counters*: These are special-purpose hardware counters that are built into modern microprocessors to store the counts of hardware-related activities within a CPU context. The output of these counters is used to forecast common workload behaviors, in terms of CPU utilization (cache, pipeline, idle time, stall, thermal).

- *Memory performance counters*: Memory performance counters identify memory access patterns, bandwidth utilization, dynamic random access memory (DRAM) power consumption, and proportions of DRAM command activity (read, write), which can be useful for characterizing the memory-intensive behavior of a workload. It is possible to characterize workload patterns by observing the proportion of read/write cycles and time in the precharge, active, and idle states.

- *I/O performance counters*: Three major indicators of I/O power are (1) direct memory access (DMA), (2) uncacheable access, and (3) interrupt activity. Of these the number of interrupts per cycle is the dominant indicator of I/O power. DMA indicators perform suboptimally, owing to the presence of various performance enhancements (such as write combining) in the I/O chip. I/O interrupts are typically triggered by I/O devices to indicate the completion of large data transfers. Therefore, it is possible to correlate I/O power with the appropriate device. Because this information cannot be obtained through CPU counters, it is made available by the operating system, using performance monitors.

- *Thermal data*: In addition to the foregoing performance counters, you may also consider using thermal data, which are available in all modern components (CPU, memory, and so on) and accessible via PECI Bus.

- *Workload performance feedback*: Control theoretic action initiates a defensive response, based on hysteresis, to reduce the effects of variation in resource demands. This response needs to be corrected if it interferes with the performance requirements of useful work. Excessive responses can slow down the system and negatively impact the effectiveness of the control action. State feedback communicates the optimal fulfillment of performance demands (or service-level objectives) at a given time. This feedback has to be estimated by forecasting the attributes of the fitness function that is related to the behavior of the work being performed and its dynamic requirements. Continuous state feedback trains the system-specific control actions and saves the recipe for those actions by relating it to a unique state-phase fingerprint that can repeat in the future.

Model Reduction Block

A *model reduction block* (MRB) is responsible for reducing the dimensionality of a dataset by retaining key uncorrelated and noncolinear datasets. This allows us to retain the most significant datasets—those that are sufficient to identify the phases of workload operation that demonstrate time-varying behavior. Input to the MRB model is time series data related to microarchitectural performance counters, workload performance counters, and analog sensors (measuring power, temperature, and so on). These data can be collected, using one of the many interfaces (PCI Express, SMBus, PECI Bus, and so on) illustrated in Figure 5-6.

You can use *principal component analysis* (PCA) for reducing the dimensionality of data without loss of information (see Chapter 2). The resulting output variables are the principal components, which are uncorrelated. For example, PCA transforms N inputs $Y = (y_1, y_2, y_3, \cdots, y_N)$ to M principal components $X = (x_1, x_2, x_3, \cdots, x_M)$, with very little information overlap $\left(Cov(x_K, x_L) = 0\right)$. Furthermore, variance of each principal component is arranged in descending order $(Var(x_1) \geq Var(x_2) \geq \cdots \geq Var(x_M))$, such that x_1 contains the most information, and x_M, the least. Each principal component defines the dimensionality of an observation.

Emission Block

An *emission block* (EB) is responsible for collecting noncorrelated emissions as time series data. The raw data that are collected from sensors are noisy and have to be filtered to extract quantifiable information. The noise-reduction procedure identifies a simple dynamic system that is a good representation of the data. During the training cycle the noise reduction scheme consists of a representative distribution that fits the incoming data for a modeling window of δt. Sensor data streaming to the receiving blocks (see Figure 5-7) are delayed by a configurable time period δt. The behavior of data within the δt period is governed by the underlying equation, which is trained to reject (or reconstruct) the datapoints.

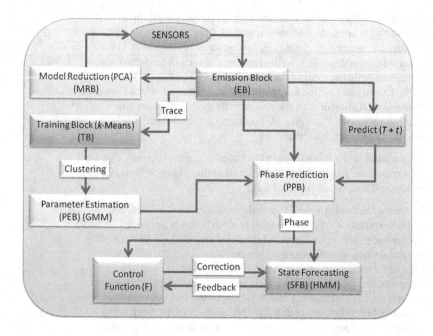

Figure 5-7. *Phase detection model, using GMM*

The output of a sensor block is processed into an EB, which processes the sequence of polled sensor data to generate a continuous observation sequence. Additionally, an MRB scales down the number of sensor inputs by synthesizing those that are significant and providing independent characteristics. You may use a discrete set of weighted Gaussian PDFs, each with their own mean and covariance matrix, to enable better modeling of phase detection features, using continuous emission. The Gaussian mixture forms parametric models, whose parameters are estimated iteratively from training data, using Equations 5-14 and 5-15. In workload phase detection a d-dimensional Gaussian (independent emission) of k mixtures is modeled as a weighted sum of Gaussian densities (see Equation 5-16).

Training Block

Dynamic systems are characterized by temporal features, whose time-varying properties undergo changes during the operational period. These systems produce a temporal sequence of observations that can be analyzed for dynamic characteristics. A *training block* (TB) facilitates the construction of a forecast model by feeding it with metric vectors and the corresponding forecast variable for workloads with varying characteristics (such as system power). A TB performs unsupervised classification and builds data structures by partitioning the data into homogeneous clusters, such that similar objects are grouped within the same class. In the simplest case, you may use the k-means clustering algorithm, which partitions the d-dimensional emissions into k clusters, such that each emission belongs to the cluster with the nearest mean. For a given a set of emissions $(x_1, x_2, \cdots, x_n)$, the k-means clustering algorithm partitions the emissions into k sets $G = (G_1, G_2, G_3, \cdots, G_k)$ by finding the minimum distance to observation of all the k clusters:

$$\underbrace{arg\ min}_{G} \sum_{i=1}^{k} \sum_{x_j \in G_i} \| x_j - \mu_i \|^2.$$

Each *G* element acts as a single-component Gaussian density function for *k* single-density states, each representing a distinctive workload phase; μ_i represents the mean of cluster *i*.

Parameter Estimation Block

You can use GMM to represent feature distributions in a workload phase prediction system, in which individual component densities model an underlying set of latent classes. A *parameter estimation block* (PEB) is responsible for estimating the parameters of the model λ_k that fits the data for that model. In the beginning, the model's input data are the output sensor data from the TB, which classifies (labels) the observations as a cluster number? The classifier uses the minimum distortion, or nearest-neighbor, approach to classify the input vector, which selects the best Gaussian component from the mixture. Once the training data are buffered for each model for a time interval δt, they are used to estimate the Gaussian mixture parameters of that model. In the absence of an a priori model, a PEB initializes the number of mixtures and estimates the model parameters (c_k, μ_k, U_k). You can use the estimation maximization (EM) method, which maximizes the likelihood $\mathbb{P}(X \mid \lambda)$ of the cluster-tagged data (see Chapter 1). The fundamental idea behind the EM algorithm is to introduce a variable (a Gaussian mixture component) that will simplify the maximization of likelihood. The EM algorithm is a two-step method:

1. *E-Step*: Estimate the probability distribution of each Gaussian mixture component for a given emission (X) and model (λ).

2. *M-Step*: Estimate the joint probability distribution of the data and the latent variable (Gaussian mixture component). This step modifies the model parameters of the Gaussian mixture component to maximize the likelihood of the emission and the Gaussian component itself.

Beginning with an initial model λ, the EM algorithm estimates a new model $\bar{\lambda}$, such that $\mathbb{P}(X \mid \bar{\lambda}) \geq \mathbb{P}(X \mid \lambda)$. The new model then becomes the starting model for the next iteration, and the process is repeated until a convergence threshold is reached. For a given sequence of *d*-dimensional emission vector sequences $X = (x_1, x_2, \cdots, x_n)$, the a posteriori probability for the *k*th mixture component is given by

$$p(k \mid x_t, \lambda) = \frac{c_k \cdot G(\mu_k, U_k)(x_t)}{\sum_{k=1}^{M} c_k \cdot G(\mu_k, U_k)(x_t)}.$$

The formula used in reestimation of the model parameters is

$$\text{Mixture weights}: \bar{c}_k = \frac{1}{n}\sum_{t=1}^{n} p(k \mid x_t, \lambda)$$

$$\text{Mixture mean}: \bar{\mu}_k = \frac{\sum_{t=1}^{n} p(k \mid x_t, \lambda) \cdot x_t}{\sum_{t=1}^{n} p(k \mid x_t, \lambda)}$$

$$\text{Diagonal variance}: \bar{U}_k = \frac{\sum_{t=1}^{n} p(k \mid x_t, \lambda) \cdot (x_t - \mu_k) \cdot (x_t - \mu_k)^T}{\sum_{t=1}^{n} p(k \mid x_t, \lambda)}$$

This block aids in categorizing the sequence of observations to the kth Gaussian component. You can expand a single-state GCHMM into a single-density, multistate GCHMM.

Phase Prediction Model

Workload patterns that can be represented as application phases exhibit certain repetitive behaviors. You need methods to identify and predict repetitive phases to apply feasible dynamic management responses proactively. With a *phase predictor block* (PPB), you can estimate the observation sequence ahead of time by a configurable period δt (see Figure 5-8).

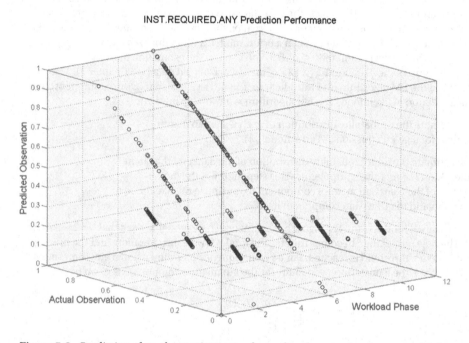

Figure 5-8. Prediction of an observation vector for twelve phases, using an exponential smoothing function

PPB analysis is of particular interest when the workload is operating at phase boundaries, and control action has to be optimized for an anticipated phase. To build a simple prediction model, you estimate the future d-dimensional observation vectors, using the observation vector exponential smoothing model. Exponential smoothing can generally be represented as

$$y_{t+1} = \alpha x_t + (1-\alpha)y_t ; 0 \leq \alpha \leq 1; t > 0$$

$$y_{t+1} = y_t + \alpha(\in_t) \text{ where } \in_t = x_t - y_t,$$

where y_t represents the predicted output of the smoothing function at instance $t - 1$, and x_t (our standard notation) represents the raw emission from various sensors. $\in_t$ represents the prediction error at instance t. Exponential smoothing takes into account all past data, but the proportional contribution of older samples is diminished geometrically. This allows us to tune the value of a for two different models. In Figure 5-7 this is illustrated by the "*Predict T + t*" block. Figure 5-9 demonstrates the prediction process, in which a control process consumes the estimated phase signature and associates with a control action. The same action is repeated if the phase appears in the future.

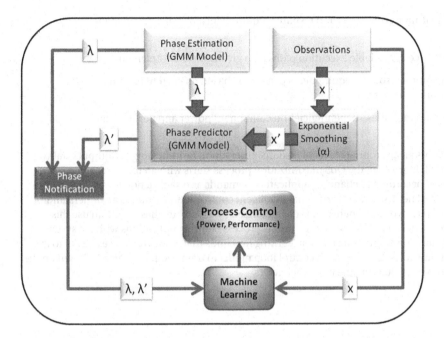

Figure 5-9. *Phase prediction block; control processes use the prediction model and sensor observations to tune the process variables proactively*

State Forecasting Block

In the context of workload characterization, a *state* represents an interesting attribute of a feedback function that, when forecasted, triggers a corrective response proactively to avoid reactive action. Reactive response lags the control action during which the function performs housekeeping and identifies the cause of behavioral change. To prevent performance degradation, you identify a key process variable that, if predicted, can generate a proactive response. A *phase* represents that unique behavioral characteristic of a workload that varies with time and that needs to be predicted to avoid reactive tuning.

System Adaptation

The preceding sections examined a systematic approach for detecting workload phases in dynamic systems with time-varying properties. Now, the question remains as to why we need to detect system phases.

Typically, workloads are subjected to arbitrary performance and environmental stresses, which are compensated for by using adaptive systems. Adaptation may have to serve functions that are mutually hostile and that pull in different directions. This results in needing to make compromises among solutions to maximize the fitness of the overall solution. An adaptation function will optimize power in a manner that delivers the desired performance, as perceived by the application. The desired performance may not necessarily be the highest performance. In real systems it is impossible to improve all aspects of the target policy to the same degree simultaneously. Therefore, systems develop various feedback control schemes that operate in hardware, software, or software-assisted hardware scenarios. Control objectives include

- Monitoring resource conditions in a continuous mode

- Determining how and when adaptation should be performed by modeling feedback control behavior

- Identifying real-time constraints and resource requirements for a given workload behavior

- Identifying choice of available execution paths for a given autonomic element

- Provisioning future resource requirements of a server, based on current resource usage and work behavior

- Discovering inherent phase dependencies on component power and performance tuning

The QoS profile governs an appropriate level of resource reservation by indicating the output quality levels in a dynamic fashion. In general, the QoS maximization process starts with an initial resource allocation, which it revises, according to changing application demands and satisfaction levels. In the scenarios we have described here, it is noteworthy that intelligent control action requires an understanding of workload behavior; because workload behavior is characterized by a discrete phase, you can use this information as feedback on any control loop action. Various process control applications within a system can optimize their work function by building custom learning functions that relate the phase activity to the control action. The resulting decisions steer each control loop model to train itself dynamically, based on the historical trends, with respect to quantifiable phase behaviors.

References

Baum, Leonard E. "An Equality and Associated Maximization Technique in Statistical Estimation for Probabilistic Functions of Markov Processes." *Inequalities* 3 (1972): 1–8.

Baum, Leonard E., and J. A. Eagon. "An Inequality with Applications to Statistical Estimation for Probabilistic Functions of Markov Processes and to a Model for Ecology." *Bulletin of the American Mathematical Society* 73, no. 3 (1967): 360–363. http://projecteuclid.org/euclid.bams/1183528841.

Baum, Leonard E., and Ted Petrie. "Statistical Inference for Probabilistic Functions of Finite State Markov Chains." *Annals of Mathematical Statistics* (1966): 1554–1563. http://projecteuclid.org/euclid.aoms/1177699147.

Baum, Leonard E., and George Sell. "Growth Transformations for Functions on Manifolds." *Pacific Journal of Mathematics* 27, no. 2 (1968): 211–227. http://projecteuclid.org/euclid.pjm/1102983899.

Baum, Leonard E. "An Equality and Associated Maximization Technique in Statistical Estimation for Probabilistic Functions of Markov Processes." *Inequalities* 3 (1972): 1–8.

Juang, Bing-Hwang, Stephen E. Levinson, and M. Mohan Sondhi. "Maximum Likelihood Estimation for Multivariate Mixture Observations of Markov Chains (Corresp.)." *IEEE Transactions on Information Theory* 32, no. 2 (1986): 307–309.

Liporace, L. "Maximum Likelihood Estimation for Multivariate Observations of Markov Sources." *IEEE Transactions on Information Theory* 28, no. 5 (1982): 729–734.

Sherwood, Timothy, Erez Perelman, Greg Hamerly, and Brad Calder. "Automatically Characterizing Large Scale Program Behavior." *ACM SIGARCH Computer Architecture News* 30, no. 5 (2002): 45–57.

Rabiner, Lawrence. "A Tutorial on Hidden Markov Models and Selected Applications in Speech Recognition." *Proceedings of the IEEE* 77, no. 2 (1989): 257–286.

Stratonovich, R. L. "Conditional Markov Processes." *Theory of Probability and Its Applications* 5, no. 2 (1960): 156–178.

CHAPTER 6

■ ■ ■

Bioinspired Computing: Swarm Intelligence

Brains exist because the distribution of resources necessary for survival and the hazards that threaten survival vary in space and time.

—John M. Allman, Evolving Brains

Natural systems solve multifaceted problems using simple rules, and exhibit organized, complex, and intelligent behavior. Natural process control systems are adaptive, evolutionary, distributed (decentralized), reactive, and aware of their environment. *Bioinspired computing* (or *biologically inspired computing*) is a field of study that draws its inspiration from the sophistication of the natural world in adapting to environmental changes through self-management, self-organization, and self-learning. Bioinspired computational methods produce informatics tools that are predicated on the profound conceptions of self-adaptive distributed architectures seen in natural systems. Heuristics that imitate these natural processes can be expressed as theoretical methods of constrained optimization. Such heuristics define a *representation*, in the form of a fitness function. This function describes the problem, evaluates the quality of its solution, and uses its *operators* (such as crossover, mutation, and splicing) to generate a new set of solutions.

Ashby's (1952) book *Design for a Brain* discusses the mechanisms that shape the concept of adaptive behavior, as demonstrated in living organisms, and the adaptive behavior of the brain. The author defines *adaptation* as a form of behavior that promotes stability and that maintains the essential variables, within physiological limits. Additionally, stability is expressed as a combined function of multiple fields with changing dynamics. Therefore, stability is assumed to be associated with a coordination function between various fields. As the system and feedbacks become more complex, the achievement of stability becomes more difficult, and the likelihood of instability, greater.

Biologically, an important factor in the survival of an organism is its ability to maintain its essential variables, within viable bounds. Otherwise, the organism faces the possibility of disintegration or loss of identity (dissolution, death), or both. Adaptation provides an organismic stability criterion that contributes to the maintenance of the essential variables, within viable limits; an adaptive system is a stable system (Harvey et al. 2005, the region of stability being that part of the state space where all essential variables are within physiological limits.

In the natural world the brain exhibits the properties of a highly efficient informatics tool that gathers data (sensor function), infers and stores useful patterns in the data (knowledge base, memory), uses that data for planning and anticipating future actions (decision making), executes those actions (control functions), and learns from the consequences of those actions (learning). The brain acts as an information processing machine that enables a fast and adequate response to environmental perturbations by filtering disrupting triggers.

Jacob, Lanyon-Hogg, Nadgir, and Yassin (2004) conceptualized autonomic computing as analogous to the *autonomic nervous system* (ANS), which constitutes an essential element of the peripheral nervous system. Autonomic computing resembles the ANS, insofar as the latter is composed of a hierarchy of numerous self-governing components that give monitoring and control functions the ability to transmit messages to various organs at a subconscious level. While the ANS monitors the "operating environment," it also maintains the required equilibrium by enacting the optimal changes at a subconscious level. In general, the ANS is responsible for controlling various actions related to digestion, perspiration, heart rate, respiration, salivation, pupil dilation, and other such functions. The ANS facilitates such control systems by actively monitoring, integrating, and analyzing input stimuli via sensory channels and distributing electrochemical impulses via motor channels to generate control responses to various environmental conditions.

The brain and the ANS inspire us with design principles abstracted to informatics tools, such as *artificial neural networks* (ANNs) and *autonomic computing*. But, nature motivates us with many more naturally occurring and highly efficient computational phenomena that, when modeled effectively, can improve the use of computers in solving complex optimization problems. Such phenomena exist in the form of social interactions, evolution, natural selection, biodegradation, swarm behavior, immune systems, cross-membrane molecular interactions, and so on. Software- or field programmable gate array- (FPGA-) based agents can model these natural forms of computational and collective intelligence as evolutionary algorithms, swarm intelligence (SI), artificial immune systems, artificial life, membrane computing, DNA computing, quantum computing, and so on. The abstractions derived from natural processes formalize the distributed computing paradigm, in which independent entities improve their reactive behaviors by interacting with other entities, using a well-defined protocol, and fine-tuning their control actions.

Applications

Bioinspired computing systems confront complex problems by exploiting the design principals and computational techniques encountered in natural processes. These systems possess a deep understanding of the distributed processes that exist in nature and use the concepts of theoretical biology to produce informatics tools that are robust, scalable, and flexible.

Evolvable Hardware

Evolvable hardware (EHW) is a novel field, in which practical circuits that exhibit desirable behaviors are synthesized, using evolutionary algorithms. In their rudimentary configuration, such algorithms—such as *genetic algorithms* (GAs)—influence a population of existing circuits to synthesize a set of new candidate circuits targeted to fulfill the design specifications. The quality of the circuit is evaluated, using a fitness function that ascertains if all the design requirements are met. Such techniques are useful when design specifications merely specify the desired behavior or when hardware needs to adapt dynamically and autonomously to changing operating conditions. In both cases, design specifications lack adequate information to warrant the use of conventional methods. An evolvable circuit can be synthesized, using a simulation tool (such as SPICE), a physical device (such as an FPGA), or a configurable logic.

In an evolutionary design approach it is not necessary to have a priori knowledge of the problem domain. In many cases, it may be either too complex or too expensive to acquire such information. As the complexity of the circuitsgrows, it becomes increasingly challenging to comprehend the dynamics between the various components of the circuit. EHW envisages evolutionary design techniques that facilitate development of online hardware that adapts its architecture, according to environmental changes or perturbations.

An example of this technique is *cache quality of service* (CQoS) logic (Iyer 2004), which performs dynamic partitioning of the cache among selected cores to improve the performance of the system. The automation methodology employs central processing unit (CPU) performance counter feedback in a GA to evolve an optimal cache distribution scheme. The GA chromosome contains all the building blocks for a solution to the problem at hand in a form that is suitable for the genetic operators and the fitness function.

Each CPU core node is represented by an *n*-bit binary number, called a *gene*. These *n*-bit genes define the representation, in which each bit and its position correspond to an individual cache slice slot of the total *last-level cache* (LLC). The GA-based evolutionary algorithm dynamically partitions the cache into private and shared regions, without prior knowledge of the workload profile, and allows sharing among the cores. The advantages of evolutionary methodology in partitioning the cache are that it is practical and significantly reduces the overall miss rate of the cache, at the cost of a small evaluation (training) time overhead. This methodology ensures optimal cache partitioning, with a view to increasing the *instructions per cycle* (IPC) and reducing the cache miss rate, thus ultimately enhancing overall performance. Each slot is assumed to host the same-sized cache partition. Figure 6-1 depicts a chromosome structure with an 80-bit string (20 bits per core) that represents the association of each core with a 1MB cache slot.

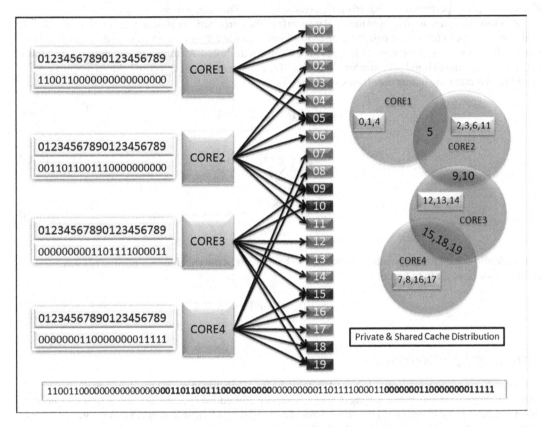

Figure 6-1. *The chromosome structure of the cache clustering, based on workload behavior, using four cores and 20 cache slots sized 1MB. For example, for core 1 cache slots, 0, 1, and 4 are private, and cache slot 5 is shared with core 2. The complete string describes the cache association of each core with a cache slot*

The cache-clustering fitness function is a weighted function capable of measuring the quality or performance of a solution—in this case, a cache-partitioning scheme that improves workload performance among CPU cores. This function is maximized by the GA system in the process of evolutionary optimization. A fitness function must include and correctly represent all or at least the most important factors that affect the performance of the system. You may need functions that represent workload-independent and workload-dependent characteristics. The workload-independent function in Equation 6-1 executes the global fair allocation of cache, without biasing the characteristic behavior of a workload. This function, where N is the number of workloads, and (ϕ_k) is the miss rate of each workload (see Equation 6-2), attempts to maximize the average performance (F_{avg}) of all workloads. The contribution of each workload k can be weighted (λ_k), based on the effect of throughput by individual workload.

$$F1_{avg} = 1.0 - \sum_{k=1}^{N} \lambda_k \cdot \phi_k, \ \sum_{k=1}^{N} \lambda_k = 1.0 \tag{6-1}$$

$$\phi_k = \frac{LLC_k^{miss}}{LLC_k^{miss} + LLC_k^{hit}} \tag{6-2}$$

The workload-dependent function (see Equation 6-3) biases the characteristic behavior of a workload and tries to improve performance, based on that characteristic. This function, where (ϕ_k) is the fraction of the miss rate of each workload over the total miss rate of the cores, and (ψ_k) is the fraction of the cache size allocated to each core over the total cache size, allows us to identify certain characteristics that may be capable of boosting the service-level objectives for a given environment. As shown in Equation 6-3, a certain bias can be generated to build pressure for allocation of cache sizes (S_k) for each core k that is proportional to the LLC miss rate ratio of that core (see Equation 6-4).

$$F2_{avg} = 1.0 - \sum_{k=1}^{N} \lambda_k \cdot abs\left(\frac{\varphi_k}{\psi_k} - 1.0\right) \tag{6-3}$$

$$\varphi_k = \frac{\phi_k}{\sum_{j=1}^{N} \phi_j} \tag{6-4a}$$

$$\psi_k = \frac{S_k}{\sum_{j=1}^{N} S_j} \tag{6-4b}$$

Finally, the overall fitness (see Equation 6-5) can be defined as the weighted proportion of each individual fitness, as given in Equations 6-1 and 6-3:

$$F_{avg} = \alpha \cdot F1_{avg} + (1-\alpha) \cdot F2_{avg}. \tag{6-5}$$

Bioinspired Networking

Communication and network technologies have gained a lot of traction in recent years, owing to advancements in *cloud-based networking* (CBN), networked embedded systems, *wireless sensor networks* (WSNs), the *Internet of Things* (IOT), *software-defined networking* (SDN), and so on. Furthermore, enterprise-class networking solutions are being developed to deliver high resiliency, high availability, and high reliability through capacity planning, traffic engineering, throughput management, and overlaying of multitenant applications, using the existing Internet infrastructure. As the network scales, the search space for the optimal route increases dramatically. The number of routing tables and the amount of traffic overhead overwhelm network bandwidth. Ideally, we would like to have efficient, self-organizing networks with low route-finding latencies (or overhead) and high probabilities of successful transmission.

Nevertheless, significant challenges prevent us from realizing the practical implementation of new networking paradigms. In addition to the need for scalability, availability, and survivability, these challenges arise from resource constraints, absence of centralized architecture, and the dynamic nature of networking. However, similar phenomena are also found in natural processes that are successfully dealt with through adaptation in biological systems. Biological communication paradigms are evolutionary; resilient to failure; adaptive to environmental conditions; and collaborative, on the basis of a simple sets of rules.

Bioinspired networks self-organize by apprehending the mutual interactions of components that produce complex patterns. These interactions facilitate behavioral responses through information transfer between interacting components as well as through the interaction of components with the environment.

Gianni, Ducatelle, and Gambardella (2005) presented the AntHocNet design for stigmergy-driven shortest-path discovery, based on a self-organizing behavior exemplified in ant colonies. Similar routing algorithms exist for packet-switched networks, such as AntNet (Di Caro and Dorigo 1998), and circuit-switched networks, such as artificial bee colony (ABC) (Schoonderwoerd et al. 1997). The AntHocNet algorithm inserts limited routing information in "Hello" messages so that the information regarding existing paths can propagate throughout the network, using node-to-node information exchange. This process is equivalent to collective ant learning behavior, in which ants swarm together to gather and maintain updated information. Artificial ants instigate the stigmergic communication process by acting as autonomous agents that update and follow the pheromone table (path). Similar to routing ants, the pheromone table explores the high-probability paths that can be used for routing data packets. Additionally, ants put their limited resources toward optimizing global behavior to identify the food source in a cost-effective manner. This behavior inspires resource-efficient networking techniques.

Given their dynamic nature and lack of infrastructure, networks are also prone to failure and delay. Therefore, networks should have capability to self-organize and self-heal in real time. Dynamic networks (especially mobile ad hoc networks) may use the bioequivalent of epidemic models both to describe and to adapt information dissemination. Papadopouli and Schulzrinne (2000) described a simple stochastic epidemic model that estimates the delay until data diffuse to all mobile devices. Carreras et al. (2006) proposed an *epidemic spreading mechanism* for efficient information dissemination in clustered networks and for opportunistic routing in delay-tolerant networks. The authors used *eigenvector centrality* (EVC) as an objective fitness measure of the ability of nodes to spread an epidemic (information) within the network. The resulting topology built using EVC defines the regions in which the epidemic spreads extremely fast. Infection fronts (information) spread toward highly connected neighborhoods (EVC), because spreading is fastest there.

Resource-constrained sensors, such as wireless sensors, are limited in energy, bandwidth, storage, and processing capabilities. Large numbers of such sensors create a sensor management problem. At the network layer the solution entails setting up an energy-efficient route that transmits the nonredundant data from the source to the sink to maximize the battery's and sensors' lives. This is done while adapting to changing connectivity resulting from the failure of some nodes and the powering up of new nodes. Khanna, Liu, and Chen (2009) demonstrated that the GA-based approach optimizes the sensor network to maximize energy usage as well as battery conservation and route optimization. Each sensor is encoded with a gene that identifies it and any other specific information it may contain. This information may be related to sensor objectivity, next hop, cluster domain, and so on. The GA adaptation process evolves optimal cluster boundaries, in terms of addition, deletion, or modified sensor objectives. The process also discovers optimal routes from cluster heads to the sink.

Datacenter Optimization

The size and complexity of modern distributed datacenter systems are expanding every day. The volume of information that must be processed in real time has been growing geometrically over the past few years, requiring peak processing capabilities to rise in concert. Despite the superior performance per watt that newer platforms deliver, handling peak loads continues to call for higher power delivery and heat dissipation capacities per cubic meter in enterprise information technology (IT) and datacenter facilities, with 63 percent of the total cost of ownership going toward powering, cooling, and electricity delivery infrastructure. In contrast to the traditional focus on delivering the highest throughput or lowest response time, unconstrained by power, these realities have made it a more compelling proposition to minimize the amount of energy consumed, relative to computational work performed, while meeting responsiveness targets. In particular, dynamically conserving power when some machines do not need to be in full use translates directly into cost savings and creates greater allowance for other, more power-constrained servers.

One way to optimize power in a datacenter is to regulate or redistribute the load of a rack-level server unit autonomously through management of job admission, distribution, and continuous balancing. Barbagallo et al. (2010) put forward self-organizing architectures for dynamic workload distribution, using a decentralized approach built on top of *SelfLet architecture*. SelfLet architecture (Devescovi et al. 2007) is a bioinspired system that possesses the capability to change and adapt its internal behavior dynamically, according to variations in the environment. SelfLet uses autonomic reasoning to facilitate self-management capabilities. SelfLet itself represents a service framework built using a self-sufficient piece of code that interacts with a group of other SelfLet individuals and that cooperates through high-level functions. Each SelfLet either offers or consumes a service and interacts via a communication framework. The authors used self-organization algorithms based on the principles of collective decision making in animal colonies. Self-organizing in these colonies is characterized by scouting, evaluating, deliberating, and decision-making functions. Self-organization in a datacenter can be summarized using similar entities, as follows:

- *Colony*: A collection of *virtual machines* (VMs) residing on the same server.

- *Scout*: Explores multiple physical servers and compares them with the original one. A scout can be characterized by its current location, lifetime, and information stored related to each server class that it examined.

- *Server manager*: Communicates with the scouts and makes decisions related to the movements of VMs.

Based on the collective data from multiple scouts, a decision is made either to permit or to inhibit migration. As in biological systems, the decision whether to migrate is not deterministic and follows a probability distribution. This avoids a reactive migration, which could result in instability and oscillatory behavior. Furthermore, like biological systems, individual servers may propagate an inhibitor flag to prevent migration in the middle of critical operations.

Li and Parashar (2003) developed *AutoMate architecture* to investigate bioinspired conceptual models and implementation designs for developing and executing self-managing (i.e., configuring, healing, optimizing, and protecting) grid applications, while dealing with the challenges of complexity, dynamism, and heterogeneity. AutoMate architecture is built on three operative principles:

- Separating policies from the mechanisms related to algorithms, communication protocols, and so on that drive those policies

- Applying context-, constraint-, and aspect-based composition techniques to applications to synthesize dynamic requirements for compute resources, performance guarantees, and QoS

- Developing proactive- and reactive-component management to optimize resource utilization and application performance in dynamic environments

Bioinspired Computing Algorithms

Bioinspired computing methods are metaheuristics that imitate methods for solving optimization problems in natural processes. These heuristics deliver a robust and decentralized compute engine that can perform in noisy ecosystems and yet deliver a desired behavior, while operating within time, energy, and power constraints. Such computing methods have been used in almost all areas of optimization, knowledge discovery, and big data analytics, including computer networks, image processing, WSNs, security, control systems, biomedical systems, and robotics. The following sections give a brief overview of bioinspired optimization algorithms that are computationally efficient alternatives to the traditional deterministic approach—an approach that does not scale well and that requires massive computational effort. Designing bioinspired algorithms involves identifying a suitable representation of the problem, developing a fitness function to evaluate the quality of solution, and defining operators to produce a set of new solutions. Broadly, bioinspired algorithms can be divided into three major classes: *evolutionary* algorithms, *swarm-based* algorithms, and *ecological* algorithms. These classes are further divided into subclasses, based on their inspiration from specific cases of naturally occurring processes involving ants, fireflies, bacteria, bees, birds, and so on.

Swarm Intelligence

Swarm intelligence (SI) is a type of artificial intelligence based on the collective behavior of decentralized, self-organized systems. The term was introduced by Beni and Wang (1989), in the context of cellular robotic systems. SI typically comprises a collection of unsophisticated agents, called *boids*, that interact locally with other agents as well as with the environment, using extremely elementary rules. No centralized control infrastructure governs an individual agent's behavior or interactions. Instead, local and random interaction between participating agents leads to an intelligent global behavior unattributable to individual agents. In other words, collective interaction at peer level leads to a sophisticated phenomenon globally. Natural examples of SI include ant colonies, bird flocking, animal herding, bacterial growth, and fish schooling. SI-inspired systems include positive feedback, negative feedback, amplification of fluctuations, and multiple interactions between multiagents.

Autonomic computing and SI are closely related. For example, through the tuning of system parameters, the self-configuration aspect can be achieved autonomically rather than manually. In the natural world the local process indicators can change, be reinforced, or reach a threshold, reflecting the actual dynamic swarm situation. Clearly, system performance can be optimized through interaction between multiple local agents. Also, system robustness can be guaranteed through this kind of parallel multiagent interaction. Finally, security and load balancing can be fulfilled with careful parameter and rule design. The appropriate tradeoff between the purely reactive behavior promoted by traditional stigmergy and the purely cognitive behavior promoted by artificial intelligence approaches has to be determined. Stigmergy is a mechanism occurring in many social animal societies that contrives to solve complex problems using a decentralized approach in a self-organized system. This system rewards positive feedback, while penalizing the negative. As a result, the system enables a complex, intelligent infrastructure that needs no planning, control, or complex interactions between the agents. The social aspects support efficient collaboration between elementary agents, which lack memory, intelligence, and even awareness of each other.

Ant Colony Optimization Algorithm

In the natural world, ants wander randomly until they find a path that leads to food. This behavior has inspired a variant of SI called the *ant colony optimization* (ACO) algorithm. In the ACO scenario (Dorigo, Di Caro, and Gambardella 1999) ants communicate with other ants to exchange status information regarding food sources through changes in the environmental medium by depositing pheromones. The status information is exchanged within a local scope, and the context is transferred only to ants at the location of pheromone deposition. After finding food, these ants return to the colony, while laying down pheromones for other ants to follow. Upon discovering the food trail, the other ants abandon their random food search and follow the pheromone trail, thereby reinforcing the original path.

Over time, however, the pheromone trail tends to evaporate and lose its attractive property. If the round-trip time between the ant colony and the food source is great, the pheromone can evaporate faster than it can be reinforced. In contrast, a short pheromone trail has a greater pheromone density and can be reinforced faster than it evaporates. The pheromone evaporation process is analogous to avoiding convergence to a local optimal; the process avoids strengthening the nonoptimal solution, while aiding the unconstrained exploration of the solution space. In general, variation in the pheromone quantity on the edge allows for the choice of a specific edge. A stable system is a network of strong edges that adapt to active variations and environmental changes. Because of dynamic variations in the interactive environment, certain edges are reinforced through positive feedback, whereas others are weakened because of negative feedback. A slight variation in the edges can result in an alternate route that remains valid until other edges exhibit stronger traits. For instance, if the pheromone trail to a single food source is reinforced, it will take much longer to discover alternate sources that may be optimally suited for the colony, in terms of distance or abundance. ACO attempts to find a path to the solution that is likely to be followed by other agents, thereby building positive feedback that eventually leads to a single path to the solution.

ACO methodologies differ from evolutionary algorithms in one main regard. In evolutionary algorithms, such as GA, all knowledge about the problem is contained in the current population, whereas in ACO algorithms a memory of past performance is maintained in the form of pheromone trails Dorigo, Di Caro, and Gambardella (1999) represented ants as playing the role of environmental signals, and the pheromone update rule, the role of the automaton learning rule. In ACO the environmental signals/ants are stochastically biased, by means of their probabilistic transition rule, to direct the learning process toward the most interesting regions of the search space. That is, the whole environment has a key, active role in the learning of good state-action pairs. The basic ACO rule can be defined by the following process (Engelbrecht 2006; Wang et al. 2007):

1. Create *nr* global ants; each ant visits each food source exactly once.

2. Evaluate the fitness of each food source; a distant food source has a lesser probability of being chosen.

3. Update the ants' pheromone and the age of weak regions.

4. Move local ants to better regions, based on the pheromone intensity, to improve their fitness; otherwise, choose new random search directions.

5. Update the ants' pheromone to all the regions they traversed.

6. After each iteration, evaporate the ants' pheromone.

Ants are attracted to the regions, based on the intensity of the pheromone at time *t*. As the pheromone evaporates, that region becomes less attractive to the ant and is finally abandoned. The probability of an ant *k* transitioning from region *i* to region *j* at time *t* is

$$P_k(i,j,t) = \frac{\tau_{i,j}(t)^\alpha \cdot d_{i,j}(t)^\beta}{\sum\limits_{n \in N_i^k} \tau_{i,n}(t)^\alpha \cdot d_{i,n}(t)^\beta}, \text{ if } j \in N_i^k, \tag{6-6}$$

where

$\tau_{i,j}(t)$ = pheromone trail region, represented by edges *i* and *j* at time *t*

$d_{i,j}(t)$ = distance between source (*i*) and destination (*j*) locations

N_i^k = feasible neighborhood of ant *k* at source *i*

α = relative significance of the pheromone trail

β = relative significance of the distance between source and destination

The positive parameters α and β define the relationship between pheromone and heuristic information. Therefore, the probability of a trail that is chosen by ant *k* is a function of distance and the density of the pheromone that already exists on that trail at time *t*. The significance of intensity and distance to the cost function is determined by α and β, respectively. Thus, the better the region is, the more attraction it has to the successive ants. The pheromone concentration in the region is updated as a function of constant evaporation (*p*) and new deposits ($\Delta \tau_k$) by the ants attracted to this region, such that

$$\tau_{i,j}(t+1) = p \cdot \tau_{i,j}(t) + \sum_{k=1}^{m} \Delta\tau_{k,i,j}(t) \tag{6-7}$$

$$if \ (i,j) \in S_k : \Delta\tau_{k,i,j} = \frac{1}{L_{k,i,j}}, \tag{6-8}$$

where

p = evaporation constant, whose value can be set between 0 and 1 and represents the rate at which the pheromone evaporates

$L_{k,i,j}$ = length of the tour by ant k, with shorter tours resulting in higher pheromone density

$\Delta\tau_{k,i,j}$ = amount of pheromone deposited by ant k in region (i, j).

The probability of local ants' selecting a region is proportional to its pheromone trail. The pheromone is affected by the evaporation rate, ant age, and growth of fitness. Thus, this pheromone-based selection mechanism is capable of promoting the solution candidate update, which is suitable for handling the changing environments in optimization.

ACO techniques can be used for knowledge discovery corresponding to learning the functional relationship between variables, changes in data pattern, and data classification. The social behavior of the ants suggests the notion of formulating an infrastructure that fosters the concept of self-organization, using natural interactions and local information to solve complex computational problems.

Dorigo, Di Caro, and Gambardella (1999) described a solution to the Traveling Salesman Problem (TSP), in which m artificial ants concurrently build a tour of the TSP. Initially, k ants are placed on randomly selected cities. At each step the kth ant applies a probabilistic action choice rule to resolve which city to visit next. The probability that an ant chooses to travel from city i to city j ($J \in N_i^k$) is given in Equation 6-6, where N_i^k defines a potential neighborhood of k cities when the ant is in city j. If $\alpha = 0$, the closest cities are more likely to be selected; if $\beta = 0$, then only pheromone amplification is used, without any heuristic bias. Each ant k retains a memory area, where it generates the tour, computes the length of the tour, and retraces the path to deposit the pheromone to the arcs of the tour. Pheromone trails are updated after all ants have constructed their tour. This is done by decreasing the pheromone by a constant factor on all arcs (evaporation) and then successively adding the pheromone to the arcs crossed by ants in their tours. Pheromone evaporation and updating are implemented in Equation 6-7. Arcs that are part of a short route and are visited by many ants receive more pheromone and are therefore more likely to be chosen by ants in future iterations of the algorithm.

Particle Swarm Optimization

Particle swarm optimization (PSO) is a stochastic computational technique that iteratively optimizes the candidate solution of a problem until it attains the target fitness (or quality) (Kennedy and Eberhart 1995). This technique is biologically inspired by the social behavior of bird flocking and fish schooling. Owing to its simplicity and computational efficiency, PSO has been successfully applied to many engineering research and optimization applications. *Particle* in PSO denotes an individual member of a population that searches for optimal behavior when subjected to velocity and acceleration in a large search space. Each particle in the swarm explores the coordinates of the solution space and records the following four vectors, relative to the best solutions (fitness) achieved in that process:

- Particle's current coordinates

- Particle's velocity, with respect to magnitude and direction

- Coordinates (position) associated with the particle's local best solution achieved up to that point (*pbest*)

- Coordinates (position) associated with the particle neighborhood's best solution achieved up to that point (*gbest*)

113

PSO can search a large solution space, while making no assumptions regarding the problem being optimized. PSO looks for an optimal solution by moving the particle in the solution space, relative to its current position, at a certain velocity and guided by a fitness function: a particle's movement is controlled by changing its velocity (accelerating), guided by its current best position (pbest) and the best position found in its neighborhood (gbest)up to that point. The gbest solution is iteratively updated as better positions are found. The combined (collective) exploration of all the particles moves the swarm toward the best solution. In their quest for the global optimum, particles in the swarm realign to cluster around the suboptimal. Once a particle is close to the global optimum, other particles are attracted to it, with a high probability of finding the best solution. In each iteration k, particle i updates its position and velocity, according to the following equations:

$$v_i^{k+1} = x_i^{k+1} - x_i^k \tag{6-9}$$

$$x_i^{k+1} = x_i^k + v_i^k + c_1 r_1 (pbest_i^k - x_i^k) + c_2 r_2 (gbest_i^k - x_i^k) \tag{6-10}$$

$$v_i^{k+1} = v_i^k + c_1 r_1 (pbest_i^k - x_i^k) + c_2 r_2 (gbest_i^k - x_i^k), \tag{6-11}$$

where

x_i^k = particle i position for the kth iteration

v_i^k = particle i velocity for the kth iteration

c_1, c_2 = weighting coefficients

r_1, r_2 = random numbers between 0 and 1

The PSO algorithm is composed of the following steps for iteration k:

1. Initialize the swarm by allocating a random position x_i^0 to each particle i of the swarm bounded by the problem space.

2. Evaluate the fitness of each particle i, relative to its current position x_i^k.

3. Compare the particle i fitness with its $pbest_i^{k-1}$; if the current fitness is greater than the pbest, set the pbest value ($pbest_i^k$) to the current fitness value.

4. Select the particle j with the best fitness ($pbest_j^k$); mark this fitness $gbest_i^k$.

5. Evaluate the new position x_i^{k+1} of particle (i), using Equations 6-10.

6. Evaluate the new velocity v_i^{k+1} of particle (i), using Equations 6-11.

The process repeats until the stopping criteria are met, or the best solution is found. Unlike evolutionary algorithms, such as GA, particles improve the PSO algorithm's fitness, using the current global optimum, without evolutionary operators.

Because of its distributed nature and ability to operate under noisy conditions, PSO can prove to be a useful technique for workload balancing, with respect to power consumption, heat generation, and QoS requirements in cloud computing. The workload has to be distributed in such a manner that power consumption is minimized, thermal hot spots are eliminated, and performance targets are fulfilled. Dynamic placement of the workload in a system (or cluster of compute machines) triggers dynamic variations in the availability of compute, memory, network, input/output (I/O), and storage resources. Optimal system operation results in complex workload distribution choices, owing to the many degrees of freedom for allocating the load in a dynamically varying resource pool. The PSO solution continuously searches for the dynamically shifting optimum to identify the placement target of the new or upcoming load.

Yassa et al. (2013) proposed *DVFS multiobjective discrete particle swarm optimization* (DVFS-MODPSO) for workload scheduling in a distributed environment. DVFS-MODPSO implements the multiobjective optimization of several conflicting goals—minimizing execution time, execution cost, and energy consumption—and produces a set of nondominated solutions to offer flexibility in choosing a schedule that meets the QoS targets. DVFS-MODPSO defines a triplet $<T_i, P_j, V_k>$ that characterizes the position of a particle and that represents a reasonable solution to the workload scheduling problem. Each triplet allocates the task T_i to a processor P_j with a voltage scaling V_k. The results demonstrate that DVFS-MODPSO generates a set of Pareto optimal solutions for execution time, execution cost, and power consumption.

Solving a global optimization problem using a traditional approach involves precise function description and gradient evaluation, which may be expensive, time-consuming, hard to achieve, or impossible. Compounding the problem, many complex optimization problems exhibit a noisy behavior that renders methods such as implicit filtering and evolutionary gradient search almost ineffective. In contrast, PSO algorithms operate in a stable and efficient manner, even in the presence of noise. In many cases, noise can be beneficial, because it helps avoid local minimum solutions and converge faster to the globally optimal solution. Owing to their simplicity, PSO algorithms have also been proposed as an alternative to gradient-based techniques for detecting Pareto optimal solutions to multiobjective optimization problems.

Artificial Bee Colony Algorithm

The *artificial bee colony* (ABC) algorithm is a swarm-based metaheuristic inspired by the foraging behavior of the honeybee that was proposed by Karaboga, Dervis, and Basturk (2007). The model consists of three groups of honey bees that facilitate an optimal search for food sources. *Employed bees* attach themselves to a specific food source and share the information regarding its profitability through waggle dancing to recruit new bees. An *onlooker bee* is an unemployed bee that evaluates the quality of the food source by observing the waggle dances on the floor and deploys itself toward the most profitable food source. A *scout bee* searches for new food sources randomly and presents information associated with their quality through a waggle dance. The employed bee whose food source has been exhausted transforms itself into a scout bee and searches for new food sources. The principal components of the ABC algorithm are as follows:

- *Food sources*: A food source represents the candidate solution to an optimization problem. To select an optimal food source, an employed bee evaluates the overall quality of a food source, as measured by its proximity to the hive, the quantity and quality of the food (nectar), and the level of difficulty in extracting the food.

- *Employed bees*: Employed bees are employed at a specific food source, which they exploit to gather nectar. The bees collect information related to the distance, direction, and quality of the food source and share it with other bees, waiting on the dance floor. An employed bee attempts to improve its solution (food source) by reevaluating the coordinates in the neighborhood of its memorized coordinates, using multiple trials.

- *Unemployed bees*: Scout bees and onlooker bees are both in this category. They evaluate the profitability of potential food sources, either through random scouting or through information shared by employed bees. This evaluation helps convert an unemployed bee to an employed bee by facilitating selection of the most profitable food source.

- *Measure of quality (fitness)*: The quality of the food source—characterized by its proximity to the hive, the quantity and quality of its nectar, and the relative difficulty of extracting the nectar—can be summarized, using a single quantity: *fitness*.

- *Knowledge exchange*: Knowledge exchange is the critical element of the ABC algorithm. Knowledge is shared within the staging area, called the dance area; here, bees exchange information related to the fitness and coordinates (angle, distance) of the food source through the waggle dance.

The ABC algorithm can be used as a technique for load balancing in a datacenter. Load balancing attempts to optimize resource utilizationresponse time, throughput, and thermal hot spots. Load balancing can be implemented by reallocating existing tasks or allocating new tasks to an existing compute node. These compute nodes act as potential candidates for hosting the workload, which, when loaded effectively, can improve the efficiency of the datacenter. Each compute node advertises its prevailing characteristics (or fingerprint) related to utilization, operational phase, time spent in that phase, cache behavior, temperature, and power consumption. The fitness function defines a compute node's ability to host new work at a future time. For example, a candidate node that can compensate for the forecasted thermal variance in its neighborhood will have a higher fitness, compared with other nodes with similar characteristics but existing in a fully balanced cluster. Each server consists of management microcontrollers that act as idle, employed, onlooker, or scout bees. Scout bees are appointed in a random manner, whereas employed and onlooker bees follow the swarm behavior that is influenced by the fitness outcome. While an employed bee (management node) records the benefits of hosting the load on the existing node, an onlooker bee (waiting in a work queue), in its effort to become employed, analyzes the collective information delivered through scout and employed bees. Once the compute target is selected, the onlooker bee attempts to host the queued work on that target. The technique of load balancing using ABC deploys the following agents:

- *Scout bee*: Acts as a random agent that constitutes approximately 2 percent of the total compute nodes in a datacenter. These agents execute the scout function, using the management agent corresponding to the compute node tagged as scout bee. Scout agents collect neighborhood-specific information related to hot spots, average power consumption, and availability of compute resources.

- *Employed bee*: Acts as an agent that assists in loading and collecting the operational statistics of the load that is executing on the compute node tagged as employed bee. These statistics include usage, memory bandwidth, noisy behavior of the cache, and I/O contention.

- *Onlooker bee*: Acts as an agent of the potential workload waiting in the queue. Each agent identifies the best target to host this workload.

Two principal factors that attract bees to a specific node or neighborhood, in this example, are the availability of thermal variance and compute resources. As the thermal variance or compute resource diminishes, that node becomes less attractive and is eventually abandoned. While a node remains attractive, an employed bee repeatedly visits that location and encourages onlooker bees to host work in its neighborhood. Scout bees identify additional targets or neighborhoods with high fitness that can be exploited by unemployed bees.

The main steps of the ABC algorithm are generalized as follows:

1. Random food sources are allocated to each employed bee. Repeat:

   a. Each employed bee visits the food source, according to the information stored in the bee's memory. The bee evaluates the quantity and quality of the food (nectar) and performs the waggle dance in the hive.

   b. Each onlooker bee observes the waggle dance of the employed bees, and some of them select the food source, based on the information communicated through the dance.

   c. Once the food source is abandoned, new sources are identified by the scout bees.

   d. The new food source is identified by the scout bees and attracts the swarm, depending on the quality of the nectar.

   e. Requirements are met.

2. Repeat.

Bacterial Foraging Optimization Algorithm

The *bacterial foraging optimization* (BFO) algorithm (Passino 2002) models the microbiological phenomenon of organized behavior in a bacterial colony. The BFO algorithm for modeling the social foraging behavior of *Escherichia coli* (*E. coli*) can be used to solve real-world numeric optimization problems. BFO is primarily composed of three processes: chemotaxis, reproduction, and elimination–dispersal.

Chemotaxis is defined as cell movement in response to a chemical stimulus. This method is used by many single- and multicellular organisms to discover their food. Bacterial chemotaxis represents the signal transduction system, which stimulates the behavior of bacterial movement. *Reproduction* characterizes natural selection, which favors the best-adapted bacteria with a higher likelihood of survival than the less-adapted bacteria. Natural selection allows the selected population in each generation to transfer the genetic material to successive generations. *Elimination-dispersal* promotes the low probability of the elimination and dispersal of randomly selected parts of the bacterial population. This fosters diversity in the bacterial population and prevents the global optimal solution from being trapped in a local minimum.

E. coli alternates between two modes of movement, called *swim* and *tumble*, throughout its entire life. *Swimming* action allows the bacterium to move in the current direction of increasing nutrient gradient; *tumble* action allows change in orientation when the nutrient gradient is no longer attractive. The alternating mode of bacterial movement enables a bacterium to locate the position of the optimal nutrient source. After a certain number of complete swims, the bacterial population undergoes reproduction and elimination, according to the fitness criteria. Each bacterium position has an associated cost and represents a possible solution. BFO simulation keeps track of the cost of current and previous positions to estimate the quality of gradient improvement or worsening. In each generation the health of the bacterium factors into its likelihood of being retained for reproduction (making replicas) or elimination.

If θ^i represents the position of the *i*th bacteria, the successive movement of the bacterium is

$$\theta^i(j+1,k,l) = \theta^i(j,k,l) + v^i(j) \cdot \phi^i(j), \qquad (6\text{-}12)$$

where

$\theta^i(j,k,l)$ = position of the *i*th bacterium in the *j*th chemotactic, *k*th reproductive, and *l*th elimination–dispersal step

$v^i(j)$ = step size in a random direction during the *tumble*

$\phi^i(j)$ = random direction of movement after the tumble

For the given position of the *i*th bacterium, $\theta^i(j,k,l)$, $J^i(j,k,l)$ represents the fitness of the bacterium at that location. If the fitness of *i*th bacterium at location $\theta^i(j+1,k,l)$ is better than that at $\theta^i(j,k,l)$, such that $J^i(j+1,k,l)$ is better than $J^i(j,k,l)$, then $v^i(j+1) = v^i(j)$, and $\phi^i(j+1) = \phi^i(j)$. If the reverse is true, then $v^i(j+1)$ takes a different step, in a random direction.

Munoz, Lopez, and Caicedo (2007) proposed a BFO algorithm for searching the best actuators in each sample time to obtain a uniform temperature over the temperature grid platform. The idea is to compensate for the cold spots by allocating or deallocating additional resources. Similar techniques can be applied to load balancing in a cluster of compute servers, as in a datacenter. Server load balancing techniques employ bacterial searches to locate the regions of nonuniform thermal behavior (high temperature variance). The fitness of the newly identified location can be evaluated by modeling the thermal variance in the temperature grid resulting from adding or subtracting quantities of unit load.

Artificial Immune System

The *artificial immune system* (AIS) is a bioinspired optimization algorithm (Dasgupta 1999) based on the principles of the vertebrate immune system. The algorithm emulates several characteristics of the human immune system: that it is highly distributed, that it is parallel, and that it uses adaptive learning and memory to solve problems related to pattern recognition and classification. The AIS algorithm learns to categorize relevant patterns through a pattern detector that associates previously -seen patterns with existing ones. The algorithm formulates a different response mechanism to deal with the effects of each pattern.

The adaptive immune system in the human body uses many agents that perform diverse functions at different locations, primarily employing negative selection and clonal selection mechanisms. *Negative selection mechanisms* exploit the immune system's ability to detect unknown antigens, while not reacting to self. *Clonal selection mechanisms* promote the proliferation of cells that possess the ability to recognize an antigen over those that do not. Therefore, self-reacting cells are eliminated, and mature cells are allowed to proliferate. The learning mechanism involves bolstering by the cloning process of those lymphocytes within a given population that contribute to the identification of an antigen. New cells are copies (*clones*) of their parents, but cloning is subject to a high rate of mutation (*somatic hypermutation*). This mutation process mimics the mechanism that reallocates the resources needed for recognition of new antigens versus previously identified antigens. The reinforced learning mechanism rebalances the population of diverse lymphocytes to promote optimal detection and mediation of pathogens.

The properties of the immune system have the following attributes (Castro, Nunes, and Von Zuben 1999):

- *Exclusivity*: The immune system is exclusive to each individual, with its own vulnerabilities and capabilities.

- *Recognition of foreigners*: The toxic elements or molecules that are foreign to the individual's body are identified, categorized, and labeled for future detection.

- *Anomaly detection*: The immune system learns to classify the unidentified foreign element as a pathogen and attempts a remedial action.

- *Distributed detection*: The cells are distributed throughout the body and are not subject to centralized control.

- *Imperfect detection* (*noise tolerance*): Pathogens are first classified as unidentified foreign elements, and their absolute recognition is not essential.

- *Reinforcement learning and memory*: The immune system continuously learns the structure of the pathogen to formulate an increasingly effective response.

Similar to that of the GA, AIS architecture comprises the following four steps (Aickelin, Dasgupta, and Gu 2014):

1. *Encoding*: Encoding is binary, numeric, or nominal representation of antigens or antibodies. An *antigen* represents the solution to a problem domain that needs to be tested for an intrusion. Antibodies represent previously identified patterns that can be used later.

2. *Similarity measure*: A similarity measure quantifies the *affinity* between an antigen and its candidate antibodies. The matching algorithm measures the extent of *agreement*, *disagreement*, or *correlation* between a candidate antibody and its target antigen. Candidates with strong agreement or disagreement may be selected for further processing (cloning or mutation).

3. *Selection*: The selection process follows an iterative procedure, in which the concentration of antibodies is regulated by cloning or removal at each step, depending on the antibody–antigen affinity measure. Upon adding a new antibody, the iterative process changes the concentration of that antibody, continuing until the AIS achieves stability. AIS iteration can be represented by the following equation (Farmer, Packard, and Perelson 1986):

$$\dot{x}_i = k_1 \left(\sum_{j=1}^{n} m_{ji} x_i y_j - k_2 x_i \right),$$ (6-13)

where

n = number of antigens

x_i = concentration of antibody i

y_j = concentration of antigen j

m_{ji} = affinity function representing the correlation between antibody i and antigen j

k_1 = rate of antibody production

k_2 = death rate

Equation 6-13 represents the iterative change in the antibody concentration, contingent on the net outcome of cloning due to antigen recognition and death in the absence of correlation.

4. *Mutation*: Antigen–antibody interaction, coupled with somatichypermutation, forms the basis of an AIS. Mutation introduces diversity in the population and facilitates effective response to antigens.

AIS uses an adaptive population of antibodies to facilitate intelligent behavior by synthesizing diverse subset solutions for a given problem domain. AIS has been applied in areas related to network security and anomaly detection.

Distributed Management in Datacenters

Datacenters are complex environments that deal with key challenges related to power delivery, energy consumption, heat management, security, storage performance, service assurance, and dynamic resource allocation. These challenges relate to providing effective coordination to improve the stability and efficiency of datacenters. The fluctuating demands and diverse workload characteristics of a large datacenter make complex the tasks of upholding workload performance, cooling efficiency, and energy targets (discussed in the following sections). In such large clusters of systems, multiple objectives compete to accomplish service-level goals by avoiding actuator overlapping and exhausting a complex combination of constraints, timing granularity, type of approach, and sequence of controls. However, the combinatorial solution space can be extremely large and may not converge to a global optimal in a bounded time. Therefore, a centralized datacenter management system may not scale well in constrained time and hence may not deliver an optimal management solution.

SI has emerged as a promising field that can be exploited to construct a distributed management methodology leading to scalable solutions without centralized control. The following sections present a control system that identifies suitable targets for workload placement, with these fundamental control elements:

- *Controlled process*: The controlled process implements the feedback control loop, which constrains the temperature and power of compute clusters, such as server racks, for a given policy. An optimal process operates within policy constraints and provisions sufficient energy to operate a workload at highest performance efficiency and lowest cooling.

- *Fitness function*: The fitness function estimates the most favorable placement of the workload, based on the existing knowledge base's expected demand and availability of resources.

- *Knowledge base*: The knowledge base acts as a finite database made up of survey data conducted by the sensor agents. This knowledge assists in identifying the most probable placement of the workload. As the dynamics of the system changes, newer data replace the old data, according to a custom data retention policy. The knowledge database increases the retention of data likely to boost the fitness of the solution and deprecates the data less likely to improve the existing solution.

- *Control parameters*: Control parameters define the optimal decision boundaries that result in placement of the workload on the selected compute node.

- *Swarm agents*: Swarm agents participate in the system optimization process by executing specific roles in a decentralized and self-organized system. These agents coordinate with each other and with the environment, ultimately leading to the emergence of intelligent global behavior.

Workload Characterization

Because workloads undergo phases of execution, phase boundaries are fundamental attributes for predicting workload behavior for scheduling or migration between clusters of servers. Additionally, phase identification enables reuse of past configurations of recurring phases to improve performance. These configurations enforce a policy for scheduling new workloads, migrating existing workloads, and eliminating thermal load imbalances between compute nodes or clusters of compute nodes.

Thermal Optimization

Given the highly dynamic environment in a datacenter, hot spots are created as a result of temporal events (such as increased workload on a set of servers) or spatial events (such as inefficiency of the computer room air-conditioning [CRAC]) units in delivering the requisite cooling to a particular region in the datacenter). Figure 6-2 depicts a thermal snapshot of a datacenter with hot and cold spots. Hot spots may trigger overcooling, degrading the *power usage effectiveness* (PUE) of the datacenter operations. Traditional cooling control solutions operate using reactive schemes, which depend on the instantaneous temperatures of racks or blades. These schemes have a fundamental disadvantage, inasmuch as the corrective action is completed long after the component's thermal or performance threshold has been crossed. In a datacenter with a large number of nodes, it is almost impossible to perform optimal workload balance in real time using a reactive approach without causing hysteresis. In the presence of dynamic variations in a cluster of configurable hardware and software, the ability to initiate a timely response to reduce temperature variance (hot spots) between clusters is essential.

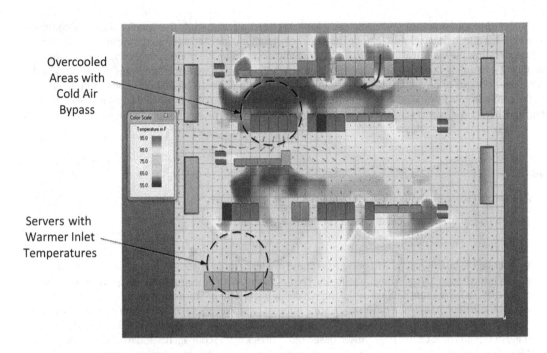

Overcooled Areas with Cold Air Bypass

Servers with Warmer Inlet Temperatures

Figure 6-2. Thermal snapshot of a datacenter

Load Balancing

Load balancing is a method for distributing workload among a cluster of compute nodes in a manner that allows fulfillment of a given policy. Load balancing optimizes resource usage, maximizes throughput, and minimizes response time. Load balancing is realized through active load migration between compute nodes, which also governs the hot-spot mitigation scheme, using workload tradeoffs and power distribution. Hot spots can be attributed to uneven load distributions leading to imbalanced compute utilization. Hot spots result in inefficient cooling and higher datacenter operating costs. In a swarm-based optimization scheme thermal variance can be equated with foraging for a source of nutrients. Regions of high thermal variance act as a source (or target) of load migration, attracting increased surveillance from the swarm agents.

Algorithm Model

The *algorithm model* consists of a server manager, a scout agent, worker agents, free agents, and a load controller. The *server manager* administers each server node and presents programming interfaces for interpreting the sensor data and synthesizing the useful metrics. The server manager exerts control at multiple levels of timing granularity, which can eventually result in heterogeneous sampling requirements specific to each one of those elements. For instance, the server manager records the performance data and processes them to synthesize the workload phase distribution by exercising built-in sensors. In a hierarchical scheme the server manager manages a cluster of compute resources and identifies the compute resource capable of hosting a candidate workload. Externally, each cluster represents a set of compute units that is managed locally, without exposing its local hierarchy.

Scout agents are randomly generated proxy instruments that evaluate their surroundings and peer clusters to identify possible sources of hot and cold spots. Owing to the dynamic nature of the systemutilization, newer sources are identified, and past sources are slowly forgotten. Scout agents employ fitness criteria to determine the suitability of the region to host the work assignment.

Worker agents are floating entities that use a feedback function to quantify the significance of the compute region and that attach themselves to a node that they select for foraging. At each scheduling instant a feedback function measures the historical impact by either boosting or shedding the node's credibility, based on the most recent scheduling decisions and preceding outcomes. If the compute region continues to host workloads successfully, it boosts its credibility; if, however, the compute region loses its bid to host or hosts infrequently, then the credibility declines. Worker agents are finite in number and can only be reused if one is released, owing to either its low impact score or its migration to newer regions. The feedback function is

$$\beta_{n+1}^k = (1-\rho)\beta_n^k + \tau_n^k, \tag{6-14}$$

where

β_n^k = impact score of cluster (or node) k at instance n

τ_n^k = incremental credit boost of cluster (or node) k at instance n

ρ = impact decay coefficient

As described in function 6-14, whenever a compute cluster or node hosts a workload successfully, it improves its impact score by receiving incremental credits. At the same time, the feedback function sheds a percentage of its score at a rate defined by the impact decay coefficient ρ. The decay coefficient lets the rate of adaptation be adjusted. At any one time, only a finite number of worker agents is allowed to operate. A worker agent transitions to a *free agent* when its fitness score falls below a certain threshold. Once this occurs, the worker agent can attach itself to a new cluster, based on feedback from scout agents and worker agents.

Whereas scout agents identify new and promising regions for exploration, worker agents help in characterizing desirable neighborhoods close to their current operating region. At all times, these agents evaluate the cluster's fitness, a measure of its ability to host a new workload. This fitness score allows the respective agents to participate in a bidding process to host the workload in the region they represent. The fitness evaluation assesses the following characteristics:

- Severity of the thermal imbalances in the attached region, as compared with other regions

- Availability of the resources needed to execute a workload successfully

- Degree of contention with respect to available resources shared among compute nodes (e.g., shared cache)

Figure 6-3 depicts the architectural interfaces of a compute node that facilitate optimal workload distribution. Worker and scout agents gather node-specific performance and environmental data, using instrumentation APIs provided by the server manager. The agents explore the viability of using the node to host a workload by measuring the node's impact score (see Equation 6-14), evaluating its resource requirements, forecasting shared resource contention, and predicting the temperature behavior that may lead to thermal imbalances. Once the node is ascertained to be a potential host, its impact score is updated for future analysis. Cold regions with sufficient availability of resources identify themselves as the preferred localities for exploration. Worker agents analyze the compatibility of each region with the workload; incompatibilities may arise, owing to lack of exclusive resources or historical evidence of noisy behavior, with respect to the sharing of resources with other workloads. The worker agent ranks the host it is attached to and makes a decision as to whether to participate in the bidding process to host the workload on that node. If it participates and wins the bid, the agent updates the feedback function; if it does not win the bid, the agent sheds a percentage of its impact score b. Once the impact score drops below a certain threshold, the worker agent transitions to a free agent. A free agent transitions its role back to worker agent by attaching itself to a new cluster (or node), based on an evaluation score received from the scout agents and worker agents.

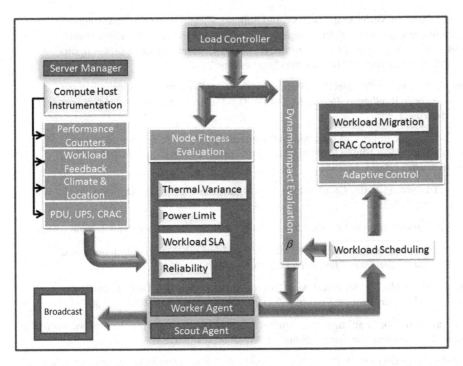

Figure 6-3. *Compute node: architectural interfaces for interpreting sensor data for evaluating feedback function and fitness function*

References

Aickelin, Uwe, Dipankar Dasgupta, and Feng Gu. "Artificial Immune Systems." In *Search Methodologies*, 187–211. New York: Springer, 2014.

Ashby, W. Ross. "Design for a Brain." New York: Wiley, 1952. https://archive.org/details/designforbrainor00ashb.

Barbagallo, Donato, Elisabetta Di Nitto, Daniel J. Dubois, and Raffaela Mirandola. "A Bio-Inspired Algorithm for Energy Optimization in a Self-Organizing Data Center." In *Self-Organizing Architectures: First International Workshop, SOAR 2009, Cambridge, UK, September 14, 2009*, edited by Danny Weyns, Sam Malek, Rogério de Lemos, and Jesper Andersson, 127–151. Berlin: Springer, 2010.

Beni, Gerardo, and Jing Wang. "Swarm Intelligence in Cellular Robotic Systems." In *Robots and Biological Systems: Towards a New Bionics?*, edited by Paolo Dario, Giulio Sandini, and Patrick Aebischer, 703–712. Berlin: Springer , 1993.

Carreras, I., D. Miorandi, G. S. Canright, and K. Engo-Monsen. "Understanding the Spread of Epidemics in Highly Partitioned Mobile Networks." In *Proceedings of the 1st IEEE Conference on Bio-Inspired Models of Network, Information and Computing Systems*, 1–8. Piscataway, NJ: Institute of Electrical and Electronics Engineers, 2006. Dasgupta, Dipankar. *Artificial Immune Systems and Their Applications*. Berlin: Springer, 1999.

de Castro, Leandro Nunes, and Fernando José Von Zuben. "Artificial Immune Systems: Part I–Basic Theory and Applications." Technical report, Universidade Estadual de Campinas, 1999.

Devescovi, Davide, Elisabetta Di Nitto, Daniel Dubois, and Raffaela Mirandola. "Self-Organization Algorithms for Autonomic Systems in the SelfLet Approach." In *Proceedings of the 1st International Conference on Autonomic Computing and Communication Systems*. Brussels: Institute for Computer Sciences, Social-Informatics and Telecommunications Engineering, 2007.

Di Caro, Gianni, and Marco Dorigo. "AntNet: Distributed Stigmergetic Control for Communications Networks." *Journal of Artificial Intelligence Research* 9 (1998): 317-365. www.cs.cmu.edu/afs/cs/project/jair/pub/volume9/dicaro98a.pdf.

Di Caro, Gianni, Frederick Ducatelle, and Luca Maria Gambardella. "AntHocNet: An Adaptive Nature-Inspired Algorithm for Routing in Mobile Ad hoc Networks." *European Transactions on Telecommunications* 16, no. 5 (2005): 443-455.

Dorigo, Marco, Gianni Di Caro, and Luca Gambardella. "Ant Algorithms for Discrete Optimization." *Artificial Life* 5, no. 2 (1999): 137-172.

Engelbrecht, Andries P. *Fundamentals of Computational Swarm Intelligence*. Chichester, UK: Wiley, 2006.

Farmer, J. Doyne, Norman H. Packard, and Alan S. Perelson. "The Immune System, Adaptation, and Machine Learning." *Physica D: Nonlinear Phenomena* 22, no. 1 (1986): 187-204.

Harvey, Inman, Ezequiel Di Paolo, Rachel Wood, Matt Quinn, Elio Tuci, and Elio Tuci. "Evolutionary Robotics: A New Scientific Tool for Studying Cognition." *Artificial Life* 11, no. 1-2 (2005): 79-98.

Iyer, Ravi. "CQoS: A Framework for Enabling QoS in Shared Caches of CMP Platforms." In *Proceedings of the 18th Annual International Conference on Supercomputing*, 257-266. New York: ACM, 2004.

Karaboga, Dervis, and Bahriye Basturk. "Artificial Bee Colony (ABC) Optimization Algorithm for Solving Constrained Optimization Problems." In *Proceedings of the 12th international Fuzzy Systems Association World Congress on Foundations of Fuzzy Logic and Soft Computing, IFSA 2007, Cancun, Mexico, June 18-21, 2007*, edited by Patricia Melin, Oscar Castillo, Luis T. Aguilar, Janusz, Kacprzyk, and Witold Pedrycz, 789-798. Berlin: Springer, 2007.

Kennedy, J., and R. Eberhart. "Particle Swarm Optimization." In *Proceedings of the 1995 IEEE International Conference on Neural Networks*, 1942-1948. Piscataway, NJ: Institute of Electrical and Electronics Engineers, 1995.

Khanna, Rahul, Huaping Liu, and Hsiao-Hwa Chen. "Reduced Complexity Intrusion Detection in Sensor Networks Using Genetic Algorithm." In *Proceedings of the 2009 IEEE International Conference on Communications*, 1-5. Piscataway, NJ: Institute of Electrical and Electronics Engineers, 2009.

Jacob, Bart, Richard Lanyon-Hogg, Devaprasad K. Nadgir, and Amr F. Yassin. "A Practical Guide to the IBM Autonomic Computing Toolkit." Armonk, NY: IBM, 2004. www.redbooks.ibm.com/redbooks/pdfs/sg246635.pdf.

Li, Zhen, and Manish Parashar. "Enabling Autonomic Grid Applications: Dynamic Composition, Coordination and Interaction." In *Unconventional Programming Paradigms: Proceedings of the International Workshop UPP 2004, Le Mont Saint Michel, France, September 2004; Revised and Selected Papers*, edited by Jean-Pierre Banâtre, Pascal Fradet, Jean-Louis Giavitto, and Olivier Michel, 270-285. Berlin: Springer, 2005.

Munoz, Mario A., Jesus A. Lopez, and Eduardo Caicedo. "Bacteria Swarm Foraging Optimization for Dynamical Resource Allocation in a Multizone Temperature Experimentation Platform." In *Analysis and Design of Intelligent Systems Using Soft Computing Techniques*, 427-435. Berlin: Springer, 2007.

Papadopouli, Maria, and Henning Schulzrinne. "Seven Degrees of Separation in Mobile Ad Hoc Networks." In *Proceedings of the 2000 IEEE Global Telecommunications Conference*, 1707-1711. Piscataway, NJ: Institute of Electrical and Electronics Engineers, 2000.

Passino, Kevin M. "Biomimicry of Bacterial Foraging for Distributed Optimization and Control." *IEEE Control Systems* 22, no. 3 (2002): 52–67.

Schoonderwoerd, Ruud, Owen E. Holland, Janet L. Bruten, and Leon JM Rothkrantz. "Ant-Based Load Balancing in Telecommunications Networks."*Adaptive Behavior* 5, no. 2 (1997): 169–207.

Wang, Xiaolei, Xiao Zhi Gao, and Seppo J. Ovaska. "A Hybrid Optimization Algorithm Based on Ant Colony and Immune Principles." *International Journal of Computer Science and Applications* 4, no. 3 (2007): 30–44.

Yassa, Sonia, Rachid Chelouah, Hubert Kadima, and Bertrand Granado. "Multi-Objective Approach for Energy-Aware Workflow Scheduling in Cloud Computing Environments." *Scientific World Journal* 2013 (2013): 350934. www.hindawi.com/journals/tswj/2013/350934/.

■ ■ ■

CHAPTER 7

Deep Neural Networks

I think the brain is essentially a computer and consciousness is like a computer program. It will cease to run when the computer is turned off. Theoretically, it could be re-created on a neural network, but that would be very difficult, as it would require all one's memories.

—Stephen Hawking, *Time* magazine

Proposed in the 1940s as a simplified model of the elementary computing unit in the human cortex, *artificial neural networks* (ANNs) have since been an active research area. Among the many evolutions of ANN, *deep neural networks* (DNNs) (Hinton, Osindero, and Teh 2006) stand out as a promising extension of the shallow ANN structure. The best demonstration thus far of hierarchical learning based on DNN, along with other Bayesian inference and deduction reasoning techniques, has been the performance of the IBM supercomputer Watson in the legendary tournament on the game show *Jeopardy!*, in 2011.

This chapter starts with some basic introductory information about ANN then outlines the DNN structure and learning scheme.

Introducing ANNs

ANNs have been successfully used in many real-life applications, especially in supervised-learning modes. However, ANNs have been plagued by a number of notable challenges and shortcomings. Among the many challenges in supervised learning is the curse of dimensionality (Arnold et al. 2011), which occurs when the number of features and training points becomes significantly large. Big data thus makes ANN learning more difficult, owing to the overwhelming amount of data to process and the consequent memory and computational requirements. Another challenge in classification is the data nonlinearity that characterizes the feature overlap of different classes, making the task of separating the classes more difficult. Primarily for these reasons and the heuristic approach to select the appropriate network architecture, ANNs lagged through the 1990s and 2000s behind the widely adopted support vector machines (SVMs), which proved to be, in many respects, superior to ANNs.

■ **Note** SVM offers a principled approach to machine learning problems because of its mathematical foundations in statistical learning theory. SVM constructs solutions as a weighted sum of support vectors, which are only a subset of the training input. Like ANN, SVM minimizes a particular error cost function, based on the training data set, and relies on an empirical risk model. Additionally, SVM uses structural risk minimization and imposes an additional constraint on the optimization problem, forcing the optimization step to find a model that will eventually generalize better as it is situated at an equal and maximum distance between the classes.

With advancements in hardware and computational power, DNNs have been proposed as an extension of ANN shallow architectures. Some critics consider deep learning just another "buzzword for neural nets" (Collobert 2011). Although they borrow the concept of neurons from the biological brain, DNNs do not attempt to model it as cortical algorithms (CAs) or other biologically inspired machine learning approaches do. DNN concepts stem from the neocognitron model proposed by Fukushima (1980). Broadly defined as a consortium of machine learning algorithms that aims to learn in a hierarchical manner and that involves multiple levels of abstraction for knowledge representation, DNN architectures are intended to realize strong artificial intelligence (AI) models. These architectures accumulate knowledge as information propagates through higher levels in a manner such that the learning at the higher level is defined by and built on the statistical learning that happens at the lower-level layers.

With such a broad definition of deep learning in mind, we can construe the combinations of the backpropagation algorithm (available since 1974) with recurrent neural networks and convolution neural networks (introduced in the 1980s) as being the predecessors of deep architectures. However, it is only with the advent of Hinton, Osindero, and Teh's (2006) contribution to deep learning training that research on deep architectures has picked up momentum. The following sections give a brief overview of ANN, along with introducing in more detail *deep belief networks* (DBNs) and *restricted Boltzmann machines* (RBMs).

Early ANN Structures

One of the first ANN attempts dates back to the late 1940s, when the psychologist Donald Hebb (Hebb 1949) introduced what is known today as *Hebbian learning*, based on the plasticity feature of neurons: when neurons situated on either side of a synapse are stimulated synchronously and recurrently, the synapse's strength is increased in a manner proportional to the respective outputs of the firing neurons (Brown et al. 1990), such that

$$w_{ij}(t+1) = w_{ij}(t) + \eta_{ij} x_i(t) x_j(t),$$

where t represents the training epoch, w_{ij} is the weight of the connection between the ith and the jth neurons, x_i is the output of the ith neuron, and h_{ij} is a learning rate specific to the synapse concerned.

The *Hebbian rule* is an unsupervised-learning scheme that updates the weights of a network locally; that is, the training of each synapse depends on the weights of the neurons connected to it only. With its simple implementation the Hebbian rule is considered the first ANN learning rule, from which multiple variants have stemmed. The first implementations of this algorithm were in 1954, at the Massachusetts Institute of Technology, using computational machines (Farley and Clark, 1954).

The 1950s also saw the introduction of the *perceptron*, a two-layer neural network model for pattern recognition, using addition and subtraction operations (Rosenblatt 1958). The model consists of four components, as depicted in Figure 7-1. The retina, or input region, receives stimulus through sensory units. The connections are called localized because their origin points tend to cluster around a certain point or in a certain area. Although units in the projection area are identical to those in the association area, the projection area receives input through localized connections, whereas input to the association area emerges from the projection area through random connections; as if the input is generated from scattered areas. The A-units receive a set of transmitted impulses that may be excitatory or inhibitory. If the stimulus exceeds a certain threshold, the units respond by firing. The random connections between the association area and the response units are bidirectional. The feedforward connections transmit synapses from the association area to the responses, whereas the feedback connections transmit excitatory synapses to the source points in the association area from which the connection is generated. Inhibitory synapses complement the source points in the association areas that do not transmit to the response concerned.

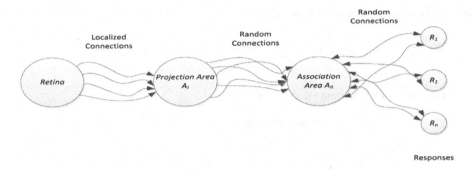

Figure 7-1. *A Rosenblatt perceptron structure*

Classical ANN

The basic structure of an ANN is the artificial neuron shown in Figure 7-2, which resembles the biological neuron in its shape and function (Haykin 1994).

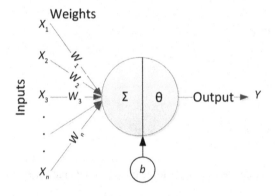

Figure 7-2. *An artificial neuron*

■ **Note**   In the human body's nervous system, neurons generate, transmit, and receive electrical signals called *action potential*. A typical biological neuron has the following three basic components:

- *Cell body*: Can have a variety of sizes and shapes

- *Dendrites*: Numerous, treelike structures that extend from the cell body and that constitute the receptive portion of the neuron (i.e., the input site)

- *Axon*: A long, slender structure, with relatively few branches, that transmits electrical signals to connected areas

---

The inputs (X) are connected to the neuron through weighted connections emulating the dendrite's structure, whereas the summation, the bias (b), and the activation function (θ) play the role of the cell body, and the propagation of the output is analogous to the axon in a biological neuron.

Mathematically, a neuron is equivalent to the function:

$$Y = \theta\left(\sum_{i=1}^{n} W_i X_i + b\right),$$

which can be conveniently modeled, using a matrix form,

$$Y = \theta\left(W.X + b\right),$$

where $W = \begin{bmatrix} W_1 & W_2 & \cdots & W_n \end{bmatrix}$, and $X = \begin{bmatrix} X_1 \\ X_2 \\ \vdots \\ X_n \end{bmatrix}$.

The activation function shapes the output or state of the neuron. Multiple activation functions can be used, the most common of which are as follows:

- *Hard limiter:* $\theta(a) = \begin{cases} 0 \ \text{if } a < 0 \\ 1 \ \text{if } a > 0 \end{cases}$

- *Saturating linear function:* $\theta(a) = \begin{cases} 0 \ \text{if } a < 0 \\ a \ \text{if } 0 \le a \le 1 \\ 1 \ \text{if } a > 1 \end{cases}$

- *Log-sigmoid function:* $\theta(a) = \dfrac{1}{1 + e^{-a}}$

- *Hyperbolic tangent sigmoid function:* $\theta(a) = \dfrac{e^a - e^{-a}}{e^a + e^{-a}}$

The bias shifts the activation function to the right or the left, as necessary for learning, and can in some cases be omitted.

A *neural network* is simply an association of cascaded layers of neurons, each with its own weight matrix, bias vector, and output vector. A layer of neurons is a "column" of neurons that operate in parallel, as shown in Figure 7-3. Each element of this column is a single neuron, with the output of the layer being the vector output, which is formed by the individual outputs of neurons. If an input vector is constituted of N inputs and a layer of M neurons, W_{ij} represents the weight of the connection of the jth input to the ith neuron of the layer; Y_i and b_i are, respectively, the output of and the bias associated with the jth neuron.

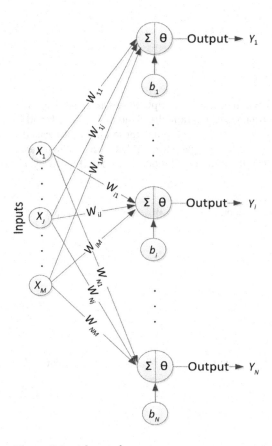

Figure 7-3. *A layer of neurons*

A layer of neurons can be conveniently represented, using matrix notation, as follows:

$$W = \begin{bmatrix} W_{11} & \cdots & W_{1M} \\ \vdots & \vdots & \vdots \\ W_{N1} & \cdots & W_{NM} \end{bmatrix}.$$

The row index in each element of this matrix represents the destination neuron of the corresponding connection, whereas the column index refers to the input source of the connection.

Designating by Y the output of the layer, you can write

$$Y = \begin{bmatrix} Y_1 \\ \vdots \\ Y_i \\ \vdots \\ Y_N \end{bmatrix} = \begin{bmatrix} \theta\left(\sum_{j=1}^{M} W_{1j}X_j + b_1\right) \\ \vdots \\ \theta\left(\sum_{j=1}^{M} W_{ij}X_j + b_i\right) \\ \vdots \\ \theta\left(\sum_{j=1}^{M} W_{Nj}X_j + b_N\right) \end{bmatrix} = \theta(W.X+b),$$

where $= \begin{bmatrix} b_1 \\ \vdots \\ b_N \end{bmatrix}$.

To aid in identifying the layer corresponding to a particular matrix, superscript indexes are used. Thus, W_{ij}^k represents the weight of the connection between the jth neuron in layer $k-1$ and the ith neuron in layer k, and Y_i^k is the output of the ith neuron of the kth layer. The network output is the output of the last layer (also called the output layer), and the other layers are called hidden layers. A network with two hidden layers is illustrated in Figure 7-4. For generalization purposes, you designate by N_k the number of hidden neurons in the kth layer.

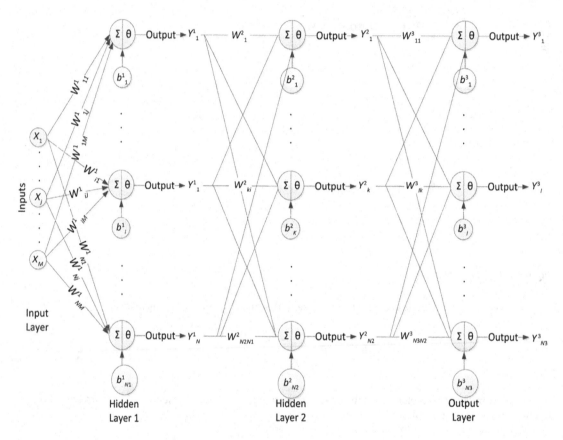

Figure 7-4. *A three-layer ANN*

The function achieved by this network is

$$Y^3 = \begin{bmatrix} Y_1^3 \\ \vdots \\ Y_i^3 \\ \vdots \\ Y_{N3}^3 \end{bmatrix} = \theta\left(W^3Y^2 + b^3\right) = \theta\left(W^3\theta\left(W^2Y^1 + b^2\right) + b^3\right) = \theta\left(W^3\theta\left(W^2\left(\theta\left(W^1X + b^1\right)\right) + b^2\right) + b^3\right).$$

■ **Note**   For the sake of simplicity, the same activation function θ has been adopted in all layers. However, multiple activation functions can be used in different layers in a network. Also, the number of neurons per layer may not be constant throughout the network.

The optimal number of layers and neurons for best performance is a question yet to be answered decisively, because this number is application dependent. A layer of hidden neurons divides the input space into regions whose boundaries are defined by the hyperplanes associated with each neuron.

The smaller the number of hidden neurons, the fewer the subregions created and the more the network tends to cluster points and map them to the same output. The output of each neuron is a non linear transformation of a hyperplane. In the case of classification, this separating curve formed by weighted inputs coming from the previous layer contributes, with other neurons in the same layer, in defining the final classification boundary. With a large number of neurons, the risk of overfitting increases, and the generalized performance decreases, because of overtraining. The network must be trained with enough data points to ensure that the partitions obtained at each hidden layer correctly separate the data.

ANN Training and the Backpropagation Algorithm

To enable an ANN to recognize patterns belonging to different classes, training on an existing dataset seeks to obtain iteratively the set of weights and biases that achieves the highest performance of the network (Jain, Mao, and Mohiuddin 1996).

In a network with M inputs, N output neurons, and L hidden layers, and given a set of labeled data—that is, a set of P pairs (X, T), where X is an M-dimensional vector, and T is an N-dimensional vector—the learning problem is reduced to finding the optimal weights, such that a cost function is optimized. The output of the network should match the target T_i and minimize the mean squared error,

$$E = \frac{1}{2}\sum_{i=1}^{P}\left\|Y_i - T_i^2\right\|,$$

where Y_i is the output obtained by propagating input X_i through the network.

ANNs can also use entropy as a cost function. Training requires at least a few epochs to update weights according to a weight update rule. It is to be noted that the backpropagation algorithm is widely adopted. It consists of the following steps:

1. *Initialization*: This step initializes the weights of the network in a random, weak manner; that is, it assigns random values close to 0 to the connections' weights.

2. *Feedforward*: The input X_i is fed into the network and propagated to the output layer. The resultant error is computed.

3. *Feedback*: The weights and biases are updated with:

$$W_{ij}^k(t+1) = W_{ij}^k(t) - \alpha\frac{\partial E}{\partial W_{ij}^k}$$

$$b_i^k(t+1) = b_i^k(t) - \alpha\frac{\partial E}{\partial b_i^k},$$

where a is a positive, tunable learning rate. The choice of a affects whether the backpropagation algorithm converges and how fast it converges. A large learning rate may cause the algorithm to oscillate, whereas a small learning rate may lead to a very slow convergence.

Because the update of the weights necessitates computing the gradient of the error (the cost function), it is essential for it to be differentiable. Failure to satisfy this condition prevents from using the backpropagation algorithm.

The computation of the gradient in the backpropagation algorithm can be simplified, using the chain rule, which calls for the following steps:

1. For each output unit $i = 1, 2, \ldots, N$ (in output layer L of Figure 7-4), the backpropagated error is computed, using

$$\delta_i^L = \frac{d\left(Y_i^L(t)\right)}{dt} \cdot \left(T_i - Y_i^L(t)\right),$$

where, T_i is the desired output; and, for the sigmoidal function,

$$\frac{d\left(Y_i^L(t)\right)}{dt} = Y_i^L(t)\left(1 - Y_i^L(t)\right),$$

resulting in the following expression:

$$\delta_i^L = Y_i^L(t)\left(1 - Y_i^L(t)\right)\left(T_i - Y_i^L(t)\right).$$

2. For each hidden unit $h = 1, 2, \ldots, N_k$ (in a hidden layer k with N_k hidden units), and moving from layer $L-1$, backward to the first layer, the backpropagated error can be computed as shown:

$$\delta_h^k = Y_h^k(t)\left(1 - Y_k^k(t)\right)\sum_{q=1}^{N_k} W_{qh}^{k+1} \delta_q^{k+1}.$$

3. The weights and biases are updated according to the following gradient descent:

$$W_{ij}^k(t+1) = W_{ij}^k(t) - \alpha \delta_i^k Y_j^{k-1}$$

$$b_i^k(t+1) = b_i^k(t) - \alpha \delta_i^k.$$

The network error is eventually reduced via this gradient-descent approach. For instance, considering a one-dimensional training point that belongs to class 1 (+1) and that is wrongly classified as class 2 (-1), the hyperplane should be moved away from class 1. Because, the hyperplane will be shifted to the left (decrease in W_{ij}^k) if $\delta_i^k Y_j^{k-1} > 0$, and it will be shifted to the right (increase in W_{ij}^k) if $\delta_i^k Y_j^{k-1} < 0$.

DBN Overview

DBNs, a deep architecture widely seen in the literature since the introduction of a fast, greedy training algorithm (Hinton, Osindero, and Teh 2006), are a network of stochastic neurons grouped in layers, with no intralayer neuron connections. The first two layers of the network contain neurons with undirected connections, which form an associative memory, analogous to biological neurons, whereas the remaining hidden layers form a directed acyclic graph, as displayed in Figure 7-5.

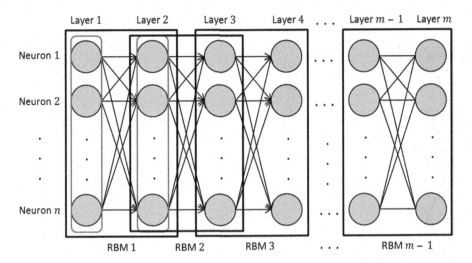

Figure 7-5. *DBN architecture*

Although a DBN can be viewed as an ANN with more hidden layers, training a DBN, using backpropagation, does not produce a good machine learning model, because the explaining-away phenomenon makes inference more difficult in deep models. When training a network, the simplifying assumption that layers are independent. *Explaining away* (also called *Berkson's paradox* or *selection bias*), makes this assumption invalid; the hidden nodes become anticorrelated. For example, if an output node can be activated by two equally rare and independent events with an even smaller chance of occurring simultaneously (because the probability of two independent events' occurring simultaneously is the product of both probabilities), then the occurrence of one event negates ("explains away") the occurrence of the other, such that a negative correlation is obtained between the two events. As a result of the difficulty of training deep architectures, DBNs lost popularity until Hinton and Salakhutdinov (2006) proposed a greedy training algorithm to train them efficiently. This algorithm broke down DBNs into sequentially stacked RBMs, which is a two-layer network constrained to contain only interlayer neuron connections, that is, connections between neurons that do not belong to the same layer.

As shown in Figure 7-6, connections between neurons in layer 1 are not allowed, and the same goes for layer 2; connections have to link a neuron from layer 1 to a neuron in layer 2 only. In a DBN the first two layers are allowed to have bidirectional connections, whereas the remaining layers have just directed connections. Therefore, interest in deep architectures was renewed, as training them became feasible and fast, involving training RBM units independently before adjusting the weights, using an up–down algorithm to avoid underfitting (Hinton, Osindero, and Teh 2006).

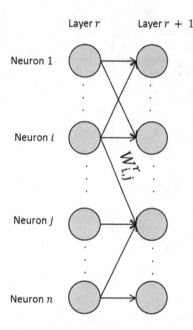

Figure 7-6. *Weight labeling*

Following is list of the DBN nomenclature adopted here:

DNN Nomenclature

$W_{i,j}^r$: Weight of the edge connecting neuron i in layer r to neuron j in layer; r is suppressed when there are only two layers in the network

$\boldsymbol{W_i^r}$: Weight vector of all connections leaving neuron i in layer r

$\boldsymbol{W_r}$: Weight vector connecting layer r to layer $r+1$

μ: Learning rate

k: Number of Gibbs sampling steps performed in contrastive divergence

n: Total number of hidden layer neurons

m: Total number of input layer neurons

$Q(.|.)$: Conditional probability distribution

h^r: Binary configuration of layer r

$p(h^r)$: Prior probability of h^r under the current weight values

v^0: Input layer datapoint $v_j^{(t)}$: binary configuration of neuron j in the input layer at sampling step t

H_i: Binary configuration variable of neuron i in the hidden layer at sampling step t

$h_i^{(t)}$: Binary configuration value of neuron i in the hidden layer at sampling step t

b_j: Bias term for neuron j in the input layer

c_i: Bias term for neuron i in the hidden layer

Restricted Boltzmann Machines

Boltzmann machines (BMs) are two-layer neural network architectures composed of neurons connected in an interlayer and intralayer fashion. *Restricted Boltzmann machines* (RBMs), first introduced under the name *Harmonium,* by Smolensky (1986), are constrained to form a bipartite graph. A bipartite graph is a two-layer graph, in which the nodes of the two layers form two disjoint sets of neurons This is achieved by restricting intralayer connections, such that connections between nodes in the same layer are not permitted. This restriction is what distinguishes BMs from RBMs and makes RBMs simpler to train. An RBM with undirected connections between neurons of the different layers forms an *autoassociative memory,* analogous to neurons in the human brain. Autoassociative memory is characterized by feedback connections that allow the exchange of information between neurons in both directions (Hawkins 2007).

RBMs can be trained in a supervised and unsupervised fashion. The weight vector is updated, using Hinton's *contrastive divergence* (CD) algorithm (Hinton 2002). CD is an algorithm that approximates the log-likelihood gradient and that requires fewer sampling steps than the *Markov chain Monte Carlo* (MCMC) algorithm (Hinton 2002). CD performs *k* steps of Gibbs sampling and gradient descent to find the weight vector that maximizes the objective function (Hinton 2010), which is the product of probabilities. As *k* increases, the performance of the learned model improves, however at the cost of a longer training time. A typical value for this parameter is *k* = 1 (Hinton 2010). The workflow of the training algorithm is shown in Table 7-1.

Table 7-1. *RBM Training Algorithm Workflow, Using CD (Fischer and Igel, 2012)*

1. Initialize the weights to 0.

2. For each sample from the training batch:

   a. Apply the sample to the network input.

   b. For 0 to *k*-1 sampling steps,

      i. for each hidden layer neuron from 1 to *n*, sample $h_i^{(t)} \sim p\left(h_i | v^{(t)}\right)$;

      ii. for each input layer neuron from 1 to *m*, sample $v_j^{(t)} \sim p\left(v_j | h^{(t)}\right)$.

   c. For each input and hidden layer neuron, compute

      i. $\Delta w_{ij} = \Delta w_{ij} + p\left(H_i = 1 | v^{(0)}\right)v_j^{(0)} - p\left(H_i = 1 | v^{(k)}\right)v_j^{(k)}$

      ii. $\Delta b_j = \Delta b_j + v_j^{(0)} - v_j^{(k)}$

      iii. $\Delta c_i = \Delta c_i + p\left(H_i = 1 | v^{(0)}\right) - p(H_i = 1 | v^{(k)})$

Based on the Gibbs distribution, the energy function or loss function used to describe the joint probability distribution is denoted in Equation 7-1, where w_{ij}, b_j, and c_i are real-valued weights, and h_i and v_j can take values in the set (Aleksandrovsky et al. 1996):

$$E(v,h) = -\sum_{i=1}^{n}\sum_{j=1}^{m} w_{ij} h_i v_j - \sum_{j=1}^{m} b_j v_j - \sum_{i=1}^{n} c_i h_i. \tag{7-1}$$

The joint probability distribution is thus computed using Equation 7-2:

$$p(v,h) = \frac{1}{\sum_v \sum_h e^{-E(v,h)}} e^{-E(v,h)}. \tag{7-2}$$

DNN Training Algorithms

Backpropagation is one of the most popular algorithms used to train ANNs (Werbos 1974). Equation 7-3 displays a simple formulation of the weight update rule, used in backpropagation:

$$w_1^r(\text{new}) = w_1^r(\text{old}) - \mu \frac{\partial J}{\partial w_1^r} \qquad (7\text{-}3)$$

However, as the depth of the network increases, backpropagation's performance degradation increases as well, making it unsuitable for training general deep architectures. This is due to the vanishing gradient problem (Horchreiter 1991; Horchreiter et al. 2001; Hinton 2007; Bengio 2009), a training issue in which the error propagated back in the network shrinks as it moves from layer to layer, becoming negligible in deep architectures and making it almost impossible for the weights in the early layers to be updated. Therefore, it would be too slow to train and obtain meaningful results from a DNN.

Because of backpropagation's shortcomings, many attempts were made to develop a fast training algorithm for deep networks. *Schmidhuber's algorithm* (Schmidhuber 1992) trained a multilevel hierarchy of recurrent neural networks by using unsupervised pretraining on each layer and then fine-tuning the resulting weights via backpropagation.

Interest in DNNs was renewed in 2006, when Hinton and Salakhutdinov (2006) proposed a greedy, layer-by-layer training algorithm for DBNs that attempts to learn simpler models sequentially and then fine-tune the results for the overall model. Using *complementary priors* to eliminate the explaining-away effect, the algorithm consists of two main steps:

1. A greedy layer-wise training to learn the weights by

    a. Tying the weights of the unlearned layers.

    b. Applying CD to learn the weights of the current layer.

2. An up-down algorithm for fine-tuning the weights

Instead of learning the weights of millions of connections across many hidden layers at once, this training scheme finds the optimal solution for a single layer at a time, which makes it a greedy algorithm. This is accomplished by tying all the weights of the following layers and learning only the weights of the current layer. Tying weights also serves to eliminate the explaining-away phenomenon, which results in poorly trained deep networks when adopting other training algorithms. As illustrated in Figure 7-7, the weights W_0 between layers 1 and 2 are learned. The weights between all the following layers are tied to W_0. Once CD learning has converged, the weights W_1, between layers 2 and 3, are learned by tying the weights of all the following layers to W_1 and fixing the weights between layers 1 and 2 that were learned in the previous stage to W_0. Similarly, when the CD converges to the optimal values for W_1, the weights of the third RBM block are untied from the second RBM block, and CD is used to learn the final set of weights W_2.

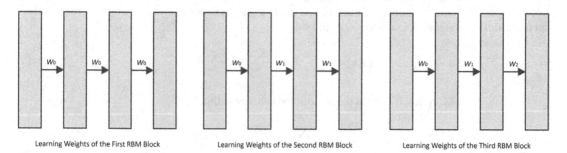

Learning Weights of the First RBM Block   Learning Weights of the Second RBM Block   Learning Weights of the Third RBM Block

Figure 7-7. *Sequential training*

This process of tying, learning, and untying weights is repeated until all layers have been processed. DBNs with tied weights resemble RBMs. Therefore, as mentioned earlier, each RBM is learned, using CD learning. However, this algorithm can only be applied if the first two layers form an undirected graph, and the remaining hidden layers form a directed, acyclic graph.

The energy of the directed model is computing, using Equation 7-4, which is bounded by Equation 7-5. Tying the weights produces equality in Equation 7-5 and renders $Q(.\,|v^0)$ and $p(v^0\,|\,h^0)$ constant. The derivative of Equation 7-5 is simplified and equal to Equation 7-6. Therefore, tying the weights leads to a simpler objective function to maximize. Applying this rule recursively allows the training of a DBN (Hinton, Osindero, and Teh 2006).

$$E\left(v^0,h^0\right)=-\left(\log p\left(h^0\right)+\log p\left(v^0|h^0\right)\right) \tag{7-4}$$

$$\log p\left(v^0\right)$$

$$\geq \sum_{all\,h^0} Q\left(h^0|v^0\right)\left(\log p\left(h^0\right)+\log p\left(v^0|h^0\right)\right)$$

$$-\sum_{all\,h^0} Q\left(h^0|v^0\right)\log Q\left(h^0|v^0\right) \tag{7-5}$$

$$\frac{\partial\left(\log p\left(v^0\right)\right)}{\partial w_{ij}}=\sum_{all\,h^0} Q\left(h^0|v^0\right)\log p\left(h^0\right) \tag{7-6}$$

Once the weights have been learned for each layer, a variant of the wake–sleep algorithm with the CD weight update rule is used to fine-tune the learned parameters. The up–down algorithm is used to backfit the obtained solution to avoid underfitting—an important concern when training in an unsupervised and greedy fashion. The up–down algorithm subjects lower-level layers, whose weights were learned early in the training, to the influence of the higher-level layers, whose weights were learned toward the end of training. In the bottom-up pass the generative weights on directed connections are adjusted by computing the positive phase probabilities, sampling the states, using the CD weight update rule, and running Gibbs sampling for a limited number of iterations. The top-down pass will stochastically activate each of the lower layers, using the top-down connections. This is done by computing the negative phase probabilities, sampling the states, and computing the predictions of the network. Appropriate adjustments to the generative and inference parameters as well as the top-layer weights are performed in a contrastive form of the wake–sleep algorithm, because it addresses issues in the sleep phase of the algorithm. The workflow for this algorithm is shown in Table 7-2.

Table 7-2. *Up–Down Algorithm Workflow (Hinton and Salakhutdinov 2006)*

1. In the bottom-up pass:
   a. Compute positive phase probabilities.
   b. Sample states.
   c. Compute CD statistics, using the positive phase probabilities.
   d. Perform Gibbs sampling for a predefined number of iterations, based on the associative memory part of the network.
   e. Compute negative phase contrastive divergence statistics, using information from step 1d.
2. In the top-down pass:
   a. Calculate negative phase probabilities.
   b. Sample states.
   c. Compute predictions.
3. Update generative parameters.
4. Update associative memory part of the network.
5. Update inference parameters.

Despite its limitations when applied to DNNs, interest in the backpropagation algorithm was renewed, because of the surge in graphics processing unit (GPU) computational power. Ciresan et al. (2010) investigated the performance of the backpropagation algorithm on deep networks. It was observed that, even with the vanishing gradient problem, given enough epochs, backpropagation can achieve results comparable to those of other, more complex training algorithms.

It is to be noted that supervised learning with deep architectures has been reported as performing well on many classification tasks. However, when the network is pretrained in an unsupervised fashion, it almost always performs better than the scenarios where pretraining is omitted without the pretraining phase (Erhan et al. 2010). Several theories have been proposed to explain this phenomenon, such as that the pretraining phase acts as a regularizer (Bengio 2009; Erhan et al. 2009) and an aid (Bengio et al. 2007) for the supervised optimization problem.

DNN-Related Research

The use of DBN in various machine learning applications has flourished since the introduction of Hinton's fast, greedy training algorithm. Furthermore, many attempts have been made to speed up DBN and address its weaknesses. The following sections offer a brief survey of the most recent and relevant applications of DBN, a presentation on research aimed at speeding up training as well as a discussion of several DBN variants and DNN architectures.

DNN Applications

DNN has been applied to many machine learning applications, including feature extraction, feature reduction, and classification problems, to name a few.

Feature extraction involves transforming raw input data to feature vectors that represent the input; raw data can be audio, image, or text. For example, DBN has been applied to *discrete Fourier transform* (DFT) representation of music audio (Hamel and Eck 2010) and found to outperform Mel frequency cepstral coefficients (MFCCs), a widely used method of music audio feature extraction.

Once features are extracted from raw data, the high-dimensional data representation may have to be reduced to alleviate the memory and computational requirements of classification tasks as well as enable better visualization of the data and decrease the memory needed to store the data for future use. Hinton and Salakhutdinov (Hinton and Salakhutdinov 2006; Salakhutdinov and Hinton 2007) used a stack of RBMs to pretrain the network and then employed autoencoder networks to learn the low-dimensional features.

Extracting expressive and low-dimensional features, using DBN, was shown to be possible for fast retrieval of documents and images, as tested on some ever-growing databases. Ranzato and Szummer (2008) were able to produce compact representations of documents to speed up search engines, while outperforming shallow machine learning algorithms. Applied to image retrieval from large databases, DBN produced results comparable to state-of-the art algorithms, including latent Dirichlet allocation and probabilistic latent semantic analysis (Hörster and Lienhart 2008).

Transferring learned models from one domain to another has always been an issue for machine learning algorithms. However, DNN was able to extract domain-independent features (Bengio and Delalleau 2011), making transfer learning possible in many applications (Collobert and Weston 2008; Glorot, Bordes, and Bengio 2011; Bengio 2012; Ciresan, Meier, and Schmidhuber 2012;Mesnil et al. 2012). DNNs have also been used for curriculum learning, in which data are learned is a specific order (Bengio et al. 2009).

DBN has been applied to many classification tasks in fields such as vision, speech, medical ailments, and *natural language processing* (NLP). Object recognition from images has been widely addressed, and DBN's performance exceeded state-of-the-art algorithms (Desjardins and Bengio 2008; Uetz and Behnke 2009; Ciresan et al. 2010; Ciresan, Meier, and Schmidhuber 2012). For instance, Ciresan et al. (2010) achieved an error rate of 0.35 percent on the Mixed National Institute of Standards and Technology (MNIST) database. Nair and Hinton (2009) outperformed shallow architectures, including SVM, on three-dimensional object recognition, achieving a 6.5 percent error rate, on the New York University Object Recognition Benchmark (NORB) dataset, compared with SVM's 11.6 percent. Considering speech recognition tasks, deep architectures have improved acoustic modeling (Mohamed et al. 2011; Hinton et al. 2012), speech-to-text transcription (Seide, Li, and Yu 2011), and large-vocabulary speech recognition (Dahl et al. 2012; Jaitly et al. 2012; Sainath et al. 2011). On phone recognition tasks, DBN achieved an error rate of 23 percent on the TIMIT database—better than reported errors, ranging from 24.4 percent to 36 percent, using other machine learning algorithms (Mohamed, Yu, and Deng 2010).

DBN produced classification results comparable to other machine learning algorithms in seizure prediction, using electroencephalography (EEG) signals, but reached those results in significantly faster times—between 1.7 and 103.7 times faster (Wulsin et al. 2011). McAfee (2008) adopted DBN for document classification and showed promise for succeeding on such databases.

Generating synthetic images—specifically facial expressions—from a high-level description of human emotion is another area in which DBN has been successfully applied, producing a variety of realistic facial expressions (Susskind et al. 2008).

NLP, in general, has also been investigated with deep architectures to improve on state-of-the-art results. Such applications include machine transliteration (Deselaers et al. 2009), sentiment analysis (Zhou, Chen, and Wang 2010; Glorot, Bordes, and Bengio 2011), and language modeling (Collobert and Weston 2008; Weston et al. 2012)—including part-of-speech tagging, similar-word recognition, and chunking. The complexity of these problems requires a machine learning algorithm with more depth (Bengio and Delalleau 2011) to produce meaningful results. For example, machine transliteration poses a challenge to machine learning algorithms, because the words do not have a unified mapping, which leads to a many-to-many mapping that does not exist in dictionaries. Additionally, the large number of source-to-target language-pair character symbols and different sound structures leading to missing sounds are just a few properties of transliteration that make it difficult for machines to do well.

Parallel Implementations to Speed Up DNN Training

Sequentially training a DBN layer by layer becomes more time-consuming as the layer and network sizes increase. Stacking the layers to form networks, called *deep-stacking networks*, and training the network on CPU clusters, as opposed to one supercomputer (Deng, Hutchinson, and Yu 2012), exploit the inherent parallelism in the greedy training algorithm to achieve significant training-time savings.

However, this method does not speed up the training time per layer. This can be achieved by parallelizing the training algorithm for the individual RBM layers, using GPUs (Cai et al. 2012).

However, use of the large and sparse data commonly employed to train RBMs creates challenges for parallelizing this algorithm. Modifying the computations for matrix-based operations and optimizing the matrix–matrix multiplication code for sparse matrices make GPU implementation much faster than CPU implementation.

As opposed to speeding up training via software, attempts have been made to speed up training via hardware, using field-programmable gate arrays (FPGAs). Ly and Chow (2010) mapped RBMs to FPGAs and achieved significant speedup of the optimized software code. This work was extended to investigate the scalability of the approach by Lo (2010).

Deep Networks Similar to DBN

One variation of DBN, called *modular DBN* (M-DBN), trains different parts of the network separately, while adjusting the learning rate as training progresses (Pape et al. 2011), as opposed to using one training set for the whole network. This allows M-DBN to avoid forgetting features learned early in training, a weakness of DBN that can hinder its performance in online learning applications in which the data distribution changes dynamically over time.

Sparse DBN learns sparse features—unlike Hinton's DBN, which learns nonsparse data representations—by adding a penalty in the objective function for deviations from the expected activation of hidden units in the RBM formulation (Lee, Ekanadham, and Ng 2007).

Convolutional DBN integrates translation invariance into the image representations by sharing weights between locations in an image, allowing inference to be done when the image is scaled up by using convolution (Lee et al. 2009). Therefore, convolutional DBN scales better to real-world-sized images without suffering from computational intractability as a result of the high dimensionality of these images.

DBNs are not the only deep architectures available. *Sum product network* (SPN) is a deep architecture represented as a graph with directed and weighted edges. SPN is *acyclic* (contains no loops), with variables on the leaves of the graph, and its internal nodes consist of sum and product operations (Poon and Domingo 2011). SPN trains, using backpropagation and expectation maximization (EM) algorithms. These simple operations result in a network that is more accurate, faster to train, and more tractable than DBN.

Deep Boltzmann machines (DBMs) are similar to but have a more general deep architecture than DBNs. They are composed of BMs stacked on top of each others (Salakhutdinov and Hinton 2009). Although more complex and slower to train than DBNs, owing to the symmetrical connections between all neurons in the BM network, the two-way edges let DBMs propagate input uncertainty better than DBNs, making their generative models more robust. The more complex architecture requires an efficient training algorithm to make training feasible. The DBN greedy training algorithm was modified to achieve a more efficient training algorithm for DBM by using an approximate inference algorithm. However, this rendered DBM training approximately three times slower than DBN training (Salakhutdinov and Larochelle 2010).

References

Aleksandrovsky, Boris, James Whitson, Gretchen Andes, Gary Lynch, and Richard Granger. "Novel Speech Processing Mechanism Derived from Auditory Neocortical Circuit Analysis." In *Proceedings of the Fourth International Conference on Spoken Language*, edited by H. Timothy Bunnell and William Idsardi, 558–561. Piscataway, NJ: Institute of Electrical and Electronics Engineers, 1996.

Arnold, Ludovic, Sébastien Rebecchi, Sylvain Chevallier, and Hélène Paugam-Moisy. "An Introduction to Deep Learning." In Proceedings of the 19th European Symposium on Artificial Neural Networks, Computational Intelligence and Machine Learning, Bruges, Belgium, April 27–29, 2011, edited by Michel Verleysen, 477–488. Leuven, Belgium: Ciaco, 2011.

Bengio, Yoshua. "Learning Deep Architectures for AI." In *Foundations and Trends in Machine Learning* 2, no. 1 (2009): 1-127.

Bengio, Yoshua. "Deep Learning of Representations for Unsupervised and Transfer Learning." In *ICML 2011: Proceedings of the International Conference on Machine Learning Unsupervised and Transfer Learning Workshop*, edited by Isabelle Guyon, Gideon Dror, Vincent Lemaire, Graham Taylor, and Daniel Silver, 17-36. 2012. http://jmlr.csail.mit.edu/proceedings/papers/v27/bengio12a/bengio12a.pdf.

Bengio, Yoshua, and Olivier Delalleau. "On the Expressive Power of Deep Architectures." In *Algorithmic Learning Theory*, edited by Jyrki Kivinen, Csaba Szepesvári, Esko Ukkonen, and Thomas Zeugmann, 18-36. Berlin: Springer, 2011.

Bengio, Yoshua, Pascal Lamblin, Dan Popovici, and Hugo Larochelle. "Greedy Layer-Wise Training of Deep Networks." In *NIPS '06: Proceedings of Advances in Neural Information Processing Systems 19*, edited by Bernhard Schlkopf, John Platt, and Thomas Hofmann, 153-160. Cambridge, MA: Massachusetts Institute of Technology Press, 2007.

Bengio, Yoshua, Jérôme Louradour, Ronan Collobert, and Jason Weston. "Curriculum Learning." In *ICML '09: Proceedings of the 26th Annual International Conference on Machine Learning*, edited by Léon Bottou and Michael Littman, 41-48. New York: ACM, 2009.

Brown, Thomas H., Edward W. Kairiss, and Claude L. Keenan. "Hebbian Synapses: Biophysical Mechanisms ad Algorithms." *Annual Review of Neuroscience* 13, no. 1 (1990): 475-511.

Cai, Xianggao, Zhanpeng Xu, Guoming Lai, Chengwei Wu, and Xiaola Lin. "GPU-Accelerated Restricted Boltzmann Machine for Collaborative Filtering." In *Algorithms and Architectures for Parallel Processing: Proceedings of the 12th International ICA3PP Conference, Fukuoka, Japan, September 2012*, edited by Yang Xiang, Ivan Stojmenović, Bernady O. Apduhan, Guojun Wang, Koji Nakano, and Albert Zomaya, 303-316. Berlin: Springer, 2012.

Ciresan, Dan Claudiu, Ueli Meier, Luca Maria Gambardella, and Jürgen Schmidhuber. "Deep, Big, Simple Neural Nets for Handwritten Digit Recognition." *Neural Computation* 22, no. 12 (2010): 3207-3220.

Ciresan, Dan Claudiu, Ueli Meier, and Jürgen Schmidhuber. "Transfer Learning for Latin and Chinese Characters with Deep Neural Networks." In *Proceedings of the 2012 International Joint Conference on Neural Networks*, 1-6. Piscataway, NJ: Institute of Electrical and Electronics Engineers, 2012.

Collobert, Robert. "Deep Learning for Efficient Discriminative Parsing." Recorded April 2011. AISTATS video, 21:16. Posted May 6, 2011. http://videolectures.net/aistats2011_collobert_deep/.

Collobert, Ronan, and Jason Weston. "A Unified Architecture for Natural Language Processing. Deep Neural Networks with Multitask Learning." In *ICML '08: Proceedings of the 25th International Conference on Machine Learning*, edited by Andrew McCallum and Sam Roweis, 160-167. New York: ACM, 2008.

Dahl, George E., Dong Yu, Li Deng, and Alex Acero. "Context-Dependent Pre-Trained Deep Neural Networks for Large-Vocabulary Speech Recognition." *IEEE Transactions on Audio, Speech, and Language Processing* 20, no. 1 (2012): 30-42.

Deng, Li, Brian Hutchinson, and Dong Yu. "Parallel Training for Deep Stacking Networks." In *Interspeech 2012: Proceedings of the 13th Annual Conference of the International Speech Communication Association*. 2012. www.isca-speech.org/archive/interspeech_2012.

Deselaers, Thomas, Saša Hasan, Oliver Bender, and Hermann Ney. "A Deep Learning Approach to Machine Transliteration." In *Proceedings of the Fourth Workshop on Statistical Machine Translation*, e233-241. Stroudsburg, PA: Association for Computational Linguistics, 2009.

Desjardins, Guillaume, and Yoshua Bengio. "Empirical Evaluation of Convolutional RBMs for Vision." Technical report, Université de Montréal, 2008.

Erhan, Dumitru, Yoshua Bengio, Aaron Courville, Pierre-Antoine Manzagol, Pascal Vincent, and Samy Bengio. "Why Does Unsupervised Pre-Training Help Deep Learning?" *Journal of Machine Learning Research* 11 (2010): 625-660.

Erhan, Dumitru, Pierre-Antoine Manzagol, Yoshua Bengio, Samy Bengio, and Pascal Vincent. "The Difficulty of Training Deep Architectures and the Effect of Unsupervised Pre-Training." In *Proceedings of the 12th International Conference on Artificial Intelligence and Statistics*, edited by David van Dyk and Max Welling, 153-160. 2009. http://machinelearning.wustl.edu/mlpapers/paper_files/AISTATS09_ErhanMBBV.pdf.

Farley, B. G., and W. Clark. "Simulation of Self-Organizing Systems by Digital Computer." *IEEE Transactions of the IRE Professional Group on Information Theory* 4, no. 4 (1954): 76-84.

Fischer, Asja, and Christian Igel. "An Introduction to Restricted Boltzmann Machines." In Progress in Pattern Recognition, Image Analysis, Computer Vision, and Applications: Proceedings of the 17th Iberoamerican Congress, CIARP 2012, Buenos Aires, Argentina, September 3-6, 2012, edited by Luis Alvarez, Marta E. Mejail, Luis E. Gomez, and Julio E. Jacobo, 14-36. Berlin: Springer, 2012.

Fukushima, Kunihiko. "Neocognition: A Self-Organizing Neural Network Model for a Mechanism of Pattern Recognition Unaffected by Shift in Position." *Biological Cybernetics* 36 (1980): 193-202.

Glorot, Xavier, Antoine Bordes, and Yoshua Bengio. "Domain Adaptation for Large-Scale Sentiment Classification: A Deep Learning Approach." In *ICML '11: Proceedings of the 28th International Conference on Machine Learning*, 513-520. 2011. www.icml-2011.org/papers/342_icmlpaper.pdf.

Hamel, Philippe, and Douglas Eck. "Learning Features from Music Audio with Deep Belief Networks." In ISMIR 2010: Proceedings of the 11th International Society for Music Information Retrieval Conference (ISMIR 2010), August 9-13, 2010, Utrecht, the Netherlands, edited by J. Stephen Downie and Rembo C. Veltkamp, 339-344. International Society for Music Information Retrieval, 2010. http://ismir2010.ismir.net/proceedings/ISMIR2010_complete_proceedings.pdf.

Hawkins, Jeff, and Sandra Blakeslee. *On Intelligence*. New York: Macmillan, 2007.

Haykin, Simon. *Neural Networks*. Upper Saddle River, NJ: Prentice Hall, 1994.

Hebb, Donald. *The Organization of Behavior*. New York: Wiley, 1949.

Hinton, Geoffrey E. "Training Products of Experts by Minimizing Contrastive Divergence." *Neural Computation* 14, no. 8 (2002): 1771-1800.

Hinton, Geoffrey E. "To Recognize Shapes, First Learn to Generate Images." *Progress in Brain Research* 165 (2007): 535-547.

Hinton, Geoffrey E.. "A Practical Guide to Training Restricted Boltzmann Machines." *Momentum* 9, no. 1 (2010).

Hinton, Geoffrey E., Li Deng, Dong Yu, George E. Dahl, Abdel-rahman Mohamed, Navdeep Jaitly, Andrew Senior, et al. "Deep Neural Networks for Acoustic Modeling in Speech Recognition: The Shared Views of Four Research Groups." *IEEE Signal Processing Magazine* 29, no. 6 (2012): 82-97.

Hinton, Geoffrey E., Simon Osindero, and Yee-Whye Teh. "A Fast Learning Algorithm for Deep Belief Nets." *Neural Computation* 18, no. 7 (2006): 1527-1554.

Hinton, Geoffrey E., and Ruslan R. Salakhutdinov. "Reducing the Dimensionality of Data with Neural Networks." *Science* 313, no. 5786 (2006): 504-507.

Hochreiter, Sepp. "Untersuchungen zu dynamischen neuronalen Netzen." Master's thesis, Technical University of Munich, 1991.

Hochreiter, Sepp, Yoshua Bengio, Paolo Frasconi, and Jürgen Schmidhuber. "Gradient Flow in Recurrent Nets: The Difficulty of Learning Long-Term Dependencies." In *A Field Guide to Dynamical Recurrent Neural Networks*, edited by John F. Kolen and Stefan C. Kremer, 237–244. Piscataway, NJ: Institute of Electrical and Electronics Engineers, 2001.

Hörster, Eva, and Rainer Lienhart. "Deep Networks for Image Retrieval on Large-Scale Databases." In *Proceedings of the 16th ACM International Conference on Multimedia*, 643–646. New York: ACM, 2008.

Jain, Anil K., Jianchang Mao, and K. M. Mohiuddin. "Artificial Neural Networks: A Tutorial." *Computer* 29, no. 3 (1996): 31–44.

Jaitly, Navdeep, Patrick Nguyen, Andrew W. Senior, and Vincent Vanhoucke. "Application of Pretrained Deep Neural Networks to Large Vocabulary Speech Recognition." In *Interspeech 2012: Proceedings of the 13th Annual Conference of the International Speech Communication Association*. 2012. www.isca-speech.org/archive/interspeech_2012/.

Lee, Honglak, Chaitanya Ekanadham, and Andrew Y. Ng. "Sparse Deep Belief Net Model for Visual Area V2." *Proceedings of NIPS 2007: Advances in Neural Information Processing Systems*, edited by J. C. Platt, D. Koller, Y. Singer, and S. T. Roweis. 2008. http://papers.nips.cc/paper/3313-sparse-deep-belief-net-model-for-visual-area-v2.pdf.

Lee, Honglak, Roger Grosse, Rajesh Ranganath, and Andrew Y. Ng. "Convolutional Deep Belief Networks for Scalable Unsupervised Learning of Hierarchical Representations." In *ICML '09: Proceedings of the 26th Annual International Conference on Machine Learning*, edited by Léon Bottou and Michael Littman, 609–616. New York: ACM, 2009.

Lo, Charles. "A FPGA Implementation of Large Restricted Boltzmann Machines." In *Proceedings of the 18th IEEE Annual International Symposium on Field-Programmable Custom Computing Machines (FCCM)*, May 2–4, 2010, Charlotte, NC, 201–208. Piscataway, NJ: Institute of Electrical and Electronics Engineers, 2010.

Ly, Daniel L., and Paul Chow. "High-Performance Reconfigurable Hardware Architecture for Restricted Boltzmann Machines." *IEEE Transactions on Neural Networks* 21, no. 1 (2010): 1780–1792.

McAfee, Lawrence. "Document Classification Using Deep Belief Nets," 2008.

Mesnil, Grégoire, Yann Dauphin, Xavier Glorot, Salah Rifai, Yoshua Bengio, Ian J. Goodfellow, Erick Lavoie, et al. "Unsupervised and Transfer Learning Challenge: A Deep Learning Approach." In *ICML 2011: Proceedings of the International Conference on Machine Learning Unsupervised and Transfer Learning Workshop*, edited by Isabelle Guyon, Gideon Dror, Vincent Lemaire, Graham Taylor, and Daniel Silver, 97–110. 2012. http://jmlr.csail.mit.edu/proceedings/papers/v27/mesnil12a/mesnil12a.pdf.

Mohamed, Abdel-rahman, Tara N. Sainath, George Dahl, Bhuvana Ramabhadran, Geoffrey E. Hinton, and Michael A. Picheny. "Deep Belief Networks Using Discriminative Features for Phone Recognition." In *Proceedings of the 2011 IEEE International Conference on Acoustics, Speech, and Signal Processing*, 5060–5063. Piscataway, NJ: Institute of Electrical and Electronics Engineers, 2011.

Mohamed, Abdel-rahman, Dong Yu, and Li Deng. "Investigation of Full-Sequence Training of Deep Belief Networks for Speech Recognition." In *Interspeech 2010: Proceedings of 11th Annual Conference of the International Speech Communication Association*, edited by Takao Kobayashi, Keikichi Hirose, and Satoshi Nakamura, 2846–2849. 2010. www.isca-speech.org/archive/interspeech_2010/i10_2846.html.

Nair, Vinod, and Geoffrey E. Hinton. "3D Object Recognition with Deep Belief Nets." In *NIPS '09: Proceedings of Advances in Neural Information Processing Systems 22*, edited Yoshua Bengio, Dale Schuurmans, John Lafferty, Chris Williams, and Aron Culotta, 1339-1347. 2009. http://machinelearning.wustl.edu/mlpapers/paper_files/NIPS2009_0807.pdf.

Pape, Leo, Faustino Gomez, Mark Ring, and Jürgen Schmidhuber. "Modular Deep Belief Networks That Do Not Forget." In *Proceedings of the 2011 International Joint Conference on Neural Networks*, 1191-1198. Piscataway, NJ: Institute of Electrical and Electronics Engineers, 2011.

Poon, Hoifung, and Pedro Domingos. "Sum-Product Networks: A New Deep Architecture." In *Proceedings of the 2011 IEEE International Conference on Computer Vision Workshops*, 689-690. Piscataway, NJ: Institute of Electrical and Electronics Engineers, 2011.

Ranzato, Marc'Aurelio, and Martin Szummer. "Semi-Supervised Learning of Compact Document Representations with Deep Networks." In *ICML '08: Proceedings of the 25th International Conference on Machine Learning*, edited by Andrew McCallum and Sam Roweis, 792-799. New York: ACM, 2008.

Rosenblatt, Frank. "The Perceptron: A Probabilistic Model for Information Storage and Organization in the Brain." *Psychological Review* 65, no. 6 (1958): 386-408.

Sainath, Tara N., Brian Kingsbury, Bhuvana Ramabhadran, Petr Fousek, Petr Novak, and Abdel-rahman Mohamed. "Making Deep Belief Networks Effective for Large Vocabulary Continuous Speech Recognition." In *Proceedings of the 2011 IEEE Workshop on Automatic Speech Recognition and Understanding*, edited by Thomas Hain and Kai Yu, 30-35. Piscataway, NJ: Institute of Electrical and Electronics Engineers, 2011.

Salakhutdinov, Ruslan, and Geoffrey Hinton. "Learning a Nonlinear Embedding by Preserving Class Neighbourhood Structure." In *Proceedings of the 11th International Conference on Artificial Intelligence and Statistics*, edited by Marina Meila and Xiaotong Shen, 412-419. 2007. http://jmlr.csail.mit.edu/proceedings/papers/v2/salakhutdinov07a/salakhutdinov07a.pdf.

Salakhutdinov, Ruslan, and Geoffrey Hinton. "Deep Boltzmann Machines." In *Proceedings of the 12th International Conference on Artificial Intelligence and Statistics*, edited by David van Dyk and Max Welling, 448-455. 2009. www.jmlr.org/proceedings/papers/v5/salakhutdinov09a/salakhutdinov09a.pdf.

Salakhutdinov, Ruslan, and Hugo Larochelle. "Efficient Learning of Deep Boltzmann Machines." In *Proceedings of the 13th Annual International Conference on Artificial Intelligence and Statistics*, edited by Yee Whye Teh and Mike Titterington, 693-700. 2010. www.dmi.usherb.ca/~larocheh/publications/aistats_2010_dbm_recnet.pdf.

Schmidhuber, Jurgen. "Learning Complex, Extended Sequences Using the Principle of History Compression." *Neural Computation* 4 (1992): 234-242.

Seide, Frank, Gang Li, and Dong Yu. "Conversational Speech Transcription Using Context-Dependent Deep Neural Networks." In *Interspeech 2011: Proceedings of 11th Annual Conference of the International Speech Communication Association*, edited by Piero Cosi, Renato De Mori, Giuseppe Di Fabbrizio, and Roberto Pieraccini, 437-440. 2011. www.isca-speech.org/archive/interspeech_2011.

Smolensky, Paul. "Information Processing in Dynamical Systems: Foundations of Harmony Theory." In *Parallel Distributed Processing: Explorations in the Microstructure of Cognition*. Vol. 1, edited by David E. Rumelhart, James L. McClelland, and the PDP Research Group, 194-281. Cambridge, MA: Massachusetts Institute of Technology Press, 1986.

Susskind, Joshua M., Geoffrey E. Hinton, Javier R. Movellan, and Adam K. Anderson. "Generating Facial Expressions with Deep Belief Nets." In *Affective Computing: Focus on EmotionExpression, Synthesis and Recognition*, edited by Jimmy Or, 421-440. Vienna: I-Tech, 2008.

Uetz, Rafael, and Sven Behnke. "Locally-Connected Hierarchical Neural Networks for GPU-Accelerated Object Recongition." In *Proceedings of the NIPS 2009 Workshop on Large-Scale Machine Learning Parallelism and Massive Datasets*. 2009.

Werbos, Paul. "Beyond Regression: New Tools for Prediction and Analysis in the Behavioral Sciences." PhD thesis, Harvard University, 1974.

Weston, Jason, Frédéric Ratle, Hossein Mobahi, and Ronan Collobert. "Deep Learning via Semi-Supervised Embedding." In *Neural Networks: Tricks of the Trade, Second Edition,* edited by Grégoire Montavon, Geneviève Orr, and Klaus-Robert Müller, 639–655. Berlin: Springer, 2012.

Wulsin, D. F., J. R. Gupta, R. Mani, J. A. Blanco, and B. Litt. "Modeling Electroencephalography Waveforms with Semi-Supervised Deep Belief Nets: Fast Classification and Anomaly Measurement." *Journal of Neural Engineering* 8, no. 3 (2011): 036015.

Zhou, Shusen, Qingcai Chen, and Xiaolong Wang. "Active Deep Networks for Semi-Supervised Sentiment Classification." In *Proceedings of the 23rd International Conference on Computational Linguistics: Posters*, edited by Chu-Ren Huang and Dan Jurafsky, 1515–1523. Stroudsburg, PA: Association for Computational Linguistics, 2010.

CHAPTER 8

■ ■ ■

Cortical Algorithms

> *If you just have a single problem to solve, then fine, go ahead and use a neural network.*
> *But if you want to do science and understand how to choose architectures, or how to go to*
> *a new problem, you have to understand what different architectures can and cannot do.*
>
> —Marvin Minsky[1]

Computational models inspired by the structural and functional properties of the human brain have seen impressive gains since the mid-1980s, owing to significant discoveries in neuroscience and advancements in computing technology. Among these models, *cortical algorithms* (CAs) have emerged as a biologically inspired approach, modeled after the human visual cortex, which stores sequences of patterns in an invariant form and recalls those patterns autoassociatively. This chapter details the structure and mathematical formulation of CA then presents a case study of CA generalization accuracy in identifying isolated Arabic speech using an entropy-based weight update.

Cortical Algorithm Primer

Initially developed by Edelman and Mountcastle (1978), and inspired by the visual human cortex, CAs are positioned to be superior to the early generations *of artificial neural networks* (ANNs), which do not use temporal and spatial relationships in data for building *machine learning* models.

   The CA model consists of a multilayered network, with the cortical column as the basic structure. The network is trained in a two-stage manner: the first learning stage is unsupervised and trains the columns to identify independent features from the patterns occurring; the second stage relies on supervised feedback learning to create invariant representations.

Cortical Algorithm Structure

The human brain is a six-layered structure consisting of a very large number of neurons strongly connected via feedforward and feedback connections. An important property of the neocortex is its structural and functional uniformity: all units in the network seem similar, and they perform the same basic operation. Like this brain architecture, CA architecture has minicolumns of varying thickness (Edelman and Mountcastle 1978). A *minicolumn* is a group of neurons that share the same receptive field: neurons belonging to a minicolumn are associated with the same sensory input region. The minicolumn is the basic structure in a cortical network, in contrast to neurons in a classical ANN. An association of minicolumns is called a *hypercolumn* or *layer*

---

[1]Marvin Minsky, "Scientist on the Set: An Interview with Marvin Minsky," in *HAL's Legacy: 2001's Computer as Dream and Reality*, by David G. Stork (Massachusetts Institute of Technology Press, 1998), p. 18.

(in what follows, the terms *column* and *minicolumn* are used interchangeably). Connections in a CA network occur in two directions: horizontally, between columns in the same layer, and vertically, between columns of consecutive layers. Although connections between nonconsecutive layers are present in the human cortex, these connections are omitted in CA, for the sake of simplicity.

Figure 8-1 displays a representation of a cortical network. The lateral inhibiting connections are not shown explicitly in the figure because their functionality is not physical; that is, these connections do not represent data propagated between neurons, but serve as a means of communication between the columns.

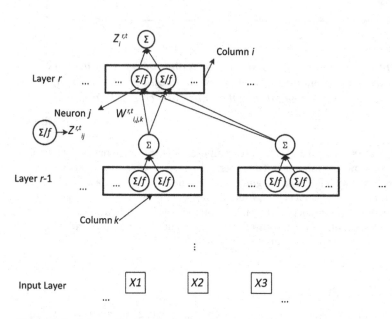

Figure 8-1. *Schematic of cortical network connectivity*

The notation adopted hereafter is given in Figure 8-2, where $W_{i,j,k}^{r,t}$ represents the weight of the connection between the *j*th neuron of the *i*th column of layer *r* and the *k*th column of the previous layer *(r-1)* during the training epoch *t*. **Bold variables** stand for vector entities, underlined variables represent matrices, and *italic variables* represent scalar entities.

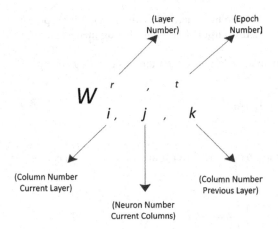

Figure 8-2. *Nomenclature conventions for the weight* $W_{i,j,k}^{r,t}$

During the learning process a connection is disabled by assigning to it a zero weight. If the network is fully connected, each neuron j in the column is connected to all the columns in the previous layer. All connections are *elastic*; that is, if a connection is disabled during the feedforward process, it can be restored during the feedback learning, and vice versa.

The *weight matrix* representing the state of a column composed of M nodes during the training epoch t is defined by

$$\underline{W_i^{r,t}} = \begin{bmatrix} W_{i,1}^{r,t} & W_{i,2}^{r,t} & \dots & W_{i,j}^{r,t} & \dots & W_{i,M}^{r,t} \end{bmatrix}. \tag{8-1}$$

The *weight vector* $W_{i,j}^{r,t}$ of the connections entering neuron j of column i in layer r, composed of L_r columns, is given by

$$W_{i,j}^{r,t} = \begin{bmatrix} W_{i,j,1}^{r,t} & W_{i,j,2}^{r,t} & \dots & W_{i,j,k}^{r,t} & \dots & W_{i,j,L_{r-1}}^{r,t} \end{bmatrix}', \tag{8-2}$$

where L_{r-1} is the number of columns in the layer $(r-1)$, L_r represents the number of columns in the layer r, and the superscript $'$ stands for the transpose operator.

Expanding $W_i^{r,t}$ yields

$$\underline{W_i^{r,t}} = \begin{bmatrix} W_{i,1,1}^{r,t} & \cdots & W_{i,j,1}^{r,t} & \cdots & W_{i,M,1}^{r,t} \\ \vdots & \vdots & \vdots & \vdots & \vdots \\ W_{i,1,k}^{r,t} & \cdots & W_{i,j,k}^{r,t} & \cdots & W_{i,M,k}^{r,t} \\ \vdots & \vdots & \vdots & \vdots & \vdots \\ W_{i,1,L_{r-1}}^{r,t} & \cdots & W_{i,j,L_{r-1}}^{r,t} & \cdots & W_{i,M,L_{r-1}}^{r,t} \end{bmatrix}. \tag{8-3}$$

The output vector $Z^{r,t}$ of layer r for epoch t is given by

$$Z^{r,t} = \begin{bmatrix} Z_1^{r,t}, & Z_2^{r,t}, & \dots, & Z_i^{r,t}, & \dots, & Z_{L_r}^{r,t} \end{bmatrix}', \tag{8-4}$$

where $Z_i^{r,t}$ is the output of column i in the layer for the same training epoch.

Considering the output of a neuron to be the result of the nonlinear activation function $f(.)$, in response to the weighted sum of the connections entering the neuron, the output of the column is defined as the sum of the outputs of the neurons constituting the column.

$Z_{i,j}^{r,t}$ is the output of the jth neuron of the ith column in the rth layer at the training epoch t, given by

$$Z_i^{r,t} = \sum_{j=1}^{M} Z_{i,j}^{r,t} \; ; \; Z_{i,j}^{r,t} = f\left(\sum_{k=1}^{L_{r-1}} W_{i,j,k}^{r,t} Z_k^{r-1,t} \right). \tag{8-5}$$

$Z_{i,j}^{r}$ is the output of the jth neuron constituting the ith column of the rth layer, and $f\left(\sum_{k=1}^{L_{r-1}} W_{i,j,k}^{r,t} Z_k^{r-1,t} \right)$ is defined by

$$\begin{cases} f\left(\sum_{k=1}^{L_{r-1}} W_{i,j,k}^{r,t} Z_k^{r-1,t} \right) = \dfrac{1}{1 + \exp\left\{ \sum_{k=1}^{L_{r-1}} W_{i,j,k}^{r,t} Z_k^{r-1,t} \cdot \left(\varphi\left(\sum_{k=1}^{L_{r-1}} W_{i,j,k}^{r,t} Z_k^{r-1,t} \right) - T \right) \right\}} \\ \\ \varphi\left(\sum_{k=1}^{L_{r-1}} W_{i,j,k}^{r,t} Z_k^{r-1,t} \right) = \begin{cases} -2 \; if \; \sum_{k=1}^{L_{r-1}} W_{i,j,k}^{r,t} Z_k^{r-1,t} = 1 \\ \\ \sum_{k=1}^{L_{r-1}} W_{i,j,k}^{r,t} Z_k^{r-1,t} \; otherwise, \end{cases} \end{cases} \tag{8-6}$$

where T is a tolerance parameter empirically selected and constant for all epochs and columns. It is assumed that all weights are normalized and bounded between –1 and 1.

The nonlinear activation function is analogous to the propagation of the action potential through an axon in the neural system.

Training of Cortical Algorithms

Connectivity within the columns is modeled through the value of the synaptic weights. Initially, there is no specific connectivity between cortical columns. It is assumed that the network is fully connected before training. Also, all synaptic weights are initialized to random values that are very close to 0 to avoid preference to any particular pattern.

The training process, as introduced by Edelman and Mountcastle (1978) and developed further by Hashmi (2010), is described in the following sections, according to its main phases: unsupervised feedforward, supervised feedback, and weight update.

Unsupervised Feedforward

Feedforward learning trains columns to identify features via random firing and repeated exposure. When a pattern is presented, the input is propagated through the network. Each column has a small probability of firing, which means that most of the columns in a particular layer stay inactive. When the random firing of a particular column coincides with a particular input pattern, this activation is enforced. In other words, when activation is enforced, the column firing strengthens its weights, according to the strengthening weight update rule. At the same time, the column firing inhibits neighboring columns in the same layer from firing by weakening the weights, as presented in the inhibiting update rule.

The weight update rules are as follows:

- *Inhibiting*:

$$W_{i,j,k}^{r,t+1} = Z_k^{r-1,t} \cdot \left(W_{i,j,k}^{r,t} - \Omega\left(W_{i,j}^{r,t} \right) \right) \qquad (8\text{-}7)$$

- *Strengthening*:

$$W_{i,j,k}^{r,t+1} = Z_k^{r-1,t} \cdot \left(W_{i,j,k}^{r,t} + C_{i,j,k}^{r,t} + \rho \cdot \frac{1}{1 + e^{\frac{\left(W_{i,j,k}^{r,t} - T \right)}{\Omega\left(W_i^{r,t} \right)}}} \right), \qquad (8\text{-}8)$$

where $\Omega(W_{i,j}^{r,t})$ is given by

$$\Omega\left(W_i^{r,t} \right) = \sum_{j=1}^{M} \sum_{k=1}^{L_{r-1}} C_{i,j,k}^{r,t} W_{i,j,k}^{r,t} ; C_{i,j,k}^{r,t} = \begin{cases} 1 & if \;\; W_{i,j,k}^{r,t} > \varepsilon \\ 0 & otherwise \end{cases} \qquad (8\text{-}9)$$

and where ρ is a tuning parameter, and ε is the firing threshold chosen empirically to be constant for all epochs and columns.

With repeated exposure the network learns to extract certain features of the input data, and the columns learn to fire for specific patterns. Layers in the network extract aspects of the input in increasing complexity. Thus, lower layers detect simple features, whereas higher stages learn concepts and more complex abstractions of the data.

Supervised Feedback

Feedforward learning trains columns to identify features of the data, such that the hierarchical network starts to recognize patterns. When the network is exposed to a variation of a pattern that is quite different from the previous one, the top layer of columns that are supposed to fire for that pattern do not, and only some of the columns in the hierarchy may fire, which leads to a misclassification. Through the CA feedback mechanism, the error occurring at the top layer generates a feedback signal that forces the column firing for the original pattern to fire, while inhibiting the column that is firing for the variation. Over multiple exposures the top layer should reach the desired firing scheme (also called *stable activation*). More specifically, designated columns in the top layer learn to fire for a particular pattern. Once the columns start to give a stable activation for pattern variations, the feedback signal is propagated back to the previous layers. Each layer is then trained until a convergence criterion, expressed as an error term in function of the actual output, and a desired output (firing scheme) are reached. The feedback signal is sent to the preceding layers only once the error in the layer concerned converges to a value below a certain, predefined tolerance threshold. The excitatory and inhibiting signals follow the same update rules as for the feedforward learning.

When used for the feedback learning of the network, CA can be summarized by the following steps:

1. Following the feedforward unsupervised batch learning (i.e., after the training data are entirely propagated through the network), a desired output scheme per layer is formed by averaging the column outputs. If $Z_{i_k}^r$ is the output of the ith column in the rth layer of the network for a certain training instance denoted by k and given N instances in total; the desired output for this particular column $Z_{i_d}^r$ is given by:

$$Z_{i_d}^r = avg\left(Z_{i_k}^r \right) = \frac{1}{N} \sum_{k=1}^{N} Z_{i_k}^r . \qquad (8\text{-}10)$$

2. Starting with the last layer, compare the measured output of each column as a response to each instance k, $Z_i^{r,t}$ with the desired value of $Z_{i_d}^r$. If the desired output of a column is a firing state, whereas the actual is different, the column is strengthened (see Equation 8-8; the column is inhibited (see Equation 8-7) if the opposite occurs (i.e., if the actual output is firing, whereas a nonfiring state is desired).

3. Repeat step 2 until the error threshold is met.

4. Follow the same procedure for the previous layers, one layer at a time.

Weight Update

In CA, good accuracy is taxed with computationally expensive and lengthy training. This cost is mainly due to the computation of the exponential function invoked during the weight update process for each neuron while the weights of the network are learned.

For a particular node $W_{i,j,k}^{r,t}$, Equation 8-8 may be written as:

$$\begin{cases} W_{i,j,k}^{r,t+1} = \alpha W_{i,j,k}^{r,t} + \theta\left(W_{i,j,k}^{r,t}\right) \\ \theta\left(W_{i,j,k}^{r,t}\right) = \beta \cdot \dfrac{1}{1+\exp\left[\dfrac{W_{i,j,k}^{r,t}-T}{\Omega}\right]} + \delta. \\ \alpha = Z_k^{r-1,t}, \beta = Z_k^{r-1,t}\rho \\ \delta = Z_k^{r-1,t} \cdot C_{i,j,k}^{r,t} \end{cases} \qquad (8\text{-}11)$$

Here, α, β, and δ are variables that depend on the training epoch as well as the column considered; therefore, a suitable nomenclature would be in the form $\chi_k^{r-1,t}$. For the sake of simplicity, one can omit the subscripts and superscripts for these variables, referring to $\Omega(W_i^{r,t})$ as Ω.

As demonstrated in Equation 8-11, the parameters of the exponential weight update rule—α, β, δ, Ω, and T—depend on the state of the column considered. Therefore, it can be inferred that the strengthening rule is a family of exponential functions with varying parameters for each column. The update of a column requires the computation of the exponential function for each of the nodes—hence, the lengthy training.

Figure 8-3 shows a plot of θ, with respect to the value of the neuron weight for a random node.

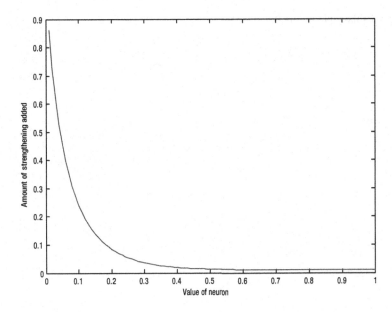

Figure 8-3. Plot of $\theta\left(W_{i,j,k}^{r,t}\right)$ versus $W_{i,j,k}^{r,t}$

The computational cost involved in the strengthening rule also comes from the calculation of the exponential function. For example, MATLAB software uses the binomial theorem (see Equation 8-12) to compute the approximate value of an exponential, and this approximation is computed up to orders ranging from 5 to 10 (Mohler 2011):

$$e^x = 1 + x + \frac{x^2}{2!} + \frac{x^3}{3!} + \cdots + \frac{x^n}{n!} + \cdots = \sum_{i=0}^{\infty} \frac{x^i}{i!} . \tag{8-12}$$

The number of operations required to compute the exponential function is summarized in Table 8-1.

Table 8-1. *Required Operations for Exponential Function*

Expression	Operations	Total Number of Operations
$i!$	$2*3*\ldots*i$	i-two multiplications
x^i	$x*x*x*\ldots$	i multiplications
$\dfrac{x^i}{i!}$	$\dfrac{x*x*x\ldots}{2*3*\ldots*i}$	$2i$-one operation
e^x	$\displaystyle\sum_{i=0}^{n} \frac{x^i}{i!}$	$\displaystyle\sum_{i=0}^{n}(2i-1)+n = n^2+n$

The workflow for CA training is displayed in Figure 8-4.

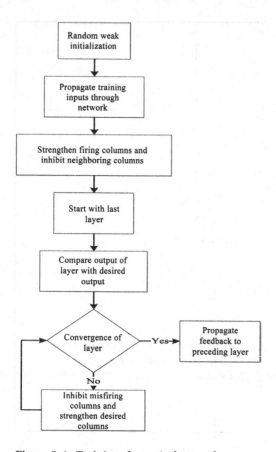

Figure 8-4. *Training of a cortical network*

Experimental Results

Experimental results for various pattern recognition databases obtained from the University of California, Irvine, Machine Learning Repository (Bache and Lichman 2013) show CA superior performance, as detailed for the following datasets:

- *Letter Recognition dataset*: This dataset consists of a collection of 20,000 black-and-white images to be classified as one of the 26 capital letters of the English alphabet (Slate 1991). Each instance is represented by a set of 16 features of integer type, normalized into a range of 0-15 representing aspects of the image, such as horizontal and vertical position, and width and length. The best accuracy reported for this dataset is 97.58 percent (Bagirov and Ugon 2011).

- *Image Segmentation dataset*: This dataset is collection of images sized 3 × 3 each, represented by 19 attributes describing features of the image, such as average intensity, saturation, and hue (Vision Group 1990). The dataset is divided into a training set consisting of 210 instances and a testing set of 2,100 instances; each image belongs to one of 7 classes. Dash et al. (2003) achieved an accuracy of 98.6 percent.

- *ISOLET (Isolated Letter Speech Recognition) dataset*: The task in this experiment is to classify a collection of isolated spoken English letters as one of 26 classes (A-Z). The dataset is composed of 2,800 instances uttered by 150 speakers, each instance represented by a set of 617 features, including spectral coefficients, contour features, sonorant features, presonorant features, and postsonorant features (Cole and Fanty 1994). The reported accuracy of this database is 96.73 percent (Dietterich 1994).

- *PENDIGITS (Pen-Based Recognition of Handwritten Digits) dataset*: This experiment consists of pen-based recognition of handwritten digits. The database collects 10,992 samples from 44 writers, each sample being a sequence of (x, y) coordinates representing the trajectory of the pen during the writing process. The sequences have been resampled to obtain a fixed-length attribute vector equal to 16 (eight pairs of (x, y) coordinates) and normalized to eliminate the effect of artifacts resulting from different handwritings. The 10,992 samples are divided into a training set of 7,494 instances and 3,498 instances for testing. The accuracy of this dataset reached 98.6 percent (Alpaydin and Alimoglu 1998).

- *Multiple Features dataset*: This dataset consists of 649 features, for a total of 2,000 patterns of handwritten numerals (`0'--`9') extracted from a collection of Dutch utility maps (Duin 2013). These digits are represented in terms of six feature sets: 76 Fourier coefficients of the character shapes; 216 profile correlations; 64 Karhunen-Loève coefficients; 240 pixel averages, in 2 × 3 windows; 47 Zernike moments; and six morphological features. The best accuracy achieved is 98 percent (Perkins and Theiler 2003).

- *Abalone dataset*: The task for this dataset is to classify the age of a collection of 4,177 abalones from a total of eight physical measurements, such as height, weight, diameter, and length. This dataset is characterized by a highly unbalanced class distribution and has achieved an accuracy of 79.0 percent (Tan and Dowe 2003).

Table 8-2 compiles the recognition rate, training time, and total number of required iterations for convergence, based on a fourfold cross-validation, using the mean squared error (MSE) and the well-formed *cross-entropy* (CE) cost functions at the output layer.

Two experiments were performed:

- *Experiment 1*: CA with the exponential weight update rule and MSE as a cost function

- *Experiment 2*: CA with the exponential weight rule and CE as a cost function

Table 8-2. *Experimental Results*

Dataset	Measure	Experiment 1	Experiment 2
Letter Recognition	% Accuracy	98.3	98.8
	Training time (min)	223	235
	Number of epochs	237	225
	Number of operations	$8.9 * 10^{12}$	$1.1 * 10^{13}$
Image Segmentation	% Accuracy	99.3	99.7
	Training time (min)	45	52
	Number of epochs	77	69
	Number of operations	$22 * 10^{12}$	$2.5 * 10^{12}$
ISOLET	% Accuracy	98.1	98.7
	Training time (min)	54	67
	Number of epochs	147	131
	Number of operations	$2.6 * 10^{12}$	$3.2 * 10^{12}$
PENDIGITS	% Accuracy	99.8	100
	Training time (min)	135	154
	Number of epochs	94	82
	Number of operations	$6.5 * 10^{12}$	$7.4 * 10^{12}$
Multiple Features	% Accuracy	98.7	99.1
	Training time (min)	35	42
	Number of epochs	66	53
	Number of operations	$1.4 * 10^{12}$	$2.0 * 10^{12}$
Abalone	% Accuracy	91.8	92.2
	Training time (min)	56	68
	Number of epochs	70	62

On average the CE cost function results in better classification accuracy. However, this is achieved at the expense of an increase in computational complexity and training time.

■ **Note**   Despite their superior hypothetical performance, CAs remain less widely used than ANNs, owing to their longer and more expensive training and computational requirements. These make them unattractive for online learning, energy-aware computing nodes, and large datasets with stringent restrictions on the training duration.

Modified Cortical Algorithms Applied to Arabic Spoken Digits: Case Study

Because CAs have not been extensively implemented for *automatic speech recognition* (in particular for the Arabic language), the following sections show how CA strengthening and inhibiting rules originally employed during feedback were modified with weighted entropy concepts that were added to the CA cost function and the weight update rule.

Entropy-Based Weight Update Rule

During the feedback learning stage of a CA, the output of each layer is compared with a desired state of firing, and the weights are updated until an error term is reduced to a minimum threshold value. Using the least squares criterion, large error values influence the learning process much more than smaller ones. For a class of problems, the gradient descent algorithm, with the MSE as a criterion for weight updates, can be trapped in a local minimum and so it will fail to find the optimal solution. In contrast, the well-formed CE criterion, employing a gradient descent algorithm, guarantees convergence to the optimal solution during learning (Wittner and Denker 1988).

The three properties of a well-formed error function of the form $J\left(W_{i,j,k}^{r,t}\right)=\sum h(W_{i,j,k}^{r,t})$ are as follows:

- For all $W_{i,j,k}^{r,t}$ the derivative of $h(W_{i,j,k}^{r,t})$, defined as $h^{'}\left(W_{i,j,k}^{r,t}\right)$, must be negative.

- There must exist an $\epsilon > 0$, such that $-h^{'}\left(W_{i,j,k}^{r,t}\right) \geq \epsilon$ for all $W_{i,j,k}^{r,t} \leq 0$.

- The function h must be differentiable and bounded.

CE as a cost function criterion can be written as

$$J^{r,t} = \sum_{i=1}^{L_r} Z_{di}^{\ r} \ln \frac{Z_i^{r,t}}{Z_{di}^{\ r}},$$

where $Z_{di}^{\ r}$ is the desired output of the *i*th column of layer *r* at epoch *t*.

If you adopt the same procedure for the feedback learning, and assume that training convergence of each layer happens when the entropy measure falls below a predetermined threshold value, the weight update rule becomes:

- *Inhibiting*:

$$W_{i,j,k}^{r,t+1} = \frac{\Delta J^{r,t}}{\Delta Z_i^{r,t}} \cdot Z_k^{r-1,t} \left(W_{i,j,k}^{r,t} - \Omega \left(W_i^{r,t} \right) \right)$$ (8-13)

- *Strengthening*:

$$W_{i,j,k}^{r,t+1} = \frac{\Delta J^{r,t}}{\Delta Z_i^{r,t}} \cdot Z_k^{r-1,t} \cdot \left(W_{i,j,k}^{r,t} + C_{i,j,k}^{r,t} + \rho \cdot \frac{1}{1 + \exp\left[\frac{W_{i,j,k}^{r,t} - T}{\Omega\left(W_i^{r,t} \right)} \right]} \right)$$ (8-14)

One advantage of using the proposed gradient descent weighted rules is that the CE cost function diverges if one of the outputs converges to the wrong extreme; hence, the gradient descent reacts quickly. In contrast, the MSE cost function approaches a constant, and the gradient descent on the least square will wander on a plateau, even though the error may not be small.

Experimental Validation

Using a CA of six hidden layers, starting with 2,000 columns of 20 nodes for the first hidden layer and decreasing the number of columns by half between consecutive layers, four experiments, employing the weighted entropy weight update rule, were performed based on a fivefold cross-validation:

- *Experiment 1*: CA trained using the MSE cost function and the original weight update rule

- *Experiment 2*: CA trained using the MSE cost function and the proposed weight update rule

- *Experiment 3*: CA trained using the CE cost function and the original weight update rule

- *Experiment 4*: CA trained using the CE function and the proposed weight update rule

Simulations were executed, using MATLAB R2011a software on an Intel i7 at 2GHz and 6GB RAM on a Windows 7 Home Premium operating system, using a modified central nervous system (CNS) library. Developed at the Massachusetts Institute of Technology, by Mutch, Knoblich, and Poggio (2010), the CNS library is a framework for simulating cortically organized networks.

The database was obtained from the UCI Machine Learning Repository and consists of a collection of 13 Mel frequency cepstral coefficient (MFCC) frames representing 8,800 spoken Arabic digits—one of ten classes (0-9), uttered by 88 different speakers, obtained after filtering the spoken digits, using a moving Hamming window. Several techniques were validated on this database; the best achieved result shows a 97.03 percent recognition rate, based on a threefold cross-validation, using a multiclass SVM classifier (Ji and Sun 2011).

TREE REPRESENTATION FOR ARABIC PHONEMES

As the first language in 22 countries, Arabic ranks fifth among the most spoken languages in the world (Mosa and Ali 2009). Although applications treating speech recognition have increased significantly (e.g., iPhone 4S Siri interface), implementation for the Arabic language is limited, mainly because of its morphological complexity. For Arabic automatic speech recognition, the recognition of phonemes constitutes an important step in continuous speech analysis. Most research proceeds by extracting isolated phonemes or small phonetic segments (El-Obaid, Al-Nassiri, and Maaly 2006; Awais 2003; Gevaert, Tsenov, and Mladenov 2010; Al-Manie, Alkanhal, and Al-Ghamdi 2009) for analysis of longer speech signals (Abushariah et al. 2010) and broadcast news (Al-Manie, Alkanhal, and Al-Ghamdi 2009), using several techniques, such as ANN (Essa, Tolba, and Elmougy 2008), fuzzy HMM (Shenouda, Zaki, and Goneid 2006), fuzzy logic, concurrent self-organizing maps (Sehgal, Gondal, and Dooley 2004), and HMM (Satori, Harti, and Chenfour 2007; Bourouba et al. 2010; Biadsy, Moreno, and Jansche 2012).

Spoken in the Middle East and North Africa, Arabic has different dialects. However, Literary Arabic (also called Modern Standard Arabic) is the official form used in documents and for formal speaking in all Arabic-speaking countries. One of the differences between spoken and written Arabic is the presence in the latter of diacritics (marks used to indicate how a letter should be pronounced). The complexity of Arabic is the result of its unusual morphology: words are formed using a root-and-pattern scheme, in which the root is composed of 3 consonants, leading to several possibilities from one root. Phonetically, Arabic has 28 consonant segments and 6 vowels (Newman 1984). Phonemes can be grouped according to the articulation of the lips and tongue during speech, as shown in the classification of Arabic phonemes.

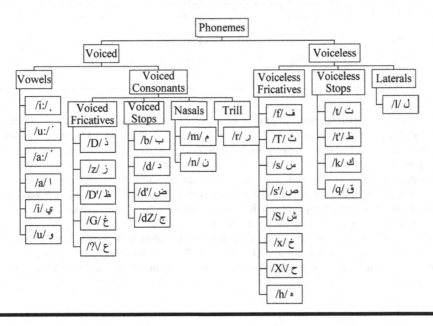

■ **Note** MFCCs can model the acoustic content of speech independently of the source (speaker). MFCCs are calculated by mapping the logarithm of the spectrum into the Mel scale and converting the obtained signal back to the time domain, using discrete cosine transform (Klatau 2005).

For consistency, the first experiment with the data used the 13 MFCCs provided and then added the first and second derivatives of the MFCCs, that is, coefficients with a feature vector of size 39. Tables 8-3 and 8-4 show a comparison of the results obtained for all experiments with the average recognition rate obtained, training time, and number of epochs required for convergence.

Table 8-3. *Results for the Spoken Arabic Digit Dataset, Using 13 MFCCs*

	Experiment 1	Experiment 2	Experiment 3	Experiment 4
Recognition rate (%)	97.4	98.4	97.9	99.0
Training time (min)	90	110	100	115
Number of epochs until convergence	240	232	235	220

Table 8-4. *Results for the Arabic Spoken Digit Dataset, Using 39 MFCCs*

	Experiment 1	Experiment 2	Experiment 3	Experiment 4
Recognition rate (%)	98.2	99.1	98.6	99.7
Training time (min)	125	142	137	156
Number of epochs until convergence	335	298	322	280

Tables 8-3 and 8-4 demonstrate that training of the cortical network, using the entropy cost function and the proposed weight update rule, performed better than the original training parameters. This improvement is achieved at the expense of a small worsening of the required training time. Despite the lengthy training time, however, the proposed weight update rule requires fewer training epochs to converge, compared with the original weight update rule. This is because the amount of strengthening added using the proposed rule is proportional to the gradient of the cost function, meaning that fewer training epochs are necessary to reach convergence. The proposed weight update rule involves computing the entropy gradient, which is computationally more expensive, compared with the original weight update rule.

The confusion matrices in Figure 8-5, obtained for the image segmentation dataset using both cost functions, demonstrate that although a significant trend is observed in the confusion between classes 1, 7, and 8 with the classical distance measure, the proposed entropy-based update rule was able to correct this trend partially.

Confusion Matrix (left)

Output Class	1	2	3	4	5	6	7	
1	65 / 11.3%	0 / 0.0%	0 / 0.0%	0 / 0.0%	0 / 0.0%	0 / 0.0%	0 / 0.0%	100% / 0.0%
2	0 / 0.0%	98 / 17.0%	0 / 0.0%	0 / 0.0%	0 / 0.0%	0 / 0.0%	0 / 0.0%	100% / 0.0%
3	0 / 0.0%	0 / 0.0%	77 / 13.3%	0 / 0.0%	1 / 0.2%	0 / 0.0%	0 / 0.0%	98.7% / 1.3%
4	1 / 0.2%	0 / 0.0%	0 / 0.0%	80 / 13.9%	1 / 0.2%	0 / 0.0%	0 / 0.0%	97.6% / 2.4%
5	0 / 0.0%	1 / 0.2%	0 / 0.0%	0 / 0.0%	91 / 15.8%	0 / 0.0%	0 / 0.0%	98.9% / 1.1%
6	0 / 0.0%	0 / 0.0%	0 / 0.0%	0 / 0.0%	0 / 0.0%	87 / 15.1%	0 / 0.0%	100% / 0.0%
7	0 / 0.0%	0 / 0.0%	0 / 0.0%	0 / 0.0%	0 / 0.0%	0 / 0.0%	75 / 13.0%	100% / 0.0%
	98.5% / 1.5%	100% / 0.0%	98.7% / 1.3%	100% / 0.0%	97.8% / 2.2%	100% / 0.0%	100% / 0.0%	99.3% / 0.7%

Target Class

Confusion Matrix (right)

Output Class	1	2	3	4	5	6	7	
1	65 / 11.3%	0 / 0.0%	0 / 0.0%	0 / 0.0%	0 / 0.0%	0 / 0.0%	0 / 0.0%	100% / 0.0%
2	0 / 0.0%	98 / 17.0%	0 / 0.0%	0 / 0.0%	0 / 0.0%	0 / 0.0%	0 / 0.0%	100% / 0.0%
3	0 / 0.0%	0 / 0.0%	77 / 13.3%	0 / 0.0%	1 / 0.2%	0 / 0.0%	0 / 0.0%	98.7% / 1.3%
4	2 / 0.3%	0 / 0.0%	0 / 0.0%	79 / 13.7%	1 / 0.2%	0 / 0.0%	0 / 0.0%	96.3% / 3.7%
5	0 / 0.0%	1 / 0.2%	1 / 0.2%	1 / 0.2%	91 / 15.6%	0 / 0.0%	0 / 0.0%	97.8% / 2.2%
6	0 / 0.0%	0 / 0.0%	0 / 0.0%	0 / 0.0%	0 / 0.0%	87 / 15.1%	0 / 0.0%	100% / 0.0%
7	0 / 0.0%	0 / 0.0%	0 / 0.0%	0 / 0.0%	0 / 0.0%	0 / 0.0%	75 / 13.0%	100% / 0.0%
	97.0% / 3.0%	100% / 0.0%	98.7% / 1.3%	98.8% / 1.2%	97.8% / 2.2%	100% / 0.0%	100% / 0.0%	99.0% / 1.0%

Target Class

Figure 8-5. *Confusion matrices for the Image Segmentation dataset: left, exponential rule; right, linear rule*

Figure 8-6 compares the CE cost function with the training epochs obtained while training the cortical network using the entropy cost function for the proposed and the regular weight update rules. Note that the proposed weight update converges to a smaller MSE value, compared with the regular update, which is consistent with the recognition rates obtained earlier.

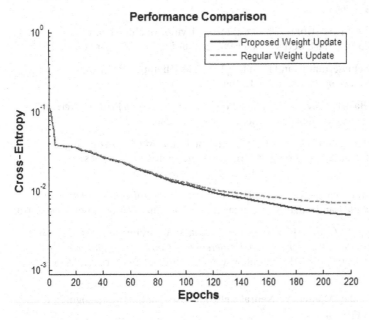

Figure 8-6. *Entropy cost function comparison for regular and proposed weight update rules*

References

Abushariah, Mohammad A. M., Raja N. Ainon, Roziati Zainuddin, Moustafa Elshafei, and Othman O. Khalifa. "Natural Speaker-Independent Arabic Speech Recognition System Based on Hidden Markov Models Using Sphinx Tools." In *Proceedings of the 2010 International Conference on Computer and Communication Engineering*, Kuala Lumpur, Malaysia, May 11-12, 2010, 1-6. Piscataway, NJ: Institute of Electrical and Electronic Engineers, 2010.

Awais, M. M. "Recognition of Arabic Phonemes Using Fuzzy Rule Base System." In *Proceedings of the 7th International Multitopic Conference*, Islamabad, Pakistan, December 8-9, 2003, 367-370. Piscataway, NJ: Institute of Electrical and Electronic Engineers, 2003.

Bache, K., and M. Lichman. "University of California, Irvine, Machine Learning Repository." Irvine: University of California, 2013. http://archive.ics.uci.edu/ml/index.html.

Bagirov, A. M., J. Ugon, and D. Webb. "An Efficient Algorithm for the Incremental Construction of a Piecewise Linear Classifier." *Journal of Information Systems* 36, no. 4 (2011): 782-790.

Biadsy, Fadi, Pedro J. Moreno, and Martin Jansche. "Google's Cross-Dialect Arabic Voice Search." In *Proceedings of the 2012 IEEE International Conference on Acoustics, Speech, and Signal Processing, Kyoto, Japan, March 25-30, 2012*, 4441-4444. Piscataway, NJ: Institute of Electrical and Electronic Engineering, 2012.

Bourouba, H., R. Djemili, M. Bedda, and C. Snani. "New Hybrid System (Supervised Classifier/HMM) for Isolated Arabic Speech Recognition." In *Proceedings of the 2nd Conference on Information and Communication Technologies,* Damascus, Syria, April 24-28, 2006, 1264-1269. Piscataway, NJ: Institute of Electrical and Electronic Engineering, 2006.

Cole, Ron, and Mark Fanty. "ISOLET Data Set." University of California, Irvine, Machine Learning Repository. Irvine: University of California, 1994. https://archive.ics.uci.edu/ml/datasets/ISOLET.

Dash, Manoranjan, Huan Liu, Peter Scheuermann, and Kian Lee Tan. "Fast Hierarchical Clustering and Its Validation." *Data and Knowledge Engineering* 44, no. 1 (2003): 109-138.

Dietterich, Thomas G., and Ghulum Bakiri. "Solving Multiclass Learning Problems via Error-Correcting Output Codes." *Journal of Artificial Intelligence Research* 2, no. 1 (1995): 263-286.

Duin, Robert P. W. "Multiple Features Data Set." University of California, Irvine, Machine Learning Repository. Irvine: University of California, 2013. http://archive.ics.uci.edu/ml/datasets/Multiple+Features.

Edelman, Gerald M., and Vernon B. Mountcastle. *The Mindful Brain: Cortical Organization and the Group-Selective Theory of Higher Brain Function*. Cambridge, MA: Massachusetts Institute of Technology Press, 1978.

Essa, E. M., A. S. Tolba, and S. Elmougy. "A Comparison of Combined Classifier Architectures for Arabic Speech Recognition." In *Proceedings of the 2008 International Conference on Computer Engineering and Systems*, Cairo, Egypt, November 25-27, 2008, 149-153. Piscataway, NJ: Institute of Electrical and Electronic Engineering, 2008.

Gevaert, Wouter, Georgi Tsenov, and Valeri Mladenov. "Neural Networks Used for Speech Recognition." *Journal of Automatic Control* 20, no. 1 (2010): 1-7.

Ji, You, and Shiliang Sun. "Multitask Multiclass Support Vector Machines." In *Proceedings of the 11th International Conference on Data Mining Workshops*), Vancouver, BC, December 11, 2011, 512-518. Piscataway, NJ: Institute of Electrical and Electronic Engineering, 2011.

Klautau, Aldebaro. "The MFCC," 2012. www.cic.unb.br/~lamar/te073/Aulas/mfcc.pdf.

Hashmi, Artif G., and Mikko. H. Lipasti. "Discovering Cortical Algorithms". In *Proceedings of the International Conference on Fuzzy Computation and International Conference on Neural Computation*, Valencia, Spain, October 24-26, 2010, 196-204.

Manie, Mohammed A. Al-, Mohammed I. Alkanhal, and Mansour M. Al-Ghamdi. "Automatic Speech Segmentation Using the Arabic Phonetic Database." In *Proceedings of the 10th WSEAS International Conference on Automation and Information*, Prague, Czech Republic, March 23-25, 76-79. Stevens Point, Wisconsin: World Scientific and Engineering Academy and Society, 2009.

Mohler, Cleve. "Exponential Function." Chap. 8 in *Experiments with MATLAB*. MathWorks, 2011. www.mathworks.com/moler/exm/chapters/exponential.pdf.

Mosa, Ghassaq S., and Abduladhem Abdulkareem Ali. "Arabic Phoneme Recognition Using Hierarchical Neural Fuzzy Petri Net and LPC Feature Extraction." *Signal Processing: An International Journal* 3, no. 5 (2009): 161-171.

Mutch, Jim, Ulf Knoblich, and Tomaso Poggio. "CNS: A GPU-Based Framework for Simulating Cortically-Organized Networks." Technical Report, Massachusetts Institute of Technology, 2010.

Newman, Daniel. "The Phonetics of Arabic." *Journal of the American Oriental Society* 46 (1984): 1-6.

Obaid, Manal El-, Amer Al-Nassiri, and Iman Abuel Maaly. "Arabic Phoneme Recognition Using Neural Networks." In *Proceedings of the 5th WSEAS International Conference on Signal Processing*, Istanbul, Turkey, May 27-29, 2006, 99-104. Stevens Point, Wisconsin: World Scientific and Engineering Academy and Society, 2006.

Perkins, Simon, and James Theiler. "Online Feature Selection Using Grafting." In *Proceedings of the Twentieth International Conference on Machine Learning, Washington, DC, August 21-24, 2003*, 592-599. Menlo Park, CA: Association for the Advancement of Artificial Intelligence, 2003.

Satori, Hassan, Mostafa Harti, and Nouredine Chenfour. "Introduction to Arabic Speech Recognition Using CMU Sphinx System." In *Proceedings of the Information and Communication Technologies International Symposium*, Fez, Morocco, April 3-5, 2007, edited by Mohammad Essaaidi, Mohammed El Mohajir, Badreddine El Mohajir, and Paolo Rosso, 139-142. Piscataway, NJ: Institute of Electrical and Electronic Engineers, 2007.

Sehgal, M. S. B., Iqbal Gondal, and Laurence Dooley. "A Hybrid Neural Network Based Speech Recognition System for Pervasive Environments." In *Proceedings of the 8th International Multitopic Conference*, Lahore, Pakistan, December 24-26, 2004, 309-314. Piscataway, NJ: Institute of Electrical and Electronic Engineers, 2004.

Shenouda, Sinout D., Fayez W. Zaki, and A. M. R. Goneid. "Hybrid Fuzzy HMM System for Arabic Connectionist Speech Recognition." In *Proceedings of the Twenty-Third National Radio Science Conference, Monufia, Egypt, March 14-16*, 1-8. Piscataway, NJ: Institute of Electrical and Electronic Engineers, 2006.

Slate, David J. "Letter Recognition Data Set." University of California, Irvine, Machine Learning Repository. Irvine: University of California, 1991. http://archive.ics.uci.edu/ml/datasets/Letter+Recognition.

Tan, Peter J., and David L. Dowe. "MML Inference of Decision Graphs with Multi-Way Joins and Dynamic Attributes." In *AI 2003: Advances in Artificial Intelligence; Proceedings of the 16th Australian Conference on AI, Perth, Australia, December 3-5, 2003*, edited by Tamás Domonkos Gedeon and Lance Chun Che Fung, 269-281. Berlin: Springer, 2003.

Alpaydin, E., and Fevzi Alimoglu. "Pen-Based Recognition of Handwritten Digits Data Set." University of California, Irvine, Machine Learning Repository. Irvine: University of California, 1998. https://archive.ics.uci.edu/ml/datasets/Pen-Based+Recognition+of+Handwritten+Digits.

Vision Group. "Image Segmentation Data Set." University of California, Irvine, Machine Learning Repository. Irvine: University of California, 1990. https://archive.ics.uci.edu/ml/datasets/Image+Segmentation.

Wittner, Ben S., and John S. Denker. "Strategies for Teaching Layered Networks Classification Tasks." In *Neural Information Processing Systems: Denver, CO, 1987*, edited by Dana Z. Anderson, 850-859. Berlin: Springer, 1988.

CHAPTER 9

■ ■ ■

Deep Learning

Any fool can know. The point is to understand.

—Albert Einstein

Artificial neural networks (ANNs) have had a history riddled with highs and lows since their inception. At a nodal level, ANNs started with highly simplified neural models, such as McCulloch-Pitts neurons (McCulloch and Pitts 1943), and then evolved into Rosenblatt's perceptrons (Rosenblatt 1957) and a variety of more complex and sophisticated computational units. From single- and multilayer networks, to self-recurrent Hopfield networks (Tank and Hopfield 1986), to self-organizing maps (also called Kohonen networks) (Kohonen 1982), adaptive resonance theory and time delay neural networks among other recommendations, ANNs have witnessed many structural iterations. These generations carried incremental enhancements that promised to address predecessors' limitations and achieve higher levels of intelligence. Nonetheless, the compounded effect of these "intelligent" networks has not been able to capture the true human intelligence (Guerriere and Detsky 1991; Becker and Hinton 1992). Thus, Deep learning is on the rise in the machine learning community, because the traditional shallow learning architectures have proved unfit for the more challenging tasks of machine learning and strong artificial intelligence (AI). The surge in and wide availability of increased computing power (Misra and Saha 2010), coupled with the creation of efficient training algorithms and advances in neuroscience, have enabled the implementation, hitherto impossible, of deep learning principles. These developments have led to the formation of deep architecture algorithms that look in to cognitive neuroscience to suggest biologically inspired learning solutions. This chapter presents the concepts of *spiking neural networks* (SNNs) and *hierarchical temporal memory* (HTM), whose associated techniques are the least mature of the techniques covered in this book.

Overview of Hierarchical Temporal Memory

HTM aims at replicating the functional and structural properties of the neocortex. HTM incorporates a number of insights from Hawkins's book *On Intelligence* (2007), which postulates that the key to intelligence is the ability to predict. Its framework was designed as a biomimetic model of the neocortex that seeks to replicate the brain's structural and algorithmic properties, albeit in a simplified, functionally oriented manner. HTM is therefore organized hierarchically, as depicted generically in Figure 9-1. All levels of hierarchy and their subcomponents perform a common computational algorithm.

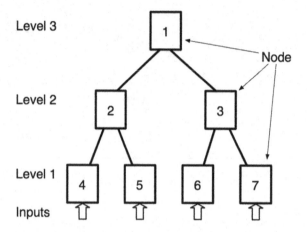

Figure 9-1. *An HTM network's hierarchical structure*

Deep architectures adopt the hierarchical structure of the human neocortex, given the evident existence of a common computational algorithm in the brain that is pervasive throughout the neocortical regions and that makes the brain deal with sensory information—visual, auditory, olfactory, and so on—in very similar ways. Different regions in the brain connect in a hierarchy, such that information flowing up coalesces, building higher and more complex abstractions and representations of the sensory stimuli at each successive level. The brain's structure, specifically the neocortex, evolved to gain the ability to model the structure of the world it senses. At its simplest abstraction the brain can be viewed as a biological data processing black box that discovers external causes in an environment that imposes massive amounts of data on its inputs (senses). The causes of this continuous stream of information are by nature hierarchical, in both space and time. These causes serve as a collection of smaller building blocks that combine to form a larger picture of the world. For instance, speech can be broken down into sentences, sentences into word utterances, word utterances into phonemes, and so on. With digital imagery, pixels combine into edges, edges into contours, contours into shapes, and, finally, shapes into objects. Every sensed object in the world reveals a similar structure perceived at varying levels of granularity. It is this hierarchically organized world that the neocortex and therefore HTM, by imitation, aim at modeling. This modeling happens in HTM at every level.

In HTM the lowest-level nodes of the network are fed sensory information. This information can be raw or preprocessed, depending on the task the network is performing. The nodes learn the most basic features of the data stream by discerning repeatable patterns and the sequences in which these patterns occur and storing them either via local memory structures or via connectivity configurations. These basic patterns and sequences are then used as building blocks at higher levels to form more complex representations of sensory causes. As information travels up the hierarchy, the same learning mechanics are used as higher and higher abstractions of the input patterns are formed. Information can also flow down the hierarchy. This enables the network to act as a generative model, in which higher levels bias lower levels by communicating their internal states to fill in missing input data or resolve ambiguity, or both (Hawkins 2007).

Hierarchical Temporal Memory Generations

HTM has seen so far two generations during its evolution. The underlying implementation in the first generation of computational algorithms, called *Zeta 1*, is strongly rooted in the *Bayesian belief propagation* (BBP) and borrows many of its computations and rules of convergence from that theory. In this earlier version, which is now sunset, HTM used a variation of BBP. BBP is used in Bayesian networks, whereby, under certain topological constraints, the network is ensured to reach an optimal state in the time it takes a message to traverse the network along the maximum path length. Thus, BBP forces all nodes in a network to reach mutually consistent beliefs. The state of these nodes is encoded in probabilistic terms, and Bayesian theory is used to process and fuse information. HTM can be thought of as a Bayesian network with some additions to allow for handling time, self-training, and discovery of causes.

The second-generation algorithms were created to make the framework more biologically feasible. Functionally, many of the concepts of invariant representation and spatial and temporal pooling were carried over by reference to principles of *sparse distributed representation* (SDRs) and structural change. Nodes were replaced with closer analogues of cortical columns with biologically realistic neuron models, and connectivity was altered to allow strong lateral inhibition (Edelman and Mountcastle 1978). Cortical columns are a collection of cells characterized by common feedforward connections and strong inhibitory interconnections (Edelman and Mountcastle, 1978).

Second-generation algorithms—initially referred to as *fixed-density distributed representations* (FDRs) and now simply called HTM *cortical learning algorithms* (CLAs)—replace Zeta 1. In lieu of the "barrel" hierarchy, with its clean-cut receptive fields, each level in the updated framework is a continuous region of cells stacked into columns that act as a simplified model of Edelman and Mountcastle's (1978) cortical columns. Figure 9-2 depicts the structure of HTM, with cells organized into columns, columns into levels, and levels into a hierarchy of cortical regions.

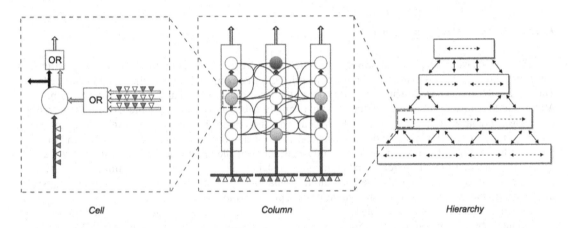

| Cell | Column | Hierarchy |

Figure 9-2. HTM structure

Whereas Zeta 1 was strongly rooted in Bayesian theory—specifically, in belief propagation—CLA is founded on the principles of SDR. To understand the underlying implementation of CLA, a discussion of SDR and how it is fundamental to HTM theory is necessary.

The architecture suggested for the first-generation HTM model was strongly influenced by the Bayesian rules it implemented. It benefited from the structural characteristics of the neocortex, namely, its hierarchical organization; however, nodes diverged from their biological counterparts. In short, functional modeling was the emphasis. In CLA, HTM abandons these roots and adheres more strictly to neocortical structural guidelines. The result is a neuron model, known in this context as an *HTM cell*. Figure 9-3 depicts the model put forward by Hawkins, Ahmad, and Dubinsky (2011). These cells are more realistic and biologically faithful than those used in traditional ANNs.

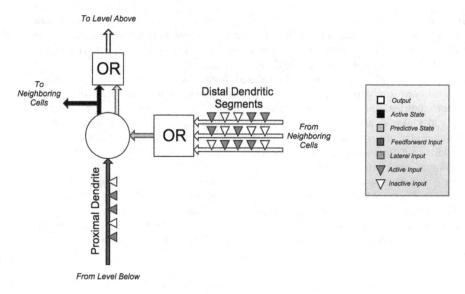

Figure 9-3. *An HTM cell/neuron model*

HTM cells have two types of incoming connection structures: *proximal* dendrites and *distal* dendrites. Dendritic segments of both types are populated by synapses that connect them to other neighboring cells. These synaptic connections are binary, owing to the stochastic nature of real neurons. Because Hawkins, Ahmad, and Dubinsky (2011) posited that any algorithm that aims at emulating the brain cannot rely on the precision or fidelity of individual neurons, HTM cells were modeled to have binary, nonweighted synapses; meaning, they are either connected or not. To account for a real neuron's ability to retract and extend to form connections, HTM cell synapses are assigned a parameter, called *permanence*. Permanence is a scalar value between 0 and 1 that is incremented or decremented, based on a synapse's contribution to activity. When permanence is above a predefined threshold, a synapse becomes connected. Therefore, all synapses in CLA are potential synapses. They are dynamic elements of connectivity.

Proximal dendrites are responsible for feedforward connectivity between regions. These dendrites are populated by a set of potential synapses that are associated with a subset of an input to an HTM region. The dendrites are shared by all the cells of a column (shared feedforward connectivity) and act as linear summation units. Distal dendrites are responsible for lateral connections across a single region. Several segments are associated with a distal dendrite. These segments act as a set of threshold coincidence detectors, meaning that, when enough connections are active at one time, they trigger a response in the receiving cell. It is enough for one segment to be active to trigger a response in the cell (OR gate). Each segment connects an HTM cell to a different subset of neighboring cells. The activity of those cells is monitored and allows the receiving cell to enter a predictive state. This is essentially the root of prediction in an HTM network: every cell continuously monitors the activity of surrounding cells to predict its own.

Finally, an HTM cell has two binary outputs. The first output, owing to proximal connections, forces the cell into an active state if enough activation is present. The second output, owing to distal connections, forces the cell into a predictive state if enough neighbor activity is present; the cell expects to be activated soon. This enables HTM to act in a predictive manner and react to sequences of input. Finally, the output of the HTM cell is the OR of these two outputs. This is what regions higher up in the hierarchy receive as input. Figure 9-4 shows an example of activation of cells in a set of HTM columns: at any point, some cells will be active, as a result of feedforward input (dark gray), whereas other cells, receiving lateral input from active cells, will be in a predictive state (light gray).

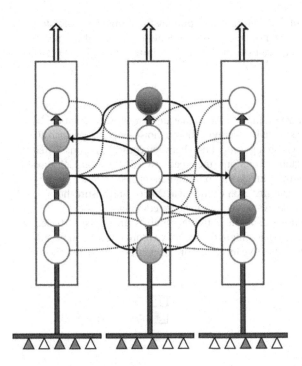

Figure 9-4. *HTM columns*

Sparse Distributed Representation

CLA borrows many of its principles of operation for its biological analogue. The neocortex is made up of more than 10^{11} highly interconnected neurons. Yet, it is still capable of reacting to stimuli with relatively sparse activation levels. This is made possible by the vast amount of inhibitory connections. Inhibition guarantees that only a small number of neurons are activated at any one time. Furthermore, CLA implements the same encoding strategy as SDR. Using lateral synaptic connections, strongly stimulated neural columns inhibit nearby activity, thus reducing the number of active columns and yielding a sparse internal representation of the input pattern or stimuli. This internal representation is also *distributed*, that is, spread out across a region.

Because active bits are sparse, knowledge of a subset of them still carries information about the input pattern, in contrast to other representations, such as ASCII code. With ASCII code an individual bit is meaningless; SDR, therefore, injects a representational quality into individual activations. Because only a tiny fraction of possibly a large number of neurons are active, whatever semantic meaning a single neuron gains becomes specific to a limited number of similar patterns. Consequently, even a subset of the active neurons of a pattern can be a good indicator of it. The theoretical loss of information that results from enforcing this kind of sparseness does not have a practical effect (Hawkins, Ahmad, and Dubinsky 2011).

Algorithmic Implementation

Contrary to the first generation, separation of the learning phase from the inference phase does not offer much insight into the rules of operation of HTM. In CLA, learning, inference, and—most important—prediction occur harmoniously. Each level of the hierarchy is always predicting. Learning by the lower nodes can be turned off when they stabilize; it occurs online in tandem with prediction, when activated.

Therefore, it is best to consider the operation of CLA in terms of its pooling functions. The following two sections discuss the theory behind spatial and temporal pooling in second-generation algorithms and show how they are implemented in the cortical network, as suggested by Hawkins, Ahmad, and Dubinsky (2011).

Spatial Pooler

The role of the spatial pooler is the same in CLA as in Zeta 1. Input patterns that are spatially similar should have a common internal representation. The representation should be not only robust to noise, but also sparse to abide by the principles of SDR. These goals are achieved by enforcing competition between cortical columns. When presented with input data, all columns in an HTM region will compute their feedforward activation. Columns that become active are allowed to inhibit neighboring columns. In this way, only a small set of strongly active columns can represent a cluster of similar inputs. To give other columns a fair chance at activation and ensure that all columns are used, a boosting factor is added. This enables weak columns to better compete.

For each of the active columns, permanence values of all the potential synapses are adjusted, based on Hebbian learning rules. The permanence values of synapses aligned with active input bits are increased, whereas permanence values of synapses aligned with inactive input bits are decreased. Figure 9-5 shows a flow chart of the phases involved.

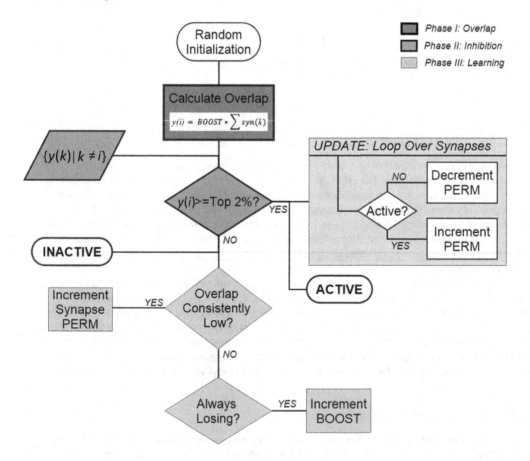

Figure 9-5. *Spatial pooler flowchart*

The spatial pooling operations are as follows:

- *Phase 0 (corresponding to initialization)*: Each column is randomly assigned a random set of inputs (50 percent of the input vector), which is referred to as the *potential pool* of the column. Each input within this pool is represented by a potential synapse and assigned a random permanence value. The choice of permanence value is decided according to the following criteria:

    - Values are chosen from within a small range around the permanence threshold. This enables potential synapses to become connected (or disconnected) after a small number of training iterations.

    - Each column has a natural center over the input region, and the permanence values have a bias toward this center, with higher values near the center.

- *Phase 1 (corresponding to overlap)*: The overlap for each column is computed as the number of connected synapses with active inputs multiplied by its boost. If this value is below a predefined threshold ("minOverlap"), the overlap score is set to 0.

- *Phase 2 (corresponding to inhibition)*: The number of winning columns in a local area of inhibition (neighborhood of a column) is set to a predefined value, N. A column is a winner if its overlap score is greater than the score of the Nth highest column within its inhibition radius. A variation of this inhibition strategy that is significantly less computationally demanding is picking the columns with the highest overlap scores for every level of the hierarchy.

- *Phase 3 (corresponding to learning)*: During this phase, updates to the permanence values of all synapses are performed as necessary as well as to the parameters, such as boost and inhibition radius. For winning columns, if a synapse is active, its permanence value is incremented; if inactive, it is decremented. There are two separate boosting mechanisms in place to help a column learn connections. If a column does not win often enough, its overall boost value is increased; alternatively, if a column's connected synapses do not overlap well with any inputs often enough, its permanence values are boosted. This phase terminates with updating the inhibition.

Temporal Pooler

With winning columns calculated by the spatial pooler, the HTM network gains insight into what pattern it may be seeing at its input. What it lacks is context. Any one pattern can occur as part of a large number of sequences, that is, in multiple contexts. Essential to HTM theory is the ability to predict through the learning of sequences. In CLA sequential learning happened using multiple cells per column. All the cells in a column share feedforward activation, but only a subset (usually a single cell) is allowed to be active. This means that the same pattern, represented by the same set of columns, can be represented by different cells in each column, depending on the context in which the pattern occurs. On a cellular level each of a cell's dendritic distal segments has a set of connections to other cells in the same region, which is used to recognize the state of the network at some point in time. Cells can predict when they will become active by looking at their connections. A particular cell may be part of dozens or hundreds of temporal transitions. Therefore, every cell has several dendrite segments, not just one.

There are three phases involved with temporal pooling. In the first phase each cell's active state is computed. Phase 2 computes each cell's predictive state. In Phase 3, synapses are updated by either incrementing or decrementing their permanence values. Following is the general case, in which both inference and learning are taking place, with the caveat that the learning phase in CLA can be switched off.

- *Phase 1*: For every winning column the active state of each of its cells is computed here. Also, a cell is designated a learning cell. If any of the cells is in a predictive state, owing to its lateral connections, it is put in an active state. If a learning cell contributed to its lateral activation, the cell is chosen as a learning cell, too. In contrast, if no cell in the column is in a predictive state, all the cells are turned active to indicate that the context is not clear—a process called *bursting*. Additionally, the best matching cell becomes the learning cell, and a new distal segment is added to that cell.

- *Phase 2*: Once all the cells in the winning columns are updated, their states can be used for prediction in the cells of other columns. Every cell in the region computes its lateral/distal connection. If any of a cell's segments are activated, owing to feedforward activation in other cells, the cell is put in a predictive state. The cell then queues up the following changes:

  - Reinforcement of the currently active segment by incrementing the permanence values for active synapses and decrementing the values for synapses that are inactive

  - Reinforcement of a segment that could have predicted this activation, that is, a segment that has a (potentially weak) match to activity in the previous time step

- *Phase 3*: This is the phase in which learning occurs, by deciding which of the queued-up updates are to be committed. Temporary segment updates are implemented once you have feedforward input and a cell is chosen as a learning cell. Thus, you update the permanence of synapses only if they correctly predicted the feedforward activation of the cell; otherwise, if the cell stops predicting for any reason, the segments are negatively reinforced.

Related Work

Zhituo, Ruan, and Wang (2012) used multiple HTMs in a content-based image retrieval (CBIR) system, which leverages the categorical semantics of a query image, rather than low-level image features, for image indexing and retrieval. Using ten individual HTM networks with some training and testing datasets of size 50 each, recall rates greater than 95 percent were achieved for four of the five categories involved and greater than 70 percent for the fifth category.

Bobier (2007) recreated a handwritten digit recognition experiment on the United States Postal Service database reported by Numenta (Hawkins's company) to have achieved a 95 percent accuracy rate. The digit images were binarized and fed to the network at varying parameters to reach a maximum rate of 96.26 percent—which, the authors noted, was not up to par, compared with other classifiers, such as support vector machine (SVM), which delivered higher rates in a fraction of the computational time.

Kostavelis, Nalpantidis, and Gasteratos (2012) presented a biologically inspired object recognition system. Saliency maps were used to emulate visual fixation and reveal only the relevant parts of the image, thus reducing the amount of redundant information presented to the classifier. The authors chose to substitute the temporal pooler with a correlation-based alternative, using the ETH-80 and supervised learning at the top node. The system outperformed other HTM-based implementations with both SVM and k-NN as top-level supervisors.

Sinkevicius, Simutis and Raudonis (2011) explored using HTM for human traffic analysis in public spaces. Two HTM networks were designed: one for human detection, the other for direction of movement detection. An experiment involving use of an overhead camera, mounted on a doorway, was performed, and detection performance was evaluated, using multiple scenarios of varying difficulties. The average accuracy achieved was 80.94 percent for pedestrian detection and 73.44 percent for directional detection.

Boone et al. (2010) used HTM as an alternative to traditional computer vision techniques for diabetic retinopathy. HTM primarily detected the optic nerve on retina images. The images were segmented into fragments the size of an optic nerve and presented with labels (0 or 1) to HTM. Following supervised training the HTM network was able to correctly classify 77.44 percent of the optic nerves presented, leading the authors to conclude that HTM is not competitive with traditional techniques, despite its promise.

Zhuo et al. (2012) supplemented state-of-the-art image classification techniques with locality-constrained linear coding (LLC), spatial pyramid matching (SPM), and HTM for feature pooling. Image descriptors were extracted and encoded using LLC. The LLC codes were then fed to HTM and multiscale SPM to form an image vector. The system was evaluated using a Caltech 101 dataset and UIUC-Sport dataset, with linear SVM as the classifier. Results showed an increase in accuracy for both datasets (73.5 percent versus 71.2 percent and 86.7 percent versus 84.2, respectively), compared with the original LLC model.

Gabrielsson, Konig, and Johansson (2012) aimed at leveraging HTM to create a profitable software agent for trading financial markets. A supervised training scheme was used for HTM, with intraday tick data for the E-mini Standard and Poor's 500 futures markets. The tuned model was used as a predictor of market trends and showed at least comparable results when evaluated against ANNs.

■ **Note** Most of the work making use of HTM has been carried out by the developer community established by Numenta. Annual "hackathons" have produced multiple demos, in which CLA was employed for traffic prediction, human movement prediction, tic-tac-toe simulation, infrared (IR) sensor prediction, and so on. One of the more impressive demos, on music analysis and prediction, shows the use of MIDI note sequencing for training; a melody was learned after 25 epochs (http://numenta.org/blog/2013/06/25/hackathon-outcome.html#jin-danny-stan). Currently, research is being undertaken on a CLA model for use in *natural language processing* (NLP). An example is available on the GitHub web site (https://github.com/chetan51/linguist). However, more research and validation are needed to compare HTM performance with the state-of-the-art machine learning approaches the model claims to be superior or similar to. With HTM reported performances, the community has yet to see where HTM has the upper hand.

Overview of Spiking Neural Networks

SNNs are biologically inspired networks and belong to the third generation of ANNs. It seems for ANNs that any improvement on the performance should be based on the neuron model. The neuron model in the second generation of ANNs is based on a simplified model of the actual neuron which ignores the actual way of encoding the information between neurons and the type of this information. SNNs are similar to the ANNs architecture which consists of one or more layers of connected neurons, but differ in the neuron's model and the type of the activation function. In contrast with the second generation of ANNs which utilize time-missing continuous activation functions, SNNs rely on the spike timing in their learning and activation phases. SNNs strive to mimic human neurons, in using spikes to transmit and learn the *spatio-* and *spectrotemporal data* (SSTD) that are encoded with the location of the synapses, for the spatial data, and with the spiking-time activities, for the temporal data.

SNNs and their variants have been used in many applications, such as character recognition (Gupta and Long 2007), sign language recognition (Schliebs, Hamed, and Kasabov 2011), visual and auditory pattern recognition (Wysoski, Benuskova, and Kasabov 2006, 2007), image clustering (Meftah et al. 2008), car crash identification (Kasabov et al. 2013), human behavior recognition (Meng, Jin, and Yin 2011), breast cancer classification (O'Halloran et al. 2011), human localization in sensor networks (Obo et al. 2011), intrusion detection (Budjade 2014; Demertzis and Illiadis 2014), electroencephalography (EEG) spatio-/spectrotemporal pattern recognition (Kasabov et al. 2013), and taste recognition (Soltic and Kasabov 2010). Generally, SNNs are not as popular as other methods of machine learning, owing to their high computational cost.

To understand how SNNs differ from ANNs, it is necessary to examine the most common models of human neurons: the Hodgkin-Huxley model, the integrate-and-fire model, the leaky integrate-and-fire model, the Izhikevich model, and Thorpe's model. These models are covered in the following sections.

Hodgkin-Huxley Model

The *Hodgkin-Huxley model* formulates the propagation of action potential in neurons and may be considered the basis of the other models. Hodgkin and Huxley modeled the electrochemical information of natural neurons after the giant axon of the squid. The model consists of four differential equations describing the change in electrical charge on the part of the neuron's membrane capacitance as functions of voltage (V_m) and current ($I(t)$),

$$C\frac{du}{dt} = -g_{Na}m^3h(u - E_{Na}) - g_K n^4(u - E_K) - g_L(u - E_L) + I(t)$$

$$\tau_n \frac{dn}{dt} = -\left[n - n_0(u)\right], \quad \tau_m \frac{dm}{dt} = -\left[m - m_0(u)\right], \quad \tau_h \frac{dh}{dt} = -\left[h - h_0(u)\right],$$

where

$I(t)$ is the input current caused by the presynaptic potentials

g_{Na}, g_K, g_L are the conductance parameters for the sodium and potassium ion channels and the leak per unit area, respectively

E_{Na}, E_K, E_L are the equilibrium potentials

m, n, h are dimentionless variables that are governed by three other differential equations

Because of the complexity of these equations, caused by the nonlinearity and four-dimensionality of the data, several simpler forms were proposed for practical implementation. We discuss some of these proposals in the following sections.

Integrate-and-Fire Model

The *integrate-and-fire model* is derived from the Hodgkin-Huxley model but neglects the shape of the potential actions. This model assumes that all potential actions are uniform but differ in the time of occurrence. As a result for the previous simplification, all the spikes have the same characteristics such as shape, width, and amplitude. The membrane capacitance and *postsynaptic potential* (PSP) are given by the equations

$$C\frac{du}{dt} = -\frac{1}{R}\left(u(t) - u_{rest}\right) + I(t)$$

$$u\left(t^{(f)}\right) = \vartheta \quad \text{with} \quad u'\left(t^{(f)}\right) > 0,$$

where

u_{rest} is the membrane potential of the neuron at the initial state

ϑ is the threshold value at which the neuron fires

$t^{(f)}$ is the spike firing time

$I(t)$ is the input current, caused by the presynaptic potentials

Leaky Integrate-and-Fire Model

The *leaky integrate-and-fire model* differs from the integrate-and-fire model, in that the membrane potential of the neuron decays over time if no potentials reach the neuron. When the membrane potential $u(t)$ of the neuron reaches a specific threshold ϑ at time t, called the spiking time $t^{(f)}$, and the $u(t)$ satisfies the $u`(t^{(f)}) > 0$ condition, the neuron emits a spike immediately. Then, the neuron goes under an absolute refractory period u_{abs} which means that the neuron will neglect any effect of the arriving spikes during this period. The refractory period lasts for a specific time d_{abs}; the membrane potential of the neuron during this period is

$$u(t) = -u_{abs},$$

where u_{abs} is the refractoriness potential.

When d_{abs} expires, the membrane potential returns to the u_{rest} value. The membrane potential is given by:

$$\tau_m \frac{du}{dt} = u_{rest} - u(t) + RI(t),$$

where

τ_m is the time constant of the neuron membrane

u_{rest} is the membrane potential of the neuron at the initial state

$I(t)$ is the input current, caused by the presynaptic potentials

R is the equivalent resistance of the neuron model.

Izhikevich Model

The *Izhikevich model* is a tradeoff between biological plausibility and computational efficiency. This model uses the following two differential equations to represent the activities of the membrane potential:

$$\frac{du}{dt} = 0.04 \, u(t)^2 + 5u(t) + 140 - w(t) + I(t)$$

$$\frac{dw}{dt} = a\big(bu(t) - w(t)\big).$$

The after-spiking action is described by the term below where membrane potential and recovery variable are reset

if $u \geq \vartheta$, then $u \leftarrow c$, and $w \leftarrow w + d$.

Here, u represents the membrane potential, and w represents a membrane recovery variable that provides -ve feedback to u. a, b, c, and d are the dimensionless parameters. Due to the simplicity of this model, large number of neurons can be simulated of a compute machine.

Thorpe's Model

Thorpe's model is a variation of the integrate-and-fire model that takes into consideration the order of the spikes as they reach the neuron. Thorpe's model is suitable for many applications, because it uses the simple mathematical representation:

$$PSP_i = \sum w_{ji} * mod^{order_j},$$

where

w_{ji} is the weight or efficiency of synapsis between neuron j and neuron i

mod is a modulation factor $\in [0,1]$

$order_j$ is the firing order of the presynaptic neuron j, where $j \in [1, n-1]$, and n is the number of presynaptic neurons connected to neuron i

The weights in this model are updated according to

$$\Delta w_{ji} = mod^{order_j}.$$

Thorpe's model makes stronger connections with the connected neurons that fire and reach the current neuron early. Spiking occurs whenever PSP_i reaches a threshold value $PSP_{\theta i}$. After the spiking, PSP_i is immediately set to 0, such that:

$$PSP_i = \begin{cases} PSP_i + P_{ji} \ when \ PSP_i < PSP_{\theta i} \\ 0 \qquad\qquad when \ PSP_i \geq PSP_{\theta i} \end{cases}.$$

This method allows a fast and real-time simulation of large networks.

Information Coding in SNN

Information coding in neurons has long been the subject of lively debate, in terms of whether the information in the neuron is coded as rate coding or spike coding. Recent studies have shown that the information is encoded as spike coding, because rate coding is insufficient as a representation of the ability of neurons to process information rapidly.

Rank coding is very efficient and can achieve the highest information coding capacity. Rank coding starts by converting the input values into a sequence of spikes, using the Gaussian receptive fields. The Gaussian receptive fields consist of m receptive fields that are used to represent the input values n as spikes. Assuming that n takes values from the range $[I_{min}^n, I_{max}^n]$, the Gaussian receptive field for the neuron i is given by its center u_i,

$$u_i = I_{min}^n + \frac{2i-3}{2} * \frac{I_{max}^n - I_{min}^n}{M-2},$$

and the width σ,

$$\sigma = \frac{1}{\beta} * \frac{I_{max}^n - I_{min}^n}{M-2},$$

where β is a parameter that controls the width of the receptive field with $1 \leq \beta \leq 2$.

Unlike the common learning methods, which depend on the rate of spiking, SNNs use a variant of Hebb's rule to emphasize the effect of the spikes' timing. The weight-updating mechanism is based on the interval between the firing time of the presynaptic and postsynaptic neurons. Two types of neurons are involved in the weights updating process; the neurons before the synapses of the current neuron (the presynaptic neurons) and the neuron after the synapses (the postsynaptic neuron). If the postsynaptic neuron fires right after the postsynaptic neuron, then the connection between these two neurons is strengthened, such that the neuron's weight is given by:

if $\Delta t \geq 0$, then $w_{new} \leftarrow w_{old} + \Delta w$, where
Δt is the difference in firing time and it is equal to $t_{post} - t_{pre}$.

If the presynaptic neuron fires right after postsynaptic neuron, then the connection between these two neurons is weakened, such that

if $\Delta t < 0$, then $w_{new} \leftarrow w_{old} - \Delta w$.

When the firing time of the postsynaptic neuron does not occur immediately after the firing time of the presynaptic neuron, the weights are not updated.

The preceding discussion addresses the excitatory connection. The inhibitory connection uses a simple process, as it does not take into account the interval between the firing time of the presynaptic and postsynaptic neurons.

Learning in SNN

The most popular algorithms developed for SNN are the *SpikeProp* and the *Theta learning* rule. SpikeProp is similar to the backpropagation algorithm that was designed to adjust the weights in the second generation of the neural networks. The Theta learning rule uses the *quadratic integrate and fire* (QIF) neuron model. Both of these algorithms are very sensitive to the parameters of the neuron model, and sometimes these algorithms suffer spike-loss problems. Spike loss occurs when the neuron does not fire for any patterns and hence cannot be recovered by the gradient method. Another approach for training SNNs is using evolutionary strategies that do not suffer from the tuning sensitivity, but these are computationally intensive and costly.

Assume **H**, **I** and **J** are the input layer, the hidden layer and the output layer respectively. Each neuron from a specific layer is represented by the lower cases **i**, **h** and **j**. The set of neurons that are preceding the neuron **i** are denoted by Γ_i while the neurons that are succeeding the neuron i are denoted by Γ^i. Each connection between two neurons in the consecutive layers is consisted of $m \in \{1..m\}$ subconnections where each has a constant incremental delay d_k and a weight w_{ij}^k with $k \in \{1..m\}$. t_i, t_h and t_j represent the spike time of the neuron in the respective layers, while $\hat{t}_i$, $\hat{t}_h$ and $\hat{t}_j$ represent the actual spike time in the respective layers.

The response function of the neuron *i* is given by:

$$y_i^k = \varepsilon\left(t \quad t_i \quad d_k\right)\big|_{t_i = t_i}$$

with:

$$\varepsilon(t) = \frac{t}{\tau} e^{1-\frac{t}{\tau}}$$

$$x_j(t) = \sum_{i \in \Gamma_j} \sum_{k=1}^{m} w_{ij}^k y_i^k(t) \big|_{t_i = \hat{t}_i}$$

Where τ is the membrane constant.

Weights updating from the output layer to the hidden layer is given by

$$\Delta w_{ij}^k = -\eta . \delta_j . y_i^k \left.\right|_{t_i = \hat{t}_i, \, t_j = \hat{t}_j}$$

where

$$\delta_j = \left.\frac{\partial E}{\partial t_j}\right|_{t_j = \hat{t}_j} \cdot \left.\frac{\partial t_j}{\partial x_j}\right|_{x_j = \hat{x}_j}$$

$$= \frac{T_j - \hat{t}_j}{\sum_{i \in \Gamma_j} \sum_{l=1}^{m} w_{ij}^l \left.\frac{\partial}{\partial t}(y_i^l)\right|_{t_i = \hat{t}_i, \, t_j = \hat{t}_j}}$$

Weights updating from the hidden layers to the input layer is given by

$$\Delta w_{hi}^k = -\eta . \delta_i . y_h^k \left.\right|_{t_i = \hat{t}_i, \, t_h = \hat{t}_h}$$

Where

$$\delta_i = \left.\frac{\partial E}{\partial t_i}\right|_{t_i = \hat{t}_i} \cdot \left.\frac{\partial t_i}{\partial x_i}\right|_{x_i = \hat{x}_i}$$

$$= \frac{\sum_{j \in \Gamma^i} \delta_j \sum_{l=1}^{m} w_{ij}^l \left.\frac{\partial}{\partial t}(y_i^l)\right|_{t_i = \hat{t}_i, \, t_j = \hat{t}_j}}{\sum_{h \in \Gamma_i} \sum_{l=1}^{m} w_{hi}^l \left.\frac{\partial}{\partial t}(y_h^l)\right|_{t_i = \hat{t}_i, \, t_h = \hat{t}_h}}$$

The weaknesses of the SpikeProp algorithm include the following:

- The membrane potential of neurons is calculated at fixed time-step intervals.

- There is no method for selecting the initial weights and the thresholds.

- A reference neuron that spikes at t=0 is required.

- Convergence is compromised owing to the insufficient spike response function.

SNN Variants and Extensions

Variants and extensions of SNNs are reviewed in the following sections.

Evolving Spiking Neural Networks

Evolving spiking neural networks (eSNNs) are a variant class of SNNs that have a dynamic architecture (Schliebs and Kasabov 2013). eSNNs use Thorpe's model and a population rank coding to encode information. eSNNs combine *evolving connectionist system* (ECoS) (Kasabov 2007) architecture and SNNs. Compared with SNNs, eSNNs have three advantages. First, eSNNs have a lower computational cost, as they are dependent on a light neuron model, namely, Thorpe's model. Second, the learning algorithm in eSNN is more effective than those in SNNs, which are unable to converge 20 percent of the time (Thiruvarudchelvan, Crane, and Bossomaier 2013). Third, eSNNs are online learning models, which gives them a clear advantage over other techniques.

Reservoir-Based Evolving Spiking Neural Networks

Reservoir computing (RC) is a framework of randomly and sparsely connected nodes (neurons) used to solve complex dynamic systems. RC is divided into *echo state machine* (ESM) (Jaeger 2007) and *liquid state machine* (LSM) (Maass, Natschläger, and Markram 2002; Maass 2010) types.

The LSM is a real-time computation model that accepts continuous streams of data and that generates a high-dimensional continuous output stream. The LSM can be seen as a dynamic SVM kernel function. The architecture of the LSM consists of a liquid and a readout function. A liquid may be seen as a filter that has a trained architecture and that is used for general-purpose problem solving, such as recognizing different kinds of objects from the same video stream. In contrast, a readout function is specific purpose, such that different readout functions are used to recognize different objects from the same liquid. The readout function should be a linear-discriminant and memory-less function.

Dynamic Synaptic Evolving Spiking Neural Networks

Dynamic synaptic evolving spiking neural networks (deSNNs) are a class of eSNNs that use dynamic weight adjustments throughout the learning process (Kasabov et al. 2013). The dynamic updating of weights makes the model more efficient at capturing the complex patterns of a problem. In deSNN the weights continue to change slightly, according to the spikes arriving at the connection, as opposed to eSNN, in which the weights are updated once.

Probabilistic Spiking Neural Networks

The neural model of the *probabilistic spiking neural network* (pSNN) (see Figure 9-6) uses three types of probabilities (Kasabov 2010):

> $P_{cj,i}(t)$, the probability that a spike emitted from neuron n_j reaches neuron n_i at a time moment t through the connection cj,i between n_j and n_i.

> $P_{sj,i}(t)$, the probability that synapse $s_{j,i}$ contributes to the $PSP_i(t)$ after receiving a spike from neuron n_j.

> $P_i(t)$, the probability that neuron n_i emits a spike after its PSP reaches the emitting thresholds.

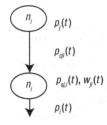

Figure 9-6. The pSNN model

The PSP of neuron n_i is given by:

$$PSP_i(t) = \sum_{p=t_0,..,t} \sum_{j=1,..,m} e_j g\left(P_{cj,i}(t-p)\right) f\left(P_{sj,i}(t-p)\right) w_{j,i}(t),$$

where

e_j is 1 if a spike has been emitted from neuron n_j, and 0 otherwise

$g(P_{cj,i}(t-p))$ is 1 with a probability of $P_{cj,i}(t)$, and 0 otherwise

$g(P_{sj,i}(t-p))$ is 1 with a probability of $P_{sj,i}(t)$, and 0 otherwise

Conclusion

This and the preceding two chapters have covered four learning algorithms that relate to deep learning: deep neural networks (DNNs), cortical algorithms (CAs), hierarchical temporal memory (HTM), and spiking neural networks (SNNs). DNN is an established technique developed from a traditional AI perspective and has shown robust results in many applications. CA, SNN, and HTM are biologically inspired techniques that are less mature but that are regarded by advocates of biologically inspired computing as highly promising. Traditional AI exponents, however, argue that DNN-related approaches will be the future winners in the learning area. Which vision will prevail is a hotly contested issue.

But, instead of asking who is right and who is wrong, we might do better to frame the question in terms of the context and aim of the learning sought. Are we seeking to create a universal form of machine intelligence that replicates the capability of human intelligence to learn by inference from a few instances for a wide variety of applications? Or, are we after computationally efficient learning frameworks that can crush with brute force the big data collected from the Internet of Things (IOT) to develop models capable of predictive and descriptive tasks?

As researchers have yet to agree on a unique definition of AI or on a golden metric for evaluating learning algorithms, the intention of the present work is to provide readers with a general background and a snapshot in time of this rapidly expanding subfield of deep learning.

References

Bobier, Bruce. "Handwritten Digit Recognition Using Hierarchical Temporal Memory," 2007.

Boone, Aidan R. W., T. P. Karnowski, E. Chaum, L. Giancardo, Y. Li, and K. W. Tobin Jr. "Image Processing and Hierarchical Temporal Memories for Automated Retina Analysis." In *Proceedings of the 2010 Biomedical Sciences and Engineering Conference*. Piscataway, NJ: Institute of Electrical and Electronic Engineers, 2010.

Budjade, Gaurav. "Intrusion Detection Using Spiking Neural Networks." Master's thesis, Rochester Institute of Technology, 2014.

Demertzis, Konstantinos, and Lazaros Iliadis. "A Hybrid Network Anomaly and Intrusion Detection Approach Based on Evolving Spiking Neural Network Classification." In *E-Democracy, Security, Privacy and Trust in a Digital World: 5th International Conference, E-Democracy 2013, Athens, Greece, December 5–6, 2013, Revised Selected Papers*, edited by Alexander B. Sideridis, Zoe Kardasiadou, Constantine P. Yialouris, and Vasilios Zorkadis, 11–23. Cham, Switzerland: Springer, 2014.

Dileep, George. "How the Brain Might Work: A Hierarchical and Temporal Model for Learning and Recognition." PhD diss., Stanford University, 2008.

Dileep, George, and Jeff Hawkins. "Towards a Mathematical Theory of Cortical Micro-Circuits." *PLoS Computational Biology* 5, no. 10 (2009). http://journals.plos.org/ploscompbiol/article?id=10.1371/journal.pcbi.1000532.

Edelman, Gerald M., and Vernon B. Mountcastle. *The Mindful Brain: Cortical Organization and the Group-Selective Theory of Higher Brain Function.* Cambridge, MA: Massachusetts Institute of Technology Press, 1978.

Gabrielsson, Patrick, R. Konig, and Ulf Johansson. "Hierarchical Temporal Memory-Based Algorithmic Trading of Financial Markets." In *Proceedings of the 2012 IEEE Conference on Computational Intelligence for Financial Engineering and Economics*, 1-8. Piscataway, NJ: Institute of Electrical and Electronic Engineers, 2012.

Guerriere, Michael R. J., and Allan S. Detsky. "Neural Networks: What Are They?" *Annals of Internal Medicine* 115, no. 11 (1991): 906-907.

Gupta, Ankur, and Lyle N. Long, "Character Recognition Using Spiking Neural Networks." In *IJCNN 2007: Proceedings of the 2007 International Joint Conference on Neural Networks*, 53-58. Piscataway, NJ: Institute of Electrical and Electronic Engineers.

Hawkins, Jeff. *On Intelligence.* New York: Times Books, 2007.

Hawkins, Jeff, Subutai Ahmad, and D. Dubinsky. "Hierarchical Temporal Memory, Including HTM Cortical Learning Algorithms." Technical report, Numenta, 2011.

Jaeger, Herbert. "Echo State Network." *Scholarpedia* 2, no. 9: (2007): 2330.

Johnson, Stephen C. "Hierarchical Clustering Schemes." *Psychometrika* 32, no. 3 (1967): 241-254.

Kasabov, Nikola. *Evolving Connectionist Systems.* London: Springer, 2007.

Kasabov, Nikola. "To Spike or Not to Spike: A Probabilistic Spiking Neuron Model." *Neural Networks* 23, no. 1 (2010): 16-19.

Kasabov, Nikola, Kshitij Dhoble, Nuttapod Nuntalid, and Giacomo Indiveri. "Dynamic Evolving Spiking Neural Networks for On-Line Spatio- and Spectro-Temporal Pattern Recognition." *Neural Networks* 41 (2013): 188-201.

Kohonen, Teuvo. "Self-Organized Formation of Topologically Correct Feature Maps." *Biological Cybernetics* 43.1 (1982): 141-152.

Kostavelis, Ioannis, Lazaros Nalpantidis, and Antonios Gasteratos. "Object Recognition Using Saliency Maps and HTM Learning." In *Proceedings of the 2012 IEEE International Conference on Imaging Systems and Techniques*, 528-532. Piscataway, NJ: Institute of Electrical and Electronic Engineers, 2012.

Maass, Wolfgang. "Liquid State Machines: Motivation, Theory, and Applications." In *Computability in Context: Computation and Logic in the Real World*, edited by S. Barry Cooper and Andrea Sorbi, 275-296. London: Imperial College Press, 2011.

Maass, Wolfgang, Thomas Natschläger, and Henry Markram. "Real-Time Computing Without Stable States: A New Framework for Neural Computation Based on Perturbations." *Neural Computation* 14, no. 11 (2002): 2531-2560.

McCulloch, W. S., and W. H. Pitts. *A Logical Calculus of the Ideas Immanent in Nervous Activity. Bulletin of Mathematical Biophysics* 5 (1943): 115-133.

Meftah, B., A. Benyettou, O. Lezoray and W. QingXiang. "Image Clustering with Spiking Neuron Network." In *IJCNN 2008: Proceedings of the IEEE International Joint Conference on Neural Networks*, 681-685. Piscataway, NJ: Institute of Electrical and Electronic Engineers, 2008.

Meng, Yan, Yaochu Jin, and Jun Yin. "Modeling Activity-Dependent Plasticity in BCM Spiking Neural Networks with Application to Human Behavior Recognition." *IEEE Transactions on Neural Networks* 22, no. 12 (2011): 1952–1966.

Misra, Janardan, and Indranil Saha, "Artificial Neural Networks in Hardware: A Survey of Two Decades of Progress." *Neurocomputing* 74, nos. 1–3 (2010): 239–255.

Obo, Takenori, Naoyuki Kubota, Kazuhiko Taniguchi, and Toshiyuki Sawayama. "Human Localization Based on Spiking Neural Network in Intelligent Sensor Networks." In *Proceedings of the 2011 IEEE Workshop on Robotic Intelligence in Informationally Structured Space*, 125–130. Piscataway, NJ: Institute of Electrical and Electronic Engineers, 2011.

O'Halloran, Martin, Brian McGinley, Raquel C. Conceição, Fearghal Morgan, Edward Jones, and Martin Glavin. "Spiking Neural Networks for Breast Cancer Classification in a Dielectrically Heterogeneous Breast." *Progress in Electromagnetics Research* 113 (2011): 413–428.

Rosenblatt, Frank. "The Perceptron: A Perceiving and Recognizing Automaton." Project Para Report No. 85-460-1, Cornell Aeronautical Laboratory, 1957.

Schliebs, Stefan, Haza Nuzly Abdull Hamed, and Nikola Kasabov. "Reservoir-Based Evolving Spiking Neural Network for Spatio-Temporal Pattern Recognition." In *Neural Information Processing* (2011): 160–168.

Schliebs, Stefan, and Nikola Kasabov. "Evolving Spiking Neural Network—a Survey." *Evolving Systems* 4, no. 2 (2013): 87–98.

Sinkevicius, S., R. Simutis, and V. Raudonis. "Monitoring of Humans Traffic Using Hierarchical Temporal Memory Algorithms." *Electronics and Electrical Engineering* 115, no. 9 (2011): 91–96.

Soltic, Snjezana, and Nikola Kasabov. "Knowledge Extraction from Evolving Spiking Neural Networks with Rank Order Population Coding." *International Journal of Neural Systems* 20, no. 6 (2010): 437–445.

Tank, D. W. and J. J. Hopfield. "Simple 'Neural' Optimization Networks: An A/D Converter, Signal Decision Circuit, and a Linear Programming Circuit." *IEEE Transactions on Circuits and Systems* 33, no. 5 (1986): 533–541.

Thiruvarudchelvan, Vaenthan, James W. Crane, and Terry R. Bossomaier. "Analysis of Spikeprop Convergence with Alternative Spike Response Functions." In *Proceedings of the 2013 IEEE Symposium on Foundations of Computational Intelligence*, 98–105. Piscataway, NJ: Institute of Electrical and Electronic Engineers, 2013.

Wysoski, Simei Gomes, Lubica Benuskova, and Nikola Kasabov. "On-Line Learning with Structural Adaptation in a Network of Spiking Neurons for Visual Pattern Recognition." In *Artificial Neural Networks–ICANN 2006: Proceedings of the 16th International Conference, Athens, Greece, September 10–14, 2006*, edited by Stefanos D. Kollias, Andreas Stafylopatis, Włodzisław Duch, and Erkki Oja, 61–70. Berlin: Springer, 2006.

Wysoski, Simei Gomes, Lubica Benuskova, and Nikola Kasabov. "Text-Independent Speaker Authentication with Spiking Neural Networks." In *Artificial Neural Networks–ICANN 2007: Proceedings of the 17th International Conference, Porto, Portugal, September 9–13, 2007*, edited by Joaquim Marques de Sá, Luís A. Alexandre, Włodzisław Duch, and Danilo Mandic, 758–767. Berlin: Springer, 2007.

Zhituo, Xia, Ruan Hao, and Wang Hao. "A Content-Based Image Retrieval System Using Multiple Hierarchical Temporal Memory Classifiers." In *Proceedings of the Fifth International Symposium on Computational Intelligence and Design*, 438–441. Piscataway, NJ: Institute of Electrical and Electronic Engineers, 2012.

Zhuo, Wen, Zhiguo Cao, Yueming Qin, Zhenghong Yu, and Yang Xiao. "Image Classification Using HTM Cortical Learning Algorithms." In *Proceedings of the 21st International Conference on Pattern Recognition*, 2452–2455. Piscataway, NJ: Institute of Electrical and Electronic Engineers, 2012.

CHAPTER 10

■ ■ ■

Multiobjective Optimization

All men seek one goal: success or happiness. The only way to achieve true success is to express yourself completely in service to society. First, have a definite, clear, practical ideal—a goal, an objective. Second, have the necessary means to achieve your ends: wisdom, money, materials, and methods. Third, adjust all your means to that end.

—Aristotle

Multiobjective optimization caters to achieving multiple goals, subject to a set of constraints, with a likelihood that the objectives will conflict with each other. Multiobjective optimization can also be explained as a multicriteria decision-making process, in which multiple objective functions have to be optimized simultaneously. In many cases, optimal decisions may require tradeoffs between conflicting objectives. Traditional optimization schemes use a weight vector to specify the relative importance of each objective and then combine the objectives into a scalar cost function. This strategy reduces the complexity of solving a multiobjective problem by converting it into a single-objective problem. Solution techniques for multiobjective optimization involve a tradeoff between model complexity and accuracy. Examples of multiobjective optimization can be found in economics (setting monetary policy), finance (risk–return analysis), engineering (process control, design tradeoff analysis), and many other applications in which conflicting objectives must be obtained.

One of the prerequisites of multiobjective optimization is to determine whether one solution is better than another. However, no simple method exists for reaching such a conclusion. Instead, multiobjective optimization methods commonly adopt a set of Pareto optimal solutions (also called *nondominated solutions*), which are alternatives with different tradeoffs between the various objectives. In the solution defined by a Pareto optimal set, one objective cannot be improved without degrading at least one other objective in the set. It is up to the decision maker to select the Pareto optimal solution that best fits preferred policy or guidelines. Pareto graphs illustrate the attributes of the tradeoff between distinct objectives. The solution can be represented in the shape of a curve, or a three-dimensional surface that trades off different zones in the multiobjective space.

This chapter discusses machine learning methodologies for solving Pareto-based multiobjective optimization problems, using an evolutionary approach. The goal is to find a set of nondominated solutions with the minimum distance to the Pareto front in each generation. Successive solutions are built as part of the evolutionary process, in which one set of selected individual solutions gives rise to another set for the next generation. Solutions with higher fitness measures are more likely to be selected to the mating pool, on the assumption that they will produce a fitter solution in the next generation (next run), whereas solutions with weaker fitness measures are more likely to be discarded. Such solutions possess several attributes that make them suitable for problems involving (1) a large and complex search space and (2) mutually conflicting objectives.

Formal Definition

A multiobjective optimization problem deals with a finite number of objective functions. In an optimization problem with n objectives of equal importance, all need to be minimized (or maximized) to serve a performance criterion. Mathematically, the problem can be expressed as a vector of objectives $f(x)$ that must be traded off in some manner,

$$F(x) = \min \left[f_1(x), f_2(x), f_3(x), \cdots, f_m(x) \mid x \in X \right], \tag{10-1}$$

where X (see Equation 10-2) is a set of n decision vectors (a *decision space*) that represents parameters for the values selected to satisfy constraints and optimize a vector function,

$$X = \left[x_1, x_2, x_3, \cdots, x_n \right]^T \tag{10-2}$$

$$x_i^{low} \leq x_i \leq x_i^{high} \quad i = 1, 2, 3, \cdots, n. \tag{10-3}$$

The relative significance of these objectives cannot be determined until the tradeoffs between them are distinctly understood. Because $F(x)$ is a vector, competing objective functions will prevent it from achieving a unique solution. You can associate each solution x in a decision space X with a point in objective space Y, such that

$$f(x) = Y = \left[y_1, y_2, y_3, \cdots y_m, \right]^T. \tag{10-4}$$

In multiobjective optimization the sets X and Y are known as *decision variable space* and *objective function space*, respectively. Figure 10-1 illustrates the mapping of the search space to the objective space. Every iteration of search space leads to a set of objective vectors that defines the objective space, in which several optimal objective vectors may represent different tradeoffs between the objectives.

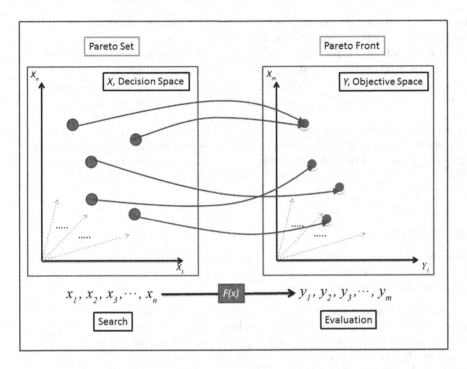

Figure 10-1. *Multiobjective optimization problem: mapping the search space to the objective space*

Pareto Optimality

Pareto optimality is a concept built on multiobjective optimization that facilitates optimization of a vector of multiple goals through tradeoffs between combinations of multiple objectives. Tradeoffs are formulated to improve the performance of one objective at the cost of one or more other objectives. As displayed in Figure 10-1, each point in the objective space represents a unique set of model variables, such that *Pareto optimality* categorizes multiple Pareto optimal solutions. The term honors Vilfredo Pareto (1848–1923), an Italian economist who demonstrated that income follows a power law probability distribution.

For an ideal case the optimal solution of a multiobjective problem is generally denoted as a *Pareto set* $X^* \subseteq X$. The corresponding outcome, or objective vector, is represented by a *Pareto front* $Y^* + f(X^*) \subseteq Y$. In practice an ideal solution is nonexistent, and solving multiobjective optimization does not typically produce an optimally unique solution. Instead, we use Pareto optimal solutions, in which one objective cannot be improved without degrading at least one of the other objectives. Therefore, when using evolutionary techniques, knowledge of the optimal Pareto set (X^*, Y^*) assists in finding a best-compromise solution.

Dominance Relationship

A solution x_1 dominates another solution $(x_1 \preceq x_2)$ x_2 if the following conditions are met:

1. For all objectives, solution x_1 is better than or equal to x_2, such that
   $f_i(x_1) \le f_i(x_2) \forall i \in 1,2,3,\cdots,m$.

2. For at least one objective, solution x_1 is strictly better than x_2, such that
   $f_j(x_1) < f_j(x_2) \exists j \in 1,2,3,\cdots,m$.

If either of these conditions is violated, then x_1 does not (Pareto) dominate the solution x_2. The dominance relationship is *nonsymmetrical*. For example, if the solution x_1 does not dominate the solution x_2 ($x_1 \npreceq x_2$), that does not imply that x_2 dominates x_1 ($x_2 \preceq x_1$); therefore, both solutions can be nondominated. However, the dominance relationship is also *transitive*. For instance, if $x_1 \preceq x_2$ and $x_2 \preceq x_3$, then $x_1 \preceq x_3$. This property allows us to identify which solutions are not dominated ($\hat{X}$) by any member of the solution set X. These nondominated sets ($\hat{X}$) of the entire feasible search space are called *globally Pareto-optimal sets*.

Generating a Pareto set can be computationally expensive. Therefore, you need to select a computationally efficient method for determining the Pareto-optimal set of a multiobjective optimization algorithm. Although you may employ many different approaches to solve a multiobjective optimization problem, much work has been done in the area of evolutionary multiobjective optimization on the approximation of the Pareto set.

Performance Measure

To evaluate the performance of a solution, it is essential to develop a measurement scheme that quantifies the quality of the nondominant Pareto front. The general performance criteria for multiobjective optimization algorithms can be summarized as follows:

1. *Convergence* (γ): Estimates the proximity of the candidate nondominated (Pareto) solutions to the best-known prediction or known set of Pareto optimal solutions. For each solution obtained using an algorithm, you can use the minimum Euclidian distance (Deb, Pratap, and Agarwal 2002) to the Pareto optimal front. The average distance can be used as the convergence measure. A smaller γ value indicates a better convergence.

2. *Diversity* (Δ): Provides a decision maker with efficient choices. Because you are interested in the solution that covers the entire Pareto-optimal region, you need to evaluate the degree of spread between the solutions obtained.

3. *Displacement* (D): In the case of algorithmic approximations or the presence of a discontinuous Pareto-optimal front, only a portion of true optimal front may be reflected. *Displacement* is used to overcome this limitation. Displacement measures the relative proximity of the candidate solution set to a known set of Pareto-optimal solutions. Mathematically, displacement can be expressed as

$$D = \frac{1}{|P^*|} \cdot \sum_{i=1}^{|P^*|} \min_{j=1}^{|Q|} [d(i,j)],$$

(10-5)

where,

P^* = Uniformly spaced solutions from the true Pareto-optimized front

Q = Final solution

$d(I,j)$ = Euclidean distance between the ith solution of P^* and jth solution of Q

A lower *displacement* value represents better convergence and coverage.

Each algorithm may select one or more performance criteria to test the quality of a solution. In many cases, the performance criteria may depend on the availability (or nonavailability) of a known collection of Pareto-optimal sets. The rest of this chapter looks at various multiobjective optimization solutions based on evolutionary learning methodologies.

Machine Learning: Evolutionary Algorithms

Generating the Pareto set can be computationally expensive, because multiobjective optimization problems no longer have a single optimal solution, but a whole set of potential solutions. Classical optimizers (Marler and Arora 2004) include weighted-sum approaches, perturbation methods, Tchybeshev methods, goal programming, and min–max methods. Although these methods can be used for multicriteria optimization, you can only obtain a single solution for each simulation run; simulation needs to execute multiple times, with an expectation that one of the solutions may lead to the Pareto-optimal solution. *Evolutionary algorithms* (EAs) are well suited to solving multiobjective optimization problems, because they mimic natural processes that are inherently multiobjective; a number of Pareto-optimal solutions can be captured in a single simulation run. Additionally, EAs are less sensitive to the shape or continuity of the Pareto front. These algorithms have been successfully applied to a wide range of combination problems, in which information from multiple sources is brought together to achieve an optimal solution. Such algorithms are particularly useful in applications involving design and optimization, in which there are a large number of variables and in which procedural algorithms are either nonexistent or extremely complicated. Generally, evolutionary methods are population-based, metaheuristic optimization algorithms that mimic the principles of natural evolution. These methods use the initial population of a solution and update in each generation to converge to a single optimal solution. Although EAs do not guarantee a true optimal solution, they attempt to find a good approximation, representing a near-Pareto-optimal solution.

EAs are typically classified into four major categories: (1) genetic algorithms (GAs), (2) genetic programming (GP), (3) evolutionary programming (EP), and (4) evolution strategy (ES). Although these algorithms employ different approaches, they all derive inspiration from the principle of natural selection. Fundamental processes involved in EAs are *selection, mutation,* and *crossover*. The first stage of an EA entails applying a *fitness* factor to evaluate the population in the objective space (which represents the quality of the solution). Next, a mating pool is created by selecting the population from previous step, using a random selection or likelihood-based selection criterion. Once the mating pool is organized, it is subjected to recombination and mutation, which produce a new population set. The recombination process performs an *n*-point crossover, with a configurable probability that allows fragments of one parent to combine with fragments of another parent to create an entirely new child population. Mating selection is a critical step in the EA process, inasmuch as it attempts to select promising solutions, on the assumption that future mating pools derived as a consequence of a high-quality selection tend to be superior. A mutation operator modifies individuals by making small changes to the associated vectors, according to a given mutation rate. Given the probabilistic nature of the mating and mutation processes, certain populations may not undergo any variation and simply replicate to the next generation.

Analogous to natural evolution, *individuals* represent possible solutions, and a set of individuals (or possible solutions) is called a *population*. Each individual is encoded, using a problem-specific encoding scheme that can be decoded and evaluated by a fitness function. The mating process iterates through the process of modifying an existing population via recombination and mutation to evolve a new population. Each loop iteration is called a *generation*, which represents a timeline in the evolutionary process.

Early work in the area of multiobjective EAs is credited to David Schaffer, who implemented the *vector-evaluated GA* (VEGA) (Schaffer 1985). Goldberg(1989) proposed calculating individual fitness according to Pareto dominance. Many variants of multiobjective EAs have since been suggested (of which this chapter considers some of the more popular).

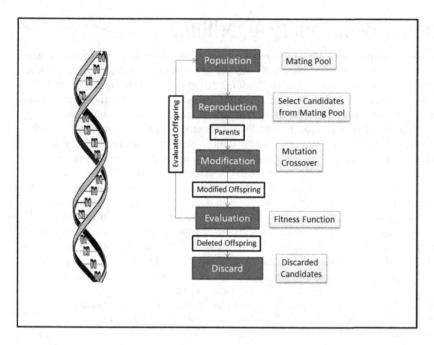

Figure 10-2. Basic flow of a GA

Genetic Algorithm

GAs follow the principle of natural selection (see Figure 10-2), in which each solution is represented as a binary (or real) coded string (chromosomes) and an associated fitness measure. Successive solutions are built as part of the evolutionary process, in which one set of selected individual solutions gives rise to another set for the next generation. Individuals with a high fitness measure are more likely to be selected to the mating pool, on the assumption that they will produce a fitter solution in the next generation. Solutions with the weaker fitness measures are naturally discarded. Typically, you can use roulette-wheel selection to simulate natural selection, in which elimination of solutions with a higher functional fitness is, although possible, less likely. In this method each possible selection is assigned a portion of the wheel that is proportional to its fitness value, followed by a random selection, analogous to spinning a roulette wheel. A small likelihood also exists that some weaker solutions will survive the selection process, because they may include components (genes) that prove useful after the crossover process. Mathematically, the likelihood of selecting a potential solution is given by

$$P_i = \frac{F_i}{\sum_{j=0}^{N} F_j},$$

(10-6)

where P_i represents the likelihood of ith solution's being selected for the mating pool, F_i stands for the operating fitness of ith individual solution, and N is the total number of solution elements in a population. GAs have proven useful in solving complex problems with large search spaces that are less understood by reason of little domain knowledge. The chromosomes of a GA represent the building blocks (alleles) of a solution to the problem that is suitable for the genetic operators and the fitness function. Candidate solutions undergo modification, using crossover and mutation functions, and result in new candidate solutions that undergo evaluation for candidacy in new mating pools.

Genetic Programming

GP is an evolutionary technique that expands the genetic learning paradigm into an autonomous synthesis of computer programs that, when executed, lead to candidate solutions. Unlike GAs, in which populations are fixed-length encoded character strings representing candidate solutions, in GP, populations are programs represented by syntax trees (also called *parse trees*). GP iteratively evolves the populations of programs, transforming one set of programs into another set by exercising the genetic operations crossover and mutation. Crossover function is implemented by exchanging subtrees at a random crossover point of two parent individuals (selected according to fitness criteria) in the population. Crossover creates an offspring by replacing the subtree at the crossover point of the first parent with the subtree of the second parent. In subtree mutation (the most commonly used form of mutation) the subtree of a randomly selected mutation point is replaced by the subtree of a randomly generated tree.

Figure 10-3 demonstrates the general flow and crossover operation of a GP methodology using two variables x and y and prefix notation to express mathematical operators. Parent 1 $[+(*(x, y),2)]$ crosses over with parent 2 $[*(+(x,1),/(y,2))]$ and produces an offspring represented by $[+(/(y,2)),2)]$. It is customary to use such prefix notation to represent expressions in GP.

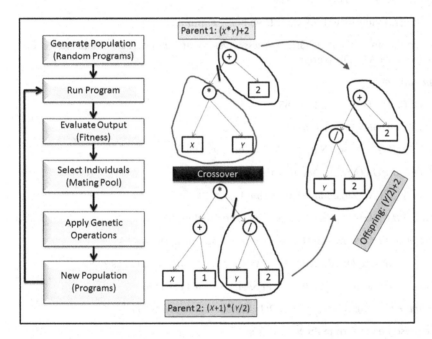

Figure 10-3. *Basic flow of GP with crossover operations; after selecting random crossover points on both parents, a portion of parent 1 attaches to a portion of parent 2 to create an offspring*

Multiobjective Optimization: An Evolutionary Approach

In single-objective optimization, to evaluate the quality of the solution, you simply measure the value of the objective function. In the case of multiobjective optimization, it may not be possible to evaluate the quality of the solution relative to optimal Pareto approximations, because you may not possess the relevant information, with respect to objective space or coverage, and thus may not be able to define the quality of solution, in terms of closeness to the optimal Pareto set and diversity of coverage. Even if one solution dominates the other solution, you may still not be able to quantify the relative improvement, because relative distance and diversity alone are not sufficient to quantify the Pareto set approximation. This brings us to the fundamental requirements for defining the strategy for implementing multiobjective EAs. These requirements can be summarized as follows:

- *Fitness*: Guiding the solution closer to the Pareto set. This requires constructing a scalar fitness function that fulfills multiple optimization criteria.

- *Diversity improvement*: Improving coverage by selecting a diverse set of nondominated solutions. This avoids a situation in which identical solutions exist, relative to objective space and decision space.

- *Elitism*: Preventing nondominated solutions from being eliminated.

Most EAs differ in the manner in which they handle *fitness*, *diversity*, and *elitism*. Listed here are some of the most popular *multiobjective EA* (MOEA) approaches:

- *Weighted-Sum approach*

- *Vector-Evaluated GA* (VEGA) (Schaffer 1985)

- *Multiobjective GA* (MOGA) (Fonseca and Fleming 1993)

- *Niched Pareto GA* (NPGA) (Horn, Nafpliotis, and Goldberg 1994)

- *Nondominated sorting GA* (NSGA) (Nidamarthi and Deb 1994)

- *Strength Pareto EA* (SPEA) (Zitzler and Thiele 1999)

- *Strength Pareto EA II* (SPEA-II) (Zitzler, Laumanns, and Thiele 2001)

- *Pareto archived evolutionary strategy* (PAES) (Knowles and Corne 1999)

- *Pareto envelope-based selection algorithm* (PESA) (Corne, Knowles, and Oates 2000)

- *Pareto envelope-based selection algorithm II* (PESA-II) (Corne et al. 2001)

- *Elitist nondominated sorting GA* (NSGA-II) (Deb, Pratap, and Agarwal 2002)

These approaches are presented in turn in the following sections.

Weighted-Sum Approach

The weighted-sum method for multiobjective optimization delivers multiple solution points by varying the weights consistently. Different objectives are merged into a single objective, and the composite function is minimized, using configurable weights. Mathematically, the weighted-sum approach can be represented as

$$F = \sum_{i=1}^{m} w_i . f_i(x) \text{ for } w_i \geq 0 \text{ and } \sum_{i}^{m} w_i = 1. \tag{10-7}$$

For positive weights, minimizing F can result in a Pareto optimal solution. Although this method is computationally efficient, the major drawback is that it cannot determine the weights that can optimally scale the objective functions for a problem with little or no information.

Vector-Evaluated Genetic Algorithm

VEGA is a population-based algorithm that extends the selection operator of a *simple GA* (SGA), such that each generation produces a number of disjoint subpopulations, as a result of a proportional selection scheme, and is governed by different objectives. For a problem with m objectives and a total population of size N, m subpopulations of size N / m are generated by their respective fitness functions. As depicted in Figure 10-4, these subpopulations are shuffled together to generate a new population of size N. The scheme is efficient and easy to implement, because only the selection method of SGA is modified.

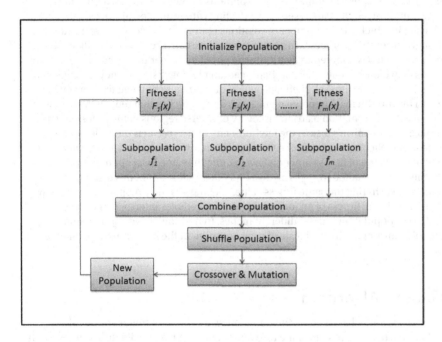

Figure 10-4. *Basic flow of a VEGA*

Because of proportional selection, the shuffling and merging operations of all the subpopulations in VEGA result in an aggregating approach. The drawback of this scheme is its inability to find a large number of points on the Pareto optimal front because each solution executes its own objective function. VEGA is prone to finding extreme solutions, owing to the parallel search directions of the axes in the objective space or simultaneous execution of multiple-objective functions.

Multiobjective Genetic Algorithm

MOGA is another variant of SGA, differing in the way fitness is assigned to a solution. In this scheme, rank R is assigned to each solution, using the expression

$$R(x_i, t) = 1 + n_i(t), \tag{10-8}$$

where n_i is the number of solutions that dominate the ith solution x_i in generation t. Once the ranking process is completed, the fitness of individuals is assigned by interpolating between the best rank (1) and the worst rank ($\leq m$) via a user-defined function. The fitness of individuals of the same rank is averaged, allowing sampling at the similar rate, while maintaining selection pressures. The fitness of certain individuals may degrade more than others, depending on the size of the ranked population. Ranking guides the search to converge only on global optima. Solutions exhibiting good performance in many objective dimensions are more likely to participate in the mating process.

Although the ranking process assigns the nondominated solutions the correct fitness, it does not always guarantee sampling uniformity in the Pareto set. When dealing with multiple objectives, *genetic drift* triggers a suboptimal behavior, in which a large number of solutions tend to converge on a lesser number of objectives, owing to an imperfect selection process. To prevent premature convergence and to diversify the population, a *niche-formation method* is adopted to distribute the population over the Pareto region, in the objective space. If the fitness of two individuals is closer than a certain niching distance, they are considered part of same niche (i.e., sharing the same fitness). Niche formation discourages convergence to a single region of the fitness function by introducing competitive pressures among niches that reduce the fitness of such locally optimal solutions. Niche formation leads to discovery of diverse regions of the fitness landscape. In nature a *niche* is regarded as an organism's task in the environment, and a *species* is the collection of organisms with the same features. Niching segments the GA population into disjoint sets in such a manner that at least one member in each region of fitness function covers more than one local optimal. In one such method, you define a parameter niche radius (σ_{radius}). Any two individuals closer than this distance are considered part of the same niche, sharing the same fitness value. Niching lets the GA operate on the new shared fitness instead of on the original fitness of an individual. Niching reduces interspecies competition and helps synthesize a stable subpopulation around different niches. In multiobjective optimization problems, a niche is ordinarily represented by the locale of each optimum in the search space, with fitness as the resource of that niche.

Niched Pareto Genetic Algorithm

NPGA is a tournament selection scheme based on Pareto dominance, in which a comparison set of randomly selected individuals participates to determine the winner between two candidate solutions. Each of the candidates is tested to determine dominance. The candidate that is nondominated by the comparison set is selected for the mating pool. If both candidates are either dominated or nondominated by the comparison set, then they are likely to belong to the same equivalence class. As shown in Figure 10-5, for a given niche radius (σ_{share}) the selection for the mating pool is determined by the niche class count. Candidates with the least number of individuals in the equivalence class (least niche count) have the best fitness. In this example, because both candidates are nondominated, Candidate 1 is selected to the mating pool, on the basis of lower niche class count.

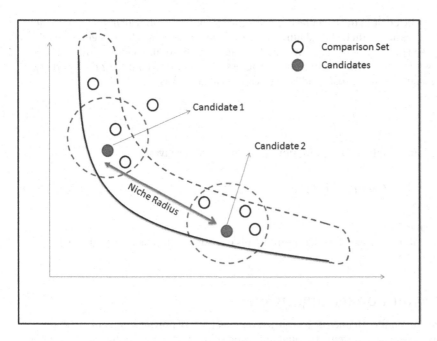

Figure 10-5. *Equivalence class sharing; candidate 1 (niche class count = 3) is a better fit than candidate 2 (niche class count = 4)*

MOGA and NPGA suffer from similar drawbacks; both methods are highly sensitive to selection of niche radius (σ_{share}).

Nondominated Sorting Genetic Algorithm

NSGA is another Pareto-based nonelitist approach that differs from SGA in the manner in which the selection operator is used. All the nondominant solutions are selected first and classified as the first nondominant front in the population. To determine the members of the second nondominant front, members of the first nondominant front are eliminated from the evaluation process, and the search for nondominance continues with the remaining population. This process of level elimination and nondominance search within a shrinking population continues until all the individuals of the population have been categorized to a level of nondominance. Levels of nondominance range from 1 to p. Fitness is assigned to each category of the subpopulation proportionally to the population size. Solutions belonging to the lower levels of nondominance have higher fitness than those belonging to higher levels. This mechanism maintains the selection pressure to select individuals to the mating pool with higher fitness (members of lower levels of nondominance), in a direction toward the Pareto-optimal front.

In the first step the initial dummy fitness, equal to the population size, is assigned to individuals in the first level of the nondominance front. Based on the number of neighboring solutions (niche class count for a given niche radius σ_{share}) sharing the same front and the same level, the fitness value of an individual is reduced by a factor of the niche count, and a new shared fitness value is recomputed for each individual in this level. For the individuals in the second nondominance level, a dummy fitness smaller than the lowest shared fitness of the first nondominance level is assigned. Similarly, individuals that are members of the third and all subsequent levels are assigned fitnesses in decreasing order, relative to the lowest fitness of the lower levels. This guarantees that the fitness of individuals belonging to higher levels of nondominance is always lower than that of individuals in the lower levels. This process continues until all individuals in the entire population have been assigned their shared fitness. Once all the fitness values have been assigned, traditional GA processes related to selection, crossover, and mutation apply. Mathematically, this process can be explained as follows: for k individuals with a dummy fitness of f_p and niche count of m_i^p, as part of p nondominance level, the shared fitness of each individual i can be calculated as

$$\hat{f}_i^p = \frac{f_p}{m_i^p} \tag{10-9}$$

dummy fitness for individuals in the subsequent nondominance level is given as

$$f_p = \min_{i=1}^{k} \left(\hat{f}_i^{p-1} \right) - \varepsilon, \tag{10-10}$$

where ε is a small positive number.

NSGA shares the same drawback as other algorithms in this category: high sensitivity to the niche radius σ_{share}.

Strength Pareto Evolutionary Algorithm

SPEA implements elitism and nondominance by merging several features of previous implementations of multiobjective EAs. Elitist selection prevents the quality of good solutions from degrading, from one generation to the next. In one of its variants, the best individuals from the current generation are carried to the next, without alteration.

Zitzler et al. (2001) defined the characteristics of SPEA by referencing the following attributes:

1. Creates an external and continuously updating nondominated population set by archiving previously found nondominated solutions. At each generation the nondominated solutions are copied to the external nondominated set. Unlike other EAs, in SPEA the relative dominance of one solution by other solutions within the population is irrelevant.

2. Applies external nondominated solutions from step 1 to the selection process by evaluating an individual's fitness, based on the strength of its solutions that dominate the candidate solution.

3. Preserves population diversity, using the Pareto dominance relationship. This EA does not require a distance parameter (such as niche radius).

4. Incorporates a clustering procedure to prune the nondominated external set without destroying its characteristics.

As stated, this algorithm implements elitism explicitly by maintaining an external nondominant population set ($\bar{P}$). The algorithm flow consists of the following steps:

1. Initialize the population P of size n.

2. Initialize an empty population $\bar{P}$ representing an external nondominant solution set archive.

3. Copy the nondominated solutions of P to $\bar{P}$.

4. Remove solutions contained in $\bar{P}$ that are covered by other members of $\bar{P}$ (or dominated solutions).

5. If the number of solutions in $\bar{P}$ exceeds a given threshold, prune $\bar{P}$, using clustering.

6. Compute the fitness of each member of P and the strength of each member of $\bar{P}$.

7. Perform binary tournament selection (with replacement) to select individuals for the mating pool from the multiset union of P and $\bar{P}(P+\bar{P})$. Tournament selection creates selection pressure by holding a "tournament" among randomly selected individuals from the current population $(P+\bar{P})$. The winner of each tournament (the individual with the best fitness) is inducted into the mating pool. The mating pool has higher average fitness, compared with the average population fitness, and helps build selection pressure, which improves the average fitness of successive generations.

8. Apply problem-specific mutation and crossover operators, as usual.

9. Go to step 3, and repeat (unless termination criteria are reached).

Strength of $\bar{P}$ Solutions

Each solution is assigned a strength $S_i \in [0,1)$. S_i is proportional to the number of individuals $j \in P$, such that i dominates j. The fitness of the solution in an external nondominated set $\bar{P}$ is given by

$$f_i = S_i = \frac{n}{N+1},$$ (10-11)

where n is the number of individuals in P dominated by i, and N is the total population of P.

Fitness of P Solutions

The fitness of solution $j \in P$ is calculated by summing the strength of all external nondominated solutions $(i \in \bar{P})$ that cover (or dominate) j. The fitness of a solution in set P is given by

$$f_j = 1 + \sum_{i \in \bar{P}, i \preceq j} S_i,$$ (10-12)

with 1 added to the fitness to maintain better fitness of the external nondominant solution. Because the fitness is minimized, lower fitness results in a higher likelihood of being selected to the mating pool.

Clustering

In SPEA the size of the external nondominated solution set $(\bar{P})$ is key to the success of the algorithm. Because of its participation in the selection process, an extremely large nondominated solution set may reduce selection pressure and slow down the search. Yet, unbalanced distribution in the population may bias the solutions toward certain regions of the search space. Therefore, a pruning process is needed to eliminate individuals in the external nondominated population set, while maintaining its diversity. Zitzler, Laumanns, and Thiele (2001) used the *average linkage method* (Morse 1980) to prune the external nondominated solution set. The clustering steps are as follows:

1. Initialize a cluster C, such that each individual $(i \in \bar{P})$ in the external nondominated solution set is a member of a distinct cluster.

2. Calculate the distance between all possible pairs of clusters. Let $d_{m,n}$ be the distance between two clusters c_m and $c_n \in C$; then,

$$d_{m,n} = \frac{1}{|c_m| \cdot |c_n|} \cdot \sum_{i_m, i_n} \|i_m - i_n\|,$$ (10-13)

where $i_m \in c_m, i_n \in c_n, \|i_m - i_n\|$ is the Euclidian distance between the objective space of two individuals, and $|c_k|$ is the population of cluster c_k.

3. Merge two clusters with minimum distance $d_{m,n}$ into the larger cluster.

4. Identify the individual in each cluster set with the minimum average distance to all other individuals in the cluster.

5. Cycle steps 2–4 until reaching a threshold of maximum number of allowed clusters ($|C| \leq N$).

SPEA introduces elitism into evolutionary multiobjective optimization. One advantage that stands out is that this algorithm is not dependent on niche distance (σ_{radius}), as are MOGA or NSGA. The success of SPEA largely depends on the fitness assignment methodology, based on the strength of the archive members. In the worst-case scenario, if the archive contains a single member, then every member of P will have the same rank. The *clustering process* also remains the critical consideration for the success of the algorithm. Although essential for maintaining diversity, this technique may not be able to preserve boundary solutions, which can lead to nonuniform spread of nondominated solutions.

Strength Pareto Evolutionary Algorithm II

SPEA-II is an enhanced version of SPEA. In SPEA-II each individual in both the main population and the elitist archive is assigned a strength value (S_i) representing the number of solutions it dominates,

$$S_i = |(j | j \in (P + \bar{P})) | \wedge i \preceq j.$$ (10-14)

On the basis of the strength value S_i, the raw fitness value R_i is calculated by summing the strengths of the individuals that dominate the existing one i,

$$R_i = \sum_j S_j,$$ (10-15)

where $j \in (P + \bar{P}), j \preceq i$.

Unlike SPEA, in which fitness is determined only by the cumulative strength of the dominating archive members, in SPEA-II, fitness is determined by the cumulative strength of the dominating members in both the archive and the population. Because the fitness is minimized, a higher fitness value signifies that the candidate individual is dominated by a large number of individuals.

To distinguish individuals with identical raw fitness scores, SPEA uses the k-nearest neighbors (k-NN) method (Silverman 1986) for estimating additional density information for each individual. Here, k is calculated as the square root of the combined sample size of P and $\bar{P}$. Each individual i measures, stores, and sorts its distance in objective space, relative to all other individuals j in the archive and the population. The kth element (distance) of the sorted list, in increasing order, is represented by σ_i^k. Density D_i is given by

$$D_i = \frac{1}{2 + \sigma_i^k},$$

(10-16)

where $D_i \leq 1$.

Finally, adding R_i (raw fitness) and D_i yields the fitness of individual i, represented by

$$F_i = R_i + D_i.$$

(10-17)

Unlike SPEA, SPEA-II maintains a constant number of individuals in the archive. After the fitness evaluation is completed, the next step is to copy all nondominated individuals from archive $(\bar{P}_t)$ and population (P_t) to the archive of the next generation $(\bar{P}_{t+1})$,

$$\bar{P}_{t+1} = \left\{ i \mid i \in (P_t + \bar{P}_t) \wedge F_i < 1 \right\}.$$

(10-18)

If the number of nondominated solutions is less than the threshold N, then the $N - |\bar{P}_{t+1}|$ best-dominated solutions $(F_i > 1)$ from the sorted list of the previous archive $(\bar{P}_t)$ and population (P_t) are moved to the new archive $(\bar{P}_{t+1})$. If, however, the number of nondominated solutions exceeds the threshold N, then the truncation process takes place by removing $|\bar{P}_{t+1}| - N$ individuals with minimum distance, relative to each other. In the case of a tie, the second-smallest distances are considered, and so on.

Also unlike SPEA, in which binary tournament selection (with replacement) selects individuals for the mating pool from the multiset population of P_t and $\bar{P}_t$, SPEA-II selects individuals from the archive population $\bar{P}_{t+1}$ only.

Pareto Archived Evolutionary Strategy

PAES is a simple multiobjective EA capable of generating diverse Pareto-optimal solutions. It is a single-parent, single-child EA that resembles (1+1)-Evolutionary Strategy. PAES uses binary representation and bitwise mutation operators to fulfill local search and create offspring. A bitwise mutation operator flips the bits (genes) of the binary coded solution (chromosomes) with a fixed probability, thereby creating a new solution. A reference archive stores and updates the best nondominated solutions found in previous generations. The best solution is the one that either dominates or remains nondominated in a less crowded region in the parameter space. This archive is used for ranking the dominance of all the resulting solutions.

First, a child is created, and its objective functions are computed. Next, the child is compared with the parent. If the child dominates the parent, the child is accepted as a parent for the next generation, and its copy is added to the archive. If the parent dominates the child, the child is discarded, and a new mutated solution is generated from the parent.

In the event that the parent and the child are nondominating, with respect to each other, then both are compared with the archive of best solutions to make an appropriate selection. If any member of the archive dominates the child, the child is discarded, and a new mutated solution is generated from the parent. If the child dominates any member of the archive, the child is accepted as a parent for the next generation, and all dominated solutions in the archive are eliminated. If the child does not dominate any solution in the reference archive, then the child is checked for its proximity to the solutions in the archive. The child is accepted as a parent in the next generation if it resides in a less crowded region in the parameter space. A copy of the child is also added to the archive.

The PAES algorithm consists of the following steps:

1. Initialize a parent, evaluate its objective function, and add it to the archive.

2. Mutate the parent, generate a child, and evaluate its objective function.

3. Compare the parent and child.

   a. If the parent dominates the child, discard the child, and go to step 2.

   b. If the child dominates the parent, accept the child as a parent for the next generation, and add it to the archive.

4. Compare the child with members in the archive.

   a. If any member of the archive dominates the child, discard the child, and go to step 2.

   b. If the child dominates any member of the archive, accept the child as a parent for the next generation, add it to the archive, and remove all dominated solutions in the archive.

5. If the child does not dominate any solution in the reference archive, then check the child for proximity to the solutions in the archive; accept the child as a parent in next generation if it resides in a less crowded region in the parameter space. Copy the child to the archive.

6. Go to step 2, and repeat until a predefined number of generations is reached.

Pareto Envelope-Based Selection Algorithm

PESA is a multiobjective EA that uses features from both SPEA and PAES. The difference is attributed to the part of the algorithm in which PESA integrates selection and diversity, using a hypergrid-based crowding scheme. Like SPEA, PESA employs a smaller *internal population* and larger *external population*. Whereas the external population archives the *existing Pareto front approximation*, the internal population comprises *new candidates* competing for inclusion in the external archive. Similar to PAES, to maintain diversity, PESA uses the hypergrid division of objective space to measure the scale of crowding in distinct regions of the external archive. Like PAES and SPEA, PESA's solution replacement scheme (archiving the best nondominated solutions) for the external archive is based on the crowding measure; however, unlike PAES (which uses parent mutation) and SPEA (which uses the fitness measure, based on the strength of the dominating solutions), the selection scheme in PESA is also based on the crowding measure.

The PESA algorithm uses two population sets: P_I representing the internal population and P_E representing the external population (also called *archive population*). The steps of PESA are as follows:

1. Initialize the external population (P_E) to an empty set.

2. Initialize the internal population $(P_I = \phi)$.

3. Evaluate each individual in the internal population.

4. Update the external population archive P_E.

   a. Copy the nondominated solution (in P_I and any member of P_E) of P_I into P_E.

   b. Remove the solution of P_E that is dominated by the newly added nondominated solution of P_I.

   c. If the solution of P_I neither dominates nor is dominated by P_E, then add the solution to P_E.

   d. If $|P_E|$ exceeds a threshold, randomly choose a solution from the most crowded hypergrids to be removed.

5. Check the termination criteria.

   a. **IF** a termination criterion has been reached, STOP; return P_E.

   b. **OTHERWISE,**

      1. Delete the internal population $P_I = \phi$.

      2. Repeat (until a new P_I is generated).

         a. Select two parents from P_E, from the less crowded hypergrid (based on the density information).

         b. Create new offspring, based on crossover and mutation.

6. Go to to step 3, and repeat.

The crowding methodology in PESA forms a hypergrid that divides objective space into hyperboxes. Each individual in the external archive is associated with a particular hyperbox in objective space. An attribute defined as the *squeeze factor* represents the total number of other individuals that reside in the same hyperbox. The squeeze factor narrows down the choice of solutions from among randomly selected solutions (from the external archive) by picking the ones with lower squeeze factors. The squeeze factor drives the search toward an emerging Pareto front by selecting members of the under represented population.

The squeeze factor is also used to regulate the population of the external archive. When the archive population $|P_E|$ exceeds a certain threshold, a random individual from the region with a maximum squeeze factor is chosen to be removed.

Pareto Envelope-Based Selection Algorithm II

PESA-II is an extension of PESA that exercises a region-based selection approach, in which the selection criteria are satisfied using a hyperbox instead of random individuals in the hyperbox. A sparsely populated hyperbox has a higher likelihood of being selected than a crowded one. Once the cell is selected, individuals with the cell are randomly selected to participate in the mating and mutation processes. Although this algorithm is computationally efficient, it requires prior information about the objective space to tune the grid size.

Elitist Nondominated Sorting Genetic Algorithm

NSGA-II improves the nonelitist nature of NSGA with a *crowded tournament selection* scheme that uses crowding distance to facilitate selection. In NSGA-II, once the population is initialized, individuals in the population undergo nondominated sorting and ranking, as in NSGA. To find the first nondominated front, each individual in the population is compared with every other individual in the population to find if that individual is dominated. The nondominated individuals in the first front are removed from the population and placed in temporary (*level 1*) storage. To find the next front, the procedure is repeated with the remainder of the population. The process continues until all the members of the population are assigned a front. In the worst-case scenario, each front contains only one solution. Each individual in each front is given a fitness value (or rank), based on the front it belongs to; for instance, an individual in the nth front is given a fitness of n. Additionally, crowding distance is measured for each individual. Crowding distance represents the measure of an individual's proximity to its neighbors, which drives the population toward better diversity. Parents are admitted into the mating pool, using binary tournament selection, based on rank and crowding distance. On completion of the nondominated sort, a crowding distance value is assigned to each individual.

If two solutions are compared during tournament selection, the winning solution is selected, based on the following criteria:

- If the solutions belong to two different ranks, the solution with the better rank wins the selection.

- If the solutions belong to the same rank, the solution with the higher crowding distance (or lesser crowding region) wins.

Once the mating pool is populated, crossover and mutation operators are applied to generate the offspring population. To implement elitism, the parent and child populations are combined, and the nondominated individuals from the combined population are propagated to the next generation. The NSGA-II algorithm is summarized as follows:

Initialization

1. Initialize a random population P_0 of size N.

2. Sort and rank the population by creating nondomination fronts.

3. Assign fitness, according to the ranks of the population.

4. Create offspring Q_0 of size N, using crossover and mutation operators.

Selection

5. The start of each generation has a combined population of $R(t) = P(t-1) \cup Q(t-1)$ size $2N$.

6. Sort and rank the population by creating nondomination fronts ($F_1(t)$, $F_2(t)$, $F_3(t)$,...,$F_n(t)$).

7. Select fronts $F_1(t)$ to $F_n(t)$ until the sum of the combined population of selected fronts exceeds N.

8. Copy the entire populations of selected fronts $F_1(t)$ to $F_{n-1}(t)$ to the mating pool of the next generation.

9. Sort the population of the last selected front $F_n(t)$ in decreasing order, by crowding distance.

10. Select the best individuals from the last front $F_n(t)$ needed to fill the mating pool slot of N.

11. The mating pool now comprises the entire population of fronts F_1 to F_{n-1} and the partial population (sorted by crowding distance) of front F_n to create a parent population (mating pool) of population N.

12. Use crossover and mutation operators to create N offspring.

13. Go to step 5, and repeat.

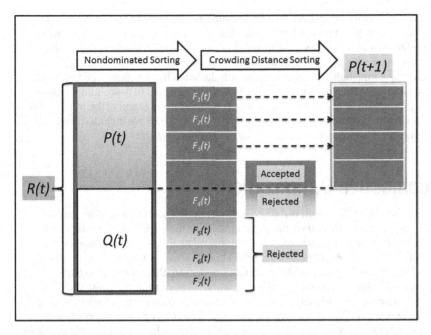

Figure 10-6. *NSGA-II procedure: the nondominated fronts $F_1(t)$ $F_2(t)$, and $F_3(t)$ are included fully in the mating pool $P(t+1)$; the crowding distance-sorted front $F_4(t)$ is included partially in the mating pool $P(t+1)$*

The crowding distance guides the selection process toward a uniformly spread-out Pareto optimal front. The crowding distance of the ith solution $D[i]$ is calculated as the sum of individual distance values corresponding to each objective m. Each objective function is normalized before calculating the crowding distance. The following steps summarize the crowding distance computation of all solutions in a nondominated set I:

1. $l = |I|$ *Number of solutions*

2. $I = \{0\}$ *Initialize all solutions to 0*
       ---------[For all objectives $k = 1$ to $k = m$]----------

3. $I = Sort\,(I,k)$ *Sort by the kth objective*

4. $D[i] = D[l] = \infty$
      --------[For $i = 2$ to $i \le (l-1)$]-----------------------

5. $D[i] = D[i] + \dfrac{\left(I[i+1].k - I[i-1].k\right)}{f_m^{\max} - f_m^{\min}}$ (10-19)

$f_m^{\max} = \max\left(I[1].m, I[2].m, I[3].m, \cdots I[N].m\right)$

$f_m^{\min} = \min\left(I[1].m, I[2].m, I[3].m, \cdots I[N].m\right)$

Step 5 is a recursive operation, in which each successive iteration evaluates the crowding distance of the sorted solutions, based on the objective fitness. Step 5 is invoked for each objective fitness. Here, $I[i].k$ represents the kth objective function value of the ith individual in the set I. The crowding distance is the Euclidian distance between each individual in the m-dimensional hyperspace. The individuals in the boundary are always selected, because they have infinite distance assignment. To ensure elitism, the offspring and parent populations of the current generation are combined to select the mating pool of the next generation. The population is subsequently sorted by nondomination. As illustrated in Figure 10-6, the new population for the mating pool is generated by filling the populations of each front F_j (low to high) until the population size exceeds a threshold size of the parent population. If by including individuals in the front F_j the total population exceeds N, then individuals in the front F_j are selected in descending order of crowding distance until the population of size N is reached. This concludes the creation of the mating pool for the next generation. In the figure the nondominated fronts $F_1(t)$, $F_2(t)$, and $F_3(t)$ are included fully, and the crowding distance–sorted front $F_4(t)$ is included partially, in the mating pool $P(t+1)$.

Example: Multiobjective Optimization

Cloud computing allows us to host workloads with variable resource requirements and service-level objectives or performance guarantees. Furthermore, the cloud enables us to share resources efficiently, thereby reducing operational costs. These shared resources primarily relate to compute, memory, input/output (I/O), and storage. Variability of resources creates thermal imbalances, over- or underprovisioning, performance loss, and reliability issues. If these problems remain unchecked, their cumulative effect can increase the cost of running a datacenter as well as degrade workload performance, owing to unplanned provisioning and unanticipated demands. The solution for efficient datacenter management rests in satisfying multidimensional constraints that may be dynamic in nature and mutually conflicting. Environmental stresses vary from time to time and create resource pressures, which may be either global or regional, creating dynamic constraints that result in revised goals that need to be achieved.

As illustrated in Figure 10-7, the operational constraints in this example can be classified as four objective functions:

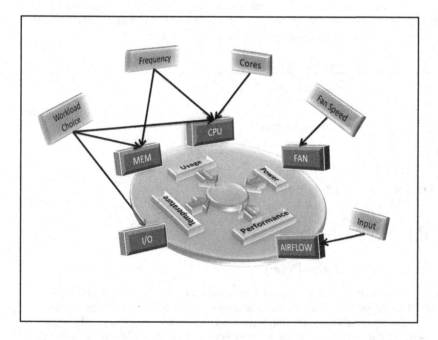

Figure 10-7. Multiobjective optimization in a datacenter with four objective functions, related to power, performance, temperature, and usage

1. *Reducing thermal stresses (F_T):* Thermal stresses occur when one or more devices approach their throttling limit or generate hot or cold spots, relative to other devices (or clusters of systems). Thermal stresses can be relieved by regulating fan speed, input airflow, or resource utilization.

2. *Meeting power targets (F_P):* Power targets are set by an external management agent, according to fair usage and availability of maximum power. System power targets can be regulated by resource utilization; fan speed; or hosting workloads that do not exceed power demands and that are nonnoisy, relative to other workloads already running on different cores.

3. *Meeting performance guarantees (F_s):* Performance guarantees are the fitness matrices defined by applications to measure *service-level objectives* (SLOs). For example, *query response time* is a measure that can quantify the quality of service when hosted on a system or cluster of systems. Performance guarantees are delivered via regulated resource utilization or by hosting workloads that are nonnoisy, relative to other workloads running on different cores.

4. *Meeting resource utilization targets (F_U):* Resource utilization targets are enforced to maximize the server usage in a unit volume of rack space, leading to a reduction in idle periods. In some cases, resource utilization is regulated to deliver service assurance or reduce thermal hot spots. Resource utilization enforcement is generally realized by using an appropriate distribution of workloads in different cores in a manner that ultimately leads to the most efficient resource utilization with the least amount of mutual noise (cache, prefetching) or contention.

The multiobjective optimization problem can be represented as a function of these four objectives,

$$F(x) = \min f\left(F_T(x), F_P(x), F_s(x), F_U(x)\right), \qquad (10\text{-}20)$$

where x represents the parameters for the values selected to satisfy thermal, power, utilization, and performance constraints. These parameters can be summarized as follows:

- Fan speed (x_1)

- Central processing unit (CPU) power limit (x_2)

- Memory power limit (x_3)

- Input airflow (x_4)

- Workload type ID (x_5)

- Number of CPU cores (x_6)

These parameters $x = (x_1, x_2, x_3, x_4, x_5, x_6)$ regulate the operating states of the resources, which result in environmental as well as system-specific perturbations that may need to be corrected as part of exploring a true Pareto-optimal front or stable system.

Objective Functions

Individual objective functions measure the quality of solutions. Multiobjective optimization methods trade off the performance between various objectives. Here, a suitable tradeoff between power, thermal, performance, and utilization objectives is sought, using the EAs. Equations 10-21–10-24 represent the objective functions for these objectives. Each of the objectives is contingent on the values of parameters (decision vectors) that define the search space to satisfy the vectors of multiple goals through tradeoffs between combinations of multiple objectives,

$$F_T = \frac{1}{N}\sum_{d=1}^{N} f\left(T^d, T_T^d\right) \ for \ T^d = f_T^d(x) \quad ; 0 \le f\left(T^d, T_T^d\right) \le 1 \tag{10-21}$$

$$F_P = f\left(P, P_T\right) for \ P = f_P(x) \quad ; 0 \le f\left(P, P_T\right) \le 1 \tag{10-22}$$

$$F_s = f\left(Q, Q_T\right) for \ Q = f_Q(x) \quad ; 0 \le f\left(Q, Q_T\right) \le 1 \tag{10-23}$$

$$F_U = \frac{1}{N}\sum_{d=1}^{N} f\left(U^d, U_T^d\right) for \ U^d = f_U^d(x) \quad ; 0 \le f\left(U^d, U_T^d\right) \le 1 \tag{10-24}$$

where T^d and U^d are temperature and utilization of device d, respectively; T_T^d and U_T^d are the respective temperature and utilization thresholds; P is the current power consumption of the complete system; and Q is the service-level agreement (SLA), or performance score, of the workload running on the system. The solution x impacts the process output, represented by the corresponding functions $\left(f_T^d(x), f_P(x), f_Q(x), f_U^d(x)\right)$, which influence the output of the objective functions. (Note that *power* and *performance* are system specific and not device specific in this context.)

The solution x evolves by maneuvering multiple dimensions of the decision space and anticipating an optimal tradeoff between all four objectives. Forinstance, setting a higher fan speed (x_1) will improve cooling (F_T) but increase power consumption, thereby degrading F_P. Similarly, the CPU power limit (x_1) may regulate power consumption but degrade performance (F_s). Therefore, the goal of the EAs is to synthesize a near-optimal solution that attempts to fulfill the inherent and often conflicting constraints of all the objectives. Solutions should reflect optimal decisions in the presence of tradeoffs between the four objectives. These decision vectors match certain workloads on specific systems, such that there is the least amount of conflict between objectives. Additional controls regulate the fan speed, CPU and memory power limits, input airflow, and allocation (or deallocation) of additional CPU cores.

Figure 10-8 displays the process of selecting the best compute node (from among a large number of nodes) for workload hosting.

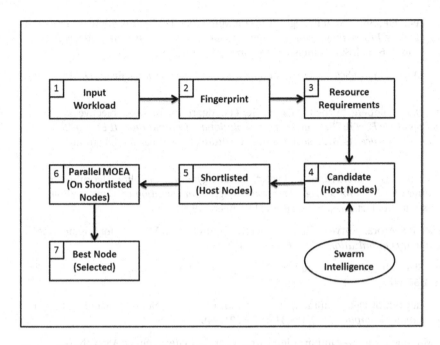

Figure 10-8. *Node selection for workload hosting, using multiobjective evolutionary optimization*

Whenever a new workload is staged for hosting on one of the compute nodes, it undergoes *fingerprinting*. This process involves matching the distinctive attributes of multidimensional features to a preexisting database. Fingerprints correlate resource utilization patterns and estimate resource requirements. Swarm intelligence acts as a mechanism whereby a few candidate host nodes are selected from hundreds of possible host nodes for further evaluation. Some nodes are eliminated because of the low likelihood of their ability to deliver enough contention-free resources. Once shortlisted, the candidate nodes represent compute resources that can host incoming workloads, although with varying degrees of resource handling. All the shortlisted nodes are evaluated for quality of hosting the new workload by running MOEA in parallel, in an effort to generate multiple Pareto-optimal fronts, one for each node. The node corresponding to the best solution is selected for hosting the workload. The MOEA evaluates the solutions (see Equation 10-20) by measuring the collective efficiency of power, performance, utilization, and temperature and iterates toward finding the tradeoff representing the best solution. The process repeats each time a new workload appears in the staging queue to be serviced by one of the compute nodes.

References

Corne, David W., Nick R. Jerram, Joshua D. Knowles, and Martin J. Oates. "PESA-II: Region-Based Selection in Evolutionary Multiobjective Optimization." In *Proceedings of the Genetic and Evolutionary Computation Conference (GECCO-2001)*. San Francisco: Morgan Kaufmann, 2001.

Corne, David W., Joshua D. Knowles, and Martin J. Oates. "The Pareto Envelope-Based Selection Algorithm for Multiobjective Optimization." *Parallel Problem Solving from Nature—PPSN VI: Proceedings of the 6th International Conference*, edited by Marc Schoenauer, Kalyanmoy Deb, Günter Rudolph, Xin Yao, Evelyne Lutton, Juan Julian Merelo, and Hans-Paul Schwefel, 839–848. Berlin: Springer, 2000.

Deb, Kalyanmoy, Amrit Pratap, Sameer Agarwal, and T. Meyarivan. "A Fast and Elitist Multiobjective Genetic Algorithm: NSGA-II." *IEEE Transactions on Evolutionary Computation* 6, no. 2 (2002): 182–197.

Fonseca, Carlos M., and Peter J. Fleming. "Genetic Algorithms for Multiobjective Optimization: Formulation Discussion and Generalization." In *Proceedings of the 5th International Conference on Genetic Algorithms*, edited by Stephanie Forrest, pp. 416–423. San Francisco: Morgan Kaufmann, 1993.

Goldberg, David E. *Genetic Algorithms in Search, Optimization, and Machine Learning*. Reading, MA: Addison-Wesley, 1989.

Horn, J., N. Nafpliotis, and D. E. Goldberg. "A Niched Pareto Genetic Algorithm for Multiobjective Optimization." In *Proceedings of the First IEEE Conference on Evolutionary Computation, IEEE World Congress on Computational Intelligence*, 82-87. Piscataway, NJ: Institute of Electrical and Electronic Engineers, 1994.

Knowles, J. D., and D. W. Corne. "The Pareto Archived Evolution Strategy: A New Baseline Algorithm for Pareto Multiobjective Optimisation." In *Proceedings of the 1999 Congress on Evolutionary Computation*, 98-105. Piscataway, NJ: Institute of Electrical and Electronic Engineers, 1999.

Marler, R. Timothy, and Jasbir S. Arora. "Survey of Multi-Objective Optimization Methods for Engineering." *Structural and Multidisciplinary Optimization* 26, no. 6 (2004): 369-395.

Morse, J. N. "Reducing the Size of the Nondominated Set: Pruning by Clustering." *Computers and Operations Research* 7, nos. 1-2 (1980): 55-66.

Nidamarthi, Srinivas, and Kalyanmoy Deb. "Muiltiobjective Optimization Using Nondominated Sorting in Genetic Algorithms." *Evolutionary Computation* 2, no. 3 (1994): 221-248.

Schaffer, J. David. 1985. "Multiple Objective Optimization with Vector Evaluated Genetic Algorithms." In *Proceedings of the 1st International Conference on Genetic Algorithms*, edited by John J. Grefenstette, 93-100. Hillsdale, NJ: L. Erlbaum, 1985.

Silverman, B. W. *Density Estimation for Statistics and Data Analysis*. London: Chapman and Hall, 1986.

Zitzler, E., M. Laumanns, and L. Thiele. "SPEA2: Improving the Strength Pareto Evolutionary Algorithm." Technical report, Swiss Federal Institute of Technology, 2001.

Zitzler, E., and L. Thiele. "Multiobjective Evolutionary Algorithms: A Comparative Case Study and the Strength Pareto Approach" *IEEE Transactions on Evolutionary Computation* 3, no. 4 (1999): 257-271.

■ ■ ■

CHAPTER 11

Machine Learning in Action: Examples

A breakthrough in machine learning would be worth ten Microsofts.

—Bill Gates

Machine learning is an important means of synthesizing and interpreting the underlying relationship between data patterns and proactive optimization tasks. Machine learning exploits the power of generalization, which is an inherent and essential component of concept formation through human learning. The learning process constructs a *knowledge base* that is hardened by critical feedback to improve performance. The knowledge base system gathers a collection of facts and processes them through an inference engine that uses rules and logic to deduce new facts or inconsistencies.

As more and more data are expressed digitally in an unstructured form, new computing models are being explored to process that data in a meaningful way. These computing models synthesize the knowledge embedded in the unstructured data and learn domain-specific trends and attributes. More sophisticated models can facilitate decision support systems, using hierarchies of domains and respective domain-specific models. Machine learning plays an important role in automating, expanding, and concentrating procedures for unearthing learnings in ways that traditional statistical methods are hard-pressed to match.

This chapter presents examples in which machine learning is used as the principal constituent of a feedback control system. We discuss machine learning usage in areas related to datacenter workload fingerprinting, datacenter resource allocation, and intrusion detection in ad hoc networks. These examples demonstrate an intelligent feedback control system based on the principles of machine learning. Such systems can enable automated detection, optimization, correction, and tuning throughout high-availability environments, while facilitating smart decisions. Furthermore, these systems evolve and train themselves, according to platform needs, emerging use cases, and the maturity of the knowledge data available in the ecosystem. The goal is to create models that act as expert systems and that automatically perform proactive actions that can later be reviewed or modified, if necessary.

A traditional system uses a collection of attributes that determine a property or behavior in current time. An expert system uses machine learning to discover the nature of the change resulting from the learning process and analyze the reasoning behind better adaptation of the process. Such a system can be either history determined or state -determined. A state-determined system can be described in terms of transitions between states in consecutive time intervals (such as first-order Markov chains). The new state is uniquely determined by the previous state. To adapt, the organism, guided by information from the environment, must manage its essential variables, forcing them to operate within the proper limits by manipulating the environment (through the organism's motor control of it), such that it then acts on the variables appropriately.

Figure 11-1 illustrates an autonomic system that is constructed by using modular functions to enact an intelligent feedback control system. Machine learning plays a significant role in modeling the knowledge function, which is used to store the rules, constraints, and patterns in a structured manner. New knowledge is synthesized, using the elements of existing structures and new learnings. The collective knowledge enacts a feedback control loop, which enables a stable and viable system. The supporting functions that facilitate an intelligent feedback control system are as follows:

- A *sensor function* to sense any changes in the internal or external environment (such as component temperature, power, utilization, and aberrant behavior).

- A *motor function* to compensate for the effects of environmental disturbances by changing the system elements, thereby maintaining equilibrium.

- An *analytical function* to analyze the sensor channel data to ascertain if any of the essential variables are operating within viable bounds, or limits.

- A *planning function* to determine the changes that need be made to the current system behavior to bring the system back to the equilibrium state in the new environment.

- A *knowledge function* that contains the set of possible behaviors that can be applied to the new environment. The planning tool uses this knowledge to select the appropriate action to nullify the disturbance; the motor channel applies the selected behavior. The knowledge function is synthesized, using the generalization process, which can be an ongoing task that effectively develops a richer hypothesis space, based on new data applied to the existing model.

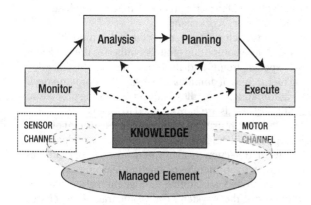

Figure 11-1. *Modular functions as fundamental elements for building autonomics architecture*

These functions enable key elements to model a practical system by using an abstracted cybernetic description (regulation theory). This description abstracts a set of interrelated objects that can receive, store, process, and exchange data. Cybernetic systems can be represented by means of control objects and control systems. Control systems transmit the control information to the controlled objects via sets of effectors. The state information on a controlled object is received through a set of receptors and is transmitted back to the control system, thereby creating a feedback loop. This feedback loop is capable of developing an autonomic system that operates an effective control system through adaptive regulation. The model comprises the following five necessary and sufficient interacting subsystems, which, collectively, constitute an organizational structure that affords system viability:

- *Infrastructure* to interact with the operational environment, which is controlled by the management process.

- *Coordination* to promote the dissemination of policy data that allow collaboration and coordination.

- *Control* for intervention rules as well as policy adherence, resource compliance, accessibilities, and responsibilities.

- *Intelligence* for planning ahead in anticipation of changes in the external environment and capabilities. Intelligence aids in capturing a complete view of the system environment and benefits the system in formulating alternate strategies, which are necessary for adapting to changing conditions to keep the system viable.

- *Policy* to steer the organization toward a purposeful goal by formulating policy functions that lead to planning activities.

Viable System Modeling

Controlled systems may demonstrate a high degree of dynamism in their interactions that may result in unpredictable behaviors. Viable system modeling facilitates a framework that allows coordination, coevolution, and survivability, using monitoring, control, and communication abstractions. Such modeling helps the system survive in a constantly changing and unpredictable environment; the modeling is built to outlast external stresses and demands variability, and it adapts to any unexpected stimuli. You abstract the framework in such a manner that variability in the usage model does not interfere with stabilizing the system within its viable limits. Unpredictable behavior, intermittent failures, and scattered knowledge generate a sizeable uncertainty, which can cause reactive or suboptimal decisions as well as rendering ineffective traditional programming paradigms, which operate on the principals of independence and static behavioral models. Programming strategies need to be built to characterize and optimize runtime patterns, using dynamic policies. This requires autonomous instantiation of mechanisms that respond to changing dynamics. Additionally, programming models must take into account the separation between policy management, activation mechanisms, computation, and runtime adaptation. Isolation can be realized using abstractions that make it possible to hide the implementation choices. Abstractions establish a common view of a component model to allow interoperability via communication semantics.

Intelligent feedback control implementation facilitates adaptation, which lets the controlled process change its configuration over time by dynamically adapting to specific needs and requirements. Adaptation is typically triggered by the rule engine, owing to faulting, or changing behavior, of a resource in platform, and is achieved through changes in the set of resources, components, or dependencies. A necessary condition for adaptation is the preservation of the existing semantics, with an ability to reconfigure and adapt to the new environment. This is supported by implementing adding, plugging, and unplugging component controllers dynamically, thereby adding or removing the functional aspect of a component. The two categories of adaptation are as follows:

- *Functional adaptation* adapts the architectural behavior of the component to new requirements or environments.

- *Nonfunctional adaptation* adapts the nonfunctional architecture of the container to the new requirements or environment (e.g., changes in security policy or communication protocol).

Adaptation functions require the ability to identify dynamically changing patterns and behaviors with these properties:

- The ability to evaluate when and how much. Heuristics are built to identify appropriate conditions that demand reconfiguration. Reactive reconfiguration or tuning can easily lead to oscillation. Additionally, the amount of reconfiguration depends on the application-specific optimization function (also called the *cost function*), which is maximized for a given policy.

- A weighted cost function to evaluate the significance of specific objectives in cases in which multiple objective functions race for adaptability.

- Low-latency evaluation and optimization of the cost function to satisfy the handling of control function in real time.

- The ability to identify and resolve resource conflicts and oscillations resulting from competing objectives.

- The ability to log resource attributes and behavioral patterns to aid in establishing a rational reasoning process for future optimizations and conflict resolutions.

Knowledge synthesis through pattern identification plays a pivotal role, modeling several behavioral trends that recur over time. These patterns are appealing for proactive analysis, which paves the way for monitoring and analyzing the process by focusing on the most significant activities. Pattern analysis is commonly used to determine workflow behavior as well as the correspondence between related actions. Pattern analysis is also used to predict the choices that are more likely to yield the desired policy compliance, thereby supporting the selection of the best action to be activated from among a set of possible candidates. The framework execution model is responsible for collecting two types of information: *raw data* logged during the execution of workload and *processed data* derived from the raw data, which are synthesized to describe behavioral patterns.

Figure 11-2 conceptualizes an adaptation framework for a *server system*, in which subfunctional components are isolated into discrete and independent blocks. The *monitor function* monitors the performance parameters and corresponding resource utilization. This is logged into the knowledge base, which traces the relationship between resource utilization and various performance attributes. The *drift detector* evaluates the deviation between measured performance and desired performance. A deviation (positive or negative) triggers a correction to the cost function as well as to the resource control block. Whereas the cost function manipulates the relative coefficients of the fitness equation, the resource control mechanism reevaluates resource allocation, based on rational reasoning and fuzzy logic. This process continues until all the objectives are met.

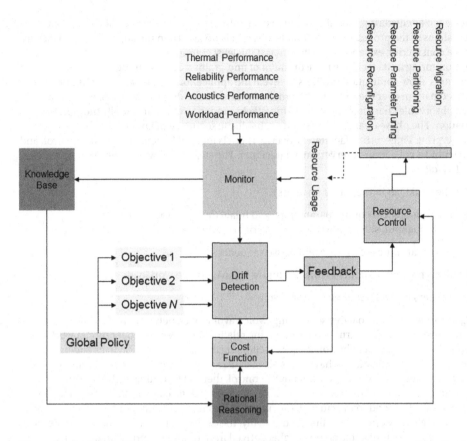

Figure 11-2. *Adaptation function of a server system; based on the feedback, the cost function block reevaluates the function weights, whereas the resource control block reevaluates resource allocation*

Example 1: Workload Fingerprinting on a Compute Node

Datacenter power consumption has increased drastically in recent years, and controlling the power intake of servers has become critical. To develop efficient servers, server platforms require online characterization to determine platform parameters for the tuning required for various system features because of the complex dependencies among them. Feedback-directed optimization of servers with insights gained from workload observation has proven to be more effective than static configurations. The server processor and chipsets expose software-configurable margins and range limits, called *control parameters*, which can be tuned to achieve a balance between power and performance. Some of these parameters are set by the platform's basic input/output system (BIOS) once at boot time and remain static throughout. One-time configuration at boot time renders the system nonresponsive to load variation.

The example given here describes a dynamic characterization technique using machine learning algorithms that determine tuned values from runtime program phases. A self-correcting workload fingerprint codebook accelerates phase prediction to achieve continuous and proactive tuning. Parameters such as memory and processor power states can be set dynamically, based on observed demand variations, by the operating system or the hardware modules. Autonomous systems then trade off system margins to gain power or performance advantages, depending on the use case. Proactive tuning prepares the system to tune itself in advance and avoids the response lag characteristic of reactive systems. Various machine learning techniques, such as clustering, classifiers, and discrete phase predictors, are applied to the data collected from subsystems of the processor. Additionally, it is crucial to ascertain the appropriate algorithms and operations, while considering extrapolative efficiency at the least computational cost.

Performance-monitoring units facilitate measurement of fine-grained events through hardware counters. These counters allow application profilers to reveal the application's time-varying phase behaviors that repeat in a defined pattern over their lifetime. A program phase can be described as a discontinuity in the time in which observable characteristics vary distinctively enough to effect an equally measurable system impact variation. The phase characteristics and probabilistic sequence of known phases are represented as a fingerprint. Fingerprints facilitate proactive models for load balancing, thermal control, and resource allocation within a collection of servers in a datacenter. The steps employed in the learning process can be summarized as follows:

1. Execute the workload in the server system(s).

2. Identify relevant process control parameters, and relate them to process goals (workload throughput, server power, thermal variance, and so on).

3. Synthesize the attributes of a phase and phase sequence.

4. Build a phase prediction model to forecast future behavior of the workload.

5. Tune the system control parameters proactively.

Workload fingerprinting allows proactive self-tuning, which avoids a lag between the feedback and the control (or the reactive control) by learning the underlying relationships between operational workload phases and corresponding application behavior, thereby facilitating dynamic adaptation in changing environments. Understanding application behavior has also been a key source of insight for driving several new architectural features, such as built-in memory power control, thermal throttling, turbo boosting, processor cache size adaptation, and link configurations. The feature-specific controls that constitute the decision space are dynamically tuned to the current and future phases through a multiobjective coordinated tuning process to achieve globally optimal results. Traditionally, the decision space of a process is defined by control parameters, which are tuned, based on insights derived from offline empirical analysis of data collected by running well-known benchmarks and establishing the average case. These control parameters are then statically programmed at boot time by the system BIOS. A better approach is to program dynamically the parametric values synthesized by proactive simulation, using a machine learning method that exploits an intelligent feedback-based self-tuning process.

Phase Determination

It is quite common to employ well-understood benchmark tools as models that approximate real-world workload behavior, because they have a finite completion time, while exhibiting unique resource usage patterns. A program phase has been defined and extended in many ways by researchers, based on the goals to be achieved. This example defines a *program phase* as a variable time interval during execution in which a set of observable characteristics exhibits spatial uniformity and distinctiveness. The example uses a multivariable phase determination technique consisting of multiple dominant variables that are both externally observable and related to the platform control variable. The measured variables m_i are the values of performance events obtained from hardware counters when running a range of bootstrap workloads. The elements of this initial dataset M $(m_i \mid m_i \in M, i \leq N)$ serve as the building blocks of the phase model.

The motivation to choose N variables to be measured comes from the objective of the study. The feature selection process is commonly applied to large datasets to filter out correlations and vastly reduce the computational complexity of algorithms in subsequent stages. To improve classifier accuracy and efficiency, special tools, such as the *correlation-based feature selection* (CFS) algorithm, are applied to reduce the dataset's dimensionality. CFS is a best-first search heuristic algorithm that ranks the worth of subsets rather than individual features. The algorithm filters out the features that are effective in predicting the class, along with the level of intercorrelation among features in the subset, by calculating the feature–class and feature–feature matrices. The features selected by CFS exhibit a high degree of correlation to the reference class, but redundant variables are removed. Given a subset S consisting of k features, the heuristic score is given as

$$Merit_{s_k} = \frac{k\overline{r_{cf}}}{\sqrt{k + k(k+1)\overline{r_{ff}}}},$$
(11-1)

where $\overline{r_{cf}}$ is the average feature–class correlation, and $\overline{r_{ff}}$ is the average feature–feature intercorrelation.

CFS transforms the measured variable set M to a reduced variable set D, yielding $(d_j \mid d_j \in D, j \leq \overline{N})$, $D = CFS(M)$, and $\overline{N} \leq N$. The next step is to build the phase model by using the selected features and applying the simple k-means algorithm to group the uncorrelated variable instances. The k-means algorithm is an unsupervised machine learning algorithm that partitions the input set into k clusters, such that each observation belongs to a cluster with the nearest mean (the Euclidean distance). The objective function of the k-means algorithm can be represented as

$$J = \sum_{l=1}^{k} \sum_{m=1}^{j} \| d_m^{(l)} - c_l \|^2,$$
(11-2)

where c_l is the chosen centroid of cluster l and $d_m^{(l)}$ represents mth datapoint in lth cluster. You consider each cluster a phase ϕ. This example, with $k = 5$, produces a model that has the mean and standard deviation of the 12 filtered variables (see Figure 11-3).

Attribute	Full data	Cluster0	Cluster1	Cluster2	Cluster3	Cluster4
INST_RETIRED.ANY	0.3769	0.2448	0.9166	0.3993	0.0791	0.4812
	+/-0.2569	+/-0.1472	+/-0.088	+/-0.0497	+/-0.1445	+/-0.0742
BR_MISP_EXEC.TAKEN_CONDITIONAL	0.2199	0.1293	0.0239	0.2896	0.0021	0.4606
	+/-0.2608	+/-0.1317	+/-0.0182	+/-0.0739	+/-0.0133	+/-0.299
ICACHE.MISSES	0.0651	0.1817	0.004	0.0055	0.0041	0.0163
	+/-0.15	+/-0.216	+/-0.0241	+/-0.0092	+/-0.0357	+/-0.051
ILD_STALL.LCP	0.1037	0.2474	0.0012	0.2242	0.0013	0.0074
	+/-0.1857	+/-0.2492	+/-0.0057	+/-0.0496	+/-0.0118	+/-0.041
UOPS_RETIRED.STALL_CYCLES	0.5227	0.8116	0.2408	0.6903	0.0118	0.5282
	+/-0.2987	+/-0.1456	+/-0.0637	+/-0.046	+/-0.0442	+/-0.0779
BR_INST_RETIRED.ALL_BRANCHES_PS	0.1555	0.131	0.1817	0.1431	0.1919	0.1573
	+/-0.168	+/-0.1042	+/-0.1235	+/-0.0152	+/-0.3694	+/-0.0494
ITLB_MISSES.MISS_CAUSES_A_WALK	0.0406	0.1207	0.0008	0.0018	0.0036	0.0031
	+/-0.1275	+/-0.2011	+/-0.0038	+/-0.0072	+/-0.0202	+/-0.0229
DTLB_LOAD_MISSES.MISS_CAUSES_A_W	0.1971	0.303	0.039	0.7877	0.0085	0.058
	+/-0.2672	+/-0.1771	+/-0.1464	+/-0.1338	+/-0.0554	+/-0.1281
OFFCORE_REQUESTS.ALL_DATA_RD	0.0336	0.0875	0.0017	0.0337	0.0009	0.0059
	+/-0.0575	+/-0.0716	+/-0.0051	+/-0.0048	+/-0.0055	+/-0.0252
RESOURCE_STALLS2.ALL_PRF_CONTROL	0.1452	0.0927	0.1794	0.8208	0.0046	0.0544
	+/-0.2412	+/-0.0924	+/-0.0966	+/-0.1321	+/-0.0241	+/-0.0764
UOPS_RETIRED.CORE_STALL_CYCLES	0.5242	0.8114	0.2387	0.6891	0.0338	0.523
	+/-0.2973	+/-0.1476	+/-0.0703	+/-0.0489	+/-0.1106	+/-0.092
UNC_M_CAS_COUNT.WR	0.1428	0.3839	0.0132	0.1237	0.0047	0.0173
	+/-0.2752	+/-0.3815	+/-0.0417	+/-0.0199	+/-0.0163	+/-0.029

Figure 11-3. Phase model: cluster mean and standard deviation

Once the phase model is trained, it can be tested against subsequent runs of the workload data. A classifier algorithm from a related class of machine learning algorithms can generate a tree, a set of rules, or a probability model to identify quickly the correct phase. One example is the tree representation obtained from a decision tree classifier algorithm upon training with the cluster data, as illustrated in Figure 11-4. This classifier achieves approximately 99 percent accuracy in phase identification.

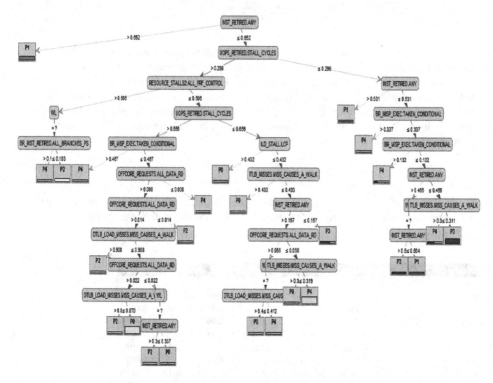

Figure 11-4. Decision tree representation of the model

The initial training data set of 37 workloads results in five clusters, with each cluster representing a workload phase (see Figure 11-5). In each phase the 12 dominant features display a diverse variation pattern, with at least one feature being the primary predictor. As mentioned earlier, a phase transition can be identified by the classifier tree, using the feature-specific threshold values.

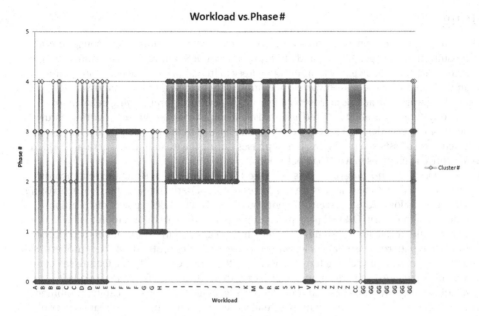

Figure 11-5. *Phase transition diagram for various workloads*

Figure 11-6 shows the workload–phase boundaries, with seven clusters found in four workloads. Each workload is characterized by a unique composition of workload phases. Once the workload is identified, it is phase characterized by its resource utilization and time series pattern. Whereas workload 3 consists mainly of phase 7, workload 1 is a complex mix of phases 3, 5, and 6. These phases discover the characteristic that is unique to a workload instance at any given time.

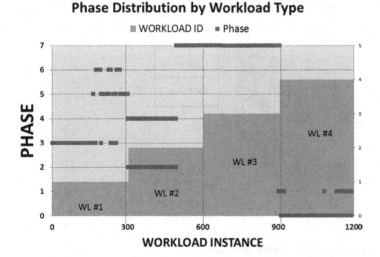

Figure 11-6. *Workload and phase dependency graph; a workload may share phase characteristics with other workloads and can cater to one or more phases*

Fingerprinting

Workloads undergo phases of execution, while operating under multiple constraints. These constraints are related to power consumption, heat generation, and *quality of service* (QoS) requirements. Optimal system operation involves complex choices, owing to a variety of degrees of freedom, with respect to power and performance parameter tuning. The process involves modeling methodology, implementation choices, and dynamic tuning. Fingerprinting acts as an essential feature that captures time-varying behavior of dynamically adaptable systems. This ability is used as a statistical output that aids in reconfiguring hardware and software ahead of variation in demand and that enables the reuse of trained models for recurring phases. Pattern detection also assists in predicting future phases during the execution of workloads, which prevents reactive response to changes in workload behavior.

As part of the *workload fingerprinting* process (see Figure 11-7), individual performance characteristics are collected at a given interval, classified, and aggregated to establish patterns representative of an existing workload or collection of workloads. System control agents, such as I/O schedulers, power distribution, and dynamic random access memory (DRAM) page policy settings, can use this information to tune their parameters or schedule workloads in real time. Fingerprinting can roughly be attributed using three properties: size, phase, and pattern. The machine learning process facilitates synthesis of these properties by measuring or data mining performance characteristics over a finite period. Generally, the feature selection process allows automatic correlation of performance matrices with occurrences of unique workload behaviors, thereby aiding in speedy diagnosis and proactive tuning. Fingerprinting data can be combined with simple statistical functions, such as optimization, visualization, or control theory, to create powerful operator tools. Furthermore, fingerprints help contain prolonged violation of one or more specified *service-level objectives* (SLOs), which involves performing proactive actions to return the system to an SLO-compliant state.

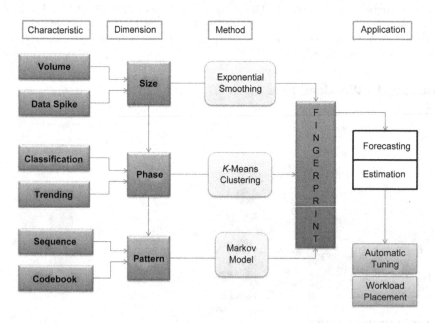

Figure 11-7. *Workload fingerprint: a quantifiable form of characterization*

Size Attribute

The *size* attribute is useful in proactive provisioning of resources. Using the size dimension provides answers to the following questions:

- What is the shape of the distribution? Which resources are more popular than others? Is there a significant tail?

- What is the spatial locality in accesses to the groups of popular objects during spikes?

Phase Attribute

A *phase* represents a unique property that characterizes the behavior of an ongoing process. In this example the phase demonstrates unique power, temperature, and performance characteristics. As described previously (see the section "Phase Determination"), this example employs a simple k-means algorithm to synthesize exclusive behaviors in the form of clusters, represented as phases. This process is executed once all the relevant feature vectors are identified. These vectors are observations that directly or indirectly reflect the unique behavior in the form of resource usage. The phases are compressed representative output that can be used in conjunction with any other statistical parameter for prediction of behavior. Sequences of phases can be seen as patterns. Patterns represent a unique time-varying characteristic of the workload. Figure 11-8a illustrates the phase sequence during one execution of a workload. Figure 11-8b displays the encoded representation of the phase sequence.

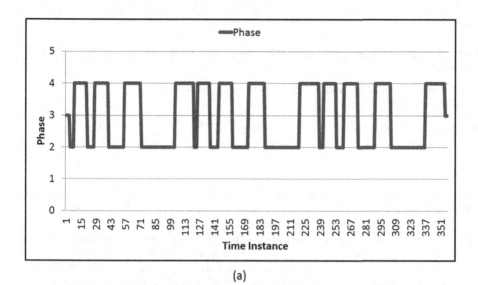

(a)

{3:3,2:3,4:11,2:6,**4:12,2:14,4:15,2:31,4:17**,2:2,4:11,2:7,**4:12,2:14,
4:14,2:31,4:17**,2:3,4:11,2:6,**4:12,2:15,4:14,2:31,4:17**}

(b)

Phase #

	0	1	2	3	4	5	6	7
0	0.943775	0.056225	0	0	0	0	0	0
1	0.384615	0.589744	0	0	0	0	0	0.025641
2	0	0	0.5	0	0.482143	0	0	0.017857
3	0	0	0	0.972826	0	0.016304	0.01087	0
4	0	0	0.201439	0	0.798561	0	0	0
5	0	0	0	0.026667	0.013333	0.946667	0.013333	0
6	0	0	0	0.04878	0	0.02439	0.926829	0
7	0	0.004902	0	0	0	0	0	0.995098

	0	1	2	3	4	5	6	7
1	0	0	0	0.613333	0	0.25	0.136667	0
2	0	0	0.186667	0	0.463333	0	0	0.35
3	0	0	0	0	0	0	0	1
4	0.856164	0.133562	0	0	0	0	0	0.010274

(Phase # rows; Workload # rows)

(c)

Figure 11-8. *(a) Test workload phases, (b) run-length encoded phase sequence, and (c) phase transition likelihood matrix and workload–phase dependency matrix; the workload 1 phase dependency is highlighted*

Pattern Attribute

A *pattern* is defined as a sequence of phases that repeats. Once a sequence is identified, it can be used to predict future phases and the duration of current phases. In the time series operations, you construct the vocabulary for the time series pattern database. Each alphabet in the vocabulary is represented by the operating phase of the workload. This phase is measured in a fixed interval of length (T). The pattern matrix can be represented as M_{ij}, where i represents the pattern, and j stands for the frequency of that pattern. As new patterns are identified, they are updated into the pattern matrix, and old and infrequent patterns are deprecated. You can use a discrete time Markov chain (DTMC) (see Equation 11-3) to identify underlying patterns in a time series sequence of changing phases,

$$\mathbb{P}(q_{t+1} = S_j \mid q_t = S_i, q_{t-2} = S_k, \cdots) = \mathbb{P}(q_{t+1} = S_j \mid q_t = S_i), \qquad (11\text{-}3)$$

where q_t represents the current state, and S_i represents one of the phases of operation. In this model a state transition (phase change) follows the Markov property and then creates transitions between states (phases), based on a learned model for forecasting. You can use a moving window to monitor real-time data and produce an autoregressive model for recently observed data, which is then matched to the state of the learned Markov model. The model also makes corrections, if necessary, to adapt to the changes. By tracing the time series progression from one phase to another, you can build a transition function of the Markov model (see Figure 11-8c).

Forecasting

The workload forecasting module detects trends in the workload and makes predictions about future workload volume. If the target workload demonstrates a strong periodic behavior, a historic forecast can be incorporated into workload forecasting. This allows the policy decision to react proactively to the workload spikes ahead of time. This also helps you take advantage of the heterogeneous compute and I/O resources offered by cloud computing providers. Furthermore, based on the extracted patterns, you may distribute the workloads in a manner that creates different performance models.

Example 2: Dynamic Energy Allocation

Controlling the amount of power drawn by server machines has become increasingly important in recent years. The accuracy and agility of three types of action are critical in power governance:

- Selecting which hardware elements must run at what rates to meet the performance needs of the software

- Assessing how much power must be expended to achieve those rates

- Adjusting the power outlay in response to shifts in computing demand

Observing how variations in a workload affect the power drawn by different server components provides data critical for analysis and for building models relating QoS expectations to power consumption. This next example describes a process of observation, modeling, and course correction in achieving autonomic power control on an Intel Xeon server machine meeting varying response time and throughput demands during the execution of a database query workload. The process starts with fine-grained power performance observations permitted by a distributed set of physical and logical sensors in the system. These observations are used to train models for various phases of the workload. Once trained, system power, throughput, and latency models participate in optimization heuristics that redistribute the power to maximize the overall performance per watt of the server.

The term *power optimization* denotes the act of targeting and achieving high levels of power-normalized performance at the application level. For a software application, such as a business transaction service or content retrieval service, the significant performance metrics include the number of requests serviced (throughput) and the turnaround delay (response time) per request. Optimizing power entails multiple dynamic tradeoffs. Typically, a system can be represented as a set of components whose cooperative interaction produces useful work. These components may be heterogeneous or presented with heterogeneous loads, and they may vary in their power consumption and power control mechanisms. At the level of any component—such as a processing unit or a storage unit—power needs to be increased or decreased on an ongoing basis, according to whether that component's speed plays a critical role in the overall speed or rate of execution of programs. In particular, different application phases may have different sensitivities to component speed. For instance, a memory-bound execution phase will be less affected by central processing unit (CPU) frequency scaling than a CPU-bound execution phase. With the execution reordering that most modern processors employ, the degree to which a program benefits from out-of-order execution varies from one phase to another. Moreover, the rate at which new work arrives in a system changes, and, as a result, the overall speed at which programs have to execute to meet a given service-level expectation varies with time. Thus, the needed power performance tradeoffs have to occur on a continuous basis.

Arguably, given the self-correcting and self-regulating aspects common in systems today, software-driven power performance should be unnecessary. For example, in power control algorithms, CPUs and DRAMs transition into lower frequencies or ultralow power modes during low-activity periods. Although circuit-level self-regulation is highly beneficial in transitioning components to low-power states, software needs to wield policy control over which activity should be reduced, and when, to facilitate the transition of hardware into power-saving modes.

Harnessing power savings on less busy servers is a delicate task that is hard to delegate to hardware-based recipes. Servers are typically configured for handling high rates of incoming work requests at the lowest possible latencies. Therefore, it is not uncommon for servers to have many CPUs and a large amount of physical memory over which computations and data remain widely distributed during both high- and low-demand periods. Owing to the distributed nature of activities, slowing down a single CPU or DRAM can have unpredictable performance ramifications; it can be counterproductive to push part of a server into ultralow power operation. At the other extreme, when power approaches saturation levels, hardware is ill positioned to determine or enforce decisions about which software activities can tolerate reduced performance and which must continue as before.

Thus, software must share with hardware the responsibility of determining when and in which component power can be saved. Here, we consider an autonomic solution for fine-grained control over power performance tradeoffs for server configurations. The solution consists of ingredients for observing, analyzing, planning, and controlling the dynamic expenditure of power in pursuance of an application-level performance objective that is specified as an SLO. This solution uses a time-varying database query workload, in which the learning machine simultaneously changes the power allocation to CPUs and DRAM and gathers performance and power readings via a set of distributed physical and logical sensors in the server. Through these observations, models are trained for various phases of the workload. Based on these models, the optimization heuristic redistributes the power to maximize the overall performance per watt of the server. Experimental measurements demonstrate that a heuristic improves performance and power, as needed or as permitted by the performance objective.

Learning Process: Feature Selection

The primary role of a learning process is to identify relationships between the total *power expended* (P) and two measures of performance: *response time* (R) and *throughput* (T). These relationships are synthesized as models, and optimization techniques use these models to achieve better power performance efficiency.

The process of generalization requires a classifier that inputs a vector of discrete feature vectors and outputs an operating phase, which can be summarized as follows:

- Fine-grained and time-aligned component-level power readings at multiple power rails of the primary components (CPU and dual inline memory module [DIMM])

- System-level readings corresponding to three quantities, each averaged over a small time interval: (1) P, the total system power; (2) T, the application-level throughput; and (3) R, the response time experienced by requests

The component-level power readings are aligned with the $\{P, T, R\}$ tuples. This entire data collection is then used to divide the $\{P, T, R\}$ space into classes (phases). Within each class or phase a linear function can relate P, T, and R to the component-level power readings. These linear relationships are used in optimization planning, whose objective may be to minimize P (total system power) or maximize T (application-level throughput), subject to R's (response time) not exceeding a specific threshold. Learning continues online. Therefore, as the workload evolves, the models and optimization planning adapt.

The *support vector machine* (SVM) technique may be employed to divide the $\{P, T, R\}$ space into different phases and to obtain linear relationships governing the $\{P, T, R\}$ variables in each phase. As discussed previously, SVM is a computationally efficient and powerful technique; invented by Boser, Guyon, and Vapnik (1992), it is employed for classification and regression in a wide variety of machine learning problems. Given a data collection relating a set of training inputs to outputs, an SVM is a mathematical entity that accomplishes these tasks:

1. The SVM describes a hyperplane (in some higher dimension) whose projection into the input space separates inputs into equivalence classes, such that the inputs in a given class have a linear function mapping them to outputs that is distinctive for that class.

2. The hyperplane whose projection is the SVM maximizes the distance that separates it from the nearest samples from each of the classes, thus maximizing the distances between classes, subject to a softness margin.

3. The SVM creates a softness margin that permits a bounded classification error, whereby a small fraction of the inputs that should be placed on one side of the projection are instead placed within a bounded distance on the other side (and are therefore misclassified); this margin allows a pragmatic tradeoff between having a high degree of separation between classes (i.e., better distinctiveness) and having too many outliers.

Equation 11-4 expresses each element of $\{P, T, R\}$ as a linear function of the five power readings per processor within each given class or phase. Whereas (V_{CPU}) yields power going into the processor, V_{DIMM} measures power in memory modules that are connected to and controlled from the processor. The variable J represents a given class, $\{P_J(t), R_J(t), T_J(t)\}$ represents a tuple from a sample numbered t in the training set, and the various power readings associated with that sample are represented by $V^*(t)$. The phases J; constants K^*_P, K^*_R, K^*_T; and coefficients $\alpha^*_\cdot$ and $\beta^*_\cdot$ are all estimated through the SVM regression technique.

$$\underline{\text{CPU Power Readings (2)}} \qquad \underline{\text{Memory Power Readings (4)}}$$

$$P_j(t) - K_P^J = \sum_{CPU=i} \alpha_{PK}^{ij} V_{CPU}^i(t) + \sum_{DRAM\,CH=i} \beta_P^{ij} V_{DIMM}^i(t)$$

$$R_j(t) - K_R^J = \sum_{CPU=i} \alpha_{RK}^{ij} V_{CPU}^i(t) + \sum_{DRAM\,CH=i} \beta_R^{ij} V_{DIMM}^i(t) \qquad \text{(11-4)}$$

$$T_j(t) - K_T^J = \sum_{CPU=i} \alpha_{TK}^{ij} V_{CPU}^i(t) + \sum_{DRAM\,CH=i} \beta_T^{ij} V_{DIMM}^i(t)$$

Learning Process: Optimization Planning

Energy and performance models have a number of degrees of freedom and conflicting objectives that are difficult to optimize collectively. For example, consider the following objectives:

- Best performance per watt

- Staying within a power limit

- Response time ≤ a service-level agreement (SLA) threshold

Conflicts can manifest themselves among these objectives, with considerations such as

- How to obtain a given throughput within a *system power budget*

- How to obtain a given throughput under a *response time threshold*

In the common case, P (total system power) is affected by both performance targets—throughput and response time. Also in the general case, performance is influenced by the power spent in both processors and DIMM modules. Thus, optimization planning must grapple with meeting a compound objective: one in which power expended toward one objective generally comes at the cost of another. Once the coefficients of the linear estimation model for power, throughput, and response time are synthesized, these models can be used as a synthetic feedback in a multiobjective optimization through a feedback control loop. This example uses an *adaptive weighted genetic algorithm* (AWGA) method to search for the global optimal in a scenario with multiple goals. In this machine learning technique a successful outcome is defined as one that redistributes power in such a way that power, response time, and the reciprocal of throughput all meet the viable limits. More generally, a set of fitness functions $\{f_n\}$, one per objective n, determines the optimality of a candidate setting (i.e., a vector describing the distribution of power among components) for each of the objectives. In AWGA, for a population ϕ of candidate settings $\{\mathbf{x}\}$, $F_n^{max} = \max(f_n(x)\,|\,x \in \phi))$ and $F_n^{min} = \min(f_n(\mathbf{x})|x \in \phi)$, you compute, respectively, the fitness bounds for each of a set of $n = 1, 2, \ldots, N$ objectives, where each x in ϕ is a vector whose fitness function represents a feasible power distribution among components, such as CPUs and DIMMs. You may then choose an N objective fitness function F that evaluates an aggregate fitness value. For example, in the case of AWGA, F can be chosen as

$$F = \sum_{n=1}^{N} \frac{f_n(\mathbf{x}) - F_n^{min}}{N \cdot (F_n^{max} - F_n^{min})}. \qquad \text{(11-5)}$$

An *evolutionary algorithm* (EA) selects parents from a given generation of ϕ (usually employing an elitism process that allows the best solution[s] from the current generation to carry over unaltered to the next), from which to produce power-feasible offspring as new candidates for the next generation. In the objective space, F_n^{min} and F_n^{max} represent extreme points that are renewed at each generation. As the extreme points, fitness bounds $\{(F_n^{min}, F_n^{max})|n = 1, 2, \ldots, N\}$ are renewed at each generation, and the contribution (weight) of each objective is also renewed accordingly.

Learning Process: Monitoring

Achieving power-efficient performance and abiding by power and performance constraints call for real-time feedback control. An autonomic system implements continuous feedback-based course correction, with the following provisions:

- *Monitoring* infrastructure to sample or quantify physical and logical metrics, such as power, temperature, and activity rates, and to obtain statistical moments of the metrics

- *Analysis* modules to distill relationships between monitored quantities (e.g., between power, temperature, and performance) and to determine whether one or more operational objectives are at risk

- A *planning* element to formulate a course of action, such as suspending, resuming, speeding up, or slowing down various parts of a system, to effect a specific policy choice (e.g., to limit power or energy consumed or to improve performance)

- A capability to *execute* the formulated plan and thereby *control* the operation of the system

Usually, a knowledge base supplements analysis and planning. The knowledge base may be an information repository that catalogs the allowable actions in each system state, or it may be implicit in the logic of the analysis, planning, and control capabilities. In a system designed for extensibility, the knowledge base typically incorporates an adaptive mechanism that tracks and learns from prior decisions and outcomes. For intelligent feedback control processes, fine-grained and lightly intrusive power performance monitoring is a key element of the adaptive power management infrastructure. The ideal monitoring mechanism operates in real time (i.e., reports data that are as recent as possible) and is not subject to the behavior(s) being monitored. In this configuration logical sensors at the operating system and software levels offer a near real-time information stream consisting of rates at which common system calls, storage accesses, and network transfers proceed. These logical sensors are supplemented with power sensing through physical sensors.

A *telemetry bus* is used to collect data from physical (hardware) and logical (software) sensors and send them to a monitoring agent. In particular, power sensing is accomplished by sensing *voltage regulator* (VR) outputs at each processor chip. The *monitoring agent,* to which the telemetry data are sent, processes the data, organizes them as a temporally aligned stream of power and performance statistics, and transmits the stream to a remote machine for further storage or analysis. The monitoring infrastructure provides the ability to obtain distinct power readings for each processor. Each processor controls distinct memory channels, with multiple DIMMs per channel; each pair of memory channels furnishes one V_{DDQ} signal; and summing those V_{DDQ} readings gives the power expended in the memory subsystem for each processor. The data collected by these sensors are refined through a succession of transformations (see Figure 11-9):

- *Sensor hardware abstraction (SHA) layer*: This layer interacts with the sensors and communication channels. It uses adaptive sampling, such that measurements are only as frequent as necessary, and it eliminates redundancies.

- *Platform sensor analyzer*: This layer removes noise and isolates trends, which makes it easier to incorporate recent and historical data as inputs in further processing.

- *Platform sensor abstraction*: This layer provides a programming interface for flexible handling of analyzed sensor data through the control procedures implemented above it.

- *Platform sensor event generation*: This layer makes it possible to generate signals. Signals facilitate event-based conversations from control procedures, thereby allowing further control to be hosted in a distributed set of containers (such as local or remote controller software and operating system modules). The prior successive refinements bridge the gap between the raw data that sensors produce and the processed, orderly stream of performance and power readings and alerts that software modules can receive and analyze further.

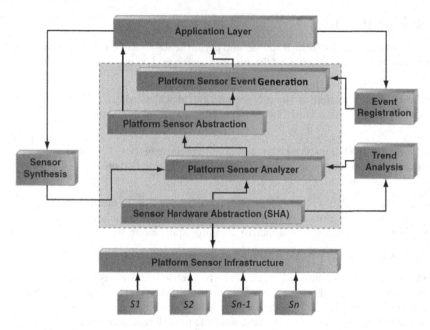

Figure 11-9. *Sensor network model: sensor network layered architecture (S1, S2, . . . , Sn) represents platform sensors (CPU/DIMM power, thermal, performance, and so on). Source: A Vision for Platform Autonomy: Robust Frameworks for Systems (Intel, 2011)*

Although a machine can be readily furnished with a metered power supply to sense total power, an instrumentation capability that yields the fine-grained decomposition of power requires nontrivial effort. Moreover, adding many physical power sensors in production machines is neither necessary nor practical, in terms of cost. Event-counting capabilities in modern machines offer a potent alternative means of estimating component power when direct measurement is not practical. One simple yet accurate way of estimating the power draw for recent CPUs is to project it on the basis of usage and power-state residencies, using trained models. Such training can be made more accurate by including execution profiles that capture what fraction of the instructions falls into each of a small set of categories, such as single instruction, multiple data (SIMD); load/store; and arithmetic logical unit (ALU). DRAM power can similarly be estimated on the basis of cache miss counts, or DRAM operations that are counted at the memory controllers and tracked through processor event monitors. DRAM power estimation permits measurement of DRAM energy at DIMM granularity with sufficient accuracy to enable efficient control of DRAM power states. Efficient control of DRAM energy allows us not only to reduce the cost of hardware infrastructure, but also to improve energy efficiency by reducing the guard bands required to compensate for underprediction. Furthermore, overprediction can also be reduced to avoid performance degradation.

Decision space that facilitates optimal distribution of power among competing components is obtained by process control methods, in which privileged software can modify its power draw. The first method, which is commonly used in Intel-based processors, is to change the P-states and C-states (Siddha 2007). The second method is to change the average power level, using a control known as running average power limit (RAPL) capability for CPUs and DRAM modules. CPU RAPL provides interfaces for setting a power budget for a certain time window and letting the hardware meet the energy targets. Specifying the power limit as an average over a time window allows us to represent physical power and thermal constraints. Privileged software can use the RAPL capability by programming to an interface register the desired average level of power to which the hardware can guide the processor via its own corrective frequency adjustments over a programmable control window. The window size and power limit are selected, such that, at either a single-machine level or a datacenter level, correction to a machine's power is driven quickly. In practice the window size can vary between milliseconds and seconds—the former to satisfy power delivery constraints, the latter to manage thermal constraints. The RAPL concept extends to memory systems as well, aided by the integration of the memory controller into each multicore processor in several recent versions of Intel platforms. Although CPU and memory energy can be regulated individually, it is possible to build a coordinated self-tuning approach, in which power regulation is part of a joint optimization function supported by the machine learning technique discussed in the following section.

Model Training: Procedure and Evaluation

For the model training the data collection module collects time-aligned readings from the power-monitoring sensors. Additionally, it gathers response times and requests completion rates from a database performance module. These readings provide the input–output training vectors $\{P_*(t), R_*(t), T_*(t), \text{and } V_{CPU}^l(t),\}$ (see Equation 11-4). The training data are obtained through a cross-product of two sets of variations:

- *Variation of demand:* This parameter controls how long each of a number of threads in the workload driver waits between completion of a previous request and issuance of a new request.

- *Variation of supply:* This control varies the CPU and memory RAPL settings, thereby varying the supply of power to CPU and DRAM.

In this example the workload uses time-varying think time varying from 0 to 100. For each think time, CPU RAPL limits are varied between 20W and 95W. SVM model training on the basis of these data is then used to categorize the data into distinct phases (J), following which the SVM model parameters for each phase $\{K_P^J, K_R^J, K_T^J, \alpha_P^{ij}, \alpha_R^{ij}, \alpha_T^{ij}, \beta_P^{ij}, \beta_R^{ij}, \beta_T^{ij}\}$ are evaluated.

The SVM-based classification yields decomposition into three phases, as shown in Figure 11-10.

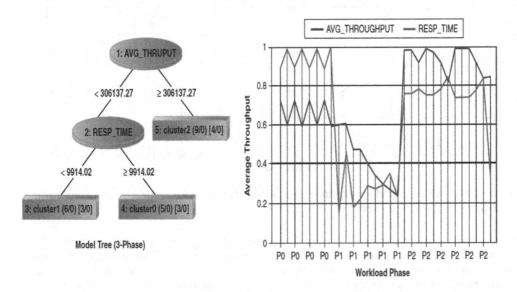

***Figure 11-10.** Model tree depicting three phases (P0, P1, P2) in a workload characterized by throughput and response time*

Accordingly, three different sets of modeling parameters (i.e., for J = 0, 1, 2) in Equation 11-4 relate CPU RAPL parameters to total system power, throughput, and response time outcomes. Figure 11-10 demonstrates how the total wall power estimated on the basis of the RAPL parameters in Equation 11-4 compares with that actually measured. Figures 11-11 and 11-12 illustrate the close agreement between estimated and measured results from the training.

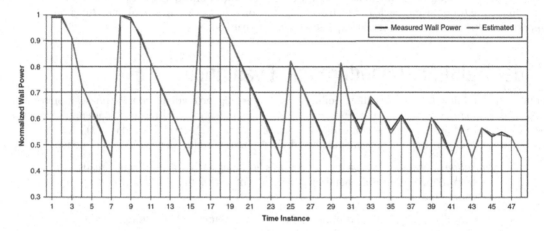

Figure 11-11. *Wall power, measured versus estimated (as function of component power)*

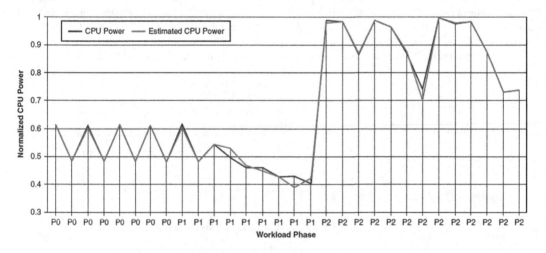

Figure 11-12. *CPU power, measured versus estimated; estimated CPU power is phase wise and based on the throughput and target latency requirements*

On average a machine learning regression function supported by SVM delivers accuracy between 97 percent and 98.5 percent. Each phase is trained for its own performance and latency model coefficients.

Figure 11-13 depicts an example consisting of four possible workload conditions on a server. On the x axis, $tt00$, $tt10$, and $tt20$ stand for think times of 0.0ms, 10.0ms, and 20.0ms, respectively. The y axis shows response times. The red multisegment line in the figure connects four workload points (W_1, W_2, W_3, W_4).

These points are randomly selected perturbations in supply and demand ; for example, W_1 results from setting a think time of 20.0ms and a CPU RAPL value of 40W; W_2 results from a think time of 0.0ms (driving a higher arrival rate than W_1) and a CPU RAPL value of 50W, and so on.

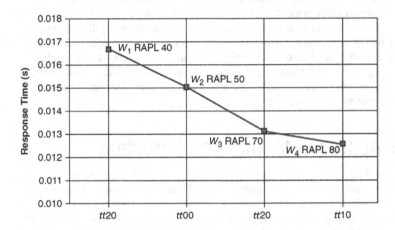

Figure 11-13. *Response time at four arbitrarily selected points, reflecting four possible workload and server conditions*

If none of the response times for W_1, W_2, W_3, and W_4 were to exceed a desired performance objective—for instance, an SLA target of $R = 20.0$ms—then it would be desirable to save power by reducing performance, so long as the higher response times were still below the target of 20.0ms. However, if at any of these workload points the response time were to exceed a desired threshold, then it would be preferable to improve performance by increasing the power to meet the SLA.

Generally, an SLA may spell out throughput and response time expectations and may include details, such as the fraction of workload that must be completed within a threshold amount of response time under differing levels of throughput. For ease of description, this example has a simple SLA setting: that the response time, averaged over small time intervals (1s), not exceed a static target value of 14.0ms; this is displayed in Figure 11-14 by the solid line, $R = 0.014$.

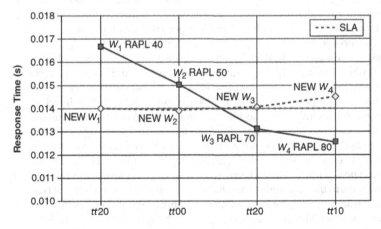

Figure 11-14. *Illustration of improvement in response time, using proactive control of CPU power employing CPU RAPL*

As you can see, new workload points (shown in diamonds) result from proactive power performance control through the use of a trained SVM model. Additionally, new RAPL settings (higher CPU power) computed using the trained model reduce the response times for W_1 and W_2 from their previous values (by 15 percent and 7 percent, respectively) to new values that are much closer to the SLA. Similarly, the model training produces lower CPU power settings for W_3 and W_4, which leads to power savings at the cost of higher response times and to 11.5 percent improvement in energy efficiency. Incidentally, the new setting for W_4 misses the SLA target by a small but not negligible margin, which could force a recomputation of the CPU RAPL setting in the next iteration. Note that to reduce frequent course correction, a control policy may permit overshooting the SLA target by a small margin in either direction. Here, because the new RAPL settings for W_1 and W_2 reduced response times, phase-aware CPU power scaling yields significant power reduction at all performance levels, relative to isolated tuning.

Example 3: System Approach to Intrusion Detection

In an era of cooperating ad hoc networks and pervasive wireless connectivity, we are becoming more vulnerable to malicious attacks. These sophisticated attacks operate under the threshold boundaries during an intrusion attempt and can only be identified by profiling the complete system activity, in relation to a normal behavior. Many of these attacks are silent in nature and cannot be detected by conventional *intrusion detection system* (IDS) methods, such as traffic monitoring, port scanning, or protocol violation. Intrusion detection may be compared to the human immune system, which, through understanding of the specifications of normal processes, identifies and eliminates anomalies. Identifiers should be distributed throughout a system with identifiable and adaptable relationships. We therefore need a model that, in each state, has a probability of producing observable system outputs and a separate probability indicating the next states.

Unlike wired networks, ad hoc nodes coordinate among member nodes to allow exclusive use of the communication channel. A malicious node can exploit this distributed and complex decision-making property of cooperating nodes to launch an attack on, or hijack, the node. This inherent vulnerability can disable the whole network cluster and further compromise security through impersonating, message contamination, passive listening, or acting as a malicious router. An IDS mechanism should be able to detect intrusion by monitoring unusual activities in the system via comparison with a user's profile and with evolving trends. Although they may not be sufficient to prevent malicious attacks if the attacker operates below the threshold, threshold-based mechanisms can be modified to monitor trends in the related system components to predict an attack. This is similar to an HMM (see Chapter 5), in which the hidden state (attack) can be predicted from relevant observations (changes in system parameters, fault frequency, and so on). Observed behavior acts as a signature or description of normal or abnormal activity and is characterized in terms of a statistical metric and model. A *metric* is a random variable representing a quantitative measure accumulated over a period of time. Observations obtained from the audit records, when used together with a statistical model, analyze any deviation from a standard profile and trigger a possible intrusion state.

This example discusses an HMM-based strategy for intrusion detection, using a multivariate Gaussian model for observations that are in turn used to predict an attack that exists in the form of a hidden state. The model comprises a self-organizing network for event clustering, an observation classifier, a drift detector, a profile estimator (PE), a *Gaussian mixture model* (GMM) accelerator, and an HMM engine. This method is designed to predict intrusion states, based on observed deviation from normal profiles or by classifying these deviations into an appropriate attack profile. An HMM is a stochastic model of discrete events and a variation of the Markov chain. Like a conventional Markov chain, an HMM consists of a set of discrete states and a matrix $A = \{a_{ij}\}$ of *state transition probabilities*. Additionally, every state has a vector of *observed symbol probabilities*, $B = b_j(v)$, which corresponds to the probability that the system will produce a symbol of type v when it is in state j. The states of the HMM can only be inferred from the observed symbols—hence, the term *hidden*. HMM correlates observations with hidden states that factor in the system design, in which observation points are optimized, using an acceptable set of system-wide *intrusion checkpoints* (ICs); hidden states are created using explicit knowledge of probabilistic relationships with these observations. These relationships (also called *profiles*) are hardened and evolve with the constant usage of the multiple and independent systems. If observation points can be standardized, then the problem of intrusion predictability can be reduced to profiling the existing and new, hidden states to standard observations.

Modeling Scheme

Parameters for HMM modeling schemes consist of *observed states*, *hidden (intrusion) states*, and *HMM profiles*. HMM training, using initial data and continuous reestimation, creates a profile that involves transition probabilities and observation symbol probabilities. HMM modeling involves the following tasks:

- Measuring the *observed states*, which are analytically or logically derived from the intrusion indicators. These indicators are test points spread throughout the system.

- Estimating the *instantaneous observation* probability function, which indicates the probability of an observation, given a hidden state. This density function can be estimated using an explicit parametric model (multivariate Gaussian) or, implicitly, from data via nonparametric methods (multivariate kernel density emission).

- Estimating the *hidden states* by clustering the homogeneous behavior of single or multiple components. These states are indicative of various intrusion activities that need to be identified to the administrator.

- Estimating the *hidden state transition* probability matrix, using prior *knowledge or random data. Prior knowledge, along with long-term temporal characteristics, indicates an approximate probability of the transitioning of state components from one intrusion state to another.

Observed (Emission) States

Observed states represent competing risks derived analytically or logically, using IC indicators. Machine intrusion can be considered a result of several components' competing for the occurrences of the intrusion. In this model the IC engine derives continued multivariate observations, which is similar to the mean and standard deviation model, except that the former is based on correlations between two or more metrics. These observations $b_j(v)$ have a continuous probability density function (PDF) and are a mixture of multivariate Gaussian (normal) distributions, expressed (Lee, Kawahara, and Shikano 2001) as

$$b_j(v) = \sum_{k=1}^{M} c_{jk} \left[\frac{1}{(2\pi)^{M/2} |\sigma_{jk}|^{1/2}} exp\left[-\frac{1}{2}(v-\mu_{jk})^T \sigma_{jk}^{-1}(v-\mu_{jk}) \right] \right], \tag{11-6}$$

where $(\cdot)^T$ denotes transpose, and

$$c_{jk} \geq 0 \ \& \ \sum_{k=1}^{M} c_{jk} = 1$$

σ_{jk} = covariance matrix of the kth mixture component of the jth state

μ_{jk} = mean vector of the kth mixture component of the jth state

v = observation vector

M = number of dimensions of an observation with a multivariate Gaussian distribution

$\theta_{jk} = (\sigma_{jk}, \mu_{jk})$ = Gaussian components

η_{jk} = drift factor of the kth mixture component of the jth state

$\lambda_{jk} = (\theta_{jk}, c_{jk}, \eta_{jk})$ = user profile components

It is the responsibility of the IC engine to reestimate the λ_{jk} parameters dynamically for all matrices and all possible attack states. Various matrices that represent dimensions of an observation are as follows:

- *Resource activity trend*: The measure of a resource activity that is monitored over a larger sampling period and that has characteristics that repeat over that sampling period. Each period of activity can be thought of as an extra dimension of activity measure.

- *Event interval*: The measure of an interval between two successive activities (e.g., logging attempts).

- *Event trend*: The measure of events monitored over a larger sampling period, with the objective of calculating the event behavior with a built-in repeatability (e.g., the count of logging attempts in a day).

Hidden States

Hidden states $S = \{S_1, S_2, \cdots, S_{N-1}, S_N\}$ are a set of states that are not visible, but each state randomly generates a mixture of the M observations (or visible states O). The probability of the subsequent state depends only on the previous state. The complete model is defined by the following probabilities: *transition probability matrix* $A = a_{ij}$, where $a_{ij} = p(S_i|S_j)$; *observation probability matrix* $B = (b_i(v_m))$, where $b_i(v_m) = p(v_m|S_i)$; and an initial probability vector $\pi = p(S_i)$. *Observation probability* represents an attribute that is observed with some probability if a particular failure state is anticipated. The model is represented by $M = (A, B, \pi)$.
A *transition probability matrix* is a square matrix of size equal to the number of states and stands for the state transition probabilities.

The observation probability distribution is a nonsquare matrix whose dimensions equal the number of states by number of observables. This distribution represents the probability of an observation for a given state. The IDS depicted in Figure 11-15 uses these states:

- *Normal* (N) state indicates profile compliance.

- *Hostile intrusion attempt* (*HI*) indicates a hostile intrusion attempt that is in progress. This is typical of an external agent trying to bypass the system security.

- *Friendly intrusion attempt* (*FI*) denotes a nonhostile intrusion attempt that is in progress. This is typical of an internal agent trying to bypass the system security.

- *Intrusion in progress* (*IP*) signals an intrusion activity that is setting itself up. This includes attempts to access privileged resources and acceleration in resource usage.

- *Intrusion successful* (*IS*) signifies a successful intrusion. Successful intrusion will be accompanied by unusual resource usage (CPU, memory, I/O activity, and so on).

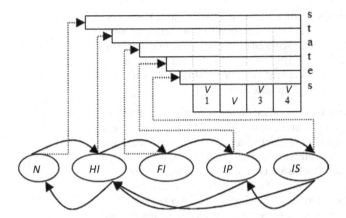

Figure 11-15. *HMM model, with five intrusion states and four Gaussian distributions for each state; each Gaussian distribution can be represented as the mixture component of an observation. (Source: Khanna and Liu 2006)*

Intrusion Detection System Architecture

In ad hoc networks an IDS is deployed at the nodes to detect the signs of intrusion locally and independently of other nodes, instead of using routers, gateways, or firewalls. In this section, we define components of the IDS that cooperate with each other to predict an attack state.

After the model is trained, it enters a runtime state, in which it examines and classifies each valid observation. The model then decides to add the observation to a profile update, reject it, or mark it "unclassified." This decision is important, because a drift in the user's normal behavior may represent an attack situation. An unclassified observation is monitored for classification in the future. This observation will later be rejected as a noise or classified as a valid state, based on the trending similarity between unclassified states tending toward a certain classification and on feedback from the state machine resulting from other, independent observations. Various components of an IDS are as follows:

> **Profile estimator** (**PE**): The PE is responsible for maintaining/reestimating user profiles, classifying an observation as an attack state, triggering an alert upon detecting a suspicious observation, or acting on the HMM feedback for reestimation of a profile. User profile data consist of PDF parameters $\lambda_{jk} = (\sigma_{jk}, \mu_{jk}, c_{jk}, \eta_{jk})$, where j represents the intrusion state, and k stands for the GMM mixture component. A new observation is evaluated against this profile, which results in its classification and drift detection.

> **Instrumentation**: Instrumentation produces event data, which are processed and used by a *clustering agent* to estimate the profile. Component identification and measurements involve setup to discern whether events should be sampled at regular intervals or whether notification (or an alert) should be generated as an event vector upon recording changes in pattern. The sensor data should be able to analyze data, either as they are collected or afterward, and to provide real-time alert notification for suspected intrusive behavior. This will require fast-acting silicon hooks that are capable of identifying, counting, thresholding, timestamping, eventing, and clearing an activity. Examples of such hooks are performance counters, flip counters (also called transaction counters), header sniffers, fault alerts (page faults, and so on), and bandwidth usage monitors.

At the same time, software instrumentation is also required to sample software-related measurements, such as session activity, system call usage between various processes and applications, file system usage, and swap-in/swap-out usage. Most operating systems support these hooks in the form of process tracking (such as process ID [PID], in UNIX). Combinations of these fast-acting hooks with sampling capability are clustered to enact an observation.

Data clustering: Observation data are dependent on the aggregation of events that are active. For instance, a resource fault event generated by a resource usage engine is further categorized as a *fault type*, such as a page fault. Page faults count, and *invalid page faults* in a sampled interval represent instances of measurement (m_1, m_2). An observation (emission) can be a set of correlated measurements but is represented by a single probability distribution function. Each of these measurements carries different weights, as in multivariate Gaussian distribution. For example, disk I/O usage may be related to network I/O usage because of the network file system (NFS). Such a relationship is incorporated into the profile, for the completeness of the observation, and reduces the dimensionality, for effective runtime handling.

Classifier: Observation data are analyzed for the purpose of subclassification as an appropriate attack state in a profile driven by different probability distribution parameters. Once the appropriate attack state is identified, an attention event is generated to initiate a corrective or logging action. Observations are also analyzed for concept drift to compensate for changes in user (or attack) behavior. Therefore, one of the objectives of the IC engine (see Figure 11-16) is to build a classifier for j (attack states) that has a posterior probability $p(j|v)$ close to unity for one value of j and close to 0 for all the others, for each realization. This can be obtained by minimizing the Shannon entropy, given observed data v, which can be evaluated for each observation as

$$E = -\sum_{j=1}^{M} p(j|v)\log(p(j|v)).$$ (11-7)

Each IC engine samples its observations independently of other observations (or emissions). Whenever it suspects an abnormal activity, it triggers an alert, which causes an evaluation of the most likely state. As the system changes its active behavior, the profile corresponding to that behavior is updated to avoid false-positive evaluations by reevaluating the model parameters, using continuous estimation mechanisms in real time. New HMM parameters are evaluated again against the historical HMM parameters by comparing the entropy of the old and the retrained models. The *expectation maximization* (EM) algorithm (Moon 1996) provides a general approach to the problem of *maximum likelihood estimation* (MLE) of parameters in statistical models with variables that are not observed. The evaluation process yields a parameter set, which the algorithm uses to assign observation points to new states. The computational complexity of the EM algorithm for GMMs is $O(i \times ND^2)$, where i is the number of iterations performed, N is the number of samples, and D is the state dimensionality. A common implementation choice is the k-means algorithm, in which k clusters are parameterized by their centroids, with a complexity of $O(kND)$. A number of other algorithms can also be used, including x-means clustering (Pelleg and Moore 2000), which reduces the complexity to $O(D)$.

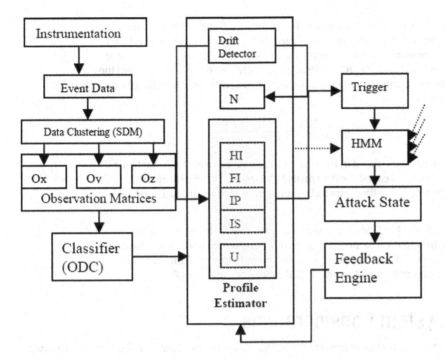

Figure 11-16. *IC engine. Reestimation of the profile uses an observation classifier and HMM feedback to the profile. The profile manager triggers an attention event if the observation classifies as an attack state or cannot be classified (U). An attention event initiates an HMM state sequence prediction, based on other, continuous observations (dotted arrows), extracted in conjunction with profiles and state transition probabilities. (Source: Khanna and Liu 2006)*

Concept drift detector (CDD): This module detects and analyzes the concept drifting (Widmer and Kubat 1996) in the profile, when the training dataset alone is not sufficient, and the model (profile) needs to be updated continually. When there is a time-evolving concept drift, using old data unselectively helps if the new concept and old concept still have consistencies and if the amount of old data chosen arbitrarily happens to be right (Fan 2004). This requires an efficient approach to data mining that aids in selecting a combination of new and old data (historical) to make an accurate reprofiling and further classification. The mechanism used is the *Kullback-Leibler* (KL) *divergence* (Kullback and Leibler 1951), in which relative entropy measures the kernel distance between two probability distributions of generative models. The KL divergence is also the gain in Shannon information that occurs in going from the a priori to the posteriori, expressed as

$$\alpha_{jkt} = KL(b_j(v \mid \theta'_{jkt}), b_j(v \mid \theta_{jkt})),$$
(11-8)

where α_{jkt} is the KL divergence measure, θ'_{jkt} is the new Gaussian component, and θ_{jkt} is the old Gaussian component of the kth mixture of the jth state at time t. You can evaluate divergence via a Monte Carlo simulation, using the law of large numbers (Grimmett and Stirzacker 1992), which draws an observation v_i from the estimated Gaussian component θ'_{jkt}, computes the log ratio, and averages this over M samples as

$$\alpha_{jk} \approx \frac{1}{M} \sum_{i=1}^{M} \log\left(\frac{b_j(v_i \mid \theta'_{jkt})}{b_j(v_i \mid \theta_{jkt})} \right). \tag{11-9}$$

KL divergence data calculated in the temporal domain are used to evaluate the speed of the drift (also called the *drift factor*) $(0 \le \eta \le 1)$. These data are then used to assign weights to the historical parameters, which are in turn used for reprofiling.

Feedback engine (FE): This component is responsible for feeding back the current state information to the PE. The current state information is reevaluated, using the current PDF model parameters. This reevaluated state information is then used for improving the descent algorithm for finding the MLE.

Profiles and System Considerations

In this section, we look at events that form input to the profile structure. We define the features as processed observations derived from one or more temporal input events, using a processor function.

Exploiting temporal sequence information of events leads to better performance (Ghosh, Schwartzbard, and Schata 1999) of the profiles that are defined for individual users, programs, or classes. Abnormal activity in any of the following forms is an indicator of an intrusion or a worm activity:

- *CPU activity* is monitored by sampling faults, interprocessor interrupt (IPI) calls, context switches, thread migrations, spins on locks, and usage statistics.

- *Network activity* is monitored by sampling input error rate, collision rate, remote procedure call (RPC) rejection rate, duplicate acknowledgment (DUPACK), retransmission rate, time-out rate, refreshed authentications, bandwidth usage, active connections, connection establishment failure, header errors and checksum failures, and so on.

- *Interrupt activity* is monitored by sampling device interrupts (nontimer).

- *I/O utilization* is monitored by sampling the I/O requests' average queue lengths and busy percentages.

- *Memory activity* is monitored by sampling memory transfer rate, page statistics (reclaim rate, swap-in rate, swap-out rate), address translation faults, and pages scanned and paging averages over a short interval.

- *File access activity* is monitored by sampling file access frequency, file usage overflow, and file access faults.

- *System process activity* is monitored by sampling processes with inappropriate process priorities, CPU and memory resources used by processes, processes' length, processes that are blocking I/Os, zombie processes, and the command and terminal that generated the process.

- *System fault activity* represents an illegal activity (or a hardware error) and is sampled to detect abnormality in the system usage. Rare faults are a result of bad programming, but spurts of activity indicate an attack.

- *System call activity* involves powerful tools for obtaining computer system privileges. An intrusion is accompanied by the execution of unexpected system calls. If the system call execution pattern of a program can be collected before it is executed and is used for comparison with the runtime system call execution behavior, then unexpected execution of system calls can be detected. During real-time operation a pattern-matching algorithm is applied to match on the fly the system calls generated by the process examined with entries from the pattern table. Based on how well the matching can be done, it is decided whether the sequence of system calls represents normal or anomalous behavior (Wespi, Dacier, and Debar 1999).

- *Session activity* is monitored by sampling logging frequency, unsuccessful logging attempts, session durations, session time, and session resource usages.

Sensor Data Measurements

Sensor data are collected and statistically processed so that they can be used to measure historical trends, capture unique patterns, and visualize abnormal behavior. The data are classified and then analyzed for use in prediction of abnormal activity. Sensor data measurements comprise various components that perform either a statistical processing function or an infrastructure function (such as generating priority events), as follows:

> **Sensor data measurement (SDM)** hooks reduce system complexity and increase the possibility of software reuse (see Figure 11-17). SDM accelerates the combined measurement of the clustered components with an ability to send alerts, using a system's policy. Hardware and software act as glue between transducers and a control program that is capable of measuring the event interval and the event trend and of generating alerts upon deviation from normal behavior, as defined by system policy. The SDM hardware exists as a multiple-instance entity that receives alert vectors from various events spread throughout the system. A set of correlated events that forms a cluster is registered against a common SDM instance. This instance represents the Bayes optimal decision boundaries between a set of pattern classes, with each class represented by an SDM instance and associated with a reference vector. Each SDM instance can trend and alert and integrates the measurements from the event sensors into a unified view. Cluster trending analysis is very sensitive to small signal variations and capable of detecting the abnormal signals embedded in the normal signals via supervised self-organizing maps (Kohonen 1995), using *learning vector quantization* (LVQ). The strategy behind LVQ is to effectively train the reference vectors to define the Bayes optimal decision boundaries between the SDM classes registered to an SDM instance.

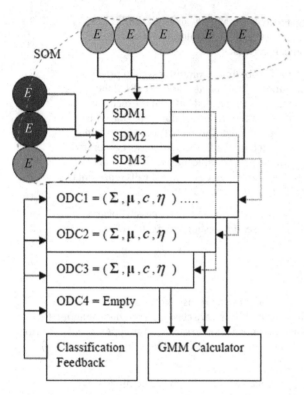

Figure 11-17. *Illustration of the relationship between events (circles), sensors (SDM), and classifiers (ODC). Clusters of events (marked by common colors) are registered to an SDM. Upon evaluating the event properties, the SDM generates an event to ODC, which is responsible for classification, trend analysis, and drift calculation. Classification feedback acts as a mechanism for reestimation. (Source: Khanna and Liu 2006)*

Observation data classifier (**ODC**) hooks accelerate the classification of an observation alert generated by SDM. This is multiple-instance hardware capable of handling multiple observations in parallel. Each registered observation instance of the ODC hook consists of Gaussian probability distribution parameters for each state. Upon receiving an SDM alert, the corresponding observation is then classified as a specific state. Reclassification of observed data may cause changes in the probability distribution parameters corresponding to the state. ODC can maintain the historical parameters, which are used to calculate concept drift properties, such as drift factor and drift speed, using the KL drift detector.

The **GMM calculator** calculates the probability of the Gaussian mixture for each state, using the current observation. During system setup, event vectors are registered against SDM instances. These events are clustered and processed in their individual SDMs. The processing includes trigger properties, which initiate an observation. These observations then act as single-dimensional events that are registered to their ODC. Upon receiving the trigger, ODC performs reclassification of the observation derived from the trigger and calculates the concept drift. This hardware is activated upon a trigger by its parent.

Summary

As more and more data are expressed digitally in an unstructured form, new computing models are being developed to process that data in a meaningful manner. Machine learning methods can be applied to synthesize the fundamental relationship between the unstructured datasets and information through systematic application of algorithms. Machine learning exploits the power of generalization that is an inherent and essential component of concept formation through human learning. The machine learning methodology can be applied to develop autonomous systems, using modular functions to enact an intelligent feedback control system. This approach can play a critical role in modeling the knowledge function, which is used to enact a stable and viable system. This chapter presented three examples of techniques used in machine learning. The first example employed the concept of workload fingerprinting, using phase detection to establish observable characteristics exhibiting spatial uniformity and distinctiveness. The second example was based on the concept of optimal, dynamic energy distribution among multiple compute elements. This example proposed phases as compressed representative output that can be used in conjunction with any other statistical parameter to predict future behavior. The last example suggested use of the IDS mechanism for detecting intrusions by monitoring unusual activities in the system with reference to the user's profile and evolving trends. Each example used an application-specific grouping of machine learning techniques to achieve the desired goals.

References

Becker, Suzanna, and Geoffrey E. Hinton. "Self-Organizing Neural Network that Discovers Surfaces in Random-Dot Stereograms." *Nature* 355, no. 6356 (1992): 161–163.

Boser, Bernhard E., Isabelle M. Guyon, and Vladimir N. Vapnik. "A Training Algorithm for Optimal Margin Classifiers." In *COLT '92: Proceedings of the Fifth Annual Workshop on Computational Learning Theory*, 144–152. New York: ACM, 1992.

Fan, Wei. "Systematic Data Selection to Mine Concept-Drifting Data Streams." In *KDD '04: Proceedings of the Tenth ACM SIGKDD International Conference on Knowledge Discovery and Data Mining*, 128–137. New York: ACM, 2004.

Ghosh, Anup K., Aaron Schwartzbard, and Michael Schatz. "Learning Program Behavior Profiles for Intrusion Detection." In *ID' 99: Proceedings of the 1st Conference on Intrusion Detection and Network Monitoring*. Berkley, CA: USENIX, 1999.

Grimmett, Geoffrey, and David Stirzaker. *Probability and Random Processes*. Oxford: Clarendon, 1992.

Khanna, Rahul, and Huaping Liu. "System Approach to Intrusion Detection Using Hidden Markov Model." In *Proceedings of the 2006 International Conference on Wireless Communications and Mobile Computing*, 349–354. New York: ACM, 2006.

Kohonen, Teuvo. "*Self-Organizing Maps, Third Edition.*" Berlin: Springer, 1995.

Kullback, Solomon, and Richard A. Leibler. "On Information and Sufficiency." *Annals of Mathematical Statistics* 22, no. 1 (1951): 79–86.

Lee, Akinobu, Tatsuya Kawahara, and Kiyohiro Shikano. "Gaussian Mixture Selection Using Context-Independent HMM." In *Proceedings of the 2001 IEEE International Conference on Acoustics, Speech, and Signal Processing*, 69–72. Piscataway, NJ: Institute of Electrical and Electronics Engineers, 2001.

Moon, Todd K. "The Expectation-Maximization Algorithm." *IEEE Signal Processing Magazine* 13, no. 6 (1996): 47–60.

Pelleg, Dan, and Andrew W. Moore. "*X*-Means: Extending *K*-Means with Efficient Estimation of the Number of Clusters." In *ICML '00: Proceedings of the Seventeenth International Conference on Machine Learning*, 727–734. San Francisco: Morgan Kaufmann, 2000.

Siddha, Suresh. "Multi-Core and Linux Kernel." Technical report, *Intel Open Source Technology Center*, 2007.

Wespi, Andreas, Marc Dacier, and Hervé Debar. "An Intrusion-Detection System Based on the Teiresias Pattern-Discovery Algorithm." In *EICAR Proceedings 1999*, edited by Urs E. Gattiker, Pia Pedersen, and Karsten Petersen, 1–15. Aalborg, Denmark: Tim-World, 1999.

Widmer, Gerhard, and Miroslav Kubat. "Learning in the Presence of Concept Drift and Hidden Contexts." *Machine Learning* 23, no. 1 (1996): 69–101.

Index

Printed in the United States
By Bookmasters